ALBRECHT DÜRER
Selbstbildnis / Portait de l' artiste / Self‑portrait / Autorretrato. 1493. Paris, Louvre

ROBERT-HERMANN TENBROCK

A HISTORY
OF GERMANY

Translated from the German
by
Paul J. Dine

MAX HUEBER · MÜNCHEN

FERDINAND SCHÖNINGH · PADERBORN

First edition 1968
© 1968 by Max Hueber Verlag, München and
Ferdinand Schöningh, Paderborn
Production: Westfalen-Druckerei and Ferdinand Schöningh, Paderborn
Printed in Germany

To my wife Ulrike

TABLE OF CONTENTS

PREFACE

The tendency today is for Germans to fight shy of any concern with their own history. The period of the Third *Reich* weighs heavy upon all—either as a feeling of guilt or as a painful memory. To the youth of today this epoch appears almost incomprehensible; they regard it as an ill-fated heritage taken over from their fathers. The present, with all its external splendour and material prosperity, cannot blind us to the fact that the struggle to find a new stay and focus for the German spirit is not yet decided; it is still impossible to say in what direction the national and European destiny of the German people will develop. This inner insecurity regarding their past and their future has given rise to a sense of unease where history is concerned. This goes even further than the sharp criticism of Germany's development since Frederick the Great which was so current in Germany immediately after the defeat in 1945. One might almost think that Germans, especially those living in the Federal Republic, were gradually losing all historical consciousness and that those living east of the Elbe and the Werra were only able to view their history in the light of Marxist Leninism.

If such is the case, one might seem justified in asking whether it would not be better for the Germans to jettison their national history and thus prepare themselves for a more unshackled entry into a supranational community. However, to approve such an attitude would be tantamount to forgetting that it is an essential component of man's nature not only to have a history but also to be conscious of the historical implications of his acts. For a German this would mean, in addition, disavowing his destiny, which has placed him in a definite community. Again, as a European, he would also misunderstand Europe if he were not clear about the peculiar nature of Europe's history. After all, each of the peoples of this continent has its own individuality which has been moulded by its history. Here, without a doubt, lies the true source of the great cultural wealth and the remarkable cultural variety of Europe, although we should not forget that the overemphasis of national individuality has also been the cause of numerous European wars. Thus, the question to be answered by Europe today is whether its peoples will succeed in discovering what is common to them as Europeans in their national individuality in order thus to attain to a new European community consciousness.

The present account of Germany's history cannot aim at confining the reader's view within the limits of national prejudice, for German history, too, has always been, from its very beginnings, only a part of European history. The author must remember that Germany's destiny is intertwined with that of Europe, although, of course, he can only take the latter into consideration in so far as it has had a direct influence on the course of the former. This presentation of Germany's individual development will be, in essentials, a statement of accounts which, in offering a sober evaluation of the history of the German people, will try to show why this development led to such results.

Any attempt to present the long, and at times somewhat obscure, history of Germany within such a brief compass must inevitably bear the stamp of the provisional. This remark also applies to the history of modern times, on which the author lays by far the greatest stress. Seen as a whole, this work can only give a first general survey and arouse the reader's interest to such an extent that he consults the scholarly studies which deal exhaustively with the various individual issues.

Wiesbaden, December 1964.

R.-H. Tenbrock

Chapter One

THE BEGINNINGS

Germany in the Shadow of the Roman Empire

About the beginning of the Christian era, the Roman Empire embraced the entire Mediterranean basin. To safeguard its frontiers, which, in keeping with the military requirements of the time, had to follow as far as possible river courses, mountain ranges or the confines of deserts, it had, in the process of subjugating the Celtic Gauls in presentday France, advanced under its great general Gaius Julius Caesar, to the Rhine from its source to its mouth. This campaign brought Rome for the first time into direct contact with the region settled by the German tribes. Hitherto, throughout its long history, with its wars of conquest and defence, it had encountered the Germanic people only outside their own settlements, when individual tribes decided to migrate southwards and thereby violated the territories of the Roman Empire itself or of countries within its sphere of interest.

In contrast to the majority of peoples living within the Roman Empire, who had all either benefited from or played an important part in fashioning that Greco-Latin civilisation which was to prove so important for the development of Europe, the Germans at this time were still living in the obscure twilight of prehistory. Certainly there were enterprising traders, bent on acquiring commercial articles unknown to the Mediterranean, who had penetrated as far as the lands of the Germans and had introduced many aspects of civilisation there. But in general the life of the people who inhabited the area to the east of the Rhine had been lived at the same tempo for centuries. Thus they could not but appear primitive to all southern peoples, leading as they did a life entirely taken up, from cradle to grave, by the simple task of providing nourishment for themselves and their families.

In this latter regard, nature seemed rather to frown than to smile upon their efforts. The climate was damp, foggy and cold. Vast pine and deciduous forests, which aggravated the humidity, covered mountains and plains like a great virgin forest. These gave rise to the

9

impression that the country was unpopulated, since the few villages and farmsteads or the infrequent roads crudely cut through the woods were concealed behind the impenetrability of their trunks and boughs.

If one did come across a settlement, it was very soon evident that an organised community life was not unknown to the Germans. The family was organised on a strictly patriarchal basis, though within the limits of their functions in home and fields women were accorded a measure of equality. This raised them, especially in times of emergency or danger of war, to the level of men's true partners. In conformity with the monogamous character of marriage, adultery was forbidden equally to man and wife, and was severely punished. The natural division of work consigned to the man the tasks of building the home and the sheds for livestock, of hunting, and of defence and attack, whereas the cultivation of the fields and garden, the upbringing of the children and the care of the domestic animals—swine, cattle, goats, sheep and dogs—fell to the woman's share. The horse, the pride of the German peasant warrior, was entrusted to the care of both partners. The Teutonic way of life presupposed a fixed dwelling-place. Only when the pasturage, which was shared by all, proved no longer sufficient for the community's needs, a decision was taken to migrate to new and better lands where its members could settle and start afresh to make a living. The community, in this context, was that of the clan, the social unit to which every German consciously belonged from birth to death. Although his personality was often strongly imprinted on his home and farm, the individual nevertheless felt himself linked by the closest bonds to all those who were members of the same clan and honoured the same elder as its head. When a girl married she gave up her clan and was assimilated into that of her husband. Insult to, or actual attack on, a clan member brought the revenge of the entire clan in its wake and not infrequently led to bloody engagements between clans (the blood feud). Several clans together made up a tribe, which, especially in time of war, chose an experienced warrior as its chief. In some tribes the chief bore the title of duke; in others, imitating non-Teutonic peoples, he was known as king.

The communal life of the tribes was organised according to well-defined principles. Yet there can be no talk of any formation into a state, in the real meaning of the term, for another hundred years to come. Great importance was attached to the assemblies of all freemen at the time of the new moon, in the "Thing", for then not only were questions of a general character discussed, but also judgment was passed on capital crimes and decisions taken on matters of war and peace. On

10

the other hand, there was no administrative apparatus, no codified law, and no form of government, apart from the privileged position of authority granted to the duke or king in time of war.

The distinguishing characteristic of the German was his freedom. Clan and tribe were associations of free men. Outstanding achievements in battle were rewarded with increased respect in the community. The men so honoured were singled out from the mass of the free as "Edhelingi", or nobles. Younger men often attached themselves to one of these "Edhelingi" to form his retinue and placed themselves under him to carry out special feats on the battlefield or in hunting. Their chosen leader, in turn, entered on a relationship of mutual loyalty with his followers. This union between an outstanding personality and his followers had its roots in a distant past and continued in later centuries to take the place of the links between governor and governed which arose from the abstract idea of the state which had been spread by Rome throughout the lands of the Mediterranean.

The greatest dishonour which could befall a German was to yield to an external enemy. In war he fought to the death; even the women sacrificed their lives rather than let themselves be taken as slaves. Among members of the same clan, however, the German not infrequently staked his freedom and that of his family when the gambling mania seized him. His future might be decided by the final throw of the dice. He was prepared to become serf to a freeman. If he lost he forfeited, like any prisoner of war, the freeman's right to carry arms and to take his place in the "Thing", though he was still far from slavish subjection. His human dignity was rarely violated. It is a fact, however, that there was no penalty attached to killing a serf.

The religious life of the Germans was determined, in all essentials, by a simple nature myth. Nature was thought of as animated by superterrestrial and superhuman beings. Water, spring, stream and river, mountain, tree and plant, air, wind and storm were either the external manifestations of divine powers friendly to man or of the superterrene forces and powers inimical to him. In keeping with these concepts there was no special place set aside for the worship of the divine, no specific picture, no statue in which the divine was considered as especially dwelling. Even the nominal attribution of certain divine powers did not necessarily carry with it attribution of divine personality.

The most exalted artistic expressions of Mediterranean civilisation in antiquity were inspired by religious notions which had been developed by the Egyptians, Greeks or Romans about the nature of the divine or of life after death. Although the Germans shared with these peoples their awe before the divine and their belief in a future life, they never had such a tangibly concrete idea of a hierarchy of gods or of the place which awaited the souls of the deceased, as was, generally speaking, so characteristic of the southern lands. Prayer, sacrifice and religious worship were offered up in some sacred grove by a man or, more often, a woman who was believed to enjoy a special relationship with the divine. This explains why shrines or representations of the gods in stone or wood were completely unheard of among the Germans. The dead were laid to their eternal rest either under burial mounds constructed of heaped earth, or under erratic boulders which were dragged to the place of interment. Numerous funerary offerings in gold or bronze which were buried with them as articles of daily use (such as sword, shield or dagger, or ornaments for the neck or arm) bear witness to the artistic abilities of the men of that time and to their manual skill. Sword-pommel and dagger, necklace, armband and belt buckle give us, in their rich chasing, some idea of the artistic inventions of the Germans, who are thus shown to have been just as much at home in metalwork as were the great civilised peoples of the Mediterranean.

The Rhine boundary, which the Romans had accepted as the north-west limit of their empire, soon proved insufficiently secure in consequence of the frequent border violations by the Germans.

For this reason, the great Augustus (31 B.C.—A.D. 14), the first Roman Emperor, resolved to extend the Roman Empire to the north and east, to subjugate the Germans and bring them into Rome's imperial orbit. The Elbe was now to become the frontier of the empire. The Romans in fact succeeded, before the dawn of our era, in expanding their empire north towards the line of the Danube. From their large garrisons at Moguntiacum (later Mainz) and Castra Vetera (later Xanten) on the west bank of the Rhine, the Romans thrust eastwards into *Germania* and reached the Elbe in 9 B.C. A Roman fleet rounded the Skaw in north Europe; a Roman army kept winter quarters on German soil; and German nobles served in Roman armies. However, not all Germans were willing to view the military decision as final. Soon after the turn of the century a secret conspiracy against the Romans was formed and open rebellion finally broke out under the leadership of one of the tribal princes named Arminius. In the late autumn of A.D. 9 he succeeded in defeating the Romans in a three-day battle in the Teutoburg Forest and wiped out their forces. This battle brought about a complete reversal in Roman policy towards the Germans. Augustus decided to withdraw his world back to the Rhine-Danube frontier in the north and north-east, and to limit the Roman effort to the defence of this frontier. How right he had been in this decision was confirmed under his successor Tiberius by the outcome of Germanicus's campaign (A.D. 14—16), which was robbed of lasting effect by German resistance. From now on *Germania* continued to exist alongside the Roman Empire as an independent power within Europe, although internally it had not yet arrived at any form of state organisation and the individual tribes continued to fight bloody battles among themselves for the ascendancy. Among these the Chatti (Hessians) were for a time the most important. The Emperor Domitian took up arms against them as the constant troublemakers along the Rhine frontier (81—96) and vanquished them.

To strengthen the frontier he caused the fortified line of the *Limes* to be built, connecting the Rhine with the Danube. This started at presentday Rheinbrohl on the right bank of the Rhine, and incorporated the Taunus mountains before joining the river Main, whose course it followed roughly as far as Miltenberg; thence it continued with a double line of fortifications reaching on one side to the river Neckar and on the other to the present town of Lorch. From there it extended eastwards to connect with the upper course of the Danube in the region of Eining. This extensive fortification system, which had to be constructed almost entirely by the hand of man, was completed under the Roman Emperor Hadrian (117—138). The frequency of legionary camps of importance, which later grew into towns (e. g. Mainz, Koblenz, Augsburg, Regensburg), indicate Rome's assessment of the German danger. In the safeguarded hinterland a Roman city-civilisation flourished, centred on Trier (Treves), which was for a time one of the capitals of the Roman world empire. Its many architectural monuments (the most important being the Porta Nigra) still bear witness to its Roman past. The Moselle and Rhine regions were opened to Roman civilization and economy. The vine was introduced to the land of the Germans, where it was to find a permanent home along the banks of the two rivers.

Inside the *Limes* area an extensive trade, often carried on by Jews, developed between the Roman Empire and the free Germans. In this part of the Roman Empire as well the Jews had, after their expulsion from Palestine, found a new home and occupation. This accounts for the fact that, until very recent times, Jewish settlements were more numerous in the Roman areas on the banks of the Rhine than in the remainder of Germany. However, even these close commercial relations with the Romans did not lead to any substantial alteration

13

in the German outlook on life or the German social structure. The inhabitants of free *Germania* remained loyal to their traditional ways and habits, and continued as a people of peasant farmers.

Within the north-eastern area of German settlement around the Baltic, however, a few of the large tribes had, as early as the beginning of the Christian era and probably as a result of overpopulation, started to leave their settlements and migrate southwards. The great majority of these migrants first settled down again in the wide-open spaces of south-east Europe, in some cases with the sanction of the Roman overlord. The west German tribes remained unaffected by this migratory wave. Slav tribes thronged into the areas vacated around the Baltic and into the Oder-Vistula regions. Individual German tribes in the west undoubtedly made incursions into imperial territory, but, on the whole, the Romans were able to contain them and either to enroll the Germans in their armies as allies or to settle them as peasants on the great *latifundia*. This slow infiltration of German soldiers and settlers presented no immediate danger, but when the frontiers of the Roman Empire collapsed once and for all under the onslaught of more sizable federations of German tribes, it was these very Romanised Germans who turned out to be the best qualified to set the pace in the transition from Roman rule in Europe to German, since they were already versed in Roman military administration and economic tradition.

The First Steps Towards the Formation of an Independent State

The advent of the Huns, an Asiatic people who swept into Europe on their swift ponies, provided the decisive stimulus for the formation of an independent state. The first to make way before them were the German tribes settled in south-eastern Europe (southern Russia and the northern Balkans), who in turn forced their way into the Western Empire and founded German states on Roman imperial soil (Italy, Gaul, Spain and North Africa). The capital of the Western Empire was transferred from Rome to Ravenna. Most of the west German tribes were overrun by the Huns, whose kingdom, at the beginning of the first century, stretched from the Urals to the Rhine, and, for a short time, enjoyed friendly relations with Aetius, the most important Roman general of the day. With outstanding success he had defended the Roman province of Gaul against those German tribes who had crossed the Rhine. Although the Huns were defeated by Aetius in the same year in which they invaded Gaul (451), this victory also meant

14

the liberation of the Germans from Hunnish rule. For this reason it led to no abatement in the German pressure on the Western Empire and its frontiers. Their continual incursions into imperial territory led to the eventual disorganisation of the Roman Empire of the West in the second half of the fifth century. A German general, proclaimed emperor by the German soldiery, set himself at its head.

During the period of Hunnish rule over the Germans to the east of the Rhine, Frankish tribes, inhabiting the Lower Rhine and the regions along the Moselle and the Meuse, had united to form a confederacy. Over each tribe were set "Gau-kings", among whom the Merovingian line was preeminent. About the middle of the fifth century they had conquered Gaul as far as the Somme.

In 481, Clovis, a young man of sixteen, became King of the Franks. His sights were aimed higher than those of the other German conquerors who until now had invaded the territory of the Roman Empire. He was not simply concerned with satisfying the hunger for land of his Frankish fellow warriors. His ambition was to found a state which in extent and organisation would stand on an equal footing with, if not be superior to, the states already existing in the territory of the former Western Empire. But whereas practically all other German tribes made their conquests, cut off from their original settlement territory, and thus after they had severed their ties with their tribal lands, Clovis maintained his connections with the homeland even when he had penetrated far into the Roman Empire. This factor made a decisive contribution to the consolidation of the Merovingian-Frankish state during its formation.

Right at the beginning of his reign Clovis succeeded in wresting from the Romans the last independent Roman province on Gaulish soil, an area lying between the Somme and the Loire, and in bringing it under his rule. This success brought him into the direct vicinity of those regions under German rule on Gallo-Roman soil, which had in part come into being with the understanding of Rome: the territories of the Visigoths and the Burgundians. The kingdom of the Visigoths in south-western Gaul fell to him, whereas south-eastern Burgundy was incorporated into the Frankish kingdom only under his successors. He also forced his sovereignty on the Alemannic tribes settled on the left bank of the upper Rhine.

The conquest of what had formerly been Roman Gaul had brought Clovis and his Frankish peasant warriors into contact with the civilisation, state administration and economic system of the Romans, and with the new faith of Christianity. This last was far from being united in its doctrine. Whereas the original Roman population of the former Western Empire professed the religious point of view which saw its centre and fulcrum in Rome, as the seat of the Pope, whom they held to be the head of the Church in doctrinal teaching and ritual, the majority of the German conquerors had adopted the views of a priest of Alexandria, Arius, condemned by Rome. Arius had, through his heretical teaching that Jesus Christ and God were not identical, opposed himself to the generally received view of the Early Church. In contrast to all other Germans, Clovis accepted the Roman profession of faith, and was baptised with three thousand Franks by a Roman bishop. In this way he did not just avoid opposing his own beliefs to those of his Roman Catholic subjects, a situation which had persisted in most of the other German states on Roman soil. As things turned out, he determined thereby the religious development of Western and Central Europe, and thus of Germany, for centuries to come, along the lines of Catholicism and the Roman cultural legacy. Certainly the Franks accepted the new faith only gradually, and Clovis's and his successors's membership of the Christian church in no way meant that Christian morals and customs from then on determined the political activity and aspirations of these men—rather the opposite must be admitted to have been the case. But the disciplined organisation and religious orders of the Roman Church were to prove effective in making the Christian faith supreme, during the course of the next three hundred years, among the majority of the German tribes.

Of similar far-reaching significance was the adoption by the Frankish nation of certain Roman forms of administration and some parts of the Roman social structure. Whereas originally the "Gau-kings" of the Frankish tribes were of equal rank with Clovis and the power of each king was limited by the popular and warrior assemblies (in the "Thing"), Clovis succeeded in eliminating these rivals by arranging for their deaths by overt or underhand means. He appropriated their spheres of influence and power to himself and built up, on the model of Rome, an absolute monarchy whose power, as a consequence of the size of the kingdom, could no longer be held in check by the popular assemblies. Their place was taken by the king's followers, from among whom the royal officials and army chiefs were taken.

The king placed dukes (*duces*) subordinate to himself over the subjugated German tribes. The sole supreme judicial authority of the realm was the king, in whose name the judges of the lower courts passed sentence. The execution of the sentence was incumbent upon the counts appointed by the king. The king's court was above the legal

kilometres
0   200   400   600
0   200   400
miles

ARMENIA

REGNUM PARTHORUM

SYRIA

JUDAEA

ARABIA

CAPPADOCIA

BITHYNIA

GALATIA

CILICIA

ASIA

AEGYPTUS

Alexandria

CYRENE

THRACIA

MOESIA

MACEDONIA

EPIRUS

ACHAIA

Athenae

CRETA

DACIA

PANNONIA

ILLYRICUM

GERMANIA

Vindobona

NORI CUM

RAETIA

Castra Regina

Colonia Traiana

Colonia Agrippina

Confluentes

Mogontiacum

Augusta

Treverorum

GERM. SUP.

GERM. INFER.

BELGICA

Lutetia

GALLIA CISALPINE

GALLIA

ITALIA

Roma

SARDINIA

SICILIA

AFRICA

NUMIDIA

Massilia

Londinium

BRITANNIA

HISPANIA

BAETICA

MAURETANIA

The Roman Empire

assembly as it originally existed in the "Thing". As long as the Roman monetary system still persisted, the king drew his revenues, the so-called *regalia,* from the dues arising from customs, marketing, and the guilds. When payment in kind became prevalent, the monarch was more and more dependent on the income arising from the extensive royal domains.

The reward for services rendered to the king by members of his retinue usually took the form of a royal gift in fee of great estates. Such property was termed a fief (literally: thing loaned). On the death of the beneficiary the property reverted to the king; in the event of the king's death his successor had to reconfirm the feoffee in his fief. The holders of the Roman *latifundia* (large landed properties), where they had not fled before the Frankish onslaught, also asked for their possessions to be ratified by the king. They and the Frankish feudal owners developed into the new nobility. For the feudal nobility subordinate to the king, with graded rights and duties, the service in the army became a special prerogative. (This came to be known as the feudal system, from the Latin *feudum*—fief.)

To particularly deserving seigneurs the king guaranteed immunity (from the Latin *immunis*, meaning free from public dues). When this happened, the administration of justice was also in the hands of the seigneur, where his own employees or those living on his property were involved. Already at a relatively early date the king or great landowners made donations to the Church from their property or erected churches or monasteries on their lands. The appointment of the priest or the nomination of the abbot, the monastic superior, then became the prerogative of the donor. Churches and monasteries had also to pay dues to the landowner (the so-called "tithes").

The free peasantry slowly but surely lost its importance, since it was no longer able to fulfil the obligations which weighed so heavily upon it. Military service in time of war and attendance at the popular assemblies were not compatible with well-regulated cultivation of the fields. For this reason many peasants gave up their freedom and placed themselves and their property in the vassalage of a feudal lord. They exchanged their personal freedom for economic security for themselves and their families, and were susceptible to serfdom. In this way the early social structure of the free German warrior peasantry was superseded.

When Clovis died, his inheritance was divided equally among his sons in accordance with Frankish custom. His four sons at first pursued their father's policy of conquest together. The unity of the kingdom was thus assured, with the result that under a grandson of the founder the state stretched, about the middle of the fifth century, from the Mediterranean to the North Sea. But the authority of the Merovingian house was undermined all too soon by fraternal strife and patrimonial disputes which favoured the rise of the nobility to the dominant position within the kingdom. The non-Frankish German tribes were also thus enabled to free themselves more and more completely from the Frankish yoke.

The increasing impotence of the royal authority constrained the nobility to take over the conduct of foreign affairs as well. At the beginning of the eighth century the Islamic Arabs had succeeded in conquering Spain and in advancing, in an unprecedented victorious campaign, right into the heart of Frankish Gaul. This meant that this part of Europe, which had only recently been Christianised, was brought face to face for the first time with the problem of its future religious and cultural development. Should it continue to be formed in the spirit of Christendom, which in Roman Catholicism had absorbed substantial portions of the classical tradition? Or was it to be determined by the spirit of Mohammedanism, which, although it had also been influenced by Judaism and Christianity in its religious conceptions, was still at that time at a relatively lower cultural level? The decision here no longer lay in the hands of the Frankish kings but of the court nobles in the different parts of the kingdom who had gained considerable power as stewards of the royal household or of their sovereign's properties. Among these the Austrasian-Frankish, non-Romanised stock of the Carolingians enjoyed a reputation apart. Already towards the end of the seventh century a Carolingian had, with the agreement of the realm's nobility, taken over the administration of the entire land, without thereby infringing upon the nominal rule of the Frankish royal house. In fact the kings were only shadows of their former selves. This explains why the historically important victory the Franks won over the Saracens on the battlefield between Tours and Poitiers in 732 is associated with the name of Charles Martel, the mayor of the palace. In this capacity he had organised the preparations for the defence of the kingdom against the Moslem menace and had won the victory with the cavalry hosts he had himself assembled. The Arabs withdrew from Gaul into Spain; there they consolidated their position on European soil for centuries to come.

The importance of his victory in 732 naturally meant that Charles "the Hammer" was recognised as the undisputed first man in the kingdom of the Franks. It was to be his son, Pepin the Short, however, who was to exercise a still more decisive influence on the future internal constitution of the country. Pepin had himself nominated king by the assembly of the Franks in place of the Merovingians, now kings only in name. Already before he had entered into close relations with Boniface, the most important bishop of the day in the Frankish ecclesiastical world. This great missionary and apostle of the German tribes settled east of the Rhine had, from the very beginning of his work of Evangelisation, made it his aim to establish close organisational links between the bishoprics of Germany (whether new or long-established) and the head of the Catholic Church in Rome. To all intents and purposes the Frankish royal house, in spite of Pepin's assumption of the kingship, still reigned. For this reason Pepin required some legitimation, of his kingship by an authority, recognised by the entire people, which would carry more weight than the mere possession of royal blood. There was only one such authority in those days: the pope in Rome, successor of Simon Peter, the prince of the apostles, who, it is said, had laid down his life for his Master in that very city and who was venerated by all German Christians. Certainly Rome was still technically subject to the authority of the eastern emperor in Constantinople and the pope's political position as *Patricius Romanorum* (Protector of the Romans) was anything but well-defined. However, the contemporary political situation made the position of the pope as protector of the former Roman capital against the threatening inroads of the Germanic Lombards crucial. Constantinople was in no position to meet its military obligations for the defence of Rome and the Italian peninsula. As it was, the north was already firmly in the control of the Lombards, whose kings were increasingly successful in their efforts to extend the orbit of their power further south. The papacy itself was forced in its military weakness to look for an ally capable of defending Rome and its hinterland better than the Byzantines.

At this precise moment Pepin asked the supreme head of the Christian Church whether it was a good thing that in the land of the Franks those should be kings who had no power. The pope's reply was: it is better for him who exercises the royal power to enjoy the royal title. Accordingly Pepin was anointed and crowned by no less a person than Boniface, acting on behalf of the pope and with the approval of the great men in the land. In this way the lack of royal birth was offset by the authority of the Church and the ecclesiastical act of coronation (751).

The fall of Ravenna, then the capital of the surviving Western Empire, served to underline the acuteness of the danger for Rome.

The reigning pope thus decided to request the help of the Franks, the most considerable military power in the West, in meeting the Lombardic threat. In the autumn of 753 the Bishop of Rome crossed the Alps in person for the first time in the history of the papacy. He aimed at overcoming the reluctance of the Franks to wage war on their Christian fellow-Teutons, the Lombards, by launching a personal appeal. Pepin gave the pope his royal protection. An assembly of the Franks held at Easter 754 approved the resolution to march against the Lombards. The Franks also declared their readiness, in the event of a Frankish victory, to hand back to the Romans the regions wrested from the Lombards. The pope crowned Pepin and his sons, Charles and Carloman, in the Abbey of St. Denis. In this way those who could boast of no royal birth received both throne and consecration from the hands of the sovereign pontiff. That same pope made Pepin protector (*Patricius*) of Rome, the seat of papal government, although the city was by rights still under the jurisdiction of the eastern emperor in Constantinople.

The Franks defeated the Lombards in two punitive expeditions. By the Second Peace of Pavia they forced the Lombards to cede their conquests in northern central Italy. Pepin conferred the region around Ravenna and Rome on "Saint Peter and the Church". The Bishop of Rome, until now only the spiritual head of western Christendom, became a temporal ruler as well, though his authority was at first still dependent on the support of the secular powers of the West. Pepin's foundation of what was to become known as the Papal States marks the first stage in a development which was destined to determine the course of European history for nigh on 800 years: the struggle between the spiritual power of the pope and the temporal authority of the emperor.

Chapter Two

THE REVIVAL OF THE ROMAN EMPIRE IN THE WEST

Charlemagne

Pepin died in 768. The transference of royal power to his two sons, Charles and Carloman, took place smoothly. Carloman's death, three years later, brought the joint rule of the two brothers to an end. Thereupon Carloman's widow hurried off to the Lombards to win their support for the claims of her sons, whom Charles had deprived of any right to the throne. The pope was not directly involved in the renewal of hostilities between the two Teutonic peoples, the Franks and the Lombards, which ensued, but his sympathies were all on the side of the former. He saw the Lombards as his most dangerous enemy and, what is more, cherished hopes of seeing his temporal possessions extended. Charles emerged completely victorious from this campaign. The Lombard king was forced to abdicate in his conqueror's favour, so that Charles henceforth styled himself "King of the Franks and Lombards and Patrician of the Romans". Nevertheless the Lombard kingdom was not incorporated into that of the Franks; it remained a kingdom in its own right. But as an autonomous power the Lombards now (774) disappear from history once and for all. The Papal States, contrary to the expectations of the pope, received but negligible additions.

With his war against the Lombards Charles had embarked on the path of conquest, a policy which was to characterise his reign for some thirty years to come. His aim was, first and foremost, the safeguarding and extension of the Frankish state, and in this his overriding concern was the union of all the German tribal communities of central Europe. In realising this aim, Charles came up against two important opponents: in the south, the Mohammedan Moors, who under the Caliph of Cordoba held sway over the Spanish peninsula and its Germano-Roman Christian population; in the north-east, the German tribe of the Saxons, who in the teeth of all attempts to missionise them persisted in the paganism of their ancestors. Charles's campaigns against the Spanish caliphate were virtually devoid of success. Only one narrow strip along the north-east of the Iberian peninsula became a Carolingian march in Spain and therefore outside the orbit of Islamic rule and culture.

One factor rendered the wars against the Saxons especially difficult: in the Saxons the Franks came up against their equals in the field who, while defending their native soil, sought at the same time to maintain their independence of an alien social order and a foreign religion which they rejected with savage determination. These campaigns were not brought to a successful conclusion until 804. In their course Charles evolved his conception of the duties of a Christian ruler, which was to become fundamental for all medieval thinkers. It was based on one of the most important works of the late patristic period, a treatise written by St Augustine, the Bishop of Hippo in North Africa. From the viewpoint of the Christian message of salvation this great Father of the Church tried to interpret the epoch-making changes brought about by the conquest of the Roman Empire of the West by German tribes. In his view, there are two realms: the City of God or *Civitas Dei* (hence the Latin title of the work *De Civitate Dei*), whose members are all those who prove their faith in charity, and the City of Satan *(Civitas Diaboli)*, composed of the enemies of God. God alone knows to which city the individual belongs. It was not long, however, before a new construction was put upon this theory of St Augustine. This interpretation regarded the community of all baptised Christians as the "City of God" on earth, against which all the unbaptised and heterodox were ranged as the "City of Satan". According to this understanding of Augustine's mind, the history of mankind is nothing but a continual struggle between the "Children of Light", marked out for eternal salvation, and the "Children of Darkness", predestined to eternal damnation. The supreme task of the Christian ruler is, accordingly, the expansion and realisation of the kingdom of God on earth, with its religious centre in Rome, the seat of the supreme Christian pastor, the pope. According to this view of history, which Charles, too, adopted as his own, wars against pagans and their subjection to a Christian prince were the fulfilment of a divine charge, for, when the vanquished were converted to Christianity, the spread of the "City of God" was served. True to this conviction, Charles incorporated the Saxon tribal community completely into the orbit of Frankish rule and faith after the successful outcome of the war. Nevertheless, the faith which had at first been forced upon the Saxons very soon became a matter of interior adherence and personal conviction. Important monasteries, whose members were almost exclusively Saxon, sprang up and became centres of Christian piety and Romano-Frankish civilisation. The ecclesiastical organisation of the country into bishoprics and parishes was, very soon after the conclusion of hostilities, able to rely on native priests and bishops. At the same time these latter were, along with the tribal nobility, the most faithful servants of the Frankish King Charles.

Among those tribes within the Frankish kingdom which had already accepted Christianity, the Bavarians had, as early as the reign of Pepin, broken away from the confederation and founded their own Duchy anew. Thus it was that, after the overthrow of Lombardic independence and the alliance of this kingdom with the Carolingian, the all-important Brenner Pass lay in hostile hands. When the Duke of Bavaria refused to comply with Charles's invitation to recognise Frankish sovereignty, Charles went to war against him and dissolved the Bavarian Duchy. The country was then divided into regions administered by Frankish counts.

After Charles had been on the throne for some thirty years, he had, in his drive to extend his empire, enlarged his domains to the limits of what was then feasible. Seas, rivers and mountain ranges guaranteed his gains; at the same time they constituted natural barriers to further expansion. (In the north: the North Sea and the river Eyders which formed his boundary with the Danes; in the east: the Elbe and Enns rivers, beyond which were the Slavs; to the south: bordering on the Papal States, the sphere of influence of the East Roman Constantinople in south Italy on the one hand, and, below the line formed by the Ebro and the Pyrenees, the Islamic territories ruled by the Saracens on the other; to the west: the Atlantic Ocean.) He created strong marches administered by trustworthy margraves to secure his still pregnable northern and eastern frontiers. The remainder of his realm Charles ruled through Frankish counts, who also dispensed justice in his name; he hoped in this way to prevent the original tribal dukes from growing strong again.

Both in its extent and administration Charles's empire represented the first broadly conceived attempt to unite both Germans and Romans in one closely knit kingdom based on the Christian religion and a Christian conception of the state. Although he was himself of German extraction and spoke a German dialect as his mother tongue, he loved Latin as the language of learning, and a more advanced civilisation, and the Christian religion as he knew it from the liturgy and the Scriptures. In the government of his kingdom he carried on the tradition of the Romans which the Franks had taken over from former Roman Gaul, without however relinquishing certain of his German ideas. These were reflected above all in the administration of justice, in the political significance accorded the free peasantry, and in the personal relationship of loyalty that bound the ruler and his free subjects to one another. It was precisely because of the way in which he appeared to succeed in combining contraries harmoniously that many a medieval ruler took this great Frank as a revered model worthy of imitation. In so doing, however, they only too often forgot that the many and varied tensions which determined the history of the Middle Ages and thereby to a very large extent that of the Germans too during that period, and later, were to be traced back to Charles and the conception of the empire which he made a reality in the revival of the Roman Empire.

Doubtless it has never been adequately explained whether Charles had himself aspired to the imperial dignity which was conferred on him by Pope Leo III on Christmas Day in the year 800. Charles's protracted efforts to obtain recognition by the emperor of Constantinople as his equal seem to favour the view that the Frankish king definitely regarded the empire he had created as the lawful continuation of the former Western Empire, whose ruler had the right to the title of emperor (*Imperator*). That he had no desire to receive the crown from the hands of the pope is certain. In 813 he caused his son Louis to crown himself emperor. Undoubtedly this was a way of giving striking expression to his claim that he owed his sovereignty and that of his descendants not to the pope but to his own unaided efforts. Inversely, by the act of coronation the papacy emphasised in no uncertain way the dependence of the temporal power on the spiritual—in conscious opposition to Constantinople where the Christian Church was so subservient to the imperial will that it was almost one with the Byzantine state.

In recognition of his achievements in constructing and organising his empire, Charles already received the honorary title of "Great" during his own lifetime. He has thus come down to us as Charles the Great or Charlemagne. Later historians have not disputed his right to this title, even though the "Carolingian" empire, named after him, survived him by barely thirty years. But, in a way similar to that of the empire of Alexander the Great, states developed out of the Carolingian legacy which, although they had very little in common with the original creation in either their extent or their internal organisation, were neither able nor willing to part with what they had inherited from Charles. This

1. Porta Nigra,
   Trier (Treves).

2. The Imperial Throne of
   Charlemagne, Aachen
   (Aix-la-Chapelle).

5. Ivory Book Cover, c. 870.

legacy endured in the close union of the Christian faith of medieval Rome, the classical civilisation and culture of ancient Rome, and the ethos of the Christian state. In this sense both Germans and French regarded themselves as the rightful heirs to the Carolingian empire and the conception of empire embodied in it, whatever the diversity of their historical development, of the tasks set them, and their slowly developing national independence. The national consciousness of these peoples only awoke and grew as a result of the turmoils which overwhelmed them when Charlemagne's empire dissolved and hostile peoples poured into the former Carolingian territories in the course of the ninth century.

The Disintegration of the Carolingian Empire and the Formation of the European National States

Charles's only heir and successor was Louis the Pious, in contrast to his father a thoroughly weak ruler who never even succeeded in asserting his authority among the members of his own family. During his lifetime his three sons quarrelled about their inheritance, which was to be divided among them in accordance with Frankish custom. After his death these three grandsons of Charles the Great each agreed to take one third of the kingdom. The Middle Kingdom was called Lotharingia (Lorraine) after its last ruler Lothar, while the western and eastern parts of the kingdom were long known as the East and the West Frankish Kingdoms. Since the Lotharingian dynasty soon became extinct there were two further partitions, that of Mersen in 870 and that of Ribemont in 880. Lotharingia fell almost entirely to the East Kingdom; Burgundy and north Italy, originally parts of the Middle Kingdom, set themselves up as autonomous states. The frontiers between the East and the West Kingdom coincided almost entirely with the great language divide which began to sunder the East Franks from the West Franks soon after the death of Charlemagne.

Here a new and weighty factor entered on the scene which had formerly not played any part whatsoever in the relations between the tribes who had once been united under one king: language. This was brought home to the peoples settled on either side of the Rhine and the Moselle for the first time in 842. They were then called upon to swear loyalty to each other at Strasbourg as soldiers of Louis's sons. Two versions of the "Strasbourg Oaths" had to be prepared, one in Old High German and the other in Old French, so that both armies could understand them. The later partitions, originating from purely dynastic considerations, were to result in the wider and more significant partition between French and German.

The adoption of the language of the Gauls and Romans by the Franks settled in what had been Gaul and by other German tribes—a language which developed from the transformation of Latin into Old French—was the most fundamental part of the legacy handed down by the ancient Romans to the new inhabitants of this former Roman province. Because the German tribes which had settled in eastern Gaul and the northern Moselle and Meuse basins and their tribal relatives east of the Rhine clung to their hereditary German dialects, the languages went such separate ways that men who had formerly been members of one and the same tribe could no longer understand one another. To distinguish their language from the Latin then usual everywhere in ecclesiastical and scholarly circles, the tribes who had remained faithful to their German dialects designated their tongue "diutisc" or "national", "belonging to the people". From this "diutisc" there developed through many intermediate transformations over the centuries *Deutsch* (German). And finally what had originally been the designation for one particular tongue gave an entire people its name: whereas we still know them by their Latin name, Germans call themselves *Deutsche*.

But, in addition to the partitions of the empire and the language division into French and German, there was a further influence which contributed to the lasting disintegration of the empire and prepared the way for the formation of the national states: the numerous wars in which the former kingdom of Charles was embroiled in the course of the ninth century. The Norse Normans represented a threat to West and East Franks equally, whereas the forays of the Hungarians were directed principally against the East Franks. Both these invaders, instead of launching concentrated attacks at particular points, made isolated raids on widely separated areas in search of plunder and loot. Such tactics rendered it almost impossible for the assailed to organise a common defence in an effort to crush the enemy and, where required, pursue him back to his base. The weakness of the royal authority was to prove even more decisive here. Throughout the whole of the ninth century neither the heirs to the throne of the western part of the empire nor those called to wear the crown in the east, proved themselves capable of guaranteeing the security of their subjects against external foes.

Chapter Three

THE EMPIRE OF THE GERMANS

Kingship and Tribes

The tribal dukes took advantage of this troubled situation to regain the power which they had lost when Charlemagne, in keeping with his idea of a centralised state, had crushed and replaced them by counts responsible only to the king. With the approval of their fellow tribesmen the dukes now took over tasks which strictly speaking came under the royal jurisdiction. In the process the solidarity of the tribes was once again established, so that the dukes were in a position to defy even the power of the king. This was bound to lead to the eventual disintegration of the still surviving East and West Kingdoms into smaller tribal states, unless the monarchy was in a position to defend its rights against the dukes. This developed into an acute threat to the existence of the East Frankish Kingdom during the reign of Conrad I, (911—918), formerly Duke of Franconia. On the extinction of the East Frankish Carolings he had been chosen by the tribes as their king because of his wife's kinship with the Carolingian house.

Conrad was thus the first German to become king. Since his ambition was to strengthen the royal authority at the expense of ducal rights, the dukes of Saxony, Bavaria, and Swabia refused him their allegiance. Right from the outset, the Lotharingian duchy recognised the West Frankish king in Paris as its sovereign. Although the dukes had shown by electing a king that they recognised in principle the unity of the East Frankish state, it was still not clear from their attitude to the king's centralist pretensions how the royal and ducal claims were to be reconciled. Conrad was a failure in both internal and external politics. However, he did recognise the dangers threatening the still unconsolidated state, and sought to avert them on his deathbed by handing over the royal insignia to the strongest representative of the tribe-ducal interests, Henry, Duke of Saxony, with an offer of the succession.

By his acceptance Henry did not just become the first king to sever the East Kingdom's blood-ties with the earlier Carolingian kingdom.

27

He also placed the state on a new footing. Collaboration between king and dukes was now to take the place of the rivalry between royal and tribe-ducal authority. Henry thought his kingship granted him the position of a *primus inter pares,* declined to be anointed and crowned by the archbishop of Mainz, and took pains to win over by patient and wise negotiation those territorial dukes who had not been in agreement with his election. By diplomatic negotiations and the concession of privileges to the Bavarian Duchy, Henry prevailed upon the Bavarian duke, who himself had just been elected "King of the Germans", to make honourable submission. Swabia recognised Henry very soon after his election. The reincorporation of Lotharingia in the East Frankish Kingdom in the year 925 was the outcome of both diplomatic and military endeavours. For the first time in their history West Franks and East Franks, French and Germans, were fighting against each other. The West Frankish king had also refused to acknowledge Henry as King of the East Franks. But the military and diplomatic superiority of the Saxon duke soon proved decisive. Besides the subjection of Lotharingia to the East Frankish monarchy, Henry obtained the recognition of his kingship by the West Frankish ruler in Paris.

In those days the Lotharingian Duchy was considerably larger than the French Lorraine of later times. It included present-day Holland, Belgium, the western Rhineland, with the exception of Alsace which came under the Duchy of Swabia, and, in the south, extended as far as the headwater region of the Moselle. Burgundy had retained its independence.

With the exception of a number of western regions, Lotharingia belonged to the German language group. Frisians had made their home in the north, while the Meuse, Moselle and western Rhine regions were settled predominantly by Franks who had retained their original dialects in spite of their proximity to the French. In this respect, then, they were more akin to the German-speaking area in process of formation, but culturally they were superior to the inhabitants east of the Rhine. Their already important city-settlements like Cologne and Trier (Treves) could trace their origin back to the Romans. Classical tradition had partially survived, Christianity had struck deeper roots, the peasantry and the economy were further advanced. The acquisition of Lotharingia thus represented a gain for the East Frankish state. Furthermore, the annexation of this region by the East Frankish federation fixed the western frontier Germany shared with France for centuries to come. (The only question left undecided was that of sovereignty over Burgundy and north Italy—both successor states of the Carolingian empire.)

Henry's efforts to win recognition for his kingship from the tribal dukes were therefore successful. They were to prove of historical importance in as much as they once again heavily underlined the special structure of the East Frankish Kingdom. In contrast to the centralist monarchy of the Carolings, Henry's sovereignty was based upon the union of tribes enjoying equal status, whose dukes had surrendered part of their authority to the first among them, whom they themselves had nominated king. Thus, from the very beginning of her independent history, Germany was marked by that tension which must arise from the harmony or disharmony of royal and ducal authority. The typical expression of this tension is above all to be seen in the fact that Germany had for centuries no universally accepted capital.

The royal authority was bound up entirely with the person of the ruler and was effective wherever he succeeded in asserting it against that of the territorial lords. It was not first and foremost institutional but personal. Its power and significance was entirely dependent on the personality of the ruler, but had its foundation in the cultural and economic development of the tribes on the one hand and in the attitude adopted by them towards the monarchy on the other. Germany's political position in nascent Europe was dependent, far more than in the other states of the continent, on its rulers' ability to direct, on every occasion, the complex of cultural, economic and political expressions of the life of the tribes and territories, and their aspirations towards an objective agreed by and binding on all, without thereby hindering the development of the individual tribal character.

For this reason the "German" has, right from the beginning, eluded confinement within one universally valid definition. Wherever he has shared in the collective development, we can point to certain common characteristics; where, however, overemphasis of what distinguishes his tribe from the others, or geographical or political conditions have led him to go his own way, then, in spite of the common language, his idiosyncrasies come to the fore. In order to appreciate the influence this has had on the course of German history down to the present day, we must take a short look at the tribes who in the early tenth century transformed the East Frankish part of the former Carolingian empire into the empire of the Germans and say something, too, about their geographical distribution and their characters, which were already quite clearly formed, even at this early stage.

The Duchy of Bavaria controlled the Danube waterway and the Brenner Pass, and had a march in what was later to become Austria. Its *Nordgau* or northern region bordered on the Thuringian March and Franconia in the north and on the river Lech in the west. Merano, Bolzano (Bozen), and Bressanone (Brixen), towns in the region of the rivers Adige and Isarco, were Bavarian possessions in the south. Part of Bavaria's territory extended as far east as the river Enns.

The region later destined for settlement by the Bavarians came under Roman rule at the beginning of the Christian era and, after the Romans had abandoned all thought of further conquest, formed the northern frontier stronghold of the Roman Empire. Numerous fortified encampments were established along the Danube which later developed into towns and, in the course of the Christianisation of the area, became episcopal sees (Augsburg, Regensburg, Passau). During the great Migration of the Peoples the *Baivarii* or *Baiuvarii,* moving down from Bohemia, settled the area; the Celts withdrew before them, partly into isolated mountain valleys. At a very early date the Bavarians were converted to Christianity and organised on state lines. Their incorporation into the Merowingian-Frankish-Carolingian kingdom did not presage the end of their independent development, which was characterised by great pride in their tribal peculiarities, and had successfully resisted all attempts at assimilation. The Bavarian is in both thought and deed a conservative man of the soil. His close ties with his native surroundings bind him to his soil and traditions; his lively temperament inclines him to elemental outbursts, but awakens in him only rarely a spirit of adventure and a thirst for the unknown. The non-Bavarian, let alone the foreigner, he is apt to treat with a certain consciousness of his own superiority. His pride in his ancient cultural traditions has survived down to the present day.

In Swabia or Alemannia, whose eastern border was formed by the Lech, the tribal settlements proper were concentrated around the Lake of Constance and, in the Swabian Jura range ("Rauhe Alb") and the Black Forest regions. The settlements in Alsace to the west and Raetia to the south went their own separate way. Raetia and Rhaeto-Romance Graubünden took in the upper Rhine region, with the addition of Glarus and the Engadine, whose population was mainly Rhaeto-Romance. Here the Swabians controlled the *Bünder Passes* (Canton Graubünden, Switzerland).

The tribal territory of the Swabians and Alemanni had been ruled by the Romans for a considerable period of time. The area was occupied by the Swabians and Alemanni in the course of the Migration of the Peoples, but came under Frankish rule as early as the reign of Clovis. Irish monks brought Christianity to the region. A duchy formed here only on the decline of the Frankish kingdom but was later dissolved by Charlemagne. The original unity of the tribe was very soon lost as a result of the fragmentation of the Carolingian empire, but, nevertheless, certain striking tribal characteristics have survived. The Alemannic or Swabian German combines his decided individualism with a pronounced bent towards philosophic interpretation or poetic glorification of the world on the one hand, and with a marked sense for a realistic and practical view of things on the other. Whereas the mountain dwellers are more inclined to be reserved and conservative in outlook, the inhabitants of the lowlands and pleasant uplands offer the stranger a ready welcome and quickly adopt what suits them. A close attachment to the land of their forefathers draws emigrants home from foreign parts, so that tribe and land have remained homogeneous over the centuries.

The Duchy of Franconia was the region around the Main and the middle Rhine. It split into two parts. Riparian Franconia took in Hesse and extended from Cassel in the north to Weissenburg in the south; it thus included parts of present-day Württemberg and Baden, and the Rhenish Palatinate. The frontier then continued east of the Rhine beyond Andernach and ran in a north-easterly direction towards Westphalia. East Franconia occupied the upper and middle Rhine, where the name has survived down to the present day.

The Franconian tribe was composed of several peoples who, soon after the collapse of the Roman Empire, extended their settlements over broad areas of the former West Roman Province (Gaul) and there began to form a state. At the same time they became the earliest and most active mediators of Christian and classical cultural influences. The inhabitants east of the Rhine received their Christianity principally from Anglo-Saxon monks (Boniface) and very early built up a stable ecclesiastical organisation (Fulda and Mainz). The Franconians have always been an open-minded, cheerful and intellectually versatile people easily accessible to anything new or novel.

The Saxon Duchy, to which Holstein and Thuringia belonged (since 908), had the Elbe and Saale as its eastern boundaries, though its frontier marches brought it as far as the Oder. Its immediate neighbours to the south were Franconia and Lotharingia. In the north-west Saxony adjoined the territory of the Frisians.

The Saxons were already settled here, at the time of their first appearance in history about the second century of the Christian era. They were one of the few tribes which were not involved in the Migrations of the Peoples, apart from the inroads which sections of this tribe (Anglo-Saxons) made into the British Isles and their settlement of south England in the course of the fourth and fifth centuries. When Charlemagne embarked on his wars of conquest, the Saxons had spread over the north-western German plain and enjoyed some measure of political organisation. They ferociously resisted all attempts to Christianize them. This stubborn attachment to traditional conventions sanctified by long generations of their Saxon forebears reveals one of the predominant traits of the Saxon character. However, once they have abandoned some traditional practice or belief because, in their sober, objective judgment, the new is better, they will cling to this in its turn just as tenaciously. This explains how Christianity very soon found its most sincere adherents and most courageous champions in Germany among the members of this tribe. The Saxons have always united a decided tendency towards individualism with a robust faculty for state formation and cultural productivity. Their spirit of adventure springs more from their contempt for danger than from any soaring imagination, and is nearly always directed towards some definite goal which is bound up with personal material advantage. The more intellectually inclined Saxon easily gets wrapped up in speculative thought; his artistic creations show signs of bizarre fantasy. Thus the Saxons are considered a combination of strong mental contrasts which have often enough influenced German history in a positive or negative way.

In his efforts to win recognition from the German tribes for his position as *primus inter pares,* Henry I had also pursued foreign political objectives. For decades it had been impossible to quell the Hungarian threat. In 924 Henry purchased a nineteen-year ceasefire from them, years which he employed in building up an effective cavalry. In 933 he succeeded, with the aid of Bavarian troops, in defeating the Hungarians for the first time, thus justifying his kingship. During a campaign against the Danes which took place the following year he subdued what was later to become the Schleswig march.

Henry saw the king's tasks as circumscribed. In discharging them completely, he laid the foundations for the rise of his house under his son Otto the Great.

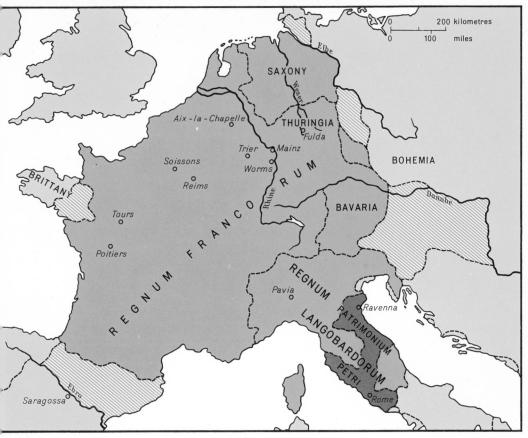

The Frankonian Empire under Charlemagne (768-814)

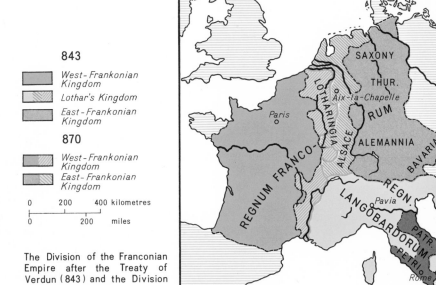

843

West-Frankonian Kingdom

Lothar's Kingdom

East-Frankonian Kingdom

870

West-Frankonian Kingdom

East-Frankonian Kingdom

The Division of the Franconian Empire after the Treaty of Verdun (843) and the Division of Lotharingia (870)

Henry had recommended his son Otto to the tribal dukes as his successor. On Henry's death Otto was duly and unanimously elected. This episode demonstrates that it was generally recognised that the monarchy was necessary to hold the young state together and that the eldest son had the right of succession. However, it is also clear that the right to elect the king, which was the prerogative of the aristocratic representatives of the tribes, was regarded as every bit as vital.

Although Otto realised fully the importance of the dukes, he tried, from the very outset, to place his kingship on an independent footing by reviving the Carolingian tradition. He had himself crowned king amidst great splendour on Charlemagne's throne in the great cathedral his great predecessor had built in Aachen. In the medieval Christian view of things consecration and unction by a bishop conferred a specially privileged position on the king, akin to that enjoyed by the priesthood, and a preeminent share in divine grace. He was thus enabled to fulfil his responsible office as a Christian ruler for the good of his subjects and the Church. In accordance with this conception Otto and his successors looked upon themselves as God's representatives. Such a view must inevitably be reflected in the king's attitude to the tribal dukes. At his coronation banquet Otto assigned the dukes the position of privileged servants of the king by allotting them functions similar to those of the old German court nobility. His aim here was the conversion of ducal authority into an office granted by, and discharged in the service of, the king and the royal authority. The dukes answered these efforts with revolts in which members of Otto's own family took part. Otto succeeded in crushing all rebellion but he was forced to recognise that the territorial lords would put their own interests and those of their clan before those of the nascent kingdom, and were not prepared to bow unconditionally before the authority of the king. The dualism involved in the interplay of royal authority and ducal authority did not appear to meet the needs of the kingdom.

In this decisive hour for the unity of his kingdom Otto cast about for a new support for his authority and found it in the Church. From time immemorial the Church had for religious, political and organisational reasons regarded a strong central secular authority as highly desirable. Papacy and Papal States needed the secular arm for their own protection; bishops and abbots could fulfil their religious and cultural obligations best if peace was assured. Moreover, diocesan and monastic boundaries were but rarely coterminous with those of the tribal territories. The more powerful the central authority, the more safely the Church could carry out her varied tasks. On the other hand the secular power had frequently to avail itself of the services of the clergy. The clerical was the only class in those days whose members had to have a higher education and some knowledge of Latin. Otto's own father had made the archbishop of Mainz chancellor for this very reason. The preparation of official documents was also the work of clerics who, as court officials in the royal chapel, performed secular as well as spiritual functions. The clerics in question were mainly drawn from the ranks of the younger sons of the higher nobility in all the German tribal communities. From now on the king chose bishops and abbots from their ranks when a vacancy arose, assigned them secular duties, including those of a knight in the royal service and of the provision of soldiers from their dioceses, and rewarded them for faithful service with rich fiefs from the royal domains. Certainly the prelates of the Church still continued to be elected by clergy and people, but, since the royal will was gladly accomplished by the Church, these elections had by this time become a mere matter of form. Otto himself selected only worthy incumbents for the higher ecclesiastical offices so that the ecclesiastical authorities tended to look on the new arrangement rather as an advantage. Since the higher clergy were bound to celibacy, there was no question of their bequeathing their royal fiefs, as was the case with the temporal lords. Clerical fiefs had therefore to be redistributed by the king after the death of their holder. This meant that the king could fill these offices-cum-fiefs in a way best suited to his and the kingdom's interests. As a symbol of their authority the higher clergy carried a staff (crosier). Like the pope in Rome, the German princes of the Church were temporal lords as well. Otto's policy for the imperial church was characterised by the selection and installation of the lords spiritual from the viewpoint of their usefulness for the royal will. The higher clergy gradually took the place of a civil service drawn from the dukes and counts of the empire, who, since the merger of fief and office, were no longer ready to serve in this capacity. From now on the clergy formed the largest single body serving the king and bore the burden of the upkeep of Otto's itinerant court.

The Hungarians had not discontinued their raids, especially into the southern parts of the kingdom, in spite of their defeat under Henry I (933). In 955 they had penetrated in great numbers as far as Swabia. On the Lechfeld Otto opposed them at the head of a great army to which all the tribes had voluntarily contributed contingents and to which the spiritual lords had sent a high levy. On this occasion he inflicted such a crushing defeat on the Hungarians, that they gave up their ways of plunder and ravage and became sedentary in bulding up farming communities along the banks of the Danube and the Tisa.

Once again the might of the Germans when united for a common end had been demonstrated. Once again the lesson had been driven home that a common danger could only be effectively encountered by all the tribes acting in concert. Not only this, but Otto's fame spread far afield, for by this victory he had shown the whole people and both spiritual and temporal lords, even more spectacularly than his father before him, the need for a strong central authority. Otto's praises were sung even beyond the German frontiers and his contemporaries got into the habit of calling him Otto "the Great". The defeat of the Hungarians on the river Lech near Augsburg also marked the close of the troubled period of the "Völkerwanderung" in Europe and gained a new mission field for Roman Christianity. In the year 1001 Stephan, King of the Hungarians, embraced the Christian faith.

Even as Saxon duke Otto had been brought into closer contact than any other of the German tribal lords with the problems raised by the unfortified and unpacified eastern frontiers of the kingdom. The geographical conditions in north Germany favoured the inroads of the Slav tribes who, in the course of their migrations, had advanced to settle areas as far west of the Oder as the middle and lower course of the Elbe. Charlemagne had tried to find an answer by creating strong marches which would contain the Slavs and halt their further advance. Otto took up this policy again, laid the Slavs between the Elbe and the Oder under tribute, and secured the territory thus gained by a chain of strong military bases. Not content with this, he even tried, in imitation of his revered model, Charlemagne, and inspired by the Augustinian concept of the "City of God", to convert the Slavs to Christianity and to provide them with an ecclesiastical organisation focused on Magdeburg. In a similar way, he tried to forge strong links between Bohemia and the *Reich* by creating the bishopric of Prague, with the complete agreement of the Bohemian duke. By this measure he hoped to give Bohemia a Church centre of its own whence missionary activity could be effectively carried out. However, Otto was only able to realise both these ends, because of a historical event which was to determine Germany's position in Europe for centuries to come and to lay a responsibility on its king which greatly exceeded that of the government of a still young and unconsolidated kingdom.

The event alluded to took place in 962. The decline of the Carolingian monarchy had brought in its wake a period of political and moral decay for Rome and Italy, from whose effects the papacy had not been excluded: in ecclesiastical history the ninth and early tenth centuries have come down to us as the Dark Age of the Church. As early as 951 Otto had made his first Alpine crossing and had received homage in Pavia as the King of the Lombards. This was the first indication he gave of his intended resumption of Carolingian policy in Italy. In 960 the pope turned to Otto for protection against anti-papal elements and promised him the imperial crown as his reward. Early in 962 Otto arrived in Rome accompanied by his queen. On 2 February he was solemnly crowned by the Vicar of Christ. In a special agreement the new Roman emperor confirmed the ancient donations and augmented them with new ones. The pope promised for his part that popes elect should swear their loyalty to the existent treaties before their coronation. This amounted to the concession of the right of confirmation to the emperor in papal elections. Otto made use of this newly acquired right for the good of the Church before his three-year stay in Italy was over. The German kings in their capacity as emperors, and thus as protectors of Rome and the Church, always endeavoured to raise the credit of the papacy of their day by advancing men who were morally above reproach, and to strengthen the papal office for the fulfilment of its lofty duties. It is one of the tragic developments of German history that the papacy was to attempt, a century later, to break free from this dependence on the emperor and aspire after a position of supremacy over all secular powers.

Otto also tried to arrange a marriage between his son and a Byzantine princess. He hoped in this way to gain the support of the eastern emperor in Constantinople for his newly revived western imperial dignity, and to bring about a relaxation in the tensions between East and West Rome. The eastern emperor, however, was extremely put out by Otto's assumption of the title "emperor" of the Romans. Otto's envoy was therefore informed in no uncertain terms that his master was neither emperor nor Roman, in fact nothing more than a barbarian king. There could thus be no question of a marriage between his son and an imperial Byzantine princess. In the end a marriage took place with the Greek Theophano, a distant relative of the Eastern Emperor. But Theophano was not an imperial princess.

The imperial coronation did not bring any external increase of power to the German king. But the imperial office did raise the king above all the dignitaries of the Christian West. It placed a special obligation on him. He was now bound to give priority to the defence of the common supranational Christian inheritance, and to the protection of this in its visible institutions, the papacy and the Church; national interests took second place. It was in this sense that medieval imperial policy with its reference to the whole of western Christendom was seen as the fulfilment of a God-given task. This special primacy of honour was granted to Otto in the first place because of his distinguished political services; later it devolved upon the German king as a matter of course. The imperial office also founded Germany's close relations with Italy and Rome.

In this sense the year 962 marks a turning-point in German history. It cannot be denied on any, even the strictest, standards of historical criticism that from this time onwards the policy of many German kings was inspired by an ideal conception which transcended both nation and state and which it was their high purpose to realise. The conviction that the kingdom of God could be made a reality here below through the Christianisation of mankind lay at the back of political measures which may seem incomprehensible to the presentday observer, accustomed as he is to view politics from the single aspect of the selfish extension of power.

The erection of the archdiocese of Magdeburg as the centre for the Slav missions, one of Otto the Great's pet schemes, led to a serious conflict with the imperial chancellor, the Archbishop of Mainz, who saw a threat to his ecclesiastical and temporal power in this removal of a great diocese from the sphere of his jurisdiction. In this way Otto came into conflict with the very princes of the Church he had promoted to the rank of his chief helpers in an effort to provide a counterweight to the territorial powers. Just thirty years later his grandson, Otto III, was to go a step further. He made Gnesen (Gniezo) an archiepiscopal see and thereby severed the entire Slav mission from the sphere of influence of the German Church; by placing Kolberg, Breslau and Cracow under the new archdiocese he laid the basis for the formation of a separate Polish church, which later became one of the chief pillars of the Polish state. Both the creation of the see of Prague by Otto the Great and the erection of the Hungarian bishoprics by Otto III were the result of purely ecclesiastical considerations, for, although they were filled with German bishops, as in the case of Hungary, they were not subordinated to the hierarchy of the German empire but placed under the direct jurisdiction of the pope. Nevertheless there was at the outset no noticeable decline in German religious and cultural influence in these lands.

The extension of Germany's power over northern Italy and, via the protectorship of the pope, over Rome and the Papal States as well, may appear considerable from the purely territorial viewpoint. But it should not be forgotten that in those centuries, when the economy was based entirely on barter, the king and his court were entirely dependent on the various payments in kind made by his subjects, or on the produce from the royal properties. Furthermore the network of communications was but little developed. The fulfilment of the functions of government thus made enormous demands on the ruler, because, in the last analysis, everything was bound up with his personal presence. The concept of the state as something independent of the person of the ruler was almost unknown in those days. For this reason the local powers were only too ready to take advantage of the king's absence to feather their own nests. And yet, frequent Italian or Roman expeditions, imperative if the emperor was to meet his obligations, were unpopular in Germany and were only possible at the cost of concessions to the tribal duchies or to the spiritual lords. Concessions were all the more necessary, since such expeditions demanded a well-equipped armed force. Of course, the protracted campaigns beyond the Alps, the protectorship of Rome, and the struggle against Arab penetration in south Italy, all strengthened German self-confidence, but the price paid for this expansion of power could just as easily appear too high, when whole armies were decimated in battle or devastated by malaria. More often than not such reverses also had repercussions in Germany. When, for example, Otto's son, Otto II, was defeated by the Arabs in southern Italy, the Danes and Slavs rose up against the Germans and all territorial acquisitions were lost save for Meissen and Zeitz. The rivers Eider, Elbe and Saale once again formed the boundaries of the empire. The situation became still more perilous for Germany under Otto III, who had completely committed himself to a quasi-mystical Christian ideal of world domination. To free the papacy from the harmful influences of the contending parties among the Roman nobility, he put on the papal throne his cousin Bruno, who thus became the first German to sit on the chair of Peter. Pope and emperor were now to cooperate so closely that Rome would once again become the capital of the Christian world. The Roman aristocracy thwarted this plan by inciting a popular rising. The emperor was forced to flee the city, after making a futile speech to "his Romans". Even the Germans showed little enthusiasm in rallying to his call for the reconquest of Rome. During this campaign the emperor died of malaria.

The failure of the last of the Ottos shows how completely out of tune his policy was with the real needs of the day. No matter how vital the exalted idea of a Christian West united under emperor and pope may have been, it was still not strong enough to effect a lasting and peaceful compromise with the nationalist aspirations which were awakening in Poland, Bohemia and Hungary—not to mention western and northern Europe.

The experience gained during the reign of Otto III, who died unmarried, caused his more down-to-earth successor, Henry II (1001—1024), to place German policy on a new footing. Certainly he, too, sought imperial coronation from the pope and treated the German claims over the Lombards, who wanted to deny him his royal prerogatives, just as seriously as his predecessor had done, but he regarded his primary task as the internal and external consolidation of Germany. Where the imperial Church was concerned he followed Otto the Great's line. In it he saw the chief mainstay of his authority and, although he backed all plans designed to ensure the best possible preparation of the monastic and parochial clergy for the performance of their religious and spiritual functions, he did not hesitate to appoint princes of the Church to their office according to his own, completely independent appraisal of them, from the viewpoint of their usefulness to him in spheres that had little or nothing to do with their spiritual calling. But since Henry II only entrusted such offices to persons above reproach by ecclesiastical standards, the Church reformers, whose centre since the beginning of the tenth century had been the Abbey of Cluny, raised no objection, although their declared aim was in fact to harness the temporal sphere as well to the service of the Church, which meant, in the last analysis, the subordination of the king and emperor to the pope of Rome.

More critical, at the time, was Germany's first great conflict with her eastern neighbour. Out of the West Slav tribes, peasant settlers between the Vistula and the Oder, the non-Slav stock of the Piast princes had, starting in the reign of Otto the Great, fashioned the beginnings of a state of the Poles (i. e. "field-dwellers") by adopting the Roman Catholic faith and making use of the pre-existent ecclesiastical organisation. The initial close collaboration with the Ottos, whose overlordship the young state at first acknowledged, led to a considerable extension of the area they ruled over, until, by 990, their territory stretched as far as the Baltic in the north and Silesia in the south. In creating the archbishopric of Gnesen Otto III concurred in the transfer of the Polish kingdom to Saint Peter (i. e. the pope) to the extent that he nominated the Polish Duke Boleslaw Chrobry (992—1025), Roman Patrician, or, in other words, his viceroy. Poland was no longer to be subject to German rule but to enjoy equal rights as a part of the empire at whose head Otto the emperor stood. The early death of Otto III frustrated these plans. Boleslaw's campaigns of conquest, which led to the annexation of Bohemia and other great areas east of the Elbe under German suzerainty, drove Henry II to defend German rights and to enter on a war which was to last more than fifteen years (1003—1018). Bohemia was, indeed, once again subjected to the empire and given a duke of its own, but the areas east of the Elbe had, in spite of long-drawn-out fighting, to be left in Boleslaw's hands as a German fief. Only the Meissen march was won back for Germany. However, soon after the death of Boleslaw, Polish power disintegrated and the German fiefs reverted to the empire. Notwithstanding his war with the Polish state, Henry kept up his efforts to promote the Slav mission. For this reason, as early as 1212, he had made Bamberg an episcopal see, which became a bulwark of Christian Germanity in the upper Main area and a base for missionary activity among the Main Slavs. He provided it with an extremely well-stocked library, enriched with numerous French and Italian as well as German manuscripts. In this way, Bamberg developed into a spiritual and cultural centre for the whole area.

Henry, in contrast to his youthful predecessor, had set himself a realistic objective for his reign: the restoration and internal consolidation of the "Empire of the Franks", as Germany is still known in the Latin documents of the time. In this respect he was entirely successful. Following his death without issue the transition of the crown from the Saxon to the Salian or Frankish house took place peacefully. Conrad II (1024—1039) was elected by the German dukes because of his relationship to the Ottos (he was great-great-grandson of Otto the Great). The claims of blood still took priority over the right to elect.

The kings and emperors of the Saxon house had, to the end, seen the basis of their high dignity in their unreflective assumption that all sovereignty derives from a direct divine mandate to the person it is invested in. Accordingly the subject, whether secular or ecclesiastical, stands in a sort of mystical relationship to the king-emperor comparable to that of the latter to God. In a sense empire and Church were therefore faced in the rule of their sovereign with the main characteristics of the divine rule. These notions were drastically altered under the new king. For this reason people have been tempted to regard him as a sort of freak appearance among medieval rulers. For him the

6. The Bernward Portal, Hildesheim.

7. St George's, Reichenau.

8. Maria Laach.

9. Spires Cathedral.

10. Worms Cathedral.

11. Bronze grave slab in
the Cathedral,
Magdeburg.

empire was an objective, autonomous institution, independent of the person of the sovereign, which both ruler and ruled were called upon to serve in the same way. When representatives of the Lombards pleaded the death of Henry II in mitigation of their destruction of the imperial castle in Pavia, Conrad replied: "When the king dies, the kingdom still lives." And in this spirit Conrad performed the duties of his office. The trials of strength with the dukes, which he also had to undergo, occasioned yet another attempt to rid the empire of the tensions arising from the tug-of-war between central and territorial authority. Conrad allotted the duchies to members of his own family and created in the lower gentry of counts and freemen, the so-called subvasalls, i. e. the vasalls of the princes, an utterly loyal instrument of government and an important counterbalance to the ducal powers. In return for their services the king protected these subvasalls against tyrannisation by their feudal lords and converted their fiefs into hereditary properties. The new class, among which were also the sons of country gentlemen, was utilised by the king for both military and administrative functions; many of them were able to read and write.

Completely failing to recognise the true mission of the imperial Church, Conrad regarded it as an organ of state and treated it accordingly. Royal preferment to a spiritual office became more and more dependent on what taxes the future prelate was prepared to pay the king. The moral worthiness of the proposed beneficiary, a factor which until now had always played a leading role in the allocation of such offices, receded more and more into the background; in the foreground was the candidate's financial and political usefulness to the king. Yet it cannot be denied that Conrad possessed a personal, if also very conventional, piety. He did much to promote churches and monasteries, even when Christian reform was preached in them which stood in marked contrast with the political practices of the king and his obsequious clergy. The latter were intent more on filling their coffers with worldly riches than on fulfilling their spiritual duties. He laid the foundations of one of the most splendid early-medieval Romanesque cathedrals, that of Spires (Speyer), which he intended as mortuary church for the Salian Franks. He also subsidised the Salian family monastery of Limburg-an-der-Haardt.

In an effort to cement the bonds between Germany and Italy Conrad encouraged marriages between German nobles and Lombardic families. He countered the archbishop of Milans's efforts to assert his independence of both empire and papacy with his deposition. In this conflict

41

he skilfully exploited both the pope and the archbishop's Milanese opponents for his own ends. The opposition to the archbishop was composed of Milanese citizens and members of the lower nobility who had joined forces against the aristocratic camp, from whose ranks the archbishop had been chosen. The cathedral chapter served the aristocracy's interests, too. Conrad could exploit these contending factions all the more easily since he completely controlled the papacy, without however deducing any obligations towards the Church from this power. When he raised a man to the papal throne, the candidate's malleability and not his worthiness was paramount in his eyes. The imperial office represented for Conrad power over both pope and Church, the subordination of the religious and ecclesiastical sphere to the interests of the empire, and an instrument for the expansion of the German king's power.

Conrad made this abundantly clear at his imperial coronation, which took place in Rome three years after his election. The ceremony was performed amidst unprecedented pomp in the presence of two kings (Canute the Great of England and Denmark, and Rudolph III of Burgundy), eight archbishops (three Italian and five German), and a great number of bishops and abbots. The German king could rightly regard himself as emperor, and consequently as ruler of the Roman Catholic part of Christendom. Even the East Roman Byzantine emperor stood on friendly terms with him. In south Italy the Normans, having become sedentary, acknowledged the overlordship of the empire, and Monte Cassino, the oldest monastery of Roman Christianity, elected a German as abbot.

As far back as the reign of Henry II the German throne had acquired the right of reversion over Burgundy. However, when the Burgundian royal house became extinct, Odo of Champagne asserted his claims to the throne. By skilfully exploiting the confusion prevailing around the French throne, Conrad succeeded in foiling Odo's designs on the Burgundian crown. This he received himself in the Cluniac abbey of Peterlingen (today Payerne in Canton Vaud, Switzerland) in the year 1033. He received the homage of the Burgundian nobility in Geneva. Burgundy represented a considerable safeguard of German authority in Italy and rounded off the Empire in the west.

Independent Cultural Development Within the Shadow of the Church

The Germans had organised themselves into a state earlier than the other peoples of Europe. Geographically this state ended at the confines of the German tribal settlements, but its sovereign obligations extended far beyond the German language area and were as far-reaching as those of the Roman Catholic Church with her universal pretensions. On this point the Germans were as completely oblivious as the Catholic Church of the internal tensions arising from the conflict between this claim and reality. It is not surprising that no one alive at the time suspected that one day this same power exercised over the Church might come into conflict with a changed conception of the nature and mission of Christianity and its visible embodiment, the Church. After all the Church had adapted itself in many respects to the external forms of the secular state. Just as the state was founded on the personal relationship of the individual subject to the next in station above him in a social scale culminating in the king, so the Church, too, was organised on hierarchical lines. The leading positions in the Church were occupied by men drawn from the same class, whose way of thinking and acting differed little from that of their secular counterparts. Roman Catholics were only very vaguely conscious of the changes Christianity had undergone owing to their close relations and in the adaptation to the views and ways of the German peoples. This is why no contradiction was at first sensed between genuine Christian teaching and Christian reality as practised throughout the empire and Church.

The culture of that time was also borne to a very large extent by the same class which had the monopoly of the leading positions in the Church. This meant that it was moulded equally by both the Christian and the German spirit; it flourished in those monasteries and convents where the monks and nuns, very soon after the coming of Christianity, were men and women of the German tongue. In literature Latin works at first greatly outnumbered German compositions; historians wrote in the language of the Church. In both cases the foreign language was handled with an astonishing assurance, which was one of the decisive reasons why the authors were able to weave personal ideas and opinions into their narrative. This German influence becomes still more noticeable in the early works written in their native tongue by members of the religous communities. Naturally enough the subject matter is Christian in inspiration; themes were generally taken from the pages of the New Testament itself. However, everything is unmistakably seen through German eyes. Where the authors found it impossible to harmonise Christian and German conceptions, they simply gave the German their preference, without causing any raised eyebrows among contemporaries. There is accordingly an element of inconsistency in all these works: although the writers are obviously thoroughly at home in the world of Christianity, the influence of their German pagan tradition is still so strong that they cannot break with it entirely.

We are nevertheless surprised to see that, once the alliteration of Old German had been discarded, the vulgar tongue, so recently discovered as a literary medium, adopted classical models for its poetry with amazing rapidity. In this respect early German poetry stands in splendid isolation in the Europe of its days, since there are hardly any outstanding works in other European tongues to be compared with the German creations in extent and significance.

The most important contribution the Germans made was in the field of ecclesiastical and monastic architecture. Under Charlemagne, the peoples north of the Alps had already begun to build in stone after the classical example (the palace chapel in Aachen is one instance of this). But it was not until the Saxon kings of the tenth century that building in stone became the rule throughout the whole of Germany. The basilica form reached its culmination in Bishop Bernward's Church of St Michael in Hildesheim, in the colonnaded basilicas of the monastic reformer, Poppo von Stablo, in Limburg and Hersfeld, in the cathedrals of Bamberg, Worms, Spires, Würzburg and Mainz. In the new episcopal sees erected in the Saxon and Wendish regions stone churches were raised whose groundplan was, generally speaking, similar to that of the basilica.

Only in one respect did the church of these early times depart from the pure basilican form, and that was in the development of the cruciform groundplan and the emphasis placed on choir and transept. The change in the function of the church can clearly be seen here. Monastic and episcopal church buildings were first and foremost for the priest and the liturgy he performed; the area set aside for the laity had accordingly to be curtailed. The cruciform groundplan was not merely a Christian symbol; it also made possible a clear-cut division between priest and layman inside the church.

The decisive change in ecclesiastical and monastic architecture came with the adoption of the Roman art of vaulting in what has become known as the Romanesque style, which would in fact be more correctly named the German style, since it represents the first really independent achievement of medieval Germany. And a remarkable achievement it was, too. It not only presupposed exact previous calculation and planning; it also called for a sure sense of proportion in the artistic partitioning of the church interior and for the finest anticipation of the effects of lights and shades within the church, which was divided by vaulting, columns and windows. The capacity of individual master-builders to give an individual character to each building, in spite of the identical basic structure, was also remarkable. The pleasure they experienced in ringing formal changes and in giving virile and striking expression to their own entirely personal experience of the mysteries of the Christian faith is unexpectedly reflected in the bronze-work of the doors, the stone-work of the capitals, the mural paintings in the church—of which but few have survived—and the first attempts at plastic expression.

The legacy of art on a smaller scale is considerably richer. Here book illumination took pride of place, because it was concerned almost exclusively with the artistic decoration of the "Book of Books", the Bible. Initially here, too, foreign influence was great. The Irish monks who had missionised southern Germany had developed their own forms and modes of expression. But as early as the ninth and tenth centuries German book ornamentation had cast aside the foreign model. The same process took place in the extremely widespread ivory-carving, which was under marked Byzantine influence (via Venice) and only gradually found its way to independent forms of expression.

The monks, however, in contrast to their eastern brethren, had never, since the days of their founder, St Benedict of Nursia, confined their activities to the sphere of religion and art. Very early on they had shown themselves to be major pioneers in the field of agriculture, especially in connection with their missionary activity. To provide wine for liturgical use they had brought the vine to areas climatically less suited. Furthermore, by clearing new ground, better soil management, the improvement of numerous indigenous plants, and the introduction of practical agricultural machinery, they made a major contribution towards extending the area suitable for settlement east of the Rhine. The monks thus enlisted the good will of the secular aristocracy, with the result that the latter handed over great areas for cultivation and as sites for monasteries, in return for moderate dues and a decisive say in the election of the abbot. Speaking in general, the monasteries became wealthy in the space of but a few decades. Even the nobility began to look upon the life of a monk, and still more of an abbot, as an extremely desirable calling which scarcely differed from purely secular professions and involved no obligation to lead an ascetic religious life. In this way monastic discipline gradually relaxed.

The reform movement which emanated from the monastery of Cluny in France reacted against this development at the beginning of the tenth century. By the end of that same century the movement began to make its influence felt in Germany, too. The reformers saw the restoration of the original monastic independence and the guarantee of the free election of abbots as their essential objectives. The Cluniac reform movement took on political significance when it turned its attentions to combatting the simoniacal practice of buying and selling spiritial benefices and dignities. Here it clashed with the practice of the German king and other temporal authorities who demanded payment for the conferment of a bishopric or abbacy (this was known as "lay investiture", i. e. installation in a spiritual office by a layman).

The harmful influence of secular princes on monastic life was to be eliminated. The reform movement thus had repercussions in the entire economic and medieval social order. For this reason the success of the reform meant for the monarchy the loss of considerable revenues, and for the larger land-owning nobility the loss of rights in filling abbacies or parishes, where the benefices in question were founded by them. The reformers also strove to restore the celibacy of the parochial clergy.

The reform movement gave rise to a conflict in medieval man between what he thought right and what he held necessary. On the one hand, he wanted to see the ecclesiastico-Christian concept of the nature and duties of the spiritual office put into practice, since the German of this period was first and foremost a Christian. On the other hand, this concept was very often opposed to the political and economic needs which arose from the structure of the medieval state, from the pressure of political responsibilities, and the natural tendency in men to augment economic gain and to defend their acquired rights. The eleventh century was moulded by this internal conflict and the appearance of the reform movement.

The Holy Roman Empire and the Ecclesiastical Reform Movement

By the reign of Conrad II the Cluniac ideas had also found adherents in the German monasteries. Originally they had aimed purely and simply, especially in Germany, at a reform of monastic life; with time, however, the movement's objectives gradually became more comprehensive, until its goal was a thorough transformation of the world by the Christian faith. The reformers did their utmost to win the support of the temporal and ecclesiastical aristocracy. Henry III (1039—1056), Conrad II's successor, was captivated by their ideals as a youth, and as ruler tried to carry them into practice. In this he was encouraged by his wife, Agnes of Poitou, whose Aquitanian background had given the Cluniac reform movement secular expression in Christian chivalry. In his endeavour to combine Cluniac demands with the political necessities of the empire, Henry III formed his idea of the Christian ruler, which he tried to realise during his reign. In contrast to his father, who had secularised the Church, he tried to "desecularise" the empire. Certainly he, too, invested prelates in their offices, but the criterion for their nomination was not their political or military abilities, not noble birth or kinship with the royal house, but theological knowledge and ecclesiastical piety alone. Thus, under him, an episcopacy came into being which, while conscious of its close links with the ideas of the reformers, was nevertheless also fully aware of its duty to show the king unswerving loyalty, because it saw in him one of the Church's strong supports for the Christianisation of this world. In order to give external expression to the bishop's close ties with his see, Henry handed to the bishop-elect, in addition to the crosier or pastoral staff, a ring symbolising the bishop's "marriage" to his church.

The personal life of the king was also in keeping with his deep piety. On many occasions he confessed his sins publicly before his people. He himself observed the custom taken over from France of suspending feuds from Wednesday evening until Monday morning in memory of the Passion, Death and Resurrection of Christ and he insisted that the German knights also keep this "Treuga Dei" or "Truce of God".

Henry's efforts on behalf of the reform of the imperial Church culminated in the Synod of Sutri (1046), at which he deposed three popes at loggerheads for political reasons, and promoted a German bishop, a member of the Cluniac reform party, to the highest office in Christendom. By him Henry was crowned emperor. At Sutri the emperor was also legally granted the decisive influence in papal elections. He raised four Germans in succession to the papacy. And it was these same popes who placed themselves at the head of the reform movement to make the Church independent of the secular powers. They restored to the papacy its universal character in the West. However, the definitive division of Christendom into the western Roman and the eastern Orthodox churches also took place under these reform popes (1054). Insignificant as the occasion was (a dispute about the form the ecclesiastical ritual in south Italy should take), the break was to prove portentous as marking the beginning of the final split in what had been the homogeneous world of Greco-Roman culture.

Missionary activity made progress in the north of the empire under the Bishop of Bremen. The work was directed not only to Scandinavia but ranged as far afield as Finland, the Orkneys, Greenland and Iceland. Under Henry III the authority of both emperor and empire was almost unchallenged in the West and, especially by his eastern neighbour. Together with the papacy he had purged, Henry felt himself to be the king and emperor of the kingdom of God on earth. He was penetrated through and through with the consciousness of the exalted nature of his office; humble before God, he was full of sovereign haughtiness and royal reserve in his dealings with the temporal and the spiritual princes. In his hands the Christian empire had risen rapidly to the height of its intrinsic possibilities, and at no time in the process had he ever neglected the worldly interests of his realms in his sober estimation of what was attainable. The severity with which he fought for the ends which in his view were right won him but few friends among people of either great or low estate. But so strong was the respect felt by all for his integrity that his return from an Italian expedition was sufficient to break up a conspiracy initiated by the princes in his absence. When, shortly afterwards, he fell seriously ill, Pope Victor II and the German princes came to visit him on his deathbed. He died in 1056, at the age of thirty-nine, having reigned for seventeen years. His son Henry IV (1056—1106), a boy of six, was chosen to succeed him.

DIE KAISERKRONE DES HEILIGEN RÖMISCHEN REICHES DEUTSCHER NATION

Der Kronenkörper besteht aus acht Platten und stammt aus dem 10. Jahrhundert. Kreuz und Bügel wurden im 11. Jahrhundert hinzugefügt.

LA COURONNE IMPÉRIALE DU SAINT EMPIRE ROMAIN GERMANIQUE

La couronne consiste en huit plaques datant du 10e siècle. La croix et l'arc ont été ajoutés au 11e siècle.

THE IMPERIAL CROWN OF THE HOLY ROMAN EMPIRE

The band consists of eight plates and dates from the 10th century. The cross and hoop were added in the 11th century.

LA CORONA IMPERIAL DEL SACRO IMPERIO ROMANO GERMÁNICO

El cuerpo de la corona está formado por ocho placas y procede del siglo X. La cruz y el aro fueron añadidos en el siglo XI.

A COROA IMPERIAL DO SACRO IMPÉRIO ROMANO DE NAÇÃO ALEMÃ

A coroa própriamente dita é formada de oito chapas e procedente do século X. Cruz e arco foram acrescentados no século XI.

Hofburg, Wien

Chapter Four

EMPIRE AND PAPACY IN THE STRUGGLE FOR SUPREMACY OVER THE CHRISTIAN WEST

The Investiture Struggle

With the death of Henry III the German empire, regarded by reason of the imperial status of its king as the lawful continuation of the *Imperium Romanum*, had reached a decisive turning-point in its history. For the first time in the history of the Christian West, a German king had given an interpretation to the Christian message, in the spiritual sphere as well as the secular, which viewed all authority as a mere means to the full realisation of the Christian message on earth. Such a view, completely overlooked the question. Is this interplay of two powers equal in status and rights, whose fields of jurisdiction can be clearly distinguished into spiritual and temporal, necessary in the first place? This question never even occurred to Henry. Still less did he ever doubt that the king-emperor was privileged to exercise the supreme power over the spiritual sphere as well. It is not difficult for us today to see, in the light of later developments, a fundamental error in Henry III's behaviour. But such a judgment neglects the fact that it was only during the period between Henry's death and the independent rule of his son (1056) that the papacy, in which the spiritual authority was embodied, itself clearly realised the essential difference in the nature of its mission from that of the emperor, and its supremacy over all worldly power. From this at first merely theoretical consideration, the papacy drew practical political conclusions which were to strike at the very roots of the previous cooperation between the spiritual and the temporal authority.

The controversy about the problem of the right relationship of the spiritual to the temporal flared up around the investiture of spiritual dignitaries in their offices by the secular ruler. Cardinal Humbert of Silva Candida was the protagonist in Rome of the Cluniac viewpoint that any bestowal of a spiritual office by a layman is in itself simony and therefore forbidden. But this view would mean that the monarchy in Germany would be deprived of the very foundations of its authority

49

over clerics, and that the secular lords would lose a substantial part of their economic power arising from the dues of the clergy invested by them. In Cardinal Humbert's opinion, only such a man should be bishop who "was chosen by the clergy, asked for by the people, and consecrated by the bishops of the ecclesiastical province after confirmation by the metropolitan". With the spiritual act of consecration the property linked to the office would then automatically fall to the bishop-elect. All that remained to the secular ruler was to give his consent.

Thus the order established by Henry III was converted into a supremacy of the spiritual over the secular power. A conflict was inevitable as soon as the temporal authorities rejected this claim as incompatible with their position and rights.

During Henry IV's minority, his mother at first ruled as queen regent. After the Bishop of Cologne had got the boy into his power by kidnapping, the young king became the object of princely jealousies. The ambitious Archbishop of Bremen, a haughty cleric and lover of pomp, managed to get his way so that the boy-king's education was to be shared by him in alternation with the prince of the Cologne church. At the age of fifteen, Henry assumed the independent rule of his realm. The impressions gained in childhood had taught him to be mistrustful of the princes. His first efforts were therefore directed towards augmenting the royal properties, the most substantial part of which lay in Saxony. He hoped in this way to win independence of the territorial powers for the monarchy. At the same time, he promoted the so-called *ministeriales* (originally unfree knights) to be his advisers and took them more and more into his service. They were to underpin his authority.

The Saxon peasants resisted Henry's intention to make Saxony the solid basis of his rule by having recourse to arms under their duke. Defeated in battle, the young king had to take refuge in the city of Worms, whose citizens offered him protection and hospitality. Protracted negotiations with the south-German princes and the arrogance of the Saxons, who destroyed the royal Harzburg and desecrated the tombs of the king's ancestors, led to a reconciliation with the territorial lords.

The king considered that he could turn his attentions to the question of ecclesiastical policy, so far neglected by him, only after he had thus consolidated his position within the empire. At the outset Henry did not give a second thought to the accession in 1073, right in the middle of his dispute with the rebellious princes, of a new pope to the chair of St Peter. The monk Hildebrand, who now took the name of Gregory VII, observed ancient custom by notifying the German king of his election and petitioning for confirmation of his election. The king had not refused his consent, in spite of the opposition of many bishops of the German and Milanese church, undoubtedly because he was anxious to avoid a conflict with the Curia. He had anyway not recognised the true aims of the new pope.

However, with this pope, a turning-point had also been reached in the history of the Church. Like Charlemagne, Gregory was also governed by his understanding of the "Kingdom of Heaven". His great ideal was to realise on earth the kingdom of God founded on justice. But in contrast to Charles the Great, he believed that only the clergy was called upon to undertake this task, for, in his view, all secular power stems from the "Prince of this World", Satan. The supreme task of the Church is to transform the kingdom of this world into the kingdom of God; all earthly authority finds its only justification in its dedication to the service of this ideal. The unconditional character of this conception of the nature of the Church and its priesthood lent Gregory's measures a note of extraordinary severity. At the same time, it was his considered opinion that the spiritual kingdom of Christ should have its own secular power for its defence.

The relatively rapid and smooth settlement of small differences with the pope had given Henry IV little opportunity to form a true estimate of the new man in Rome. In spite of Gregory's severe decrees against simony and clerical marriage, the king continued, like his grandfather before him, to appoint bishops to their sees against payment of taxes, regardless of whether they were, in the meaning of the reform movement, 'worthy' clerics. At the Lenten Synod of 1075 Gregory reiterated his demands and forbade the king to dispose of bishoprics at his own discretion. When Henry refused to comply with the papal injunction, Gregory threatened the king with deposition and laid the royal counsellors under excommunication. At a "national synod" called by the king at Worms (1076), the German bishops agreed almost unanimously to declare Gregory's papacy illegitimate. Henry himself composed an impassioned epistle to "Hildebrand, no pope, but a false monk"; in the conclusion he urged Gregory: "For I, Henry, King by the grace of God, and all my bishops, say to thee: come down, come down, thou whom all ages will condemn!"

Perhaps Henry believed that the force of his words and the dignity of his office would be enough to compel the pope to resign, just as his father had forced three popes to step aside at the Synod of

Sutri. But he had, in the folly of youth, overlooked the consequences which the policy of that same king of the Sutri synod had had for the papacy and the Church in the following decade, and had forgotten what a strong personality, completely dominated by the idea of the *libertas ecclesiae,* confronted him in Gregory VII. For this reason the royal condemnation Henry had hazarded was bound to have a reverse effect. Gregory adapted himself in a masterly fashion to the religious conceptions prevalent not only among the clergy but also among the people of his day. He decreed, in the form of a prayer to the prince of the apostles, Peter, the excommunication and deposition of the king, an unprecedented occurrence in the history of the relations of the spiritual and temporal powers. In the eleventh century excommunication still involved the complete exclusion of the person thus penalised, not only from the Christian community but from society. It swept the foundations of Henry's kingship from him. The German princes now had to decide whether they should confirm the papal sentence by holding a new election, a procedure to which they were anyway inclined, since Henry had won few sympathisers among them.

In this almost hopeless situation Henry decided on a course of action which can only be understood in the light of medieval religious conceptions, just as the deposition of a pope by the king or of a king by the pope can only be understood from the standpoint of the medieval notion of the special position enjoyed by king or pope. In the depths of winter, accompanied only by his wife and baby son, the king crossed the Alps to meet Gregory VII on his way to Germany, and, after carrying out the ecclesiastical penance, to compel the supreme pontiff to lift the ban. In the mountain stronghold at Canossa, Gregory VII took the penitent back into the community of the Church and declared himself reconciled with him. As priest he could do nothing else. Henry submitted himself to the judgment and decision of the pope and guaranteed Gregory a journey to Germany.

That day at Canossa marks the climax of the conflict between the *Sacerdotium* and the *Imperium* within the self-contained world of medieval Christendom. It marked a victory for the papacy in that Henry agreed to the conditions set by the pope and recognised the papal claim to have a say also in decisions concerned with internal German questions. But it was still more a victory for the king, for by his penitential journey Henry compelled Hildebrand to seek a new foundation for his policy. At the same time Henry struck a wedge between the papacy and the German princes opposed to him, and thus saved his throne.

Furthermore Canossa represented a turning-point in the relations of the spiritual and the temporal powers. The hitherto undisputed theoretical unity of both in the government of the world had come to an end. Its place was now taken by the papal struggle for the supreme authority in the Christian world (hierocracy), while the temporal power committed itself more and more to the pursuance of objectives distinct from those purely ecclesiastical.

After the lifting of the ban nobody in Germany could refuse obedience to the king on the grounds that he was under the ban of the Church. The struggle which Henry now entered on against the anti-king and his supporters in Germany was successful in spite of the unfavourable conditions he was called upon to accept. After the death of his rival in battle, Henry was again excommunicated by the pope in 1080 for breaking the agreement entered into at Canossa. A year later Henry set off for Rome to install the anti-pope elected by the German bishops. But he was unable to force his way into Rome and enthrone his anti-pope until 1084, after liberal bribing with Greek moneys. From the hand of the anti-pope the German king received the imperial crown. Gregory was forced to take refuge with his allies, the Normans of Lower Italy. With them he withdrew to Salerno. Abandoned by the majority of his former supporters, the most important pope of his epoch died embittered (1085), convinced that he had achieved nothing. However, he had by his spiritual legacy influenced the history of the medieval papacy more than most of the occupants of the papal chair before him. The Hildebrandine concept of a papacy to which both Church and world were in the same sense subject has again and again captivated the wearers of the tiara since Gregory's day. A beginning was soon made after his death, however, in the attempt to delimit the spheres of activity of the two powers.

The struggle was at first continued, but it was no longer conducted with the same wholeheartedness as under the deceased pope. In Germany more and more princes rallied to the king, only his own son, Conrad, and the Bavarians under their duke taking the pope's part. Henry's position looked extremely precarious. Since the Bavarians had closed the passes, he had for years to look on at the course of events in Germany as a powerless spectator in Italy. In the end a diet of princes at Mainz declared the rebellious Conrad deposed, and elected in his place his younger brother Henry as successor to the throne. The king wanted to make his peace with the pope, but the latter refused and renewed the excommunication pronounced against him.

At this difficult time, Henry IV's second son rose against him. Near Bingen this son treated his father with perfidious treachery, carried him as a prisoner to a castle, and set himself off for Mainz to the princes, some of whose support he won for himself. The king was compelled by his son and the papal envoy to confess his sins and to renounce all rights to the throne. His rebellious son was acknowledged king as Henry V. Henry IV did make one more effort to rally his supporters to his cause and to lead them against his son, but shortly before the outbreak of hostilities death claimed him.

Unter Henry V (1106—1125), the struggle between *Imperium* and *Sacerdotium* continued. Not until 1122 was a treaty concluded between the two powers (Concordat of Worms). This stipulated that bishops should be elected by the clergy in the presence of an imperial envoy. The bishop-elect received the sceptre from the king and, as a sign of his spiritual authority, the ring and the crosier from the pope. This mighty trial of strength thus ended in a compromise. The bishops maintained their temporal possessions and remained in the service of the king as temporal lords, but their election was regulated by pope and Church.

Missionisation and Colonisation in the East

While the two greatest powers of the Christian West were driving each other to the verge of exhaustion in their struggle for the leadership of a misconceived "City of God", decisive changes were taking place throughout Europe at all levels of the population below the ruling classes. These concerned in the first place the peasants, numerically far and away the largest section of the population of Europe. After the Hungarians had been worsted and had settled down in the Hungarian lowlands, conditions in Europe had stabilised. There were no further inroads by foreign peoples. The only area of unrest was south Italy and Sicily, where Greeks, Saracens, and Normans, and, at the end of the 12th century, Germans too, vied for supremacy.

This political stability in Europe led to overpopulation. Apart from the Alpine valleys and the lower German coastal areas free peasants cultivating their own soil had become more or less a rarity. The feudal system offered younger sons only poor opportunities for gaining a livelihood. On the whole, the peasant's sustenance, for which he had to render definite services on the lands of his feudal lord, was calculated to provide for the bare support of his family. Nevertheless, from the 11th century onwards, recourse had to be had to the settlement of serfs on woodland or wasteland and, to the reclamation of land from the sea by dyking (Flanders and Holland). The land still remained the property of the territorial lord; the serfs did not become freemen.

As successor to Henry V the German princes had chosen as king the devout Catholic Duke of Saxony, Lothair (1125—1137), whose reign was taken up with battles for the recognition of his kingship by the powerful house of the Hohenstaufen. However, he succeeded in compelling the Polish duke to accept from his hand the recently conquered land of Pomerania with Rügen as a fief of the empire, and to recognise German overlordship.

By this act he laid the foundation for the revival of a German eastern policy, the execution of which he entrusted to proved German princes. Albert I, surnamed "the Bear", who was enfeoffed with the so-called North Mark, exploited the opportunities which his territory offered. He expanded his frontiers in bloody battles with the Slavs. In 1150 he inherited Brandenburg and, as Margrave, extended his rule over the inhabitants of the Havelland and the Priegnitz.

But Lothair also renewed the Ottonian eastern policy in his efforts to missionise these areas. By founding new bishoprics and subordinating the Polish church to the Archbishop of Magdeburg again, he tried to give the missionary activity some organisational backing.

The settlement of these areas with German peasants was to prove decisive. The peasants were drawn, in the first place, from Flanders and Holland (hence the survival of the name "Fläming" in the Brandenburg margraviate down to the present day). But other German tribal groups also responded to the call to the east, so that the settlement of the new areas of colonisation eventually developed into an achievement of the entire empire. Better economic conditions and personal freedom awaited the German settler. On an average he received some 60 acres of land as a free inheritable fee or against payment of a small rent to his feudal lord. Besides the peasants, Cistercian monks and Premonstratensian canons also played a considerable part in the colonisation and missionisation of the East.

Although the modern spirit of nationalism was entirely unknown in the Middle Ages, the new settler could not but be conscious of having established himself among a foreign people and on foreign soil. It was thus inevitable that at first there should be embittered fighting with the Slav population. However, the Slav rejection of the German peasant was in general only of short duration. Very soon the Slavs recognised the advantages of German methods of agriculture and gave up their resistance. They saw that the introduction of the iron plough and the three-field system yielded substantially richer harvests; they saw with their own eyes how waste land, marsh and uncleared woodland valleys were transformed into fertile areas of cultivation by the industry of the monks and the peasant settlers. Besides, the Slav peasants were granted personal freedom and equal economic rights with the German colonists, if they accepted Christianity. Very soon old and new settlers merged into one community. To speak German gradually became a matter of course in the regions between the Elbe and the Oder. Independent Slav princes called for German settlers too, eventually adopted the German tongue themselves, and were admitted by degrees to the ranks of the princes of the empire (Mecklenburg and Pomerania; Silesia no longer recognised Polish overlordship).

Closely related to the growth in the peasant population was the rise of the medieval city in Germany. The fall of the Roman Empire had also tolled the knell of the cities of north-west Europe. Where they had survived as episcopal seats (e.g. Mainz, Trier, Salzburg), they were exclusively centres of diocesan administration and completely dependent on the surrounding countryside for their survival. Only from the 11th century onwards did craftsmen settle in the episcopal cities and around fortresses ("*Burg*", from *burgus,* a fortified place of defence whose inhabitants became known as burghers). For these the city lord —bishop, abbot or burgrave—erected a market intended to take care of their needs. Customs and taxes flowed into his treasury; supreme jurisdiction was his. In return he provided for the defence of the city by the construction of city walls.

Outside these cities tradesmen from other parts settled, attracted thither by the storage and marketing possibilities for their goods within the walls. These trading suburbs soon developed a life of their own. The traders formed into guilds, built their own churches and lived according to their own laws.

Since these traders were financially better off than the burghers, they soon acquired a great part of the city ground, built walls around their settlements directly connected with the original city, and thus merged with the old population. The development of the city to an independent legal entity in its own right alongside the feudal powers took place, particularly in north-west Europe, during the time of the investiture struggle. In general this was the result of a combined revolution of tradesmen ("patricians") and the craftsmen of the guilds against the tutelage of their city lord. Because the originators of the freedom movement were the traders, the revolution brought into being not a democratic, but an aristocratic or patrician system of government.

56

The freedom of the city was the indispensable condition for the formation of the third order, that of the burghers. The inhabitants of the cities were not subject but could dispose at will of their property and marry without the permission of the authorities. Of course, this freedom was bound up with actual domicile within the city. Only a person who had lived for a year and a day in the town and whose return had not been demanded by his former feudal lord had a claim to this freedom ("Town-air makes free").

The towns developed their own system of law. Codes of municipal law which were considered particularly exemplary were adopted by other cities, too. New towns founded by inhabitants of older cities brought the law of the parent town with them. For these reasons, with the increasing urbanisation of the population, there were also numerous cities in the Slav regions, even as far distant as Poland, which lived according to German city law or were founded by new settlers according to its principles.

In the "council" the townsmen created the organ of their self-administration. Its task was to supervise defence and impose taxes. The colleges of aldermen had the function of guaranteeing the observance of municipal law.

Empire and Papacy in the Struggle for Supremacy in Italy

Lothair's successor, Conrad III (1138—1152), was not a strong king either. The German princes elected him precisely because of his weakness, in order not to imperil the rights they had acquired during the dispute between emperor and pope. However, he was the first emperor of the Hohenstaufen line, which was once again to intervene powerfully in the fortunes and struggles of the day. The Hohenstaufen ensured the sovereignty of a German royal house over north Italy's budding city republics, and took the checkered destiny of southern Italy and Sicily into its hands.

Conrad's own reign was entirely taken up, like that of his predecessors, with internal political struggles, above all with the powerful opponents of the Hohenstaufen, the princely line of the Welfs, who controlled important German duchies. Like the Hohenstaufen, this family had its origins in Swabia, but was related by marriage to the north Italian house of Este. Where papacy and Church was concerned, Conrad was careful not to overstep the limits which the reform curia had set the German king. He was persuaded to take part in a crusade, the first in which German contingents participated, by Bernard of Clairvaux, the most important man of his day and the great preacher and organiser of the struggle of Christian-occidental chivalry against Islam. The campaign (1147—1149) achieved nothing in the Holy Land, but seriously disrupted authority within the empire.

For this reason, after the death of Conrad, the German princes agreed to elect a king whom they hoped would be able to take care of the internal reorganisation of the empire: Frederick I Barbarossa (1155—1190), of the house of Hohenstaufen, a nephew of Conrad's and Duke of Swabia. Barbarossa actually did confer peace on the empire by redistributing possession of the territories. Henry the Lion, a member of the Welf house, which was particularly opposed to the Hohenstaufen, was granted the duchy of Bavaria. Since he was already Duke of Saxony, he was now the most powerful territorial lord in the empire. The Babenbergs, who had until this date governed the fortunes of Bavaria, were conceded the margraviate of Austria, which was raised to the dignity of a duchy and endowed with special privileges (1154).

A survey of the reign of Frederick Barbarossa from 1152—1180, that is until the fall of Henry the Lion, may incline one to speak of the age of Frederick Barbarossa and of Henry the Lion, just as later historians speak of the age of Frederick the Great of Prussia and of Maria Theresa of Austria. Both these men typified the possibilities and dangers of German policy in the Middle Ages. Whereas Frederick directed his efforts towards winning back for the emperor the power he had exercised before the great trial of strength between Henry IV and Gregory VII, Henry the Lion's political sagacity was concerned with strengthening his territorial position, which he could, as Duke of Saxony, extend almost at will in the largely defenceless east. Since Frederick's and Henry's political paths did not at first cross, German politics long presented a dual aspect.

The weak position of the German sovereign was to be explained not only by the loss of respect occasioned by the investiture dispute, but equally by the continual reduction in the royal property resulting from the need to reward services rendered by the lesser nobility. Frederick Barbarossa therefore tried to find a new basis for his power in the kingdom of the Lombards, Germany's ally. His marriage to Beatrice of Burgundy enabled him to integrate the Burgundian kingdom and Provence into the empire; in this way he ensured his communications with Lombardy.

A resumption of the Italian imperial policy inevitably aroused the suspicions of both the papacy and the prosperous burghers of the north Italian towns. Since the reign of Gregory VII, the papacy had grown more and more accustomed to regarding its temporal rule over the Papal States and its close relations with other secular powers as the basis of its coveted supremacy over all Christian rulers and over the whole of Christendom. Accordingly the re-establishment of German power in Lombardy could not but be interpreted as a direct threat to the Papal States. The economic position of the townsmen of north Italy had been so strengthened by the increased trade and new markets resulting from the crusades, that they regarded the independence and freedom of their towns as their proudest possession.

The methods adopted by Frederick Barbarossa in his attempt to break the resistance to his plans put the Italian policy of the German kings on an entirely new footing; they also raised the imperial authority in his own person and that of his son to dizzy heights once again. Initially Frederick was able to pursue his new Italian policy and yet remain on good terms with the pope. Later, however, each was forced to recognise that the policy of the other was irreconcilable with his own. The battle thus flared up anew. Relying on his strong military position, Frederick endeavoured to turn the clock back to the time of Otto the Great and Henry III (Sutri). He set up his own candidate as anti-pope to the rightfully elected pope. The papacy for its part sought military help from the Normans of south Italy, united with the burghers of the north Italian cities, and built up a system of alliances with all the European Christian powers which were ill-disposed towards the German king and the Holy Roman Empire. At first Frederick had the military advantage. Even before the outbreak of open hostilities between papacy and emperor, Barbarossa had broken the resistance of the north Italian towns and had forced them to bow to his will as supreme ruler, invoking Roman law in justification of his actions. The cities were compelled to pay heavy monetary dues to their imperial lord and to suffer the installation of an imperial representative (*podestà*). City leagues were outlawed. Imperial forts secured the roads of greatest military importance. When Milan, four years after the resumption of the imperial sovereignty, dared to rebel (1162), it was razed to the ground and its inhabitants dispersed in four village settlements under a stern imperial overseer. Frederick maintained his powerful position undisputed for 12 years. Even the papal system of alliances was not able to endure for long against Frederick's skilful diplomacy. The anti-pope took possession of Rome and crowned Frederick's queen as empress.

However, the papal-Lombardic party had not remained inactive either. The Milanese finally built their town up again, the Lombards founded a new city and named it Alessandria, after Pope Alexander, the emperor's opponent on the chair of Peter. As long as the papacy and the Lombard cities remained so closely allied, Frederick held a reconciliation with the pope to be entirely out of the question. For this reason he was determined to break the league by force of arms. However, in the decisive battle of Legano in 1176 Milanese cavalry and Lombard infantry were victorious over the imperial knights. For the first time in the history of the development of the medieval city, burghers had, in the struggle for their freedom, proved more than a match for an army of knights tried in war and arms. It is only fair to add, however, that Frederick's army was numerically inferior, because Henry the Lion had refused to send his imperial lord military reinforcements.

As a result of this defeat Frederick concluded a peace with the pope, and an armistice—in some cases a peace—with the cities. The antipope was quietly dropped, the papal schism ended. The Lombards, though still recognising the overlordship of the empire, were conceded municipal self-government. The period of purely feudal overlordship thus came to an end for Italy.

The consequences of this same defeat were to prove more decisive in Germany. For the last 25 years the emperor had concerned himself with the political changes taking place inside Germany only in so far as they had stood in the way of his plans for the empire. This meant that Henry the Lion had been able to pursue his own plans without imperial interference. Henry's efforts were aimed at extending his possessions, thus building up a well integrated and organised territory which would provide him with the powerful backing he needed if he were to challenge even the king himself and the other territorial lords with impunity. He succeeded in incorporating the Baltic Sea region (Mecklenburg, Pomerania) in his territory. A large proportion of the Slav population had been decimated by long wars; their place was taken by German settlers. The economic and cultural development of this area was placed in the hands of the Cistercians, whom Henry called in and generously endowed with lands from Doberan to Oliva. Lübeck, the only favourable harbour along the Baltic Sea coast, was extorted from its founder, and superbly enlarged by Henry. He established a marital union with Denmark to protect his work from interference from that quarter; he was also son-in-law of the king of England. His energetic endeavours transformed the duchy of Saxony into the largest and best administered territory in Germany.

Until now Frederick Barbarossa had never seen Henry's political activities and the expansion of his territorial power as a threat to his own authority and position. The king had always taken Henry's part when the latter's neighbours among the lesser lords had complained of the Duke's unjust encroachments on their property. Henry had been misled perhaps by the emperor's good will, when he refused to come to the emperor's aid during his Italian campaign. But on this occasion Frederick felt his position as emperor impugned. For this reason he imposed the imperial ban on Henry the Lion at a court held at Würzburg (1180) and pronounced that he had forfeited his right to his imperial fiefs. The Saxon duchy was partitioned: the Cologne archbishop received the diocese of Cologne and Paderborn as duchy of Westphalia, whereas the remainder of the duchy of Saxony was conferred on a count of Anhalt. Bavaria was granted to Otto of Wittelsbach, whose house remained on the Bavarian throne until 1918. The Steiermark duchy was newly created and separated from Bavaria. These counter-measures of Frederick's gave the death blow to Germany's tribal duchies. From now on the empire was organised and built up on a strictly feudal basis.

The dualism between the Italian policy of the emperor and the eastern policy of the territorial lords seemed at first to have been surmounted in the emperor's favour by his authoritative reaction here. Nevertheless, the conception that Frederick's and Henry's policies represented two possible approaches to political decisions on German soil had taken deep root in the consciousness of contemporaries in Germany and elsewhere. In certain circumstances this might later affect the destinies not only of Germany, but also of large areas of Europe.

Henry the Lion's efforts transformed the name of his house, Welf, into a party name for all those within the western empire who were prepared to sacrifice the idea of the universal empire for the reality of vigorously developing territorial units of various types (north Italian cities, national kingdoms, German territories). Outside Germany, people called the exponents of this viewpoint Guelphs. In contrast, Frederick Barbarossa was seen in his Italian policy as the great anti-pole to the territorial and eastern policy of Henry the Lion. He thus became the model for all those who saw the universal empire as a possible anti-dote to the break-up of western unity, which was now threatening as a result of the formation and consolidation of autonomous territories independent of the emperor. Like the name Welf, the name of Barbarossa's house, Waibling, developed into a battle cry for the parties (in Germany: "Hie Welf, hie Waibling!"); in Italy the supporters of the Hohenstaufen became known as the Ghibellines. Until long after the time of Dante, the great Italian poet, the internal politics of every important city in north Italy were riven by the unbridgeable rivalry of Guelph and Ghibelline.

In view of its consequences, we might be tempted today to view the marriage of Frederick's son Henry to Constance of Sicily in 1184 as the climax of the Italian policy of this great Hohenstaufen. But Constance was the aunt of William, the reigning Norman King of Sicily. From the human point of view it was highly improbable that William would die childless and thus leave the way open for Henry to succeed to the throne through his queen. The marriage was therefore designed in the first place to bring about a reconciliation between Germany and Sicily.

In advanced old age Frederick Barbarossa, in his office of "Protector of Christendom", placed himself at the head of the third crusade (1189—1192). Jerusalem was to be wrested from Saladin. Frederick took up the cross in 1188. At practically the same time the king of France was reconciled with Richard Coeur de Lion of England, and both resolved to take part in the crusade, too. The German crusading army set off from Regensburg taking the overland route via Hungary for Constantinople. The East Roman emperor's somewhat hostile attitude was overcome by treaty; the army embarked for Asia. Frederick Barbarossa met his death bathing in the Salef, a mountain stream in Cilicia.

After Barbarossa's death Frederick of Swabia, his son, took over the leadership of the crusade. The "Teutonic Order" was founded before the walls of Acre. With the help of the English King Richard Lionheart and Philip II of France Acre was taken and a truce signed with Saladin. Christians were granted the possession of the coastal area from Tyre to Jaffa and the right of pilgrimage to the Holy Places.

Frederick Barbarossa had endeavoured to restore the empire of Charlemagne. Undoubtedly the great dispute between the temporal and spiritual powers had caused a change in the character of the imperial office: its original religious bias had begun to give way more and more to secular interests. Nevertheless Frederick's goal was still the unity of the empire under an emperor whose inspiration was religious. Seen from this point of view his political measures, for whose execution he used the means determined by the circumstances of his day, were essentially an expression of the sense of duty which he felt towards his office. Thus, in the course of his reign, he became the foremost representative of the mentality which characterised the secular knights of the day. They strove to unite into one great synthesis the Church's call to refashion the world in the spirit of Christianity and in accordance with the natural conditions of man's existence. His attitudes of mind and his behaviour towards others caused Frederick to appear in literature and to the people as the perfect knight who had made moderation the ideal of his life. The Italians gave him the nickname Barbarossa ("Red Beard") with which he has gone down in history.

In 1189, while Frederick Barbarossa was still at the head of his army on crusade against Islam, the unexpected had happenened. William, the King of Sicily, had died without issue. The south Italian Norman-Sicilian kingdom had thus passed to the nearest in line to the throne, Constance, the wife of Henry VI, the German king. The dream of many German kings of a permanent link between Germany and Italy appeared to have come true at last in the person of a ruler who, as hardly any other before him, united the ability and the will to rule. Latin he spoke like his mother tongue; he was perfectly versed in Canon and Roman law. He seemed in his natural element in the world of western chivalry. Indeed he was a refined and talented writer of knightly poetry. He had been regent for Italy in 1186/7 and had been appointed regent for both parts of the empire for the duration of the crusade. He had been elected king and successor to Barbarossa by the German princes in 1184. But the world of his day was only in a very qualified sense his world. In him the idea of an empire ruled over by an emperor who believed himself bound, both personally and officially, to the fulfilment of a religious task yielded to the concept of world dominion as it appeared to have been realised in antiquity by Alexander the Great or the Roman emperors. Thus, the prime motivating force of his person and policy was power for its own sake. Certainly he had relatively rapid success in getting the better of those opposed to his rule in both Sicily and Germany, but the means he employed to obtain this end were out of keeping with the conceptions of his day. The soul of the opposition to the Hohenstaufen was the outlawed Henry the Lion. A conspiracy of the German princes which was supported by the Norman states of Sicily and England, compelled the king to interrupt his progress to Sicily after his imperial coronation in Rome, in order to break the rebellion in Germany. Here chance came to his aid. The English King Richard Coeur de Lion, had fallen into the power of Duke Leopold of Austria on his return from the crusade. Henry arranged for the English king to be handed over into his power and imprisoned him in the castle of Trifels. In so doing he violated the unwritten law by which all Christian rulers were to afford protection and assistance to every crusader. He thus placed himself beyond the pale of Christian chivalry. Still he did win a superior bargaining position for himself by this move. The opposition in Sicily was deprived of its most important support; the conspiracy of German princes collapsed. Richard Coeur de Lion accepted his own kingdom of England as a fief from the hands of the emperor. On Christmas day of that same year, Henry VI was crowned king of Sicily in the cathedral of Palermo. Sicily, then the jewel of the Mediterranean, important also because of its distinguished culture (a fusion of elements drawn from Arabic, Islamic, Norman and Christian influences) was ruled over by a member of the Hohenstaufen royal and imperial house.

The basis of Henry VI's power was now located outside the actual kingdom of Germany. True, the Mediterranean was still culturally and economically superior to the rest of Europe, and represented an extremely favourable starting-point strategically for the realisation of the king's far-reaching ambitions both in the east (Byzantium, Jerusalem) and in the west (the Spain of the Moors). Armenia, the Island of Cyprus, Jerusalem and the El Mansur, the Spanish caliph, already recognised Henry's overlordship. However, if the imperial throne was to recover its universal significance from the viewpoint of power politics, then it was dependent on the good will both of the pope and of the German princes, spiritual and temporal, whose military contingents were still extremely important. This sober assessment of the situation gave rise to Henry's plan to transform the empire into a hereditary monarchy.

His project granted the German temporal princes the hereditability of their fiefs also through the female line. In this way they became the unrestricted owners of their territories. The spiritual princes were to be released from all their obligations to the throne. In exchange, the princes were to renounce their right to elect and recognise the right to the succession of the eldest son of the Hohenstaufen house. But they rejected this scheme. They were convinced that they would be able to achieve their aim, the unrestricted possession of their fiefs, without any further concessions. They gave their consent only to the election of his recently (1195) born son, Frederick, as German king. The emperor himself had to put down a new rebellion in Sicily. The means used in the process were, even by medieval standards, so exceptionally cruel that the men closest to the king refused to approve them. During the preparations for a new crusade, Henry VI fell ill with dysentery. When the German crusading fleet had already put out to sea at Messina, he succumbed to its effects (1197). He was buried in the cathedral at Palermo. Frederick, his son and heir, was two years old.

In the eight years of his reign, which coincides in time with the climax of chivalry in Germany, Henry VI had, thanks to his singleness

PRUSSIA

HOLSTEIN
BRANDENBURG
POMERANIA
Elbe
FRIESLAND
SAXONY
LAUSITZ
MEISSEN
SILESIA
LOWER
LOTHARINGIA
THURINGIA
BOHEMIA
MORAVIA
FRANKONIA
Rhine
UPPER
LOTHARINGIA
SWABIA
BAVARIA
AUSTRIA
BURGUNDY
TYROL
CARINTHIA
STEIERMARK
Danube
A R E L A T
VERONA
KRAIN
SAVOY
LOMBARDY
Po
PROVENCE
ROMAGNA
ANCONA
TUSCIEN
SPOLETO
CORSICA
PATRIMONIUM
PETRI
BENEVENT
SARDINIA
SICILIA

| 0 | 100 | 200 | 300 | 400 | 500 kilometres |

| 0 | | 100 | | 200 | | 300 | miles |

The Kingdom of the Staufers (1190)

of purpose and energy, brought the universal imperial sovereignty of the Hohenstaufen to a height of power never to be achieved again. At the same time he had clearly thrown into relief the extent to which the medieval imperial ideal was in jeopardy both in his own policy and in the measures taken by his opponents. The papacy was now more than ever inspired by the idea of Gregory VII that a strong temporal power was needed as the sure foundation of its spiritual rule. The pope felt his encirclement by Hohenstaufen power a most dangerous threat to his independence. The Lombard cities aspired to complete freedom from and independence of German rule. The German princes feared for their territorial sovereignty. The national kingdoms in process of formation in Europe rejected the universal claims of the empire. Therefore with the consent of Pope Innocent III (1198—1216), Otto of Brunswick, a son of Henry the Lion, was elected king by the German princes. The few supporters of the Hohenstaufen cause agreed on Philip of Swabia, a brother of the deceased emperor. This meant civil war for Germany. Everywhere in Italy German sovereignty collapsed. Even Henry VI's widow dismissed her German advisers and officials. Her son Frederick she handed over to Pope Innocent III to educate as his ward.

Otto renounced all rights in respect of the papacy which were still due to the German kings in accordance with the Concordat of Worms and recognised Innocent III's arbitrary territorial aggrandizement of the Papal States. The imperial church founded by Otto the Great ceased to exist. But in spite of the great resources at his command, Otto was denied fortune in war. Philip of Swabia was already in a position to believe that he had once again assured the crown for his house, when he met his death as the result of a private feud (1208). Tired of further civil war the Hohenstaufen supporters also recognised Otto as king. Hardly was he in undisputed possession of the throne, however, than Otto, a Guelph, took up the Hohenstaufen policy for emperor and empire once again, renewed the German claims to sovereignty over the Lombard cities, and disputed the pope's right to extend the Papal States. This provoked the embittered enmity of Innocent III. Negotiations with the German opposition to the Guelphs finally led to a new election. Frederick, the son of Henry VI, and the pope's ward, became king (1212). Innocent considered this Hohenstaufen more amenable to his wishes than the Guelph, especially as Frederick had renounced the union of Sicily and Germany for all time and to endorse this intention had named his eleven-year-old son King of Sicily. In Germany Frederick took possession of the Hohenstaufen houselands and, aided by the king of France's generous financial assistance, quickly extended his power over central and southern Germany. In the presence of the French king he was crowned King of Germany at Frankfurt in 1212.

Anglo-French relations were dictated at this time by the French desire to bring the Norman possessions of the English crown on French soil under French sovereignty. This was the cause of the Hundred Years War between the two countries. Otto, as a relative of the English royal house, saw the French king as his main adversary. For the first time German policy was bound up with that of western Europe. In 1214 a decisive battle between the two west European rivals took place in France. Otto fought on the side of the English king. Since France won the battle, however, Otto's fate was also sealed. By a military engagement decided outside Germany, Frederick II (1212/15 —1250) became undisputed ruler in Germany.

By this means the young king had attained his first political objective. In reality, however, he did not place any value on the German throne. It was a mere means to provide him with the opportunity of winning back Hohenstaufen sovereignty over Sicily and north Italy—the Sicilian and Norman blood in his veins as well as his upbringing at the papal court had made him more Italian than German. After his coronation as emperor in 1220 he set foot only once more on German soil. The government of the country he left for the most part to his sons, in order to be able to devote himself entirely to the political development of his Sicilian inheritance. Here his achievement was extraordinary. But his entire attitude of mind, his scepticism before anything traditional, his toleration of all religious viewpoints, his striving to be guided in all his actions by the light of pure reason alone, his understanding of the importance of effective propaganda as one of the essential props of his policy, his dubious morals (in many respects well documented), make him seem almost a product of modern times, or at least, a ruler who tried to realise the ideas of the later Renaissance as early as the first half of the 13th century.

His resumption of his father's policy inevitably met with the uncompromising resistance of the papacy and of the north Italian city states. The relentless nature of the struggle and the employment on both sides of every available means were decisive reasons for the emperor's seeking an agreement with those powers in Germany whom it was imperative to prevent from stabbing him in the back while he was pursuing his Sicilian and Italian objectives. These were, of course, the temporal and spiritual princes who by this time expected from the emperor not just strict respect for their territorial sovereignty but also the rejection, or rather the restriction, of the libertarian rights of the now important city communities. With this in view he first granted territorial sovereignty to the spiritual princes, relinquishing his rights over imperial church property and to *regalia*. This concession he extended some time later to the temporal princes, renouncing in their favour, too, the royal prerogatives of jurisdiction, minting, marketing and customs, and restricted city rights to the area enclosed by the city walls. In this way he deprived the towns of the very real possibility of gaining new citizens by immigration or settlement in the environs of the city.

Frederick's tendency to make Germany a power reservoir for his Sicilian and Italian undertakings was to be clearly seen in his treatment of the imperial property. This, like the family lands of the Staufen in Alsace, was submitted to very rigorous administration by officials. The new pass over the St. Gotthard was guaranteed by the acquisition of the most important access area of Uri and the bestowal on Schwyz of the privilege of immediate subjection to the empire. However, apart from the attempt to guarantee the law in the empire by the General Peace Law *(Landfriedensgesetz)* of Mainz and thus call a halt to the rampant abuse of frequent feuding, from the days of Frederick II the actual and complete authority lay in the hands of the appropriate territorial lord.

In spite of his indisputable accomplishments as a politician and of his achievement, far in advance of his times, in constructing a modern state in Sicily and lower Italy, victory was withheld from Frederick in his conflict with the papacy. The concept that the law of the state must be respected by everyone, even by the pope and the Church, and that in certain circumstances even the Church might have to bow to the interests of the state, found general rejection. The papacy was thus sure of many allies. At the height of the struggle, Frederick died at the age of 56 and was buried in Palermo cathedral. His memory is still fresh among the Sicilian people, who regard him to this day as one of the greatest rulers their island has known. The house of Anjou, which was now enfeoffed with Sicily by the pope, persecuted Frederick's successors with unrelenting hatred. His grandson, Conradin, the last of the line, was publicly beheaded in the market-place of Naples in 1268.

The victory of the papacy over the Hohenstaufen marked the end of the universal empire. The national kingdoms of Europe and the German territorial lords also shared the spoils of this victory. At the same time the defeat of the empire was also the occasion for the rise of the

Lombardic city states, which, as the irreconcilable opponents of the Ghibellines, were able to strengthen their position, which was based on trade and money, and become the representatives of a new spirit in Europe.

As early as 1247 the German princes elected William of Holland king. But he was unable to extend his power beyond the lower Rhine. After his death in 1256, two foreigners were elected to the throne in a double election, but they hardly troubled themselves about the *Reich*.

The Age of Chivalry

The end of Hohenstaufen imperial rule, and thereby of the universal empire too, marked at the same time the end of one of the most peculiar phenomena of the Middle Ages: Christian chivalry and the culture it inspired. This knightly culture was something common to the whole of Europe. It was the fruit of the change wrought in the status of the soldier under the influence of Christianity. The Christian Church had turned her attentions to the soldiers among the faithful relatively late in the day. Only the increased preoccupation with the world of the laity, in whom the Cluniac reformers saw comrades-in-arms in the fight for the kingdom of Christ, opened up the purely ecclesiastico-Christian spheres to the layman in the army without his having thereby to abandon his obligations in the world. It was presupposed of course that he looked upon himself and his profession as being primarily dedicated to the service of God and His Church, as involving the duty to fight and act for the spread of the kingdom of God on earth.

As a consequence of the changes which had taken place in the art of warfare from the 8th to the 10th century, general conscription among the people had given way more and more to the professional army of mounted and heavily armed men. These performed their military service partly in the immediate vicinity of their commander-in-chief and partly in the outposts, the outlying fortresses. From their ranks rose, on the basis of special services rendered, the *ministeriales* and the hosts of retainers often originating from the peasant class. Within the ranks of the mounted soldiery there developed at a very early date certain forms of military service and behaviour which imparted a definite character to the members of that class. As long as the regions entrusted to him to defend were externally menaced and there was a strong supreme authority in the land, the life of the knight was in general fully occupied by his service. When conditions in Europe became stabilised and the kings in France, and at times in Germany, grew weak, the knights took to feuding among themselves; their differences were often decided without any thought or consideration for those who had no part in the dispute. Eastern France especially suffered from the consequences of such feuds. Here the Cluniac reform movement intervened decisively for the first time by giving special support to the movement originating in Aquitaine, the *Treuga Dei*, the Truce of God. A second decisive factor here was the enlistment of knights to meet the great challenge facing the Church represented by Islam. In this way, for the first time in her history, the Church entrusted the military class with a religious charge. Since their mission transcended all national and racial ties, it united all those taking part in such a holy war against Islam in a special brotherhood. This feeling of solidarity was still more strengthened by their unique experience of the strange world of the Orient.

As with the clergy, a man was not born a knight, he became one. Admittedly the ranks of the knights also included those who were specially "called", that is those who because of their birth or the circumstances of their lives were particularly marked out for the knightly status (nobles by birth and service). However, it was the accolade alone by which a man was solemnly received into the ranks of the knights. This was the symbol of membership of a class of men who attempted to combine in one great synthesis the courage and bravery of the warrior, thirst for action and a spirit of adventure, devotion to one's needy neighbour, the service of womankind, and the fight for Christ and His Church in such a way that the virtue of moderation exercised in any single task qualified the knight for the fulfilment of all tasks.

The knights' consciousness that they were creating something entirely new and exemplary by their achievement (especially in the crusades) and by their influence on their surroundings and on the lives of men, gave rise to a literature inspired by chivalry itself. It was the fruit of the pleasure they experienced in singing the praises of western chivalry's combined achievement. The knightly poets sought the subject matter of their great epic poems in the traditions stemming from the times of the western *Völkerwanderung*, in the Carolingian period, or in their experience of the world of the Orient (the Dietrich legend, the Nibelungenlied, the Gudrun epic, the Rolandslied, the Alexander Epic, King Arthur and the Grail). At the same time these subjects were well suited to give artistic expression to the knightly ideal and to be held up as models for present and future generations (especially in the King Arthur and the Grail Epic). Moreover, the consciousness of the personal dignity of the individual was of tremendous importance for the development of western man. This transformed the expression of one's own value into a universally valid statement of the value of human beings in general. This led to the birth of the *Minnesang,* at first a glorification of the conventional homage paid by the knights to the fairer sex and later of love between the sexes.

In this context there arose in western Europe (France, England, and Spain) and in Germany the great poems written in the vernacular, which did not in any way involve any restriction within national boundaries. The most important German poets were Hartmann von der Aue, Wolfram von Eschenbach (Parsival), Gottfried von Strassburg (Tristan and Isolde) and Walther von der Vogelweide, the greatest of the lyric and political poets.

Chivalry was the most significant supranational movement in the West and one of the greatest shared experiences. For some 200 years (until about the year 1250), the West was the fatherland of men who all participated in some way or other in what gave it its peculiar significance. Stimuli, opinions, forms and styles were constantly fused. And what resulted from this fusion and endured was always more than the mere expression of something narrowly national—it was part and parcel of the Christian world of the West.

The languages of the peoples who provided cultural leadership in Europe at this time have all retained an epithet which has survived to the present day to characterise a man who places his perfectly harmonised powers of intellect, spirit and body at the disposal of his fellow men. In English we still describe such a man as chivalrous.

Chapter Five

NEW FORCES AT WORK IN THE COLLAPSING EMPIRE

The Territorial Princes

German development from Otto the Great to the end of Hohenstaufen rule was characterised by the idea of the universal empire, which, even if often unexpressed, has left its mark on German history also in its furthest ramifications. This explains why the personality of each individual ruler was of such decisive importance: the expression given in each case to the "universal empire" idea was essentially dependent on his will and energy of purpose. In contrast, the pattern of the late Middle Ages was no longer determined by the emperor. Where he intervened at all in the order of the empire, it was rather as a type of territorial lord who happened to be the bearer of the royal and imperial titles than as the executor of the power of king and emperor. For this reason, we can omit a detailed presentation of the various emperors. It is more important to concentrate our attention on those powers which were the real formative elements, namely the princes and the cities. Whenever the emperor succeeded in winning their support he was strong; whenever they were against him, his power was indistinguishable from that of one of the princes themselves.

What, however, began especially at the end of the Hohenstaufen era and influenced German history decisively was the completely different development of East and West, in other words of the colonial area and the old fatherland, the cultural centre. The conflict between Frederick Barbarossa and Henry the Lion had not been simply of the type frequent in the early Middle Ages between feudal lord and subject. It had also thrown some light on the difference in the conception of the task of the empire as these two men saw it: the emperor viewed this as the protection of the old universal idea with its emphasis on the cradle of western culture, Italy and Rome; Henry the Lion conceived it as the expansion of the empire over the undeveloped East with all its bright promise for the future. The more imperial power declined, the greater was the influence of the princes and of the burghers, the latter with all their new-found self-confidence, on local history and the history of the colonial regions, and the greater, too, the tendency to leave the new land, especially as it was unburdened by tradition and but recently conquered, to develop its own individual existence. Thus that dualism of imperial and territorial power which has given its special character to German history right up to the 20th century dates from the late 13th and early 14th centuries.

The division of the higher nobility into princes, magnates and *Freiherren* was already a reality under Frederick Barbarossa. In 1237 Conrad IV had been elected to the German throne by the votes of the Archbishops of Cologne, Mainz and Trier, the Count Palatine of the Rhine, the Duke of Saxony, the King of Bohemia and the Margrave of Brandenburg, while the remaining princes could only give their approval. In this way, the right to elect, probably in imitation of papal elections by the college of cardinals, had been restricted to a small circle of privileged spiritual and secular princes. The college of electors had been formed without any special foundation in law. If we examine its composition, it is easy to understand that the three Rhenish archbishops should have acquired the privilege of election on the basis of the antiquity of their sees. In contrast, the successful assertion of the claims of the four secular princes—with the exception perhaps of the Duke of Saxony—cannot but surprise us, at least in the cases of Brandenburg and Bohemia and the Count Palatine of the Rhine. In the first two instances there is question of downright newly settled territory; the latter was of only second rate importance when compared with Baden, Württemberg and Bavaria. However, the March of Brandenburg had developed into one of the most important of the larger territories in the empire under the successors of Albert the Bear, while Bohemia had already been raised to a kingdom in feudal dependence on the empire under Premysl Vladislav II (1140—1174). Perhaps there was an added reason for the designation of the two eastern lords as electors: it gave special emphasis to the cohesion of East and West, of the new and the old lands.

The character of the old duchy had been tribal. The territorial powers now in process of formation have nothing in common with the original tribal duchies. Their development is entirely dependent on the political dexterity of their respective rulers. The more numerous the forces struggling for authority, the smaller the territories became; the more the forces in these territories held together to extend their territorial possessions, the stronger became the political authority wielded by the territorial lord. This also meant that the disintegration of the whole

72

12. The Margravine Uta, Naumburg Cathedral.

13. Trumpeting angel, Strasbourg Cathedral.　14. The Bamberg Rider. ▷

15. Freiburg Minster.

caused by the struggles of the territories among themselves and as united against the king-emperor became ever more apparent. This development was not peculiar to Germany but common to the whole of Europe. The new state with its division into estates was trying everywhere to supplant the old feudal state. But whereas in the other European states the monarch prevailed over the princes, the opposite was the case in Germany. When they acquired the right of levying taxes on their subjects, originally an exclusively royal prerogative, the princes, already endowed with the rights granted them by the kings of previous centuries, held supreme political power in their territories. Of course they acquired this right only very gradually, but its acquisition was decisive for the internal political development of all the territories. Originally taxes consisted of voluntary tributes paid to the feudal lord. These he had requested from the great ones of the land—the representatives of the estates, of the nobility and of the Church, and of the cities subject to the spiritual and temporal lords. Thus the territorial lord was in this respect as much dependent on the estates as the king was on the princes. While, however, the princes were jealous of their hold on the king, they increasingly restricted the influence of the representative organs of the estates. Where the administration of justice was concerned, the jurisdiction of the princes, exercised through officials, won the day from the end of the 13th century onwards. Right into the 17th century still further rights were acquired, until the territory was entirely centred on the person of the prince.

A map of Germany during the 13th to the 15th centuries which would attempt to reproduce the multiplicity of the German territories would have to be many-coloured indeed. But it would make clear at a glance the differences obtaining between the eastern and the western empire.

In south Germany, after the extinction of the Zähringe, whose properties lay in present-day Switzerland and the upper Rhine region, and of the Hohenstaufen with their lands around the upper Danube, power passed first and foremost to the Habsburgs, who extended their original possessions in Alsace, Breisgau, Aargau, Zürichgau, and Lucerne as far as the Vorarlberg and, in the 14th century, as far as Tyrol. Their Swiss possessions, however, they lost during the course of the 14th and 15th centuries.

The counts of Württemberg were, indeed, not as rich as the Habsburgs in territorial possessions, but were, for all that, similar to them in their insatiable acquisitiveness; they were raised to the rank of dukes in 1495. The third greatest territorial power in south Germany was Baden, which, following the course of the eastern upper Rhine, had extended into originally Swabian and Alemannic territory. Within these three larger territorial domains a multitude of smaller properties endured which were always in danger of being swallowed by the greater as a result of purchase, marriage or feud.

The principality of Bavaria alone—granted to the Wittelsbachs as a duchy in 1180—had maintained the strongest links with the old tribal duchy. Only the later Austrian territories had been separated from it. In their place the Wittelsbachs had in 1214 acquired the Palatinate; this territory was later lost to them again as a result of testamentary partitioning by which it became an independent territory with the Upper Palatinate.

In central Germany the Wettins had extended their sway from the Saale, both to the east (Saxe-Wittemberg) and to the west (Thuringia). Hesse, its nearest neighbour, had developed into the most important landgraviate in the course of protracted rivalry with the archbishop of Mainz and the Wettins. Along the Rhine and Main, the great territories of the spiritual lords lay, so that the Rhine-Main area had been dubbed quite simply "Parsons' Way". To the north the Frisians were almost entirely independent of the empire; Schleswig and Holstein fell under Danish rule in 1460 after the extinction of the dukes of Schleswig and the counts of Holstein. The Brunswick-Lüneburg territories had lost their importance after the fall of Henry the Lion. Saxe-Wittemberg, after it had been raised to the dignity of an electorate, inherited Saxony's great tradition as a powerful duchy. The eastern half of the empire presented a far more unified picture. Mecklenburg had been fully Christianised under its Slavonic princes, had become German and was raised to a duchy in 1342. Pomerania likewise was, at first as a vassal of Brandenburg, under a Slavonic ducal house.

Brandenburg was the creation of Albert the Bear. By the 13th century, his successors had already acquired possession of the Old Mark, the Priegnitz, the Havelland, the Uckermark, the New Mark, and Upper and Lower Lusatia. The cities of Berlin-Kölln, Landsberg, Frankfurt-on-Oder, creations of the margraves, flourished. But the feuds and rapacity of the Brandenburg branch of the Ascanians (the Wittelsbach and Luxembourg dynasties), which became extinct in 1320, led to the disorganisation of the territory and made the threat of invasion from Poland very real. The grant of the margraviate to the Burgrave of Nuremberg, Frederick of Hohenzollern, in 1417, called a halt to this decline. He successfully joined battle with the rapacious nobility, and thenceforth Brandenburg took its place among the well administered territories of the empire.

Like Mecklenburg and Pomerania in the north, Silesia in the south had adopted Christianity and become a German duchy, thanks to the efforts of its Slavonic dukes. Bohemia alone had, in spite of its close connections with the empire and its Habsburg kings, remained Slav both in speech and in national character and heritage. Only its border region had been gradually won over to the German way of life by German settlers.

The Teutonic Order

A German territory outside the limits of the empire, particularly remarkable both in its origins and its structure, was Prussia, the state ruled by the Teutonic Order. The Order itself was purely German, founded by Frederick Barbarossa's son for the protection of the Holy Land. Like the other orders of knighthood it consisted of knights, priests and serving brothers. The habit of the members of the order was a white mantle bearing a black cross (the Prussian flag was later created from these two colours). The members of the Order designated themselves Knights of Christ and of the Hospital of St. Mary of Jerusalem. They regarded the conversion of the heathen, above all of the followers of Islam, as their main task. When they were no longer able to work for this end in the Holy Land, they were sent into action against the heathen Cumans in Transylvania. In 1225 the Polish Duke of Masovia asked the grand master of the Order, Hermann von Salza, for help against the heathen Prusi (Prussians), peasant warriors who had settled east of the Vistula. Frederick II, the Hohenstaufen emperor, and friend of Hermann von Salza, granted the knights permission to wage war against the Prussians. The pope and Conrad of Masovia guaranteed the Order all the land it succeeded in wresting from the Prussians. An imperial deed solemnly confirmed the foundation of an autonomous Order State in Prussia, put under command of the empire and subsequently also of the pope. Thus, this territory stood outside the empire and its constitutions until the foundation of the new German empire in 1871.

The subjugation and missionisation of the Prussians proved extremely difficult and beyond the Order's capabilities. The crusade against the eastern heathen was therefore preached throughout the empire. Fortified positions, from which the cities of Thorn, Kulm, Marienwerder, and Elbing later developed, were founded by the knights as centres from which they could either organise punitive excursions against the refractory or preach Christianity to the heathen. But progress was still laborious and slow. The Order found powerful support for its labours in King Ottokar of Bohemia. In his honour a castle built on the Pregel was called Königsberg or "King's Hill" (since 1945 Kaliningrad). In the end it took the Order fifty years of bloody warfare to subjugate Prussia. In collaboration with the Knights of the Sword, the Order also subdued Courland, Estonia and Livonia. Marienburg on the Nogat, a channel of the Vistula, became the seat of the grand master, who until then had resided in Venice. The Order began to cultivate the land and partition it among numerous German settlers. Germans had responded to the call to the East, but in disappointing numbers. While Prussians and Germans merged to form one new people of German tongue and culture, the remaining lands of the Order, the so-called Baltic Provinces, were little touched by German rule, at least as far as the people's way of life and traditions were concerned. Only the cities here were of German foundation and inhabited by German burghers, e.g. Riga, Reval (Tallinn), Dorpat Tartu.

During the period of its moral and military greatness, the Order carefully planned for Prussia's future and succeeded in transforming it into a flourishing territory which soon achieved great wealth by reason both of the far-reaching commercial connections of its most important cities (like Danzig and Königsberg) and of the industry and ability of its peasant settlers. The important architectural monuments in the flourishing city communities and the castles built by the Order still bear witness today to the wealth and cultural creativeness of the German settlers.

It should not, however, be forgotten that all the territories between the Elbe and the Gulf of Finland were originally colonial areas settled by all the German tribes and estates without distinction. Often they developed along economic, social and political lines which made them markedly different from those regions within the old frontiers of the empire. In nearly all areas the new settlers merged in the end with the earlier Slavonic or Baltic settlers. The city settlements extended far into the Baltic Provinces; the peasant settlers preferred fertile to poor soils. The deserted character of the tracts of land brought under the plough and the cheap manpower represented by the Slav population encouraged the emergence of large landed properties. The possibility of building where nothing had stood before encouraged systematic town-planning, but the protective influence of tradition was often lacking. The feudal lord was able to rule without restriction, the organisation could be tighter. The territory and its size could be made the measure of political bargaining with less risk of challenge than in the empire.

The disintegration of the empire into a patch-work of secular and ecclesiastical territories and of free imperial cities hindered Germany's development into a centralised kingdom. German history therefore took a course which was different to that of western Europe. The main weight of political power gradually shifted to the territories. The king-emperor was forced to seek an adequate counter-balance in his own territory, since the imperial dignity was now an empty title bereft of political power. With the fall of the Hohenstaufen, the German kings lost their suzerainty over Italy. The same event heralded the decline of the king-emperor's power in favour of the territorial princes. This meant that he was faced by a new political necessity: his policy had now to be directed towards acquiring more dynastic power to compensate for the regions lost to the empire in Italy and to provide a counter-poise to the territorial princes.

Since the end of Hohenstaufen rule the attempt had been made to get along, for all practical purposes, without a king by electing princes who were too weak to assert their sovereignty over the empire. This experiment had proved a failure. Therefore, in 1273, the princes decided to elect a man who should bring order again to Germany's disorganised internal affairs, which were in a sorry state because of the general weakness of the law and the widespread abuse of feuding. They agreed upon Rudolph of Habsburg (1273—1291), an unimportant elderly count whose possessions were widely scattered throughout Alsace and Switzerland. The Habsburg itself, the castle from which the family drew its name, lay in Swabia between the Aar and the Reuss.

A second candidate for the throne was Ottokar of Bohemia, a Premysl and a powerful prince of the empire, who was not only Duke of Austria, Carinthia, Carniola and Styria, but also King of Bohemia. Through his mother he had received a German education. He was a convinced supporter of the adoption of the German tongue and culture, and had, as king, promoted the German colonisation of his native land. In this he was following the example of the Princes of Silesia, Pomerania, and Mecklenburg. He gave notable help to the Teutonic Order.

After Rudolph's election, Ottokar refused to surrender Austria and the remaining Alpine duchies as fiefs of the empire. Rudolph took up arms against him and defeated him in 1278 at the Battle of Dürnkrut. The victor bestowed the imperial fiefs of Austria, Styria, and Carniola on his sons. The fulcrum of Habsburg power thus shifted from the south-west to the south-east region of the empire. This fact predestined the Habsburgs to the role of champions of both the empire and western Christendom against the Turks a few centuries later.

Rudolph's success within the empire was negligible. He was able to reduce the rampant feuding somewhat, and to restore to some extent the rule of law, but he was not able to restore respect for the monarchy.

After his death the internal weakness of the kingdom assumed even greater proportions because of the dissensions among the princes. This period is characterised by rivalries to secure the throne, the efforts of the territorial rulers to extend their dynastic power during their reigns, and papal interference in German disputes about the succession.

Henry VII (1308—1313) of the house of Luxemburg had tried to take up medieval Italian policy again, for the first time since the collapse of Hohenstaufen rule. In contrast to all his predecessors he had formed an alliance with the burghers of the Italian cities and skilfully exploited the new enthusiasm for antiquity which was sweeping the peninsula. On his Roman campaign in 1310 the Ghibellines, supporters of Henry VII's and Frederick II's Hohenstaufen conception of empire, had received him with enthusiasm; Dante, too, had hailed his coming. The poet had dedicated his *Monarchia* to him, in which for the last time the Holy Roman Empire is seen as the coping-stone of the world order established by God. Henry did see his efforts rewarded by imperial coronation in Rome but, on an expedition against Naples, he fell victim to the southern climate. Louis the Bavarian (1314—1346), a candidate of the Luxemburg party, was elected to succeed him. In 1322 Louis defeated the candidate put forward by a rival camp. This was Frederick of Austria, the son of the Emperor Albert (1298—1308). Although the authority of the papacy had been weakened by its close ties with the French crown since Pope Clement V's move to Avignon (the beginning of the period known as the Babylonian captivity of the Church, 1309—1377), popes still attempted to meddle in German dynastic disputes.

Pope John XXII feared that Louis the Bavarian would take up the Italian policy of the emperors again, and this time with Italian support. In 1324 the pope placed him under the papal ban, but this no longer carried any weight in Germany. In 1327 Louis set out for Rome, received the imperial crown and set up an anti-pope. Louis could count on the support not only of a great number of the Italian burghers but, in Germany especially, of the mendicant orders, some of whose members placed the law of the state above that of the Church. Their most telling spokesman, Marsiglio of Padua, drew his weapons against the Church from Roman civil law. Although Louis was unable to maintain his position in Italy, his dispute with the pope had important consequences for the institution of the empire. The German princes also rejected papal interference in German affairs. In order to define once and for all their own and papal rights in respect of the German crown, the electors meeting at Rense on the Rhine in 1334 unanimously declared that their elect was legally king and invested with full imperial rights; the only right the pope had was that of coronation. In the "Golden Bull"— which got its name from the golden capsule in which the seal was enclosed—King Charles IV confirmed the electoral right of the seven electors (1356).

In 1346 the electors had deposed Louis the Bavarian because they disapproved of his policy of acquisition and had elected Charles IV of the house of Luxemburg in his stead. But this king was no sooner elected than he too moved into line with the traditional policy of his predecessors since Rudolph of Habsburg and tried to gain great power for his house in Bohemia. On his mother's side he was closely related to the Premysl. Prague became the main focus of his power, which he increased by the acquisition of Lusatia and the March of Brandenburg. Silesia and Moravia were already part of the Bohemian kingdom before Charles IV ascended the imperial throne. During his reign Prague acquired its distinctive features and its importance. The year 1348 saw the foundation of the first German university there, right in the heart of the Slavonic region. Charles intended this university to be a centre where the new Italian spirit of the Renaissance should be fostered north of the Alps. Petrarch, the greatest representative of this movement, was a friend of the king. Charles also kept in contact with the new popular movement in Italy which centred around the person of Cola di Rienzi and which aspired to found an empire based on the sovereign will of the people. But his practical spirit grasped clearly that such a movement was not yet in a position to gain real significance, because its foundations were too narrow. He used it without expecting from it any real revival of the empire and the imperial ideal. What was, however, to grant him enduring significance was the eminence he gave to the city of Prague, and his encouragement of the German tongue in his chancery, a German modelled on the finely phrased and highly cultured literary language of Italy. German literature owes to Charles's efforts the work of Johannes von Saaz: *Der Ackermann aus Böhmen* (The Ploughman from Bohemia).

Sigismund (1410—1437), an energetic emperor once more raised the sovereign claims of the medieval empire and took over the guidance of the realm. He saw the healing of the papal schism, in existence since 1378, as his most important task. He understood his imperial dignity as a charge to reestablish the unity of the Church and of the Christian West. Compared with the proceedings at Rense, by which the respective competencies of the spiritual and the temporal authorities were clearly defined, Sigismund's policy towards the Church, which he summoned to the Council of Constance, resembles more the early medieval conception of the emperor's duties. Besides condemning the Bohemian John Huss as a heretic, the Council of Constance (1414—1418), the first on German soil, succeeded in bringing the papal schism to an end. Sigismund did not restrict his efforts, as his predecessors had done, to the aggrandizement of his house. He retained Bohemia only with difficulty, and was able to defend Hungary against Turkish aggression. He also entertained thoughts of reforming the empire in order to consolidate the political unity of his realm.

While Sigismund was investing the Hohenzollern Frederick with the March of Brandenburg at the Council of Constance, an event unimportant in itself which was only to take on significance because of its consequences, important changes had been taking place in eastern Europe. An extensive Slavonic-Baltic state had been formed by the union of Poland and Lithuania. The new state came into conflict with the region ruled by the Teutonic Order because it coveted an outlet to the Baltic Sea and aimed besides at uniting the north Slavonic tribes. In this way it succeeded in winning the Order's dissatisfied German subjects as allies. In 1410 the Knights were defeated by this coalition at Tannenberg, Henry of Plauen managing, however, to save the Marienburg. The Peace of Thorn guaranteed once more the regions ruled by the Order.

The Order's decline continued because its interests were at variance with those of the German population, particularly of the cities and of the landed nobility. Moreover since its original purpose had been achieved when Lithuania embraced Christianity, internal dissensions began to appear. In the second Peace of Thorn (1466) the Order had to surrender to Poland West Prussia with Danzig and the Marienburg, and the Ermeland. East Prussia became a Polish fief. Poland had gained the coveted access to the Baltic.

Sigismund's successors were hardly worthy of the name of emperor. They devoted their attentions even more to dynastic aggrandizement. In this respect the extremely long reign of the Habsburg emperor Frederick III (1440—1493), who, by the marriage of his son Maximilian to the daughter and heiress of Charles the Bold of Burgundy (1477), secured for his house the right of succession to Burgundy and the

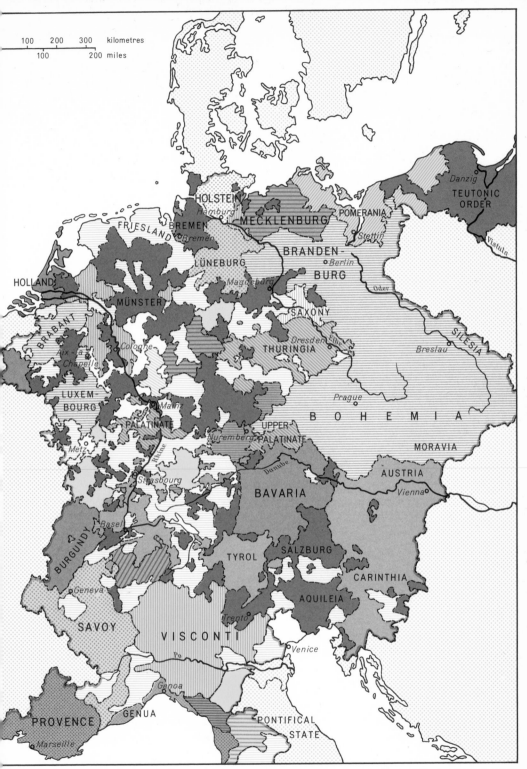

Central Europe at the Time of Charles IV (1347–1378)

Netherlands, was to prove of historical importance. This union made Maximilian the most powerful territorial lord in the empire, but it also laid the foundations of the centuries of armed conflicts at first between France and the Habsburgs, and later, as history took its course, between France and Germany. Admittedly the empire had exercised sovereignty over Burgundy, a land of both German and French origins, since the days of Conrad II, but this possession had never gone unchallenged. Some areas owed feudal allegiance to the French king. With the growth of national consciousness the attachments of the people, no matter how irrelevant these may have been in dynastic disputes, had inevitably come to weigh more and more in favour of the French claims. Thus, in this respect also, France could appeal to its "national" right, when, after the final defeat of England in the Hundred Years War, she turned her attentions to the east and north with the aim of territorial aggrandizement. Nevertheless, it would be historically inaccurate to see Maximilian's marriage as the only cause of innumerable wars. France would have wanted to round off her territory in the north and east, no matter who had succeeded to the Burgundian heritage. And Germany would eventually have been drawn into these conflicts in any case, since the immediate interests of the empire were also involved.

Compared with all the other German princes, the Habsburgs were by this time the most powerful of the territorial lords. Hardly any other prince of the empire was strong enough to contest their right to wear the German royal and the Holy Roman imperial crown. In fact this challenge was hardly ever attempted. The claim advanced by Francis I, King of France, to be accepted along with the Habsburg contender as a possible successor to Maximilian only serves to show how undisputed the position of the Habsburgs within the empire itself was.

Maximilian (1493—1519) was also unsuccessful in his efforts to provide the empire with a new and stable order. He was not able to translate into reality the "Ewige Landfriede", the Perpetual Peace, proclaimed by him at Worms. The partition of the empire into ten regions, and the constitution of the imperial chamber (*Reichskammergericht*) to judge offences against the peace, also achieved no practical result. Not even the imperial tax, the "gemeiner Pfennig", could be collected in all parts of the empire. For all practical purposes the Swiss confederates won full independence of the empire in 1499. For the first time in the history of the German-speaking peoples a highly gifted section of the tribe of the Swabians and Alemanni had deliberately broken away from the empire and taken its political

6 R. H. Tenbrock, A History of Germany

destiny into its own hands. On the eve of the Reformation the internal situation of the empire was insecure. The king's and emperor's authority over both princes and people was now founded less than ever before on the prestige of the imperial office, but rather on the actual power he wielded on the basis of the extent of his territories and their economic and political strength. By the marriage of Maximilian's son Philip to Johanna, heiress to the Spanish kingdoms, Spain was added to the Habsburg possessions in central Europe. Spain was at this time a well-integrated and economically flourishing country with possessions in both Italy and America. This recently discovered continent was destined to become one of the most important sources of Spanish wealth.

City and Burgher

The vigour and vitality of the German people as a whole resulting from the diversity of its tribes, estates, and territories, stand in striking contrast to the internal and external weakness of the imperial authority during the two and a half centuries preceding the close of the Middle Ages. During these centuries the enterprise of the burghers gave the city its characteristic form and the peasants made the hitherto uncultivated fields productive. At the same time the steady influx of settlers transformed eastern Germany into a permanent part of the sphere of German colonisation, language and culture. Finally, the intellectual life of the nation, always open to stimulation from outside, made great advances which contributed to the gradual development of the modern age.

The cities had for a time been retarded in their development by the imperial legislation of Frederick II. But the end of Hohenstaufen rule marked a turning-point for the cities, too, to the extent that they increasingly threw off the restraints which temporal or spiritual lords had imposed on them. It is true that the city community at first also followed the normal medieval social pattern and was organised in estates—nobility, patriciate, guilds. But the more feudalism and chivalry lost their importance as the formative forces of the period, the stronger those forces developed in the city whose will for economic expansion burst the traditional social barriers. For this reason the distinctive feature of the new urban development within the German-speaking area was the determination of the burghers continually to extend their rights and those of their city, and to safeguard their commerce outside the city limits so that they could safely carry their trade across broad areas not subject to city rule. Cities which did not obtain the freedom of the empire but persisted under the seignory of a territorial lord (these were the *Landstädte,* the mediate or mesne towns) often attained far-reaching autonomy in the course of the late Middle Ages. Towards the close of the 15th century the cities acquired the right of participation in the imperial and territorial diets, a right roughly comparable to that which the City of London alone among English towns, obtained in the Magna Charta as early as 1215. The free imperial cities were the most powerful champions of the imperial idea and could be relied upon to support the emperor in his struggle with the territorial powers.

With the decline of the imperial power, the cities united in leagues in order to protect their economic interests better. In 1254 the League of Rhenish Cities was formed, and in 1331 and 1376 the Swabian League. These leagues represented an attempt to organise the political power of the cities in order to strengthen the royal power, and at the same time to safeguard law and order. At the outset, even ecclesiastical and lay lords joined these leagues because they, too, were interested in finding a way of solving the most important problem facing the empire, namely how to secure the public peace *(Landfrieden).*

A league between the monarchy and the cities would, as in the west European national states in process of formation, have been able to give the king the backing he required in his struggle with the territorial powers. However, the elective character of royalty in Germany forced the king to take another political course. Dynastic aggrandizement transformed the king into just another territorial lord, so that he, too, came into conflict with the cities; moreover, the king-elect had to make numerous concessions to the territorial lords at the expense of the cities in special pre-election agreements *(Wahlkapitulationen).* However, the cities themselves never made an attempt to turn their economic power to effective political account by uniting in a general league, and this omission was to prove decisive. Hence the princes had no difficulty in eliminating the cities and burghers as a factor of political importance. Leaving aside for the moment the north German Hanseatic League, the military and political power of the south German city leagues was broken as early as 1388 by the victory of a coalition of princes over the Swabian cities. A year later the cities of south Germany were forced to disband their leagues. The princes had proved stronger than the cities and the burghers.

In contrast, the north German Hanseatic League rose to the height of its power during the same period. This was undoubtedly the most important of all city leagues. It had arisen from the association of German merchants abroad and the leagues of the north German cities, especially of Lübeck and Hamburg. About 1350 the name *Hanse* became the usual designation for these cities. Lübeck became the leading city in northern Germany and as such embodied the political power of the German burghers.

The *Hanse* members abroad enjoyed a position apart because they were subject to their own jurisdiction and maintained their own German law, manners and customs. The Hanse was organised along typically medieval lines. Membership of the League bound the individual to its regulations. Free competition was forbidden, but this was offset by the protection and security it granted its members in their economic existence. The resolutions of the Hanseatic cities harmonised the economic and political interests of the individual with those of the Hanseatic organisation as a whole.

From the middle of the 14th century to the beginning of the 16th the history of the Baltic is essentially the history of the Hanseatic League. It is also closely bound up with the destinies of the Scandinavian states. Fortunes in the struggle for sovereignty over the Baltic region at first fluctuated, but in the war against the Danish King Waldemar IV, the League succeeded in securing the help of the Teutonic Order, of Sweden and of Norway. With their help it defeated the Danes. In the Peace of Stralsund (1370) Waldemar had to relinquish Scania to the *Hanse*. The Baltic thus became a German sea and the Hanseatic League the most important economic and political power in northern Europe. At times more than 80 cities large and small, from Amsterdam to Novgorod in north Russia, acknowledged Lübeck's leadership. Within the League various groupings were formed, based on geographical situation and particular economic interests: the Livonian group with Riga, Dorpat and Reval; the Prussian (the territory of the Teutonic Order) with Thorn, Elbring and Danzig; the Saxon with Brunswick, Lüneburg and Bremen; the Wendish with Hamburg, Rostock and Wismar, Stralsund and Lübeck; the Lower Rhenish-Westphalian with Soest, Dortmund and Cologne. All over Europe the League had its counters: in London the "Steelyard", in Bergen the "German Bridge", in Novgorod the "Petershof", in Antwerp the "House of the Easterlings". In their disciplined organisation they were an example to all. Even in Russia men tried to imitate them. English relations with the *Hanse* were so close that the Hanseatic money (Easterling) became England's currency (sterling).

In spite of the major successes the League could point to in the fields of economics and politics, it found no support in the empire. But without this, it could not in the long run carry on the fight against the Nordic states. In 1397 the latter entered into a political union known as the Kalmar Union. So long as the three Scandinavian states were prevented from taking energetic and concerted action against the League by their political and economic divisions, the economic supremacy of the League was assured. The gradual development of a national consciousness in those states in which the *Hanse* had enjoyed a privileged position until now (Denmark, England, Holland and Russia), and the strengthening of the north German territorial powers, who forced the cities under their seignory to withdraw from the League, were to prove decisive. Lübeck came to grief at the beginning of the 16th century when it sought once again to regain the Hanseatic mastery of the Baltic in a trial of strength with Denmark. At the same time the Hanseatic privileges in the rest of Europe were also lost. In the north the national state and the princely state succeeded to the heritage of the cities.

Culture and the Late Medieval Town

The culture of the burgher-dominated Middle Ages, i.e. of the period from the 13th to the beginning of the 16th century, is bewildering in its profusion and variety. The reasons for this are every bit as diversified as was the life of the later Middle Ages, splintered as it was in estates, territories and cities. It is also difficult to define the fundamental attitude of mind of late medieval man, not only because traits of a stronger individualisation were beginning to show but because the communal thought and conduct so peculiar to the medieval period continued to develop just as vigorously. These two trends intermingled and fertilised each other, until the day finally came when the individual severed his ties with the community. This stage in the process occurred late in the period, at any rate in Germany. Furthermore, the efforts of the individual estates—nobility, clergy, burghers, and peasants—to develop a separate life of their own imposed a variety of tensions on the cultural expression of the late Middle Ages. The explanation of these tensions is to be sought, on the one hand, in the burgher's pride in the independence he had at long last won and in his conviction of the value of his own creative contribution to the culture of his day, and, on the other, in the refusal of the knightly order to have anything to do with the new forms and ways of life. This also explains why the culture of the late Middle Ages lacks in many of its forms the evenly balanced harmony of a well-developed sense for life and religion. Late medieval culture had its roots in a section of the German people, whose general attitude towards life was determined by the task which had to be performed anew every day in the sweat of their brow. The resulting attitude to life in general, which was by no means always negative, led to a reappraisal of the contents and concepts of its Christian faith.

Nothing is perhaps more characteristic here than the change in the way men regarded the founder of the Christian religion, his earthly mother, and the numerous saints, with whom medieval man especially stood in a particularly familiar relationship. Christ was looked upon, until far into the age of chivalry, as first and foremost the hero victorious over life and death; no one doubted that his reign in heaven, as on earth, was that of a king. Mary and the saints took a prominent place in men's lives because they were the visible guarantee of the heavenly reward promised for an exemplary life on earth. In this view the "Heavenly Jerusalem" complemented the earthly. The terrestrial order of things was a reflection of the blessed order of eternity, from which it alone received its justification. But the earthly order had collapsed amidst the upheavals during the time of the last Hohenstaufen and the rise of the burghers. The experience of the burgher and the peasant was different to that of the knight and the noble. Their interpretation of the Christian message was accordingly different. Christ once again became the son of a simple workman. His life and death were no longer a mere pledge of a great victory but also the symbol of the sufferings of men during their lives on this earth. And Mary and the saints provided the proof that precisely the least among men, after having led a model life, can take the first place in heaven. More than ever before, the religious figures became intimately associated with every aspect of daily life, not only of the individual but of the entire burgher community in town or village. Certainly Christ and the saints lost something of their grandeur in the process, but the lack of remoteness contained in the new relationship signified a definite gain for religious life. The line of demarcation between spiritual and temporal, between creator and creature became blurred, and heavenly and earthly constantly mingled. In this soil thrived the mysticism which aspired to an experience of God within himself. The outstanding names among these mystics were Master Eckhart (1263—1327), Henry Suso (1295—1366), and Johann Tauler (1300—1361). However, an extreme form of primitive piety which found at times bizarre expression in pilgrimages and processions, an exaggerated belief in miracles, and the efficacy of self-castigation, in the cult of relics and justification by works, proliferated exuberantly and wildly, and as good as asked for a reformation.

Against the backcloth of such superstitition and a false interpretation of the Christian faith, the first great outbreak of anti-Semitism also occurred in Germany in connection with the ravages wrought by the Black Death, which swept the whole of Europe in 1349. It is true that there had been an outburst of Jew-baiting in the cities along the left bank of the Rhine (Spires, Worms, Mainz) during the first crusades, but at that time the temporal and spiritual authorities were still strong enough to protect the Jews against excessive vexation. Medieval German Jewry had found a strong protector above all in Henry IV. The motives for the persecutions were in both instances pseudo-religious. In the 14th century the persecution was particularly remarkable since the great bulk of the burghers and peasants were, for the first time, in sympathy with it and the Jews obtained no help worthy of mention either from the secular or from the ecclesiastical authorities.

However, it would be wrong to let our view of the burghers and their religious life during the late Middle Ages be so warped by these negative features that we allow them to blind us to the magnificent achievements which, though fruit of the same soil, mirrored the thriving and healthy side of this same burgher society. For the very centuries which made it clear what aberrations a misunderstood Christianity can trap men into have also gone down in history as the age of Gothic architecture and art. Originating in France, this had triumphed in Germany between the years 1250 and 1350. In 1248 the foundation stone of Cologne cathedral was laid and in 1250 that of Strassburg minster. At first the Gothic style was nothing more than a further development of the Romanesque round arch. By making skilful technical improvements, however, the French had evolved a system which gave more variety to the church interior and lent it not only more movement and spaciousness, but at the same time a certain quality of grace and other-worldliness. The horizontal gave way to the soaring perpendicular which created the light-flooded spaces apparently no longer bound to this earth. The cathedral groundplan ceased to be the expression of massiveness and restriction to this world; it had now to embody man's heavenward strivings. Thus, the nave was built higher; it was meant to stand out and be particularly conspicuous above the lower side aisles. To emphasise still more effectively the heavenward tendency of the Gothic cathedral, it is surrounded by the small dwellings of the city. The double towers of the Romanesque period were often replaced by a single tower which forms the west end of the cathedral, and the façade was diversified by a mighty portal straining upwards. The worshipper's attention was thus caught at the entrance and directed towards heaven.

Apart from the great cathedrals, the greatest of which in Cologne, Ulm and Freiburg were centuries abuilding, there developed in Germany, from the middle of the 14th century onwards, the Gothic hall churches, in which aisles and naves are of the same height, so that the nave here lost its dominant position. This provided the best solution for a "burgher church", for it made an unobstructed view of the pulpit and altar possible from all parts of the church, which was precisely what the burgher demanded. In addition, as little emphasis as possible was to be given to the distinction between clergy and laity. Just as the burgher built his own church so also he had the right to choose his own clergy.

A peculiar and special form of the Gothic church is to be seen in the brick Gothic which has left its stamp on most of north-eastern Germany.

One a level with the Gothic cathedral was the town hall, frequently just as important from the architectural viewpoint. This was the communal expression of burghers grown conscious of their freedom and importance. Among the most beautiful of Gothic town halls are those of Münster (North Rhine-Westphalia), Brunswick, Tangermünde, Breslau, and Prague.

Sculpture is inseparable from Gothic architecture. Their union was closer than any attained before or since. This architectural sculpture found its most vigorous and genuine expression in the 13th century (Strassburg, Bamberg, Naumburg). Here it is the expression of great nobility of mind and deep-felt piety.

The numerous commissions to decorate the interior of churches gave artists the opportunity, particularly during the 15th century, to express themselves individually. Their works were not mere products of pure craftsmanship and were completely independent of the prescriptions of the handicraft schools. Foreign, particularly French, models no longer dominated, and the German masters, famous far beyond the limits of their own land, succeeded in giving expression to late Gothic mentality as if it were some special gift of their own (examples are: Hans Multscher: the high altar of the parish church in Sterzing; Joerg Syrlin: the choir stalls of Ulm cathedral; Adam Kraft: the Rebeck epitaph; Michael Pacher: the high altar of St. Wolfgang; Veit Stoss: the high altar of St. Mary's, Cracow; Tilman Riemenschneider: Adam and Eve from the south portal of St. Mary's, Würzburg; the Lady altar in the Herrgottskirche in Creglingen, and the tomb of Emperor Henry II and Empress Cunigunde in Bamberg cathedral).

Where stained glass was concerned, the newly won independence of stone made even finer and more profound design possible. Mary, the

16. Festal Refectory of
    the Marienburg.

17. The Town Hall,
    Thorn.

18. Riemenschneider: Adam and Eve.

19. Pacher: Coronation of Mary.

20. Vischer: A portrait figure of the artist himself.

infant Jesus, and God the Father appear again and again, but in a disciplined concentration which seems to merge heaven and earth.

This concentration yielded, nonetheless, in the 14th and 15th centuries, to a growing joy in more striking, more emphatic artistic expression. The burgher element asserted itself in the wider range of subjects chosen. A wealth of forms was developed, and the two poles of Gothic, the human and the divine, entered on a sensuous union. Glass painting became the most fertile source of inspiration for the popular imagination, insatiable in its thirst for new stimulation.

Whereas mural painting lost in importance as a consequence of the limited wall surfaces of Gothic architecture, and wood cutting and copper-engraving were still only in their beginnings, painting on wooden panels came to the height of its development. At first the best panel paintings originated from the Austrian region at the beginning of the 14th century, Giotto and the Italian school without a doubt exercising the greatest influence. The paintings of Klosterneuburg give perhaps the best impression of this form of art. But shortly afterwards Cologne and the Westphalian school brought this type of painting to the peak of perfection. Stephan Lochner and Conrad von Soest, never again to be equalled, can be named here as the most important among many others of importance.

There is little in the literature of the late Middle Ages that is worthy of mention. Its forces were spent in the imitation of knightly poetry which catered for the popular taste and was for the most part interested in themes rich in intricate plots and improbable adventures. Folk ballads and epics, and *Fastnachtsspiele* (carnival comedies) flourished in the highways and byways of the city. Spiritual poetry with popular appeal maintained a fairly high standard in the religious passion play. Ecclesiastical and love songs in the vulgar tongue were popular; earlier than the other peoples of Europe, the Germans created their own hymnody in the vernacular. Moreover in the course of the 15th century polyphonic music and counterpoint also came to the fore.

In spite of the fact that Johannes Gutenberg's invention of the printing press in Mainz in the mid-fifteenth century had greatly furthered the speedier and wider propagation of the written word, Germany was left almost untouched by the Renaissance and by Humanism, the two great intellectual movements which exercised such a profound influence on the cultural development of Italy from as early as the 14th century. Economic reasons undoubtedly had a large part to play here. In the north Italian states capitalistic ideas and practice had broken the bounds of the burgher's medieval community at an early date, and had forced the individual citizen to become aware of his own individuality. This newly awakened individualism sought its inspiration in pagan antiquity and not only found its own philosophic sanction there but at the same time determined anew the function and status of man in this world and his relation to the next. A man's most essential task was considered to be the development of his free personality, whereby his human gifts and powers were to be harmoniously integrated and brought to perfection. In the process of discarding the medieval modes of thought and life, men now developed a new relationship to the art of antiquity, which they looked upon as their model to be imitated in all creative work. In Italy men had progressed beyond Gothic before it had been able to exercise any decisive influence.

In contrast, the burghers of Germany did not discard the order they had taken over from the Middle Ages until far into the 16th century. Of course this did not mean that the German merchant limited his transactions to the confines of Germany; on the contrary, his trade connections were with the whole of Europe. German goods, acknowledged as the products of highly developed handicrafts—the first clocks came from Germany, for example—were greatly prized and fetched a good price. In addition, Germany with its most important towns lay at the heart of the commercial network of Europe, linking north with south and east with west. But the special structure of the late medieval empire hindered the city from developing along the lines of the north Italian cities, for example, in their development into city-states. In Germany the city continued to be a world apart, and early capitalistic economic forms only found a place in it when strong personalities like the Fuggers of Augsburg, influenced by the Italian example, had the upper hand. A similar development occurred at the intellectual level. German Humanism as an intellectual and artistic movement was confined to a small circle. Its greatest representative was Erasmus of Rotterdam (1466—1528), who strove for a purified Christianity and looked upon the great philosophers of Greek antiquity as the forerunners of Christ. Such views found little favour even within the ranks of German scholars. The writings of the humanists exercised a deeper influence, when they attacked abuses in the Church, especially among the regular clergy, or again when they demanded that the Church be mindful of her real origins in the Bible. Here they were sure of a hearing among the people. Indeed, acute religious unrest was perhaps the most characteristic feature of the German mind at the turn of the 16th century, a feature which we must still regard as a legacy of the Middle Ages rather than as a forecast of the future.

Chapter Six

THE REFORMATION IN GERMANY

Martin Luther and His Religious Convictions

The Austin Friar Dr. Martin Luther gave general popular expression to the religious unrest widespread in Germany, when, on 31st October 1517, he posted up his 95 Latin theses on the door of the Castle Church in Wittenberg. Translated into German by some unknown hand, they spread like wildfire wherever German was spoken and evoked an unexpected response in Luther's favour. A sermon on indulgences preached by the Dominican John Tetzel not far from Wittenberg was the occasion for nailing up the theses. In accordance with university practice of the day, Luther's theses represented a challenge to a disputation about the worth and efficacy of indulgences and the related questions of penance, guilt, punishment, and purgatory. His intention was not a breach with the Church, but her reform. His view of the truth, the result of years of lonely wrestling with the articles of faith, was partially embodied in these theses. With them his thought made its entry on the stage of world history.

Martin Luther was born in Eisleben, a town near the city of Halle, on 10th November 1483. His father was of peasant stock but had been able to improve his lot somewhat because the economic situation of the day was favourable to mining. He was a member of that class of provincial burghers whose sons were glad of the opportunity to improve their social position offered by the study of law. From 1501 onwards the young Luther had pursued his studies at the university of Erfurt, but unexpectedly entered the monastery of the Augustinian Canons of that city as the result of a personal religious experience. The order was strict and of high moral standard. It counted among its members a number of gifted scholars. In the solitude of his cell the young friar hoped to attain that blessed certainty of a soul saved by Christ. However, the exact observance of the Augustinian rule did not grant him this grace. Instead he was tormented more and more by the certainty of his own worthlessness and insignificance in the eyes

91

of God, the Judge Who is infinitely remote from man and implacable in His punishments, before Whom no works of man can stand scrutiny. In this agony of heart he sought consolation in the Bible, from which he drew two certainties: that man is utterly damnable in God's eyes, and that salvation is only possible through Jesus Christ by the grace of faith in Him and His act of redemption. "Then I began to understand the justice of God as the justice by which the just man lives by God's gift, namely by the gift of faith; and apprehended that the meaning of the phrase 'the Gospel reveals the Justice of God' is that passive justice by which the merciful God justifies us by faith, as it is written, the just man lives by faith. Then I felt myself born entirely anew, and it was as if I had entered Paradise by an open door." This new insight, which Luther had experienced in himself some time during the years 1512/13, had a twofold significance: man's relationship to God is not dependent on his own actions, but on God's fatherly grace; the experience of this grace by faith in Jesus Christ takes place solely within the individual person and does not require the intervention of a priest. In these conclusions Luther deviated from Catholicism in two essential points. According to the Catholic view, man has indeed been corrupted by original sin, but is still able to save his soul by his own powers; the Church's treasury of grace is there to help him. Moreover, man stands in need of the Church, since she alone is the steward and dispenser of divine grace. Since, however, Luther's new insight had grown out of the study of the source of Christian faith, the Bible, the absolute authority of the Old and New Testaments was for him as incontestable as the personal divine guidance of the believer in all religious things.

Many of Luther's theses were completely in accord with Catholic teaching; only a few gave an inkling of the Wittenberg friar's new experience of the faith. Unfortunately, the general and voluble criticism of the Church as such, sparked off by the theses, caused considerable alarm in Rome. For the Roman curia Luther's act was not the expression of heart-felt concern about the human failings which he thought he detected everywhere in his Church; it was nothing less than an unjustified act of rebellion against the authority of the pope. For this reason, the means adopted by Rome in an attempt to force Luther to retract his theses and abandon his criticism were also entirely in accord with traditional practice. Theological disputes with the representatives of the ecclesiastical authorities did not bring any change in Luther's attitude; on the contrary, they led rather to a more precise formulation of Luther's views and finally to his appeal to Holy Scripture as the sole and final authority in matters of faith. The pope countered Luther's stand with a bull in which Luther was threatened with papal excommunication if he did not recant. Luther parted ways with the Church of his birth when he burnt this bull outside the Elster Gate in Wittenberg in the presence of jubilant students.

Luther's activity can be compared to the great reform movement which emanated from the monastery of Cluny in the Middle Ages. He, too, was concerned with the reform of the Church and of religion in the spirit of the gospel and of tradition as he understood them. Like the monks of Cluny, Luther was a religious man, a believer, not a politician. But, again like them, he came at a time when religious demands amounted to a challenge to a political decision which might prove to his advantage or against it. For this reason, it was impossible that the Reformation set in motion by Luther should be confined to the religious sphere alone; it was inevitable right from the very outset that it would have repercussions on the entire political structure of the areas it affected.

Following medieval custom Luther's case had now to be handed over to the secular arm to decide. The emperor was called upon to execute the ban. Charles V, however, could not bring himself to do this without first giving the monk a hearing. A diet at Worms was to decide Luther's case in the presence of the emperor.

The Reformation and Its Political Consequences

In 1519 Maximilian, Holy Roman Emperor and King of the Germans, of the house of Habsburg, died. Francis I of France, and Charles, Maximilian's grandson and King of Spain and her colonies, heir to Austria and her territories, to Burgundy and the Netherlands, to Naples and Sicily, both offered themselves as candidates for the German throne. The candidature of the French king was understandable, for it was to be expected that France should fear total encirclement by regions under Habsburg sovereignty. However, for the electors political considerations took second place to hopes of material gain. Each of the pretenders sought to gain a majority of the voters for himself by bribery. Charles had made certain of the support of the Fuggers, a merchant family of Augsburg and the greatest bankers of the day. And it was to their money that Charles owed his election to the German throne. He ascended the throne of Charlemagne as Charles V (1519—1556).

The circumstances surrounding the election of Charles V show clearly to what a pass the empire had come. Its destiny now lay in the hands of a banking family. The princes were no longer strong enough to place their own interests (jeopardised by the excessive power wielded by both pretenders) above temporary material benefits. Still they did try to protect their interests against extravagant imperial demands. They made Charles promise in "electoral capitulations" not to undertake a foreign war without the consent of the German princes, and not to station Spanish troops in Germany. The emperor broke his word in both respects.

Charles V had been King of Spain since 1516. Decisive changes had taken place in that country since the conclusion of the "Reconquista" (the reconquest of Spain and the expulsion of the Moors from the peninsula in 1492). Unbaptised Jews had been exiled by royal edict in 1492, baptised Jews had been placed under the supervision of the Inquisition. In 1502 all unbaptised Moors were banished from the kingdom. Spain not only enjoyed legal, economic and administrative unity, which her kings had won for her during the course of the "Reconquista", but now had enforced unity of faith as well. Christopher Columbus's voyages of discovery had enabled Spain to build up a colonial empire across the Atlantic. As an immediate result the main burden of trade shifted from the Mediterranean to the western seaboard of Europe and huge quantities of precious metals flowed into the Spanish exchequer. This new wealth was the foundation of Spain's hegemony and policy during the 16th century. Right from the early days of the reign of Charles V as Roman emperor, Spain bore the financial burden of the Habsburg world-wide monarchy.

The idea of *one* Christendom, whose secular head was the emperor, was perpetuated in Charles V's conception of empire. He therefore saw his chief task as the safeguarding of the unity of Christendom. For him the only possible form *one* Christendom could take was as *one* faith in *one* Church. In politics as well the Catholic faith was for him inviolable. This provides the key to his policy in the sphere of politics as in the province of religion and morals. His conception of the nature of the empire differed radically from that of the princes. Because of the actual distribution of power, Charles's rule in Germany was bound to lead to conflict.

The peculiar political situation in Germany was characterised by the break-up of the medieval Holy Roman Empire into a multiplicity of territories. Elsewhere in western Europe the Church had lapsed into a condition of dependence on the state. And in Germany, too, a regional Church had evolved by degrees. The struggle to reform the Church in the 14th and 15th centuries was at the same time an attempt to

94

weaken papal power and strengthen national Church tendencies. The Church was compelled to concede more and more privileges to the princes. Encouraged by the regional character of German ecclesiasticism, the princes tried to gain not only political power but also the control of the Church in their territory. The popes, in their struggle with the emperor, by their concordats with the princes and the repeated grants of privileges to the territorial lords, had themselves contributed towards the success of the princes' efforts in this direction.

The decline of the empire had also especially compromised the economic existence and the legal freedom of some classes of the German population. The blame for this they laid at the door of the papacy, which they also severely criticised because of its growing financial demands. Thus a strong anti-Roman feeling was rife among the knights of the empire, the imperial cities and the peasants.

After he had received an assurance of safe conduct, Luther had declared his readiness to plead his cause personally at the Diet of Worms, which the emperor had called for April 1521. His progress to Worms was like a triumphant procession; wherever he arrived, he was received with enthusiasm and the pealing of church bells. On April 17 he stood before Charles V and the assembled estates of the empire. The summons to retract as erroneous the teaching which he had propagated in word and writing, he countered the next day with:

"I neither can nor will recant, since it is both difficult, unsalutary and perilous to act against one's conscience. So help me God. Amen." Thereupon the emperor promulgated the Edict of Worms which placed Luther under the ban of the empire. The reformer, however, was able to evade the consequences of this imperial act; he allowed himself to be "imprisoned" in the Wartburg by his overlord, the Elector Frederick of Saxony.

The "common people" often reached their decision for or against Luther's views, and thus for or against a break with Rome and the ancient Church, from religious considerations. But these very soon came to be mixed with political, economic, and social motives. The reform movement soon passed far beyond the objectives that Luther had set it. Many of the German ecclesiastical princes remained loyal to their Church in the early days. The Teutonic Order accepted Lutheranism under its grand master Albert of Brandenburg, who, in 1525, put himself under command of the Polish king and accepted him as feudal lord. The knights who remained Catholic transferred the grand master's residence to Bad Mergentheim. Many of the lower clergy and many monasteries adopted Luther's teaching, with the result that soon only reformed worship was held in a great number of churches, and the monasteries were empty. In Wittenberg itself there were repeated disorders because the abolition of ecclesiastical customs and institutions was not proceeding fast enough for Luther's supporters. Luther spoke out against these radical elements in daily sermons. He condemned them as fanatics and forced them to leave the town.

Luther's views found general and undivided approval among the burgher population of the cities. Where the free imperial cities were concerned, the anti-Rome feelings abroad in the nation undoubtedly played an important role, too. Those mesne towns (Landstädte) which were still subject to the princes of the Church saw in the Reformation a welcome opportunity to free themselves from spiritual overlordship.

The situation became critical for Luther and his cause when the knights and peasants decided to have recourse to force, in an all-out effort to obtain their political and social demands in the name of the Gospel.

The knights of the empire had, as a class, inseparably linked their destiny to that of the Roman emperor at the height of the Middle Ages. The change which had taken place in the art of war, with the increasing infrequency of the emperor's Roman campaigns and the discovery of gunpowder by the German monk Bertold Schwarz, had deprived the knights of their essential functions. The small fief—a castle with its adjoining village—provided its holder with but a meagre living. Moreover, the princes of the empire wanted to deprive the knights of their imperial freedom and transform them into their subjects and officials. In 1523 the knights met this threat to their freedom by taking up arms under Franz von Sickingen. They demanded that their independence be guaranteed, the Reformation be enforced, and the ecclesiastical principalities abolished. Their most eloquent spokesman was the humanist and poet Ulrich von Hutten. Franz von Sickingen first engaged his forces against the Prince Archbishop and Elector of Trier. Contrary to all expectation, the inhabitants of Trier remained loyal to their ecclesiastical lord. But even Lutheran territorial lords supported the cause of the princes of the Church. The imperial knights had no chance against these superior forces. With the capture of the Castle of Landstuhl near Kaiserslautern in the Palatinate by a princely army, and the death on the battlefield of Franz von Sickingen, the revolt of the knights of the empire collapsed. The knights were now finished as a political factor to be reckoned with.

At the beginning of the 16th century the economic situation of the German peasants, especially in the south, was, generally speaking, not

MATHIAS GRÜNEWALD

Isenheimer Altar: Auferstehung

Retable d'Isenheim: La Résurrection

Isenheim Altarpiece: The Resurrection

Retablo de Isenheim: La Resurrección

Retábulo de Isenheim: A Resurreição

1513—1515. Musée d'Unterlinden, Colmar

at all hard. Land reclamation, marketing facilities for their agricultural products in the nearby towns, improved agricultural methods, and the extensive adoption of monetary exchange had assured the peasants a tolerable existence. Many younger peasant sons had risen by the study of law into the highly respected profession of *doctores* at the courts of the territorial lords. But, the peasants were despised as a class by both burghers and nobility. The old relationship of dependence still existed. Often the peasant stood in a relation of complete villeinage to his lord, dues and services were high out of all proportion and his share in the communal rights (hunting and fishing) was very small indeed.

As early as the 15th century the peasants had banded together to assert their claims by force. Their uprisings were always unsuccessful, because the nobles and ecclesiastics took common cause against them.

In 1525 another peasant rising took place that surpassed all earlier ones both in violence and in extent (nearly the whole of southern Germany). The peasants based their demands first on natural law by appealing to medieval teaching on the natural rights of man, secondly on religion by invoking the Bible and divine revelation, and finally on history by recalling early German times, when their forefathers enjoyed freedom and independence. The movement received its main impetus from Luther's teaching, "A Christian is free lord of all things, and subject to no man", which Luther had naturally meant in a religious sense. But for the peasants Luther was *the* deliverer without reservation.

Knights of the empire also provided the peasants with leadership, especially in military matters. The best known among them were Götz von Berlichingen and Florian Geyer von Giebelstätt. Luther at first supported the just demands of the peasants as expressed in their 12 articles.

In his "Exhortation to Peace in Response to the Twelve Articles of the Swabian Peasants" he took the princes to task and exhorted them to clemency in keeping with the Gospel. But at the same time he also expected the peasants to show unconditional obedience towards the constituted authorities. He did not recognise any right to revolt. When revolt broke out after all, he addressed himself with severity "Against the Murderous and Thieving Peasant Bands". The rising itself was crushed because of the superiority of the princes' mercenaries and was put down at the cost of severe bloodshed among the peasants. No new social order resulted. For centuries to come, the peasant class lost all say in the political and cultural life of Germany.

Luther made a strict distinction between the spiritual and the secular orders. In contrast to Catholicism and Calvinism, he renounced any

7 R. H. Tenbrock, A History of Germany

role in shaping political and social life. Of all the former guarantors of order only the territories and the free imperial cities had survived, and this was still true, even after their adoption of the Reformation. If Luther wanted some degree of order in his church in spite of his fundamental view that the individual stands alone before God, then he had to join forces with the territorial lords. This alliance between his reform movement and the secular authorities was facilitated by his distinction between the spiritual and the secular orders; for the sake of the "pure doctrine", he abandoned the world to the secular authorities whom he made answerable to God alone. In his view of things, the state had been instituted by God on account of the wickedness and weakness of men. The relation of the individual to the authorities was to be one of obedience and subordination, no matter how much his sense of justice might rebel against the measures of secular authority. Luther also gave his approval to the establishment of regional churches under the *summus episcopatus* of the princes.

Because of his brutal rejection of the Peasants' Revolt, Luther has been held responsible for hindering a development which, by releasing the peasant order from its feudal ties, would slowly but surely have led Germany as a whole out of the age of feudalism. However, anyone passing such a judgment fails to understand both the nature of a religious movement and the real point of Luther's undertaking. Reference has already been made to the comparison one may justifiably draw between the Cluniac reform movement and that of Luther. Cluny, too, pursued neither political, economic, nor social objectives. And yet the realisation of the Cluniac reform concept had brought political, economic and social changes in its wake. Luther's experience was similar. To require that he should have both recognised and, what is more, encouraged the secular side-effects of his religious efforts is certainly demanding too much of him. The intrinsic integrity of Luther's personality and his astonishing power to influence men were both founded essentially on his view that religious considerations alone were at the centre of his thoughts and actions, indeed of his whole life. This world had value in his eyes only in so far as it served the realisation of his religious objectives. The social order inherited from the Middle Ages had importance for him only to the extent that it could be modified to serve that end more wholeheartedly. For this reason it was a matter of complete indifference to Luther that his attitude towards the peasants had lowered his reputation in men's eyes and caused a fall in the number of his followers, especially among the members of the peasant class.

During the same decade (1520—1530) in which the face of the age was largely determined by political and social upheavals, Luther gave substance and form to the Lutheran Church by his writings and his translation into German of the Old and New Testaments. These efforts of his found their provisional conclusion in the "Augsburg Confession", composed by his collaborator Philip Melanchthon, which was at the same time an attempt to restore religious unity at the Diet of Augsburg in 1530. The institution of regional churches had with Luther's consent created in the German territories conditions similar to those most clearly to be seen in Charles V's Spain. As a consequence of the decline of the formerly Catholic monasteries and of the Catholic social institutions in the Lutheran territories, their possessions, but also the functions they had fulfilled, passed to the territorial lords concerned. With the help of their officials these then developed the regional admistration still further and step by step they strengthened their independence both of the estates within their territories and of the emperor outside, on the basis of the superior financial security the former church property now brought them. Like their Catholic opponents they too regarded unity of belief as an essential guarantee of unity of state.

The Edict of Worms and the decision of the great majority of Germans in Luther's favour had swept the Reformation and Catholicism into the field of tensions existing between the Roman emperor and the territorial lords, between the Habsburg universal monarchy and the power ambitions of individual European states. Charles V's success abroad weakened the position of the territorial lords and helped the emperor in his struggle against the new faith, whereas setbacks in his foreign policy made him dependent on the princes and thereby furthered the cause of the Reformation.

Immediately after the Diet of Worms, France and the papacy had allied for reasons of power politics to make war on Charles V. They wanted to put a stop to the encirclement of their territories by the Habsburg states (1521—1526). In the course of these conflicts France united for the first time in the history of Christian Europe with a non-European, and non-Christian power, the Turkish empire, in order to force the Habsburgs to engage in a war on two fronts. At the same time France sought and gained considerable support from the German princes of both confessions. The princes frequently refused to allow the stationing of Spanish mercenaries on German soil, demanded that the emperor respect princely liberties, and, where they were Lutheran, made their support for Charles V's wars dependent on concessions in matters of faith. The pope's political hostility towards Charles was only overcome by the entry of German troops into Rome in the year 1527. The form this invasion took unleashed feelings of revulsion and contempt for the Germans, but occasioned an internal transformation of the papacy which was to prove of the greatest historical importance. The year 1527 marks the end of the worldly Renaissance papacy and the beginning of the Reform papacy.

One year previously the first military encounter with Francis I of France had been decided in Charles's favour. Milan, Naples and Burgundy remained in the possession of the Habsburgs. In the same year Charles's brother Ferdinand had been elected King of Bohemia and Hungary on the grounds of his marriage to Anna, the heiress of the King of Bohemia. Hungary's immediate neighbour was the Ottoman empire, which crowned its irresistible advance on the Balkans, after the conquest of Constantinople, with a first thrust against Vienna (1529). Francis I chose this moment to launch an assault on Charles V (1526—1529) and thereby forced on the Habsburg monarchy the dreaded double threat to both flanks of the empire. But in spite of this advantage, success was denied both adversaries, the French as well as the Turks. The sultan had to withdraw in the face of the stubborn resistance of Vienna, and Charles V again defeated his opponent Francis, to whom he had to surrender Burgundy, but whom he was able to keep out of Italy. Reconciliation with the pope in Barcelona put an end to the armed conflict with the Papal States. It also inaugurated the period of their combined efforts against the Reformation.

The Diet of Spires (1529) created another critical situation for Luther's work. There the emperor demanded that all innovations introduced in the lands which had embraced Lutheranism should be dropped. Luther's supporters with Philip Landgrave of Hesse at their head protested against this move and demanded religious freedom of conscience and the convocation of a general council to meet on German soil. The term "Protestant" as a designation for the followers of the Reformation was coined as a result of this *Protestatio*.

The attempt of the same prince to strengthen the Evangelical front by bringing about an organisational union between the Lutherans and the Swiss supporters of the Zurich reformer, Zwingli, proved abortive. Talks between the two about the nature of the Eucharist at Marburg in the same year came to nothing because Luther remained faithful to medieval and Catholic ideas about the Sacrament.

The *Confessio Augustana* of the following year was the last great attempt to restore Christian unity. In this respect it was a failure, though it was to prove important for the internal development of

100

Protestantism. The Diet of Augsburg rejected it as irreconcilable with the Catholic faith, and demanded the restitution of all ecclesiastical property as well as the reinstatement of the clerical princes. This was the occasion for the Protestant princes to meet at Schmalkalden and unite in a league against the emperor in defence of their political and religious freedoms, if need be by force of arms. The division between Catholics and Protestants seemed to be final. Unexpectedly, however, the Catholic Duke of Bavaria joined the Schmalkaldic League because he feared the Habsburgs were getting too powerful. France, the Habsburg's natural enemy, also joined the league.

The deployment of a great Turkish army against Vienna forced the emperor to give way. In 1532 he recognised the Protestant powers and the Lutheran faith. A general council was to be summoned to meet on German soil.

Charles V's wars with France and the Turks kept the emperor away from Germany for more than a decade. During these years the Reformation was able to spread unhindered and take deep root. Nearly the whole of north, west, and south-west Germany was lost to the Catholic faith. Only Bavaria and various prince bishops remained loyal to their Catholic beliefs. Of the number of bishoprics, Osnabrück, Merseburg, Meissen, and Naumburg embraced Protestantism. In the Habsburg dominions it was especially the nobility who joined Luther; in the archbishopric of Salzburg the majority of the population was Protestant. The German colonists in Hungary and Transylvania went over to Protestantism very early. The Baltic provinces also adopted Lutheranism.

Despite the great military superiority of the French and Turks, Charles V succeeded in halting the Turkish advance on the Balkans and in liberating a part of Hungary from Turkish domination. However, North Africa fell almost entirely into Turkish hands. The engagements in the field with Francis I (1536—1544) did not shake the position of France as a great power, but assured the Habsburgs the continued possession of the Free County of Burgundy (Besançon) and sovereignty over Italy. Moreover, in the Peace of Crépy (1544) Francis I undertook to throw in his weight in the fight against the Reformation.

The emperor had promised the Protestants the convocation of a general council on German soil. As a consequence of political developments and the pope's attitude, he was not able to keep his word. It was not until the year 1546 that the pope summoned a council to meet at Trent, a town which was indeed situated on German imperial territory but whose population was Italian. In contrast to the emperor,

101

the pope demanded that questions of faith should be considered first, before those of ecclesiastical reform. The Protestants did not respond to the invitation and Luther died a year after the convocation of the council.

After successfully concluding his foreign wars, Charles V thought he could now decide the religious question in Germany by his authority alone. But the territorial princes resisted this claim not only on religious but also on economic and political grounds. The restoration of Catholicism would have meant for them the renunciation of the regional church set-up, the restitution of all secularised ecclesiastical property, and the possible loss of their almost sovereign position in their territories. Charles V, however, had resolved to break the resistance of the Protestants by force of arms and in 1547 he defeated them in the Battle of Mühlberg. The emperor was at the height of his power, the end of Protestantism seemed in sight, unity of faith looked close at hand. But the defeat awoke in Protestantism forces of resistance for which the emperor, in spite of the numerous Spanish mercenaries on German soil, was no match. In addition, the Protestants entered into an alliance with Henry II of France, whom Maurice Elector of Saxony acknowledged as "Vicar-General of the Empire" for Metz, Toul and Verdun. The allies invaded south Germany (1551—1552). Only with the greatest difficulty did the emperor escape being taken prisoner at Innsbruck. Afterwards the Turkish problem and a new and unsuccessful war against France prevented Charles from forcing a speedy settlement of the religious question in Germany. Finally a religious peace was concluded at Augsburg in 1555. Charles V wanted to have nothing to do with it in his capacity as emperor for reasons of conscience. He therefore entrusted the negotiations to his brother Ferdinand.

The Peace of Augsburg placed Lutheranism on an equal footing with the Catholic faith. Subjects were to follow the religion of their ruler, according to the principle *Cuius regio, eius religio;* the territorial ruler and the cities were therefore to decide the religion of their subjects. Unity of belief was here recognised in law as a *sine qua non* for unity of state. Dissenters were only conceded the right to emigrate. The division of Europe into Protestant and Catholic areas was now an established fact. For the time being, however, the supporters of the reformer Calvin were still excluded from this settlement.

Conscious of his failure to solve the religious question, Charles V abdicated in 1556 and withdrew to the monastery of St. Jeronimo de Yuste in Spain. He was succeeded in his Spanish dominions by his son Philip II, and in the possessions of the Austrian Habsburgs and as emperor by his brother Ferdinand I. The universal empire of the Habsburgs was thus divided.

The reign of Charles V represents the last attempt so far made in Europe to bulwark or restore the political and religious unity of the West using the means at the disposal of a world-wide empire and motivated by the medieval religious concept of one Christendom. Charles V's plans were frustrated by the political system in process of formation in the European national states and by the German territorial rulers. In addition, political and religious individualism, considerably strengthened by the intellectual movements known as the Renaissance and Humanism, had established itself so firmly that from now on it was to make a decisive contribution towards determining the history of Europe and, therefore, of Germany, too.

Cultural Development in Germany at the Time of the Reformation

During the Reformation period and until far into that of the Counter Reformation, Germany's cultural development was greatly influenced by the profound religious upheavals occasioned by Luther's break with the old Church. Since the driving force of German culture was still primarily religious, it continued along the lines laid down in the late Middle Ages. In German-speaking areas we do come across some cautious adoption of elements inspired by the Italian Renaissance, but late Gothic elements still continued to predominate in architecture, and it was only in profane buildings that the Italian Renaissance style found isolated imitators.

Strangely enough, the Church of the Reformation did not evolve a style of its own in church architecture, either at the time of the actual reform movement or after. At first Protestants were content to take over former Catholic places of worship and remodel the interiors in accordance with their own religious views. Later they built churches of their own in the style of the day, so that until the end of the 19th century Catholic and Protestant churches looked very much alike externally.

The Reformation period found its strongest expression in the field of painting. Its most important exponents, who won world-wide renown for German art, were Matthias Grünewald and Albrecht Dürer. The Renaissance and Humanism are not at all significant for Grünewald's art; his work, although revolutionary, remained true to the Gothic tradition. In contrast Dürer attempted to learn from the glories of

Italian art and then to equal its achievements. In the process he followed the dictates of his own individual genius so faithfully that he ended by giving the most vigorous expression of all to German contemporary art.

Matthias Grünewald (probably also known as Neithardt or Matthes von Aschaffenburg) died in 1528. The date of his birth is unknown. His reputation was founded, even in his own lifetime, on his splendid achievement, the altarpiece of Isenheim (Upper Alsace). For Luther the most genuine expression of his spiritual experience was the word, in the form either of an inspiring sermon, a stirring pamphlet, or a translation which, though close, conveys the spirit and exact import of the original. For Grünewald colour took the place of the word. He expressed pictorially the problem of salvation, which gave him, as a religious man, as little peace as it gave Luther. Thus the Isenheim altarpiece became the great representation of his own religious experience. This had taught him the spiritual poverty of man, the inconceivable greatness of the divine act of redemption, and the utter bliss of Jesus's triumph in the Resurrection as the pledge of personal salvation. Though Grünewald was entirely rooted in traditional Christianity, his experience of Christian truth was every bit as personal as Luther's.

Albrecht Dürer was born in Nuremberg on 21st May 1471 as the son of a goldsmith. At first he began to learn his father's trade but his talent for drawing was already so marked in his youth that his father apprenticed him to a painter. Dürer early enjoyed the special patronage of the emperors Maximilian I and Charles V. The main themes of his work were borrowed from the realm of religion, though numerous self-portraits, tracing his own development, also occupy an important place in his creative work. This interest in self-portraiture was unusual at this period. The end of the 15th century saw his sketches for the great series of woodcuts for the Apocalypse and the Passion, and various other isolated woodcuts. They are all completely medieval in character and based on medieval religious conceptions.

Dürer's many journeys to Italy also brought him into contact with the new art of the Renaissance. However, his encounter with the German humanist Pirkheimer was to prove of decisive importance for his development. To this man Dürer owes the conviction so essential to his works that beauty and perfection arise from correct proportion— a view which was also characteristic of contemporary Italian painting. During one of his longer stays in Italy he produced those works in which he achieved such perfection in the new style that artists like Raphael and Michelangelo recognised him as an equal. Nevertheless he did not continue along these lines. In Germany he devoted himself

21. Dürer: The artist's mother.

23. Heidelberg Castle.

22. Holbein, the Younger: Portrait of Thomas Howard, Duke of Norfolk.

24. Nördlingen.

25. Karlsruhe.

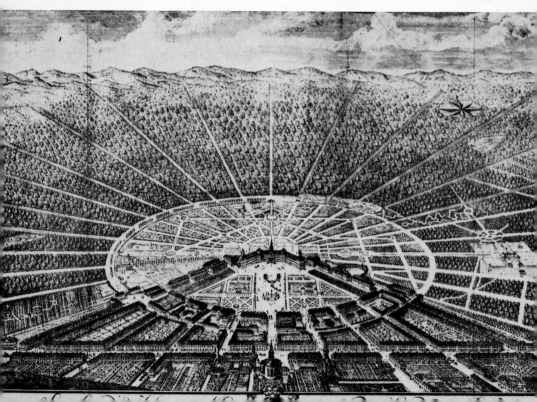

anew to woodcutting and copper-engraving. He thought these techniques offered him greater opportunity to penetrate beyond the purely pictorial to the inner meaning of human activity, which for him was determined by the religious element. As an inevitable consequence he regarded the content of his artistic creations as more important than their form. Although he did not join Luther, he tried in his famous "Four Apostles" to give Luther's new interpretation of the Gospel message an expression that would force the observer "not to accept human seduction in place of the word (of God)". Albrecht Dürer died in the town of his birth in 1528.

Contemporaries of Dürer and Grünewald were Lucas Cranach (1472—1553), Albrecht Altdorfer (1480—1538), and Hans Baldung (1480—1553). Cranach supported the Reformation and went to live in Wittenberg, where he created above all impressive portraits of the Reformer. These painters, too, were completely familiar with the new aspirations of the Italian Renaissance. However, none was successful in coming to a clear decision for or against. Thus, their attempt to find a synthesis gives their work something of the ambivalence which is to be observed in other fields at this time.

Hans Holbein the Younger (1497—1543) stands alone. He was indeed the only one who surrendered himself entirely to the new style. But since Basle, the town where he had settled, did not provide him with the background he required for his art, he left the confines of the German empire in 1532. Four years later we find him in England as court painter to Henry VIII, who offered him numerous opportunities to develop his genius for portrait painting.

The Reformation exercised a profound influence on German literature. Both literary and spoken High German trace their origins back to Luther, who transformed the dialect of the chancery of the Saxon electorate (Meissen) into the magnificent vehicle of his translations of the Bible, of his sermons, and of his polemical writings and hymns. In Nuremberg Hans Sachs, the "shoemaker poet", raised the *Meistergesang* to the summit of its development. The last product of late medieval folk literature was the publication of the *History of the Inquisitive Dr. Faust,* who sells his soul to the devil and finally becomes his prey.

Of far-reaching significance was the treatise of the canon of Frauenburg, Mikolaj Kopernik (Copernicus, 1473—1543), entitled *De Revolutionibus Orbium Coelestium* (On the Revolution of the Heavenly Bodies), in which, stimulated by ancient authors and using his own observations, he sketched the first outline of our modern picture of the universe. He explained the observed movements of the planets by reversing the generally accepted view of the universe. Not the earth but the sun lies at the centre of our planetary system. The earth is a planet just like the others and revolves around the sun. Copernicus thus started a revolution in the field of natural science. But it was not only the Ptolemaic picture of the world that collapsed. The intellectual difficulties of modern man who feels himself torn between faith and the findings of science also originated here.

The Swiss Paracelsus (1493—1541), the most learned doctor of his day and the pioneer of modern medicine, has also a claim to be numbered among scholarly humanists. He viewed sickness not as an isolated phenomenon, but tried to use it to come to an understanding of the whole man. In this way he recognised the dependence of the human organism on many long-concealed factors and discovered a series of prophylactics which answered to his conception of the interaction of all natural things. That he strayed in the process into the spheres of the occult and mysticism is to be accounted for more by the inadequate medical knowledge of his day than by his own habits of thought.

Chapter Seven

THE DEATH THROES OF THE EMPIRE

The Secession of the Netherlands

Charles V's partition of the Habsburg empire made Philip II sovereign of Spain and her colonies, of the Free County of Burgundy (Besançon), Italy, and the Netherlands. This meant that the mouths of the Scheldt and the Rhine, so important for German trade, were removed from the jurisdiction of the German King and Roman Emperor Ferdinand I, and placed under Spain, a centralised power intent on preserving the unity of faith. Philip II regarded the defence or restoration, as the case may be, of the Catholic faith as the main task he had to face as king. His chief aid in this respect was the "Society of Jesus", the religious order founded by the Spaniard Ignatius of Loyola during Luther's lifetime.

The Netherlands, which at this time embraced present-day Holland and Belgium, had grown rich during the 14th and 15th centuries on cloth-weaving and an extensive wool trade with England and Central Europe. During the age of discovery they had been able to take advantage of Antwerp's harbour and opened up trade relations with the new parts of the globe. The wealthy cities of the Netherlands housed proud burghers who clung to the freedoms of their estates in the teeth of the sovereign state of monarchical Spain. In addition the Reformation had won the sympathies of the inhabitants of the northern (Flemish) Netherlands at an early date, whereas the southern (and more Walloon) population clung to their Catholicism. The Reformation was adopted for the most part in the Calvinistic and not in the Lutheran form. In contrast to Luther, Calvin had from the beginning tuned his reform to the shaping of political and social life in the spirit of Christianity. The believer was bound to impose this Christian state by force if need be; he had the right of rebellion in a state which hindered him in the performance of the duties of his Christian faith. Not only the burghers of the cities but the nobles of the northern Netherlands had also embraced Calvinism. Their leader was the Count of Nassau and Prince of Orange (in France), born in Dillenburg castle in Hesse, who had considerable possessions in the northern Netherlands. But his Catholic peers also rejected Spanish overlordship and a compulsory conversion of the reformed Christians to the old faith. They regarded the princes of the empire as their political ideal and aspired to the liberty they had won from the emperor.

Spain's conflict with the Netherlands was an offshoot of the religious question. The open resistance to Philip's efforts to annul the Reformation moved him to initiate a reign of force and terror through the intermediary of his regents. It self-defence the seven northern Protestant provinces united under the leadership of William of Orange at Utrecht in 1579, whereas the southern Catholic provinces, after initial resistance, ultimately yielded to Spanish overlordship from religious considerations. Military reinforcements from Germany and financial support from Protestant princes made the northern provinces so strong that in 1581 they declared Philip II deposed and themselves independent. The defeat of the Armada in 1588 made it impossible for Spain to continue the struggle. A truce was finally concluded between the "United Netherlands" and Spain in 1609.

Economic Decline and Political Weakness

When Charles V divided the Habsburg monarchy, he was undoubtedly influenced not only by political but economic considerations as well. He saw that the main focus of trade was shifting from central Europe to the western seaboard of the Continent. He therefore judged it timely to attach to the Spanish half of the empire as contiguous a belt of lands as possible, so as to ensure Spanish control of important west European harbours. He thought that Spanish efforts to consolidate and extend her great colonial empire could then be successfully promoted from these ports. As early as about 1600 the Dutch succeeded in forcing their way into the American and Indian trading areas and above all in fully safeguarding the interests of Dutch spice traders. In contrast, Germany left the scene of world politics for nearly a century.

This development had already begun immediately after the Peace of Augsburg. The religious solution to which it had given formal legal approval had brought the German territorial rulers almost unrestricted sovereign powers. The territorial lords now spent themselves almost entirely in the jealous defence of these newly acquired rights. The Austrian Habsburgs, too, made no attempt to strengthen their imperial position in the empire, but regarded themselves more as territorial rulers than as emperors. Germany's "exit from history" was almost

108

total. Even in the face of the Turkish threat, both emperor and princes behaved with studied negligence. Until 1606 they tried to avert it by paying an annual tribute.

Attended with even graver consequences for the future development of German history was the passive attitude of the German towards his state, the empire, and public affairs. Even the quest for religious truth, so typical of this century, was no longer a subject for discussion, since the territorial lord decided the issue for his subjects. For this reason Catholicism tried to win back lost areas by concentrating its efforts on the regional ruler. These efforts did not go unrewarded, especially in the south of Germany. In the Lutheran territories the ruler, in keeping with his position as supreme head of the regional church, issued territorial decrees *(Landsordnungen)* which even decided details of ecclesiastical and educational policy. The Lutheran clergy was entirely dependent on him; the representatives of the estates no longer had any decisive say. The burgher spirit of enterprise in the cities, even in the surviving free imperial cities, now had no room to develop because of the displacement of trade. The cities were in no position to compete with the two sea powers, England and Holland. Within Lutheranism there were numerous theological controversies, which nevertheless contributed to the clarification of key problems in theology. But widespread religious and political quietism remained characteristic of Lutheranism for many years.

In contrast, Calvinism became ever more determinedly active in all spheres. This was why it was almost more feared by the princes than Catholicism with its new-found vigour and its authoritative attitude towards the simple people which largely corresponded to their own.

As a consequence of the weakness of the Catholic emperor, Protestantism continued to win ground, especially in the spiritual principalities. With the exception of Hildesheim, all the bishoprics east of the Weser accepted the new teaching. Although the Peace of Augsburg in what is known as its spiritual reservation clauses forbade bishops embracing Protestantism to convert their bishoprics into secular principalities, the emperor made no protest when this happened. Only under Rudolph II (1576—1612), the emperor educated by the Jesuits in Madrid, did Catholicism offer effective resistance and prevent the loss of the important west German diocese of Cologne to the Protestants after its archbishop had converted to Calvinism. In saving Cologne, Catholicism also gained an important bastion for the re-Catholicisation of Westphalia and the success of the Counter Reformation in other bishoprics.

These first major successes won by Catholicism in north-west Germany led the Calvinist princes especially to take steps in defence of their rights. The more the Bavarian Duke Maximilian encroached on Protestant rights, in their eyes unwarrantably, the more they intensified their efforts. Under pressure from the most active among the Calvinist princes, who were still excluded from the Peace of Augsburg, the majority of the Protestant princes and free cities united in a military league, the Protestant Union, against Catholicism. Frederick IV of the Palatinate and Christian of Anhalt took over the leadership. The Catholics, headed by Maximilian of Bavaria, answered this challenge one year later by forming the Catholic League, of which Count Johann Tzerclaes of Tilly was nominated general. Both alliances sought support abroad; the Catholics turned to Spain, the Protestants to England, France and the Netherlands. Bavaria vetoed the accession of the Catholic Habsburgs of Austria to the League in order to prevent the imperial authority from being strengthened. In Germany, Protestantism and Catholicism faced each other under arms.

A dispute, in itself historically unimportant, between the Elector of Brandenburg and the Count Palatine of Neuburg about the succession to small areas of territory in the Lower Rhine and Westphalia underlined once more the tense situation in Germany, especially as Spanish troops were deployed on the Catholic side. But the outbreak of open war was prevented even at this stage when both pretenders came to an agreement and divided the disputed inheritance. East German Brandenburg acquired for the first time west German territory in the duchy of Cleve (Lower Rhine), and the counties of Mark (Westphalia) and Ravensberg-on-the-Weser—an event pregnant with significance for Germany's future (1614).

The Thirty Years War and Its Aftermath

In no other country peace between Catholics and Protestants was more in jeopardy than in Bohemia. In order to safeguard their position as kings of Bohemia, the Habsburgs had granted the Bohemian estates a series of rights covering the practice of the Protestant religion, which most of them professed. This tolerance aggrieved the Catholics. They kept zealous watch that the Protestants did not transgress the freedoms granted. The Archbishop of Prague felt he was justified in ordering the closure of a Protestant church in one of the small towns, because its erection was not covered by the royal privileges. In Prague the representatives of the Bohemian estates appeared before the imperial commissioners and, when the latter were unwilling to yield to their complaints, threw them out of the window of Prague castle. It is true the commissioners escaped with their lives, but this "Defenestration of Prague" sparked off one of the most important and protracted wars of German, indeed of European, history (1618).

With the Defenestration, Bohemia threw off its allegiance to the Habsburgs and the empire. It aspired to independence on national and religious grounds. Moravia and Silesia joined Bohemia. In the mercenary soldier-count Ernst von Mansfeld and his troops it found a military commander and a powerful army. It is true that Ernst was Catholic, as were possibly many of his mercenaries, too, but for him and for them war was a trade which had to provide a man with his living. It was thus a matter of complete indifference to whom and for whom he sold his services. This attitude of Ernst von Mansfeld's was shared during the next thirty years by many others who far surpassed him in military gifts and success. But the result was always blood, tears, sufferings and death for millions. For mercenary armies did not confine their activities to the battlefield; they regarded raids on towns and countryside, and on the innocent as well as the guilty, in search of plunder and spoil as their natural right.

Ernst's army was successful in Bohemia. This made it possible for the estates to offer the Bohemian crown to Frederick, young Elector Palatine of the Rhine, instead of to the Habsburg Ferdinand. The new king was the son-in-law of James I of England and the leader of the Protestant Union. He was a prince who loved pomp and splendour, though as a Calvinist he rejected all ornament in the house of God. His military gifts were limited, indeed almost non-existent, when compared with those of his most dangerous opponent, Tilly, who, as general of the Catholic League, took the field against him. Most of the Lutheran princes remained neutral; the Protestant elector of Saxony sided with the emperor; Frederick was defeated by these superior forces in the Battle of the White Mountain in 1620, not far from his royal capital of Prague. His reign had lasted hardly one winter. Catholicism was ruthlessly restored in Bohemia. Frederick, who had fled to England, was deprived of his electoral dignity, which was transferred to the Wittelsbachs of Bavaria.

The victory of the Catholic cause seemed assured, a victory which would at the same time have decisively strengthened the emperor's position in the empire. At this juncture Christian IV, King of Denmark, intervened in the war. He was a Protestant and had his eye on the north

German bishoprics. Allied with Holland and England, he invaded Germany at the head of a strong army. This act converted the German war into a European war.

In this situation, menacing for emperor and Catholicism, which would have ended eventually, in spite of Tilly's brilliant run of victories, in a triumph for Protestantism as a consequence of the League's lack of funds, Duke Albrecht von Wallenstein offered the king an army which he proposed to support himself. This ambitious Bohemian nobleman, consumed with great political ambitions, was born of Protestant parents but had become a Catholic in his youth as a result of a Jesuit education. In contrast to Tilly, questions of faith were of secondary importance in his eyes. Private means and a talent for organisation had made it possible for him to raise at short notice an imposing army recruited from the adventurers of all European nations and only kept together by the authority of its commander, Wallenstein. What Ernst von Mansfeld had started, Wallenstein continued on a larger scale. War alone could support such a monster of an army.

With the aid of this numerically superior army, the emperor and the League were able to drive Christian IV and his followers out of north Germany and to dictate the Peace of Lübeck (1629). The Danish king gave an assurance that he would not interfere in the affairs of north Germany. Wallenstein was enfeoffed with the duchy of Mecklenburg and nominated "General of the Baltic and Oceanic Seas". He was aspiring, however, after far more than these external honours: he hoped to make the Baltic into a German sea again and to win a position for the emperor which would assure him independence of the princes. Wallenstein envisaged for himself a position at the emperor's side as the most powerful prince in the empire.

But, as it turned out, his Baltic plans came to nothing because of the resistance offered by the Protestant town of Stralsund, with the support of Denmark and Sweden. More decisive for his personal fortunes was the attempt of his imperial lord to force the Protestant princes to restore all the ecclesiastical property acquired since 1552 and thereby to agree to a reconversion to Catholicism of all north German religious houses and institutions, and numerous south German monasteries and abbeys. With the support of Catholic France and Protestant Sweden, both Protestant and Catholic princes alike resisted this demand, which was prompted by imperial and Catholic political ambition. No matter how varied their motives, Ferdinand II's opponents presented him with a united front. At first they were only intent on breaking the imperial hegemony. They were able to force Ferdinand to give way at the Diet of

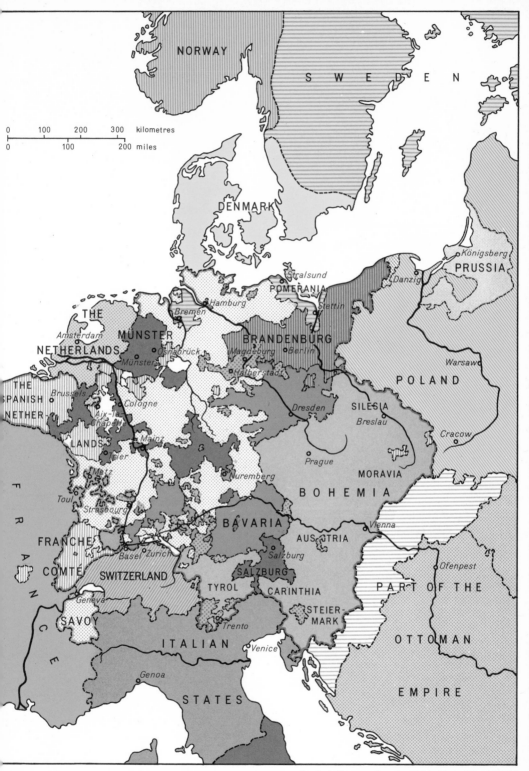

S W E D E N

0   100   200   300   kilometres
0   100   200   miles

DENMARK

Königsberg

PRUSSIA

Stralsund

POMERANIA

Danzig

Hamburg

Bremen

Stettin

THE

Amsterdam

MÜNSTER

BRANDENBURG

Osnabrück

Magdeburg   Berlin

Warsaw

NETHERLANDS

Münster

Halberstadt

POLAND

THE

Brussels

SPANISH

Cologne

Dresden

SILESIA

NETHER-

Aix-la-

Breslau

Cracow

Chapelle

LANDS

Mainz

Trier

Prague

MORAVIA

Metz

Nuremberg

BOHEMIA

Toul

Strasbourg

F R A N C E

Basel   Zurich

BAVARIA

Vienna

FRANCHE-

AUSTRIA

COMTÉ

SWITZERLAND

Salzburg

Ofenpest

Geneva

SALZBURG

P A R T   O F   T H E

SAVOY

TYROL

CARINTHIA

Trento

STEIER-

MARK

ITALIAN

Venice

O T T O M A N

Genoa

E M P I R E

S T A T E S

Central Europe after the Thirty Years War (1648)

Regensburg (1630). Wallenstein was dismissed and the imperial army reduced to 40,000 men. The reconversion of northern Germany, which had hardly begun, came to nothing because of the entry of a new Protestant opponent, Gustavus Adolphus of Sweden, on the scene.

The Swedish king was a convinced and pious Lutheran. Undoubtedly he wanted to come to the aid of his hard-pressed brothers in the faith in north Germany, but it is just as certain that he was also thinking of Sweden's power and greatness when he decided to join in the struggle between Protestantism and Catholicism, between imperial ascendancy and the independence of the princes in Germany. His objective was at least to safeguard Sweden's position in the Baltic. But to do this he had to gain control of the German coastline facing Sweden. That the Protestant princes of north Germany soon recognised the military objectives of Gustavus Adolphus is clear from the fact that the Elector of Brandenburg, up to then a neutral, only granted the Swedes the right to pass through his territory after long negotiations, although Tilly's siege of Magdeburg, a Protestant city on the Brandenburg border, was an unmistakable sign of the peril German Protestantism was in. The permission was granted too late to save Magdeburg, but this further victory for the emperor rallied practically all the Protestant princes round Gustavus Adolphus, the ranks of whose Swedish army were swollen by powerful German contingents. Tilly was no match for this superior force or for the military genius of the Swedish king. He himself met his death in battle. Almost effortlessly the Swedes fought their way through to Bavaria, the heart of Catholic resistance, and entered Munich in triumph. In this extremity Ferdinand turned once again to Wallenstein, who succeeded in raising a large army at very short notice. The two armies faced each other at Lützen in 1632. Wallenstein's men were routed, but the Swedes lost their king, the most outstanding general of the Thirty Years War.

But from now on Wallenstein seemed to regard fortune in war as unimportant. His position as commander-in-chief of all the imperial troops was more secure than ever before, and this led him to believe that he could realise his bold plans without victories in the field. Since in his eyes a war for the sake of religious beliefs was futile and unnecessary, he wanted to bring it to an end by negotiation. How he proposed to solve the numerous political and religious problems involved was not clear to friend or foe. That he had assigned himself a key position and that he would not even have shrunk from deposing the Habsburgs is certain. Although the court at Vienna had no conclusive evidence against him, he was accused of treason and the order was given to bring him to Vienna dead or alive. Deserted by a great part of his army he withdrew from Pilsen to Eger, probably with the intention of uniting with the Swedes and, with their help, restoring peace to the country. But before he could realise his plans, he was assassinated.

After Wallenstein's death, the emperor was again able to promote the Catholic cause energetically for a short time. The Swedes were defeated at Nördlingen in 1634, and Bavaria liberated. Once more the Protestants were in a tight corner, and the imperial and Catholic position seemed assured. At this juncture France determined to take an active part in the war; until now she had confined her aid to financial support for the emperor's opponents.

The rivalry between the French and the Habsburgs was confined mainly to the Spanish line of the Habsburgs during the second half of the 16th century, a period when France was weakened internally by the religious disputes between Catholics and Huguenots. But ever since the outbreak of the Thirty Years War, Madrid had been sending the Austrian Habsburgs financial assistance and, towards the end of the conflict, large contingents of Spanish soldiers, whose main theatres of operation were Alsace, the Palatinate, and the Swiss canton of Graubünden. Spain's aim here was, in addition to promoting the Counter Reformation in Germany, to regain political ascendancy over the Netherlands. For France, however, the presence of Spanish troops along the Rhine meant the renewed encirclement of her lands by the Habsburg power bloc, Spain and Austria.

After the Edict of Nantes (1598) had put an end to the internal religious wars, the French monarchy had been able to strengthen its position against the decentralising influences at work in the country. It had won independence from the estates and broken the power of the nobility. Credit for the consolidation of absolute monarchy at home was indisputably due to Cardinal Richelieu, who, although a convinced adherent of his own Church, was first and foremost a statesman and a patriot. As such, he persecuted the Protestants in France for the sake of unity of faith at home with the same zeal with which he supported the Protestants in Germany and abroad, wherever he could persuade them to take part in the struggle against the Habsburgs.

In Bernard of Saxe-Weimar the French and their Swedish allies found a military leader who was successful in defeating the Catholic emperor's army and in ridding Alsace of Spanish troops. He personally aspired to a duchy of Alsace. But death robbed him prematurely of the realisation of this dream in 1639.

The war dragged on as a war of plunder and robbery for almost another decade before peace was finally negotiated. The German people suffered appalling losses, especially during the last phase of the war. Of the estimated population of 18 million only half lived to see the conclusion of hostilities. A great part of Pforzheim, for example, was still deserted in 1667; in Baden the number of dwellings was reduced by half by the end of the war; in the Palatinate, of one million inhabitants only 50,000 survived the hostilities; the population of Berlin before the war was 12,000, after the war a mere 6,000. These are only a few figures which give some idea of what terrible toll the war had taken in Germany. In contrast, the population of France had risen to some 25 million.

The peace was negotiated and concluded in the two Westphalian towns of Münster and Osnabrück, and has therefore gone down in history as the Peace of Westphalia (1648). The real victors of the war were the German territorial rulers, France and Sweden. The territorial sovereignty enjoyed by the princes and free cities was granted legal recognition; they were also empowered to contract alliances, with the one proviso "without prejudice to emperor and empire"—a completely futile condition, since there was no competent higher authority which was strong enough to bring the princes to book. The Holy Roman Empire continued as a legal entity, the emperor kept his suzerainty over all principalities, and the empire its sovereignty, as previously, over areas outside the imperial boundaries. Savoy, the southern Netherlands, and Lotharingia (Lorraine), which also came under French suzerainty, recognised their position as fiefs of the empire. But for all practical purposes the empire had dissolved into a loose confederation of states. In the words of Pufendorf, the authority on international law, it was "a monster, hardly a geographical entity still". The way was thus open for the further vigorous development of the individual states. Though Germany was therefore spared the fate of intellectual uniformity, she fell victim to the effects of a perilous, egocentric particularism.

The Brandenburg electorate received the largest territorial additions of all German states in 1648. It was assigned eastern Pomerania and some north German bishoprics. Bavaria was confirmed in its possession of the Upper Palatinate and as an electorate. The son of the Palatine elector who had been made King of Bohemia in 1619 received the Rhenish Palatinate again and an eighth electorate was created for him.

France's possessions of Metz, Toul and Verdun were legally ratified and in addition it received possessions and sovereign rights in Alsace, which until now the Habsburgs had enjoyed. It also acquired the city of Breisach on the right bank of the Rhine. Sweden obtained western Pomerania with Stettin and Rügen, the archbishopric of Bremen excluding the town of Bremen itself, and the bishopric of Verden. The United Netherlands and Switzerland legally seceded from the empire and their independence was given international recognition.

An attempt was made to arrive at a final solution of the religious question. The situation obtaining on 1 January 1624 was to be regulative for the restitution of ecclesiastical property to the original owners. Where church properties had come into secular hands before that date, possession was confirmed, that is the properties were secularised. The religious peace in 1555 also included the Calvinists. The territorial lord was also to be obliged to grant dissident subjects the right of domestic worship. After nearly one and a half centuries of religious conflict, at times involving bloodshed, the obligation of toleration was at last recognised in a solemn international treaty.

The Thirty Years War had completed a process in Germany which had long been coming to fruition: the empire disappeared as a political power of importance within the framework of European states. It was reduced to the condition obtaining in the early days of its history. As in Henry 1's time (919—936), it existed only in its parts. But these were not governed by the will of the tribal groupings comprising them, but were subject to numerous more or less powerful princes. The political result, therefore, of the Thirty Years War was the creation of a power vacuum in central Europe. The peace treaty left it completely open which powers should fill this vacuum.

Economically, Germany had as a whole been incalculably weakened by the course of the war, whereas the economic situation in its parts varied according to whether the war had raged there continually or only occasionally. Nevertheless, those areas spared by the war were also economically depressed at first, for Germany's marginal position in relation to the new trading and production centres had its full effect only in the 17th century. Thus the German cities, where they were not administrative centres of government, inevitably stagnated and declined into country towns whose inhabitants won their living from agricultural work and drew only a negligible part of their income from the scanty trading possibilities they still enjoyed. The German burgher, source and channel of late medieval culture until far into the Reformation period, lost his importance entirely. Germany became more than ever before a land of peasant farmers.

This was by no means the only aftermath of the war. The fact that the territorial rulers had successfully concentrated political power in their hands within the nominally still-existent empire had been decisive in establishing within their domains those ideas of the nature and task of the state which, as the heritage of the Renaissance, had already formed the west European states during the course of the preceding century. France became the great model for almost all German states, no matter what their confession. Nevertheless, their economic and political power was still so small that they were more the object of international politics than its arbiters. It was furthermore to prove important for the internal development of Germany that the princes in their efforts to secure their absolute power during the build-up of the modern state destroyed precisely those powers that might have been able to prepare the way for a social order based on more liberal principles. The powers here in question were the estates. Previously the princes had been dependent in their internal and foreign political decisions on their consent. Though it is true the constitutional rights of the estates were nowhere abolished, they were mostly deprived of political influence. Except in the ecclesiastical states, the clergy had lost their former importance as an estate, especially of course in the Protestant lands. The nobles alone, on account of their extensive landed properties, were still in a position to exert political pressure and to defend their traditional rights against their territorial ruler. This was why the rulers directed their chief efforts towards breaking the nobility's resistance to princely self-aggrandizement. This they generally achieved not in open struggle but by bringing about a subtle change in the nobles' rights. In order to bind the nobility to their persons and employ them as officials or officers of the absolute state, the princes granted them almost unlimited rights over the peasants on their properties. The peasants also lapsed into villeinage and subjection in the colonial areas of the east, where from the high Middle Ages onwards an important class of free peasants had developed.

As a result of the extreme fragmentation of Germany into hundreds of territorial states, practically all of them—with the exception of a few larger ones—had a population of only a few thousand, whose experience of the absolute power of their prince was immediate and direct, in contrast to the position in the great national states of western Europe. It must not be thought that the majority of the German territorial lords were blood-thirsty tyrants, but many did collect taxes with utter ruthlessness and did not hesitate to sell their subjects to foreign rulers as mercenaries. The burghers, too, were largely dependent on the court for their economic existence. Indeed, even the majority of the industrial undertakings originated, for lack of capital, not from the burghers, but from the princes. Thus, all too easily, a certain spirit of subservience developed, which took it for granted that the indispensable condition for survival was obedience to the will of the prince.

Chapter Eight

THE HOUSE OF HABSBURG

Germany and France

After the conclusion of the Thirty Years War, Germany's real masters were France and Sweden. Both powers were guarantors of princely freedom against imperial encroachments, and both had the right to intervene at all times as arbitrators in Germany's internal affairs. Sweden owed its powerful position more to its skilful and powerful rulers than to the size of its population. For this reason its influence on German development was inevitably only transitory. It did succeed in strengthening its influence on the Baltic area in the Swedish-Polish War (1655—1660), but the Great Northern War (1700—1721) destroyed its sovereignty in the north once for all. Its place was taken by Russia, which now gained access to the Baltic region for the first time. Peter the Great shared with Louis XIV a high measure of esteem and admiration; both rulers exemplify to a high degree the spirit of the Age of Absolutism.

The absolute rule of the princes was the fruit of a development which had its origins, especially in the west European countries, in the struggle of the monarchy with the estates and feudal powers during the late Middle Ages. The monarchy had won the day in both France and Spain. The burghers of France, who had allied with the south French nobility in their resistance to royal aspirations, were bound to lose in the end. They were defeated and constrained to take over the task of sustaining, consolidating and advancing the aggrandizement of the realm. This, however, was ruled by the king by virtue of the "divine right". Indeed, the king was the embodiment of the state, and in him alone was the fulness of law and power. At the beginning of the 16th century the Italian Macchiavelli had developed his teaching about the omnipotence of the state, before which all other interests and even religious and moral considerations have to give way. At the end of the

119

same century the Frenchman Jean Bodin (1530—96) provided the theoretical basis for absolutism. Princely sovereignty was defined as absolute and eternally unlimited in power, task and time. With France as the foremost power in Europe, the 17th century became the age of the triumphant absolutist sovereignty of the princes.

This new attitude to the state as the sum of human power and to the prince as the representative of the omnipotent state had, however, inevitably to bring changes whose consequences would prove serious for Europe. The trial of strength between Charles V and France at the beginning of the 16th century had given a foretaste of what threatened Europe if the dynastic imperialism of absolute monarchs were to prevail. In his own interest the absolute monarch had to pursue a policy of unlimited conquest which took no account of geographical and language boundaries. However, the Netherlands and England, in resisting the efforts of individual powers to dominate Europe, gave birth to a new national spirit which also swayed the hearts of their peoples. This was something utterly new in European history. Of course its influence on the course of political events must not be overestimated, although it played a considerable role in the offensive wars of France and the rebuttal of French claims by others.

The 16th century had already proved that it was no longer possible for one European state to subject the whole of the Continent to its rule. Spain, for instance, had failed to impose its sovereign claims on England. The Habsburgs were not able to subdue France, and even state leagues were hardly in a position to smash existing power blocs, as had been proved once again during the Thirty Years War in the case of the Habsburgs. Thus the theory of the balance of power in Europe arose, according to which the great powers had to balance each other in power and influence in order to guarantee peace in Europe. England was the foremost advocate of this theory. She always intervened in continental wars when she feared the "balance of power" was about to be upset.

The balance of power in Europe had its Achilles' heel in the power vacuum which the peace of 1648 had created in central Europe, and which extended beyond Germany into Italy. It was inevitable that the western regions of Germany especially, as a consequence of their fragmentation into small states, should tempt France to try to gain influence in them which it could utilise at any time to obstruct an energetic imperial policy on the part of the strongest German power, the Austrian Habsburgs.

Despite the serious defeat which the Thirty Years War had inflicted on the empire and the Austrian line of the Habsburgs, the bearers of the imperial crown, the century after 1648, until the early years of the reign of Maria Theresa, was almost entirely dominated, as far as Germany was concerned, by the Habsburgs. Although the Austrian Habsburgs no longer possessed any real power within the empire, they nevertheless succeeded in taking the lead in German history after the catastrophe of 1648 because, after a period of recovery lasting almost twenty years, they assumed responsibilities which were to benefit the whole of Germany, even the whole of Europe. It would certainly be a distortion of the facts if we were to presume that the Habsburgs were conscious of fulfilling a special destiny, when they accepted these responsibilities. Like all other European rulers, they allowed themselves to be swayed merely by consideration of personal advantage. In the event, however, their victories over the Turks have exercised a positive influence on European development.

The recovery and rise of the Austrian house of Habsburg to a new position of power in Europe is linked with the reign of the emperor Leopold I (1657—1705). It was he who determined that south-east Europe should be the Habsburgs' main sphere of interest for the future. When we recall that during the age of absolutism the territorial expansion of the state was considered more important than its internal integrity based on the unity of the people's way of life, traditions and language, these expansionist aims towards the south-east become understandable. The Habsburg possessions in the west of the empire had always been in danger, and the outcome of the Thirty Years War had shown this again. French supremacy in western Europe under Louis XIV, and France's close relations with the west German territorial lords, frustrated Habsburg hopes of being able to defend their possessions in western Germany. That Austria's attitude here could cause a German ethnic area to be lost to a non-German power was a consideration of no importance to the rulers of the day. In this respect the Habsburgs were neither better nor worse than other European powers. The age of the national state still lay in the distant future.

During the 16th century the Turks had pursued a policy of conquest which had enabled them to incorporate the Balkans in their Afro-Asian empire. Hungary, too, was a Turkish province. Not until 1606 did the Ottoman Empire recognise the Roman emperor of the house of Habsburg as a sovereign of equal rank to the padishah. Constantinople's

"Sublime Porte" had not intervened in the Thirty Years War because the Ottoman rulers were hamstrung in their foreign policy by the rebelliousness of the janissaries. Only under Sultan Mohammed IV (1648—1687) did the Turks begin to pursue an active foreign policy again. Its objective was to advance the frontiers at the expense of Venice, of that part of Hungary still in Austrian hands, and of Austria itself. In 1663 the Hungarians were forced to fall back in the face of the advancing Turks. Tartar hordes appeared before the Bohemian towns of Brünn (Brno) and Olmütz (Olomouc). The German diet, the representation of the estates, declared its readiness to provide financial aid and to muster a small imperial army. A strong Austrian army, supplemented by French auxiliaries, was able to defeat the Turks in 1664. Germans and French were fighting on the same side again for the first time since the crusades. Unfortunately, it was also to be the last time for centuries to come. In the peace which was concluded after a short passage of arms, the Turks still retained half of Hungary, an arrangement which was not to the liking of the Hungarian magnates. Louis XIV fanned their indignation at the Habsburgs' "treacherous game". A rebellion of the Hungarian nobles against the Habsburg sovereignty, planned for 1670, was put down in good time.

A secret agreement between Vienna and Paris in the year 1668 marks the withdrawal of the Austrian Habsburgs from western Europe. In it Leopold I concluded a treaty of partition with Louis concerning the Spanish possessions. According to this, Louis's share in the Spanish heritage was recognised in principle and the Spanish Netherlands, Naples and Sicily conceded to him. This treaty was complemented three years later by a treaty of neutrality.

Even the successful quelling of the Hungarian uprisings by the Habsburgs had not been able to induce the Turks to restrain their expansionist aspirations in the north. In this they were supported, as in the days of Charles V, by France, to whom any weakening of Habsburg strength was welcome. The imperial efforts, too, to raise help from the empire for a war against the Turks met a cool reception from many princes of the empire and a flat refusal from Brandenburg. On the other hand, Saxony, Hanover and Bavaria were prepared to furnish troops. The combined efforts of pope and emperor were finally successful in persuading Poland to abandon its policy of friendship towards France and to take the emperor's part. Hardly, however, had the individual armies joined that of the emperor, when Europe was startled by the news that the Turks were before the gates of Vienna and laying siege to the city. The city was saved by the Battle of Kahlenberg in 1683 under the generalship of the Polish King John Sobieski. This European victory over the Ottomans marks a turning point in Europe's relations with the Turkish empire. In his efforts to crush the Turks once for all, Leopold signed a twenty years truce with Louis XIV at Regensburg (1684). In it he confirmed the problematic legal claims of the "chambers of reunion" and French possession of the city of Strassburg in Alsace. France, however, never attempted to dispute the German character of Alsace or of the city of Strassburg.

With the help of Poland and Venice, the imperial arms were able to liberate the whole of Hungary from the Turkish yoke. In 1687 Hungary was united to Austria in a personal union. While the Habsburgs and their allies were successfully continuing the fight against the Turks, France invaded the Palatinate (1688). Louis XIV based this new offensive against west Germany on the hereditary title of his sister-in-law, Liselotte of the Palatinate. At the instigation of William of Orange, who became King of England as well in 1689, the Grand Alliance was formed against France. Besides Spain, Sweden, Brandenburg, Saxony, Hanover, England, Holland, and Savoy, the Habsburgs also joined the league. The war dragged on for nine years. Its most enduring results were the devastation of the Palatinate, the destruction of Heidelberg castle, the desecration of the tombs of the German emperors in Spires cathedral, and the pillaging by French troops of many places along the left bank of the Rhine. Although the Alliance was superior at sea, it did not succeed in breaking the military supremacy of France. At the Peace of Ryswick (1697) Louis XIV was confirmed in his possession of the Alsatian territories including Strassburg; Freiburg-im-Breisgau and some areas east of the Rhine, which had been annexed by France, reverted to the empire.

After the successful conclusion of the Turkish wars, Austria secured by the Peace of Carlowitz (1699) the union of Transylvania, Slavonia and Croatia with its crown; Poland obtained parts of the Ukraine and Podolia; Azov fell to Russia. Austria had become one of the European great powers. A Turkish attempt to reconquer lost territory was frustrated by the military genius of Prince Eugene of Savoy, a great general who had offered his services to the house of Habsburg and had already won important military successes in the European war to decide the Spanish succession (the so-called War of the Spanish Succession, 1701—1713/14). The Spanish possessions in Europe, namely Milan, Naples, Sardinia, and the Spanish Netherlands (present-day Belgium) fell to Austria in consequence of the coalition of European powers formed to resist the claims of Louis XIV to the Spanish succession after the extinction of the Spanish line of the Habsburgs. In the struggle against the Turks, Prince Eugene took Belgrade in 1717; the treaty of Pasarowitz (1718) guaranteed Austria's possession of that town and of the largest part of Serbia.

Austria's acquisition of these ethnically very diversified areas established German influence in the Balkans for more than two hundred years. At the same time Austria acquired the character of a multinational state, a character particularly emphasized by its possessions in Italy and western Europe (Belgium). Its internal structure was from the beginning extremely loose because the ties of the individual parts with the reigning dynasty were founded on a wide variety of ethnic, historical, and cultural factors. Prince Eugene, who until his death in 1736 was commander-in-chief and organiser of the army, and Austria's leading statesman, tried to give new life to the imperial concept in Vienna as well, in order to create a broader German basis for Austria's new position as a great power. Here his efforts were entirely without success. His posthumous fame was wholly founded on his military gifts and the catholicity of his interests and tastes, to which he gave eloquent expression in his Belvedere Palace in Vienna, his extensive library, and his rich collection of engravings and antiquities. When he died, the young crown prince of Prussia and the future Frederick the Great remarked that in him Austria had lost "the Atlas" who had borne the burden of the imperial throne and state.

During the 17th and early 18th centuries Vienna had developed from a frontier town, the south-eastern gateway of the empire, into the hub of a great European power whose every action was closely watched not only by German states but also by the great courts of Europe. Austria, the country from which all this had grown, and Vienna, its capital, looked back on a centuries-old tradition deeply rooted in a Roman past, a history in fact very similar to that of the western regions of Germany. Christian faith and culture had been absorbed by this tradition, as had also the spirit of medieval chivalry and of the burgher of the late Middle Ages in his aptitude for the crafts and trade. The Reformation had been able to gain a footing only among the upper classes of the population, and this, too, only for a short time. With the victory of Catholicism a great second flowering of Italian and Spanish Renaissance culture blossomed throughout the land. Thus right from the beginning, Austria, without having forfeited her own special character, was geared to the culture of the whole of Europe. Most typical perhaps of life there was its moderation; differences of opinion tended to become blurred, so that there was aversion to any extreme measures.

Nature had been very helpful too. Austria had never been excessively rich, but was blessed with valuable mining areas which gave the Habsburgs their financial backing. Arable land, pasturage, and woodlands provided for the needs of its inhabitants, the Danube was an important commercial waterway, and the roads which led south—to Venice, Milan and Genoa—were short and for the most part in Austrian hands. The country thus possessed a certain natural prosperity which had been considerably increased by the Balkan conquests.

Chapter Nine

BRANDENBURG — PRUSSIA

Modest Beginnings

The Brandenburg Electorate lay in the colonial regions. Its roots reached back to the time when medieval Germany was at the zenith of its power and Germany proper had arrived at the eve of its first flowering of culture. Its destiny was determined by the law of the colonist whose every day signified a new conquest of his environment. Only when men who combined tradition with a spirit of initiative streamed into the Brandenburg Mark from the overpopulated West did it begin to take on more of the western character. Differences still remained, however. The cathedrals, which were built here as in the West, were the fruit of the same architectural inspiration, but the material used, brick, gave them their own distinctive character. Its cities were to a great extent cultural and commercial centres, but for many long years continued to be island in an alien environment which was regarded as culturally backward. Also the peasant colonist from the old country felt himself superior to his Slav compeers; the feeling of superiority over subordinates was here far more strongly developed than would ever have been possible in the West. The more the empire in the course of the Middle Ages subjugated the East and converted it into the most important settlement area for its excess population, the more strongly and inevitably it evolved the special character of a colonial territory.

All this was even more true of Prussia, the state of the Teutonic Order, in which the conqueror class was united in addition by vows of chivalry and religion. Though this meant in the first place greater emphasis on the Christian message, it cannot be overlooked that the sword was just as important an instrument for spreading the gospel as the word of God and the plough. The Teutonic Knights did not just set out to erect churches, monasteries and cities, and to preach Christianity; they were also men who took it for granted that they, or at least their community, had a right to acquire possessions and wealth. The cities and the German nobility, by now completely assimilated with the old population, combined with Poland to resist the exercise of this "right". The Order was looked upon as a foreign intruder and lost its independence to Poland.

The conversion of the electors of Brandenburg and of the Teutonic Knights to Protestantism was of far-reaching significance for the Orders' territory. The religious knights became secular lords who sought to extend their properties till they were large enough to support both present and future generations. The agricultural productivity of the areas east of the Elbe was not, generally speaking, comparable to that of west Germany. The Brandenburg Electorate was known in the Middle Ages as the "Holy Roman Empire's Sand-Pit". The peasant's holding had to be considerably larger than in the West, if the land was to support the owner and his family. The gradual oppression of the small peasant by the large landowner made considerable progress during the 16th and 17th centuries, and the reduction of the free peasant class to almost complete serfdom reached an even more advanced stage than in the West. Emigration to the West, if only in small numbers, started as early as the 17th century. Like the other territorial rulers in Germany the Brandenburg electors had the greatest difficulty in breaking the resistance of the landlords and of the influential families in the cities to the assertion of their sovereign claims in the electorate and, after 1618, in ducal Prussia. There was no notable change in this respect until late in the 17th century. In their endeavours to establish the sovereignty of the crown both at home and abroad the Hohenzollern rulers of Brandenburg were, of course, acting completely in accord with the spirit of their age. Their efforts were, however, to prove of grave significance because they were directed for more than a hundred years towards an area that knew far less the restraint of long tradition than the empire west of the Elbe and the Saale. Where difficulties arising from tradition or people were concerned, the Hohenzollern of Brandenburg and Prussia had the advantage over their peers in other parts of the empire.

Organisation and Discipline

When Frederick William I, the "Great Elector", ascended the Brandenburg throne in 1640, his land and Germany were still in the throes of the Thirty Years War. Although the original nucleal territory of Brandenburg was not at the centre of the European struggle, it still bore deep scars inflicted by the war. The Brandenburg possessions on the Rhine and in Westphalia (Cleve, Mark and Ravensberg) were situated far from Berlin, while Brandenburg and the former state of the Teutonic Knights, ducal Prussia, were separated by territory ruled by the latter's overlord, the King of Poland. The finances of the small state were in disorder and the nobility met the elector's efforts for improvement with determined resistance. Frederick William, however, was consumed by the ambition to transform his needy land into a principality which could worthily take its place alongside the other German states. Following the example of France he ruthlessly broke the resistance of the nobility, who had obstructed him especially in his plans for new taxes. With the larger state income he created a small standing army. At the Westphalian Peace Conference he successfully advanced his considerable territorial claims, without however acquiring Hither Pomerania, a fertile land with numerous harbours. Instead he acquired in the west Kammin, Minden, Halberstadt, and finally (1680) Magdeburg and Halle. This facilitated communication between the tribal territory and the western possessions.

From now on, Frederick William did all in his power to remain neutral for as long as possible in the disputes between the great powers, and to intervene only at the last moment on the side likely to win. He did not hesitate to change sides twice in the war between Sweden and Poland. Indeed his conduct during that war won him the elevation of Prussia from a Polish fief to a sovereign duchy, which he now completely incorporated into the Brandenburg state, and his own investiture as independent duke of Prussia. When Louis XIV took up arms against the Netherlands some years later, Frederick William lined up with the Habsburg emperor against France and Sweden. At Fehrbellin his army inflicted the first defeat on the Swedes, until then considered invincible. Still the hoped-for price of victory, western Pomerania, did not materialise. Without more ado the elector deserted his allies and went over in 1679 to the camp of Louis XIV, who assured him financial assistance. As a *quid pro quo* Frederick William promised him his vote at the next imperial election. But even this alliance did not bring him the coveted Hither Pomerania, although, true to his treaty obligations, he refused the emperor all help for the liberation of Vienna from the Turkish threat. The break with France did not come till 1685, one reason certainly being Frederick's disapproval of the expulsion of the Huguenots by Louis XIV after the revocation of the Edict of Nantes. The refugees were granted asylum in his land, since he realised their value as skilled craftsmen and tradesmen. Descendants of these

9 R. H. Tenbrock, A History of Germany

French emigrants have played a not inconsiderable role in the history of Prussia.

At the end of his life Frederick William entered on a league with the emperor. They came to an agreement about Silesia: the elector did not press his title to the Silesian territories and received Schwiebus in their stead.

Frederick's expenditure on his army, which he brought by the end of his reign to the imposing number of 36,000 professional soldiers, demanded a political economy furthered and guided by the state in the spirit of the mercantile system. The cornerstone of the economy was the royal domains, which the Elector reorganised and placed under loyal officials. He sought to overcome the natural poverty of the soil by settling Dutch colonists and experts, and by cultivating potatoes and tobacco, reclaiming the Havel, Oder and Warthe marshlands, and erecting factories for glass and iron. His efforts here were not without some success. He built a canal from Silesia to Berlin and opened a postal service between Königsberg and Cleve in order to strengthen the links between his subjects and the capital. Although Frederick William was not altogether successful in centralising the entire administration of the state in the hands of the ruler after the model of France, Brandenburg was to be numbered among the well-administered territories at the end of his reign. The estates, which still exercised certain sovereign powers both in the central government and in the various parts of the territory, had allowed themselves to be persuaded to surrender their political rights voluntarily. In exchange, the nobility received an extension of their rights over the subject peasants. On his death Frederick William left as his proudest heritage to his successor a standing army which commanded respect. On its maintenance he spent many times more than what other states of his day, for example France, expended on their troops. This orientation of the state to military needs—an orientation, which the Great Elector also bequeathed to his successor—concealed dangers to which the young state might one day succumb to its own undoing.

To the Great Elector's immediate successor, Frederick III (1688—1713), however, the external prestige of his country was more important than its internal stability. For this reason he strove to acquire the title of king. In 1701 the emperor granted him the right to designate himself Frederick I, "King in Prussia". Königsberg became the city where all Prussian kings were crowned.

The real founder of the centralist state of Brandenburg-Prussia was Frederick William I (1713—1740), the "Soldier King". He consistently followed in his domestic and foreign policy the political course on which the Great Elector had set the Brandenburg state. His goal was to exalt the power of the Brandenburg-Prussian state centralised in the person of its ruler. The monarchy, the army, and his officials were all epitomised in him. He aimed to make his officials the indisputable and undisputed pillars of the Brandenburg-Prussian state.

Elector Frederick William had abolished the political privileges of the nobility, when, in line with the other absolutist states, he conceded them a special economic status. King Frederick William I now restricted this, too. From 1717 onwards the properties of the knights were subject to tax. Although this did not imperil the privileged economic position of the nobility's lands in Brandenburg-Prussia, it made the nobility even more dependent on the king.

More decisive was the administrative reform he carried through. The state had two sources of revenue, the royal domains and taxes. In 1713 he united both under the General Directory and articulated the entire administration from top to bottom on the principle of individual responsibility. The officials for this work he recruited only from the ranks of the nobility.

The administrative reform abolished all the privileges still possessed by the estates or the cities. It gave the nobility a new position, for service as a royal official was proclaimed honorary service for king and state. The economic basis of the nobles who had become officials continued to be their property, whose possession the king guaranteed. The financial independence and the high standards which the king developed in his bureaucracy (after all it was an honour to serve in it) assured the Prussian official a position of great respect for a long period of his history.

Frederick William geared the state to the army to an even greater extent than the Great Elector. At the end of his reign the standing army was 83,000 strong. The country was divided into recruiting districts. Only journeymen and the sons of serfs were liable to conscription; other citizens were spared because of their importance to the economy. The soldiers were billeted on the burghers; the captains received a sum of money in advance with which they were to provide for their company. Frederick William drew his officers almost exclusively from the nobility, for whom army service was made attractive by grants of privileges and decorations.

With the exception of a late intervention in the Great Northern War, Frederick William hardly took any active part in foreign politics. His relations with the emperor remained good until 1739.

When Frederick William died in 1740, the yearly income of his state amounted to seven million thalers, of which five million were devoted to the army; the state exchequer contained eight million thalers.

Frederick William created a state that occupied a special place among the states of Germany and Europe on account of its honest, conscientious officials and its army with a corps of officers all with the same social background. This achievement was only possible because the king, also in his private life, subordinated everything to the needs of the state. Devotion to the state he regarded as a religious duty, which he imposed upon himself from a deep sense of responsibility. He demanded the same attitude from his subjects. In this way Frederick William prepared Brandenburg-Prussia to become a great power, a status to which the country's natural resources could not possibly have raised it. From the reign of Frederick William onwards there developed in the Brandenburg-Prussian state, especially in the army and civil service, certain "typically Prussian" qualities, such as unconditional devotion to duty, precision and punctuality, implicit obedience to all orders of superiors, the will to be effective and to avoid mere empty show. In addition to these undeniably positive attributes, however, the danger easily arose that all human activities were subordinated to the state, that the state stultified until it was nothing more than a soulless machine. Prussia has several times succumbed to this danger in the course of its history. A large part of later German history has been occupied with coming to grips politically, militarily and intellectually with the state created by Frederick William and the particular spirit to which it gave birth.

Chapter Ten

THE BAROQUE IN GERMANY

Antecedents

From the standpoint of the history of ideas the Baroque can be traced back to two sources: one is the Catholicism of the Counter Reformation, and the other is the absolute prince's consciousness of his power. The ecclesiastical religious source was more original; the secular and profane, however, far and away more fruitful. The Baroque was the fulfilment of a fundamental desire cherished by the princes who dominated this epoch: it bore graphic witness to their love of life, their power, and the all-inclusive nature of their rule. To substantiate their claims, both Catholicism and Absolutism appealed to man's distinguishing faculty of reason, which is capable of endowing all his other powers with meaning, purpose, and order. According to the Catholic view of things, the Council of Trent's great achievement was to lay bare the rational basis of the mysteries of the Christian religion. Although Catholicism was perfectly well aware that the Church, like many of its institutions and customs, could only be grasped in its essential nature by the believing heart, it nevertheless laid the greatest stress on the intellect as the ordering faculty, for in this way the element of irresponsibility and arbitrariness could be excluded as a danger to the Church, either as a whole or in part. In this way it achieved its monumental internal coherence without thereby losing any of the dynamism of a vigorous life of faith. In many respects Absolutism resembled Catholicism. Its goal, however, was not in the next world, but in this, not an organisation for the salvation of men's souls, but an earthly state. In the products of their cultural activity, whether church or palace, Jesuit religious drama or court poetry, the fundamental inspiration is always the same.

The artistic antecedents of the Baroque are to be sought in the Renaissance. From the latter it took the intellectual notion of symmetry, filling it with a superabundance of life. The straight line becomes the curve, the structural column gives way to its decorative counterpart, the enclosing dome opens up heavenwards, drawing the eye ever higher. The Baroque could suffer nothing to be in repose; its very principle was to transform the work of art in the restless engagement of the senses into an experience. The visual arts and literature were as one here, and music followed their example.

Religious Baroque

The Baroque's country of origin was Italy, where its most brilliant representative was Bernini. In Germany also it owed its universal adoption to the Catholic or princely need for spectacular display. In Catholicism it was above all the Jesuits who in the magnificence of their churches desired to contrast the impressive cohesion and grandeur of their faith with its conscious appeal to both senses and intellect with the plainness and disunity of Protestantism. Wherever the old faith wanted to make a breach in victorious Protestantism, it addressed itself with marked success to the people through the medium of Baroque church architecture. The Baroque churches and monasteries scattered across western and southern Germany have remained an eloquent testimony to the aims and victory of the Catholic revival. Among the churches those of St. Cajetan (Theatinerkirche) in Munich and of St. Charles Borromeo (Karlskirche) in Vienna reach the heights of artistic inspiration. A number of well endowed orders, too, built houses that look more like palaces than monasteries, but which, nevertheless, represent outstanding monuments of Baroque church and monastic architecture (the abbey of Göttweig by Hildebrandt, and Melk and St. Florian in Austria, Ebrach in Franconia, Weingarten in Baden-Württemberg, Grüssau in Silesia, Klosterneuburg near Vienna, and Maria Einsiedeln in Switzerland).

The Catholic literature of the Baroque period was also primarily a vehicle for the Church's teaching. Drama treated especially of religious, historical, and legendary subjects. Artistic demands were generally small. The technical excellence of the stage and the spectacular nature of the works performed were far more important than artistic form. The viewer was to leave the theatre a changed man as a result of the effect the performance had on him.

A certain measure of artistic excellence was attained in hymnody and mysticism. The sensitive poetry of the Jesuit Spee's hymns vies with the more vigorous productions which gush forth from the spiritual conflict of the Protestant hymnologist Paul Gerhardt. As mystics Jakob Böhme, a Protestant, and Angelus Silesius, a Catholic, attained the same height in power of expression and depth of feeling.

Profane Baroque

During the 18th century the secular authorities exercised much greater influence on their age than the Church or the Christian faith. It is not at all surprising therefore that the great creations of the Baroque age and culture stem from the absolute princes. The burgher class of the cities had exhausted its creative powers in the course of the great economic and political changes. The princes attempted, on the model of France, to give visible expression to their position as the focal point of their subjects' lives. But since Germany, in contrast to western Europe, was a land of innumerable princes, distinguished only in rank but otherwise absolute in their territories, its physiognomy was inevitably as different from that of western Europe as was its state organisation. The foreigner's idea of France was determined to a great extent by its capital, Paris; Germany, on the other hand, was the sum of its capitals. This factor was to ensure that the great diversity of the medieval cities would be preserved down to the present day, even if, as is only to be expected, the absolute princes have left their mark on many of them.

All the princes took Versailles as the model for their palaces. They tried to imitate it in the perfection of its conception, in its expression of royal authority. Thus "little Versailles", the splendour of whose execution was often far more than the financial resources of their small territories could bear, sprang up all over Germany. Vienna, Potsdam, Dresden, Würzburg and Salzburg owe their character to the century of Absolutism, and Mannheim, Karlsruhe and Bruchsal even their very existence. Nowhere perhaps did the princely will leave more striking monuments to the comprehensiveness of its claim than at Mannheim with its checkered, and Karlsruhe with its fan-shaped, groundplan, which centre the town on the hub of the state, the sovereign's palace. Besides these capitals, however, the princes often remodelled the countryside in the spirit of the 18th century when laying out their extensive palaces and grounds. Charlottenburg and Potsdam near Berlin, the Favorita and Schönbrunn near Vienna, Nymphenburg and Schleissheim near Munich, Herrenhausen near Hanover, Wilhelmshöhe near Kassel, Ludwigsburg near Stuttgart, Nordkirchen near Münster

(Westphalia) are the great living witnesses to the architectural sense of the princes and the artistic genius of their creators. Though it is true that foreign influence was of decisive importance, Johann Balthasar Neumann (1687—1753) in his Würzburg creations, Lukas von Hildebrandt (1688—1745) with his Belvedere palace in Vienna, Andreas Schlüter (1664—1714) with the Arsenal, the palace, and the equestrian monument of the Great Elector in Berlin, Fischer von Erlach (1656—1723) with the Imperial Chancellery, the Court (now National) Library, the Karlskirche and Schönbrunn palace in Vienna, and especially George Bähr (1666—1738) and Daniel Pöppelmann (1662—1723) in their magnificent Dresden creations take their place alongside their contemporaries in other countries.

Within the environment of the palace and court life, courtly poetry developed into the presentation of social behaviour and manners and into the exaltation and refinement of daily life in society. It was intended to be popular and not the expression of the soaring flights of poetic inspiration; it was designed to fit smoothly and flatteringly into the rhythm which best suited life at court. In accordance with the basically rational trend of this period, the schemes which formed the framework of this poetry could be learnt. All that was then required were the sentiments, moods and superficial feelings of court society which, put into words, were woven in and around the schemes taken over as models from abroad like so many rinceaux and arabesques. In this, Opitz (1597—1639), the man of the world, was the first to achieve mastery. At the same time, however, his *Buch von der deutschen Poeterey* reinstated German as the language of poetry.

The opera, which, starting from Italy, made a triumphal conquest of all the courts of Germany, was most adapted to the artistic needs and sentiments of the court. It succeeded in delighting both eye and ear. Its content surrounded life at court with a faint aura of adventure and romance. Italian music, which held the stage almost exclusively for a long time, was decidedly instrumental in facilitating the rise of German opera. Its exponents were Christoph Willibald von Gluck (1714—1787) and Wolfgang Amadeus Mozart (1756—1791). In this way the already extensive musical production of Germany, which was at first connected with the names of George Frederick Handel (1685—1759) and Johann Sebastian Bach (1685—1750) and later with that of Joseph Haydn (1732—1809), was made the richer by the addition of another valuable musical form. The work of Bach does not follow the trend of the age. Its ultimate root was not the desire for display, but the most profound Lutheran faith for which Bach provided

26. St Michael's, Munich.

27. Residence Theatre, Munich.

28. The Zwinger, Dresden.

29. Belvedere Palace,
    Vienna.

30. The Frauenkirche,
    Dresden.

31. Schlüter: Equestrian statue of the Great Elector.

the perfect medium of musical expression. It was not without significance either that he wrote his compositions not at the court of a prince, but as a simple cantor at the church and school of St. Thomas in Leipzig. Luther had commended the establishment and organisation of education to the princes as one of their primary duties. The absolute princes both on the Protestant and on the Catholic side were not slow in meeting these obligations, especially as they soon realised that influence over education gave them a favourable opportunity to inculcate their conception of the nature and task of the state. Primary schooling was given great encouragement at the beginning of the 18th century in a number of German states, but without being made compulsory. Duke Christian Albrecht von Holstein-Gottorp founded the university of Kiel in 1665, and Frederick I, King in Prussia, the university of Halle in 1694, which could boast an important savant and the champion of German as the language of scholarship in Christian Thomasius (1655—1728). Emperor Leopold I founded the Catholic universities of Innsbruck (1677) and Breslau (1712). The foundation of the university of Göttingen was to prove the most important, because it became the home of new sciences (e.g. history) and of numerous literary and artistic treasures of the Middle Ages.

Although the foreign influence on German intellectual life was various and strong, German scholarship was able to produce its first important representative of European rank in Gottfried Wilhelm Leibniz (1646—1716). As a man of affairs, he attempted to drive home his ideas on religious toleration and understanding among princes by rational argument. As a scholar, he hoped to further cultural progress by the foundation of princely academies (Prussian Academy in 1701). As a mathematician, he discovered the differential and integral calculus independently of Newman, and, as a physicist, the formula for the determination of kinetic energy. As a philosopher, he was convinced that he could combine conflicting views in one great harmonious system, of which diversity was the distinctive feature. Important, however, as thought was in his eyes, action was even more decisive. Human life is according to him the great arena of human achievement. Reason was to be the plumb-line, a man's delight in action to provide the impetus. Man's happiness is to be sought in the steady perfecting of the world by his work and in continual progress in education.

It was in keeping with the spirit of the age that the attempt was made to give a new legal basis to the relationships between states. Following the lead of the Dutchman Hugo Grotius (1583—1645), Samuel Pufendorf (1632—1694), historiographer to the Great Elector, studied the extent to which natural right and the natural moral law are founded in the inscrutable will of God. That they are so founded, he contended, could be proved by reason and from the nature of man. Like Grotius, he regarded the state as the instrument for the establishment of the peaceful order required by God. The state itself, however, was based on treaties. The absolute authority of the princes, too, should be restricted by treaty, and should the princes refuse such restriction, he held revolution to be justified. Such ideas as these make him the precursor of German Englightenment.

The suggestion made by Samuel Rachel, the Schleswig-Holstein diplomat, that an international law should be created to regulate relations between states represents the first attempt to outlaw war within the European family of nations. As early as 1676 he demanded an international court of law backed by sufficient power and authority to enforce its decisions on all states.

The world of the imposing churches and palaces, of scholarship and courtly poetry had barely skimmed the surface of society leaving the lower levels almost untouched. The one poet of the age, Hans Jakob Christoffel von Grimmelshausen (1610—1676), although his works were closely connected with the events of the day, illustrates this point most eloquently. Basic Christian conceptions permeate his entire work. Man must win through in this utterly evil world by his own initiative and by trust in God's goodness. At the same time Grimmelshausen was not sparing with his vigorous scorn and blunt satire about every possible circumstance of his day. His novel "Simplicissimus" is the most vivid portrayal of the Thirty Years War that has come down to us.

Chapter Eleven

THE RISE OF GERMAN DUALISM

The Struggle Between Austria and Prussia for Silesia

The youth of the Prussian Crown Prince, Frederick II, was decisively influenced by the antagonism existing between him and his father, Frederick William I. This did not develop simply out of the natural tension arising between a strongly willed father and a son very early conscious of his own individuality. It was far more the expression of the clash of two ages, whose incompatibility was all the more emphasised in the peculiar intellectual atmosphere of Brandenburg-Prussia. On his accession to the throne, his father had made a clean sweep of everything that, from the intellectual and cultural point of view, might have suggested contact between Brandenburg and the great world of European Baroque. The universities in Prussia lost their good name; the Prussian Academy founded by Leibniz languished; the intellectual life in the royal palaces was hardly distinguishable from that in the home of a Pomeranian country squire.

Frederick William I had made little use of his imposing military might for purposes of military conquest, although the army and the military were his prime concern as king. The acquisition of Hither Pomerania as far as the River Peene with the islands of Usedom and Wollin he owed mainly to favourable political circumstances. Although Austria did not keep the promise given to Brandenburg in connection with the regulation of the female succession by the Pragmatic Sanction, Frederick William did not take advantage of the critical situation which had arisen for the Habsburgs with the loss of Belgrade during the unsuccessful Turkish War of 1737—1739. If one seeks the reasons for such a passive attitude on the part of an absolute monarch, one will probably find them, among other things, in Frederick William's deep religious convictions. These and the views based on them about the duties of a sovereign were what Frederick William wanted to hand on to his son as his most important contribution to the crown prince's upbringing.

However, the influence of Sophia Dorothea of Hanover, the mother of the young crown prince, was stronger than his own. For her son she was the refined vehicle of the intellectual riches of the West and of the Enlightenment. She encouraged him in his leanings towards music and in his approving admiration of the sensuous Baroque. Thus Frederick's early inclinations were towards exact philosophic thought and artistic endeavours in the French tongue and in music. His interests did not extend to politics, economics, and soldiering. He regarded himself as so little suited to become the ruler of the Brandenburg state that in 1730 he determined to flee to England, in order to escape the rigorous discipline of his father's upbringing. The attempt at flight failed. Frederick was cast into prison together with his most faithful friend, and his father summoned a court martial at Köpenick. His friend was condemned to death and beheaded before Frederick's eyes. The crown prince was set to work in the state administration at Küstrin.

Frederick carried out his father's orders by conforming to what had been imposed upon him. But beneath the external world of obedience to duty and service of the state he created an inner world entirely of his own. From the youth who had presumed to be able to mould his life according to his own will developed the man who learnt to master his fellow men by concealing his own thoughts. The sacrifice which he seemed to make for his father in renouncing his own desires released him from all attachments. He despised men because they were not in a position to master themselves and instead blindly followed their instincts. At this stage of his intellectual development, Frederick, who developed into a fine administrative official and a good soldier, and who reconciled himself to a loveless marriage concluded in obedience to his father with Princess Elizabeth Christian of Brunswick-Bevern, came into contact with Voltaire, the most outstanding representative of the French Enlightenment. Since 1736 the crown prince had been living on his Rheinsberg estate, which he had converted into a refuge of peace and study. The friendship, at first epistolary and later personal, with the French cynic and philosopher he so admired strengthened him in his belief in reason as the final arbiter of all thought and conduct. This view was entirely in keeping with his theory that a ruler must also regard himself as bound in his conduct by an objective norm of law. War as a political expedient and the absolute prince's mania for new conquests are equally to be rejected. A prince should regard the safeguarding and maintenance of peace as the state's greatest good, and the exercise of the virtue of philanthropy as his chief concern. In 1738 Frederick consigned these views to writing in his polemical work the "Anti-Macchiavel". At the same time he also defended the viewpoint that the sovereign should subordinate himself to the interests of the state in all things, for after all he is nothing but "the first servant of the state".

Frederick had been constrained to take part in the business of government. Charles VI of the house of Habsburg had sheltered Maria Theresa, his eldest daughter and heiress to the Austrian dominions, from all political employment. She heard of the great political events as they were seen through the eyes of her tutor and instructress, or of her mother, who was of the same house of Brunswick-Bevern as Frederick's wife. Maria Theresa's world was that of a sincere and convinced Catholicism whose laws and regulations were binding on both prince and subject. The Enlightenment had no part in the intellectual formation of the young princess. All the greater, however, was the influence on her of Italian literature and music, to which she abandoned herself with characteristically feminine open-mindedness. The choice of her husband, Francis Duke of Lorraine, who in the Polish War of Succession (1733—1735) had had to cede his duchy of Lorraine to Louis XV's father-in-law, Stanislaus Leszcynski, in exchange for Tuscany, was fully in keeping with her own inclinations. She had been his play-fellow as a child and was strongly attached to him. According to her father's will, her marriage, too, was not intended to give her a political view of the world, but to provide the monarchy with a son who would protect Austria from the rule of a woman. Nevertheless Charles VI had obtained the recognition by all the great powers of the female succession in Austria, if at some sacrifice. When, however, he died in 1740, shortly after the accession of Frederick II in Brandenburg-Prussia, he left his lands to a woman who ascended the throne as queen over a great empire with nothing but her natural, feminine, open-minded approach to her tasks, a quick mind, and a big motherly heart to guide her.

After the death of Charles VI the German electors, led by Brandenburg-Prussia, chose the Elector of Bavaria as emperor, a choice which France had been assiduously advocating. Frederick II then demanded from Maria Theresa the whole of Silesia in return for an undertaking to defend the rest of the Habsburg possessions against all eventual enemies. Maria Theresa rejected this offer, whereupon Frederick gave the command for his troops to invade Silesia, while he continued the negotiations. The Prussian victory at Mollwitz (1741) led to the Peace of Breslau (1742), in which Silesia and the County of Glatz were

141

ceded to Frederick II. Two years later, East Friesland also came to Prussia as a consequence of an earlier treaty.

At the same time Maria Theresa had to fight for recognition of her accession against a powerful coalition with France at its head. Her most embittered opponent, the Holy Roman Emperor Elect and Elector of Bavaria, was driven from his electorate. However, he was able to secure his coronation to the imperial dignity as Charles VII at Frankfurt in 1742. After the conquest of Bavaria, the French were thrown back beyond the Rhine. England, Austria's ally, defeated the French at Dettingen. It almost looked as though Austria would be successful in reconquering Alsace and Lorraine, the hereditary territory of Maria Theresa's consort. Moreover, a great number of the princes of the empire, impressed by the Austrian victories, had deserted the elected emperor. At this moment favourable for Austria, Frederick II joined the French coalition (1744) and invaded Bohemia from Silesia. He was not able to maintain his position there, but won a decisive victory over the Austrians at the Battle of Hohenfriedberg (1755). The Peace of Dresden was signed in the same year. This confirmed Frederick in his possession of Silesia, but also recognised Francis of Lorraine as emperor. Subsequent to this peace treaty, Frederick was greeted by his countrymen as he marched into Berlin with the title "the Great". Brandenburg-Prussia thus took its place as one of the five great powers in Europe alongside England, France, Austria, and Russia. It must also be remembered, however, that this same Dresden peace treaty was also the foundation of the enduring quarrel between Prussia and Austria.

Charles, Holy Roman Emperor and Elector of Bavaria, died in 1745. Not only had Austrian arms proved their superiority over the forces of Bavaria and France; Charles's death also brought Maria Theresa's husband, Francis I (1745—1765), recognition as emperor. The Peace of Aix-la-Chapelle (1748) confirmed Maria Theresa in her Habsburg possessions against the Bavarian and French claims.

Frederick II devoted the next ten years of his reign to the internal administration of his territories, especially to the incorporation of Silesia into his state, which he was able to carry out with comparative ease because of his policy of strict toleration towards both Protestants and Catholics. During this interlude he also built his mansion of Sanssouci near Potsdam.

Maria Theresa found it difficult to reconcile herself to the loss of Silesia since every cession of a German territory represented a great danger to her empire, which united more foreign than German peoples under the Austrian crown. For this reason she geared her policy to a

142

renewal of armed conflict with Prussia. The world political situation, which was determined at the time by the struggle between France and England for the colonies in North America and India, was opportune for both the great German powers. At the beginning of 1756 Frederick succeeded in winning England over to his side. Prussia undertook to protect Hanover, which was linked in a personal union with the English crown; England held out prospects of subsidies. After the Anglo-Prussian agreements had become known, France, which felt that its Prussian allies had played false, was successfully persuaded into an alliance with Austria—a sensational alteration in the "Concert of Powers". Russia, which hoped for territorial aggrandizement in the west as a result of the conflict between the two great German powers, likewise joined Austria. Tsarina Elizabeth, a personal enemy of Frederick the Great, was promised the former land of the Teutonic Knights, Prussia, in the event of an Austrian victory.

In 1755 an Austrian secret conference of state had decided on a war with Prussia to take place the following year, because Austria was convinced that Frederick would take up the offensive again. In 1756 the Prussian king, alarmed by Russian and Austrian mobilisation, sent an ultimatum to Austria demanding an assurance that he "would not be attacked either this year or the next". This assurance was not forthcoming. He believed that he could only escape the impending doom by entering on a preventive war. Thus, in 1756, without a declaration of war, he invaded Saxony, which belonged to the opposing coalition. Thereupon Frederick was placed under the ban of the empire and an army was raised to meet him. Sweden joined Austria in order to win back the mouth of the Oder. France and England stood by their treaty obligations. England sent Frederick subsidies and troops, and in America fought against France and her colonies. A world war had begun. For seven long years it was to devastate Silesia and the adjacent territories.

Frederick with the aid of his powerful army of 150,000 men succeeded in occupying Saxony very rapidly. The burdens which he imposed on this land were heavy. During the first three years of hostilities Frederick emerged victor from nearly all the larger engagements. Certainly he had at times to abandon Prussia to the Russians, but he was able to defend Silesia against the Austrians and the French. The Battle of Rossbach especially, where his numerically inferior army carried the day against a larger force of French, Austrian, and imperial troops, made a great impression on the Germans in other parts of the empire. As Goethe put it, most Germans were "Frederick-minded" ("fritzisch gesinnt") at this time. They began to regard Frederick as a national hero who was fighting not against the Austrians but against the enemies of the German people. Frederick took very skilful propaganda advantage of this mood. It gave rise in later Prussian historiography to the myth of Frederick the Great as the pioneer of German unity.

From 1759 onwards, however, the manifold numerical advantage of the Russian, French and Austrian allies made itself felt. Frederick suffered his greatest defeat at the Battle of Kunersdorf. Dresden was lost; Austrian and Russian troops occupied Berlin. England, having achieved her war aims in North America, concluded a separate peace with France in 1762 and withdrew from the alliance. Canada and the Mississippi region were ceded to England. Brandenburg-Prussia was faced with economic ruin. At this critical moment for Frederick, Tsarina Elizabeth of Russia died. She was succeeded by Peter of Holstein-Gottorp, an admirer of Frederick, who promptly discontinued the war with Prussia. A year later a peace was also signed with Austria at Hubertusburg. Prussia kept Silesia.

The Seven Years War had shown Frederick conclusively that he could not obtain any extension of his territory by a war of aggression conducted against the great powers of his day. This explains why he renounced all thought of annexation during this almost hopeless struggle, and came to regard the maintenance of the territorial status quo ante bellum as his war objective. After the Peace of Hubertusburg he drew closer to Russia. In 1764 he negotiated a treaty of mutual assistance with Russia for a period of 25 years. Russia was given a free hand in Poland, where anarchic conditions prevailed. Prussia was now able to devote its energies undisturbed to the reconstruction of its territories, since it no longer had any need to fear Austria. Catherine II of Russia had her former favourite, Stanislaus Poniatowski, crowned King of the Poles, and he ascended the throne as Stanislaus II Augustus. Repeated Russian interference in the internal affairs of Poland led Turkey to declare war on Russia in 1768 as a means of strengthening the hand of the Polish opposition to Stanislaus and to Catherine II. However, the Turks were no match for the Russian land and sea forces. As a result Moldavia and Walachia were occupied by Russia. This considerable Russian expansion in the Balkans occasioned Maria Theresa to form an alliance with Turkey in 1771. A war in which Prussia—this time alongside Russia—would once again have to fight against Austria seemed unavoidable. At this juncture, however, Catherine II proposed a partition of Poland among the great powers of eastern Europe. Frederick declared himself in agreement and obtained, through the intercession of Joseph II, his great admirer and heir to the Austrian throne, the agreement of Maria Theresa as well. Prussia was granted West Prussia, Russia the territory east of the Dvina and the Dnieper, and Austria Galicia. The core of Poland survived unscathed.

The first partition of Poland represents a masterpiece of well-contrived spoliation of a territory and was entirely in keeping with the policy which Louis XIV had employed against the Netherlands and Germany. It was also, however, the expression of a policy of power and conquest which was assured of success because of the weakness of its opponent. Whereas the large land-owning Polish nobility, the real cause of Polish weakness, was easily assimilated, the burgher and peasant class, encouraged by a decidedly nationalistic Catholicism, refused to cooperate, especially with Russia and Prussia. In spite of this, both Austria and Prussia carried out the incorporation of the Polish territories into their states without any attempt at Germanisation. The settlement of German peasants in West Prussia had economic, not nationalistic objectives. As in all the other Prussian territories, this policy aimed at raising the economic prosperity of the country, and in this the Polish population also had a share. Thus the preponderantly Polish regions kept their Polish character in regard to language, religion, and culture.

Some years after the Polish partition effected in union with Austria, hostilities between the two great German powers nearly broke out anew. In 1778 the Bavarian Wittelsbachs became extinct. Whereupon the Emperor Joseph II raised claims to Bavaria. These Frederick opposed and sent troops to invade Bohemia. As a consequence of Russian mediation between Prussia and Austria there was no general engagement of troops. Bavaria ceded the Inn Quarter to Austria. The Rhenish Palatinate and Bavaria were united.

When in 1785 Joseph again tried to prevail upon the future heir of Bavaria to exchange his inheritance for Belgium (the Austrian Netherlands), Frederick countered by founding the "German League of Princes" with the object of preventing any alteration in the territorial structure of the empire. Joseph II yielded before this threat from the north. Thus the union of Bavaria with Austria, which would doubtless have set German history on a completely different course, was not achieved.

Frederick's conception of the duty of the absolute ruler to expand the territory of his state had been the guiding-star of his foreign policy, and, despite forbidding reverses, had brought him success which the rest of the world admiringly acknowledged. By his brilliant achievements in the field, Frederick had raised Prussia to the status of a European power and maintained this with enduring results. It was a matter of

10   R. H. Tenbrock, A History of Germany

complete indifference to him that in so doing he also gave the death-blow to the empire, which, in spite of its loose-knit structure, still regarded Austria as its natural head. It was precisely the spokesmen of German unity under Prussian leadership who, during the struggle to reshape and reform the German empire in the 19th century, usurped Frederick's name for their cause. They could do this because of Frederick's fame as a general and because of his domestic policy.

Absolutism and the Enlightenment

The 18th century took its course in the shadow of the Enlightenment. It was the Age of Reason. Although the absolutist form of government was considered the only effective and progressive one by nearly all continental powers, individual monarchs nevertheless still tried to face the issue involved in the new ideas which rejected the absolutist state, and to turn them to such good account for their own programme of government as was possible without endangering the unlimited power of the ruler. In this respect Frederick the Great became an important pioneer and model, not only for his own state but also for Austria—especially for his admirer Joseph II—and a number of other German territories.

Frederick the Great created the Prussian constitutional state. All his subjects, without distinction of class or confession, were equal in the eyes of the law, even if the king occasionally intervened in the administration of justice in the interest of the state. The judges were irremovable and adequately salaried. Of great significance for court cases were the *Codex Fridericianus* and a general legal procedure. The *Allgemeines Preussisches Landrecht*, the first modern legal code in German, was prepared by Frederick's orders, but appeared only after his death. It was the first royal codification of law since the code of the Roman Emperor Justinian. Its real creator was Suarez. This Prussian legal code made the law independent of the person of the ruler and placed the ruler, too, under the law in the same way as the subject. Legal proceedings were rid of antiquated methods of arriving at the truth (such as torture). This uniform code of law for all parts of Brandenburg-Prussia has, since 1793, proved a strong cementing factor in Prussian state consciousness. In the spirit of the Enlightenment, Frederick proclaimed toleration for all varieties of religious opinion. In this way he made the relation of the citizen to the state independent of religious beliefs. However, a number of restrictions remained in force in particular

146

cases. Thus, for example, Catholics were barred from taking higher office in the state; the Jews formed a nation apart within the state and were placed under a humiliating set of special laws.

Frederick's measures against any mixing of the estates preserved the strict division of society into nobility, burghers, and peasantry. The purchase of a noble's property by burghers and peasants was forbidden. In this way, in spite of the king's enlightened attitude in legal and religious matters, the system conceding an unalterably privileged position to the nobility in Prussia was preserved.

Thus the nobility remained the ruling class; for from their ranks Prussian officials and officers were exclusively drawn; the peasants were subjected to them. The burghers of the city continued to be without political rights and indifferent towards political life. The peasantry was, indeed, protected by royal decrees against acts of violence and expropriation. But in law, except on the crownlands and in the western regions of Prussia, the peasants were only chattels, mere appurtenances of landed property.

Frederick the Great viewed the state purely mechanically and rationally. For him it was something supra-personal and sublime, to which both ruler and ruled had to subordinate themselves by their service. The position of the individual was determined by the value of the service he rendered to the state. This in turn was essentially dependent on the class into which he had been born. As long as the state, embodied in the king, his army, and his officials, ruled the subject with absolute power and was far removed from the individual, enlightened absolutism could mitigate hardships but not remove them. Frederick the Great regarded himself as a member of the state which he like all others had to serve indefatigably.

Frederick replaced the bureaucratic government of the General Directory with government through a cabinet. The privy councillors elaborated the cabinet orders for the king, although it was the latter who had the final word. The ministers had to approach the cabinet in writing. Each minister of the General Directory administered a particular province with the result that not one of them had an overall view of the administration of the entire state. The individual provinces had to submit their budgets, which were then synthesised by the king in the state budget. Thus he alone had knowledge of the financial position of the state as a whole.

Frederick the Great, through his personal interest, made the Potsdam of his day a Prussian cultural centre where the culture and intellectual spirit of France were especially cultivated. The blossoming of a German culture he treated either with disregard or with disdain. Science and education he greatly promoted. The architectural works he inspired breathe, in spite of their graceful form, the spirit of Prussian temperance and austerity.

Frederick the Great, indisputably an outstanding king, was offset in his day by an empress of no less importance, Maria Theresa. Yet they were in their natures entirely different. This arose from their contrasting conceptions of the role of a sovereign. Frederick the Great saw his role as fulfilled in his service of the supra-personal "State"; Maria Theresa, on the other hand, discerned a divinely appointed mission in her care of the subjects entrusted to her. As a woman of deep Christian convictions, who always remained an exemplary wife and mother, she attempted, wherever she judged it feasible, to place her conscience above necessities of state. After the death of her husband, the Emperor Francis I, she ruled her Austrian possessions jointly with her son, Joseph II. As sole ruler she had carried through a policy of closer centralisation in her lands. The dispensation of justice was separated from the administration. The State Chancellery (ministry of external affairs) was established in addition to the Court Chancellery (ministry of internal affairs). However, when her son became co-regent, the reforms were precipitated; Maria Theresa often found herself in opposition to him.

Joseph was a fervent admirer of Frederick the Great. His character had been formed more by the spirit of the Enlightenment than by the Christian beliefs of his mother. His ecclesiastical, educational and cultural policy has gone down into history as "Josephinism". He adopted a very harsh line towards the Catholic Church. All contemplative orders were abolished. In addition he interfered in the Church's internal life of worship: processions and confraternities were forbidden; divine service and the number of feast days regulated; the candles at mass restricted for reasons of economy. For a time he even contemplated separating the Austrian Church from Rome.

During his reign Protestants received equality of civil rights and admission to public offices. The Jews were granted some amelioration of their legal position. They were allowed to enter the universities and to practise crafts, to start factories, to bear German surnames, and to dispense with their distinctive clothing.

A patent of marriage issued in 1783 declared marriage a civil contract even if, for the time being, the ecclesiastical ceremony still remained compulsory. In contrast, divorce and remarriage were permitted to non-Catholics.

148

In 1781 a secret resolution was passed provisionally lifting the death penalty. Some years later, the "Josephina", a new, humane code of law, was issued in which torture and capital punishment were officially abolished.

In order to better the lot of the peasants under the Habsburgs, Joseph became the first German sovereign to suppress serfdom in his dominions (1781). The peasants were granted the unrestricted right of marriage, of free movement, of free choice of employment, and of freedom to sell their property. By arrangement with their landlord they were to commute corvees and dues in kind, and become tenants.

Because Joseph imposed these innovations forcibly upon his people he drove them to revolution, especially by his ecclesiastical policy. He was forced to revoke many of his reforms because of the resistance of the nobility, the clergy, and the broad masses of the people. However, the patent of tolerance for Protestants and Jews, the abolition in principle of personal serfdom, and the "Josephina" remained in force. The emperor intended that all trace of national and provincial independence should disappear from the Habsburg states. The same prescripts were intended to apply on the Turkish border as in the Austrian Netherlands. For these reasons German was introduced as the official language in Bohemia and Hungary together with the German administrative system. Against this restrictive regimentation the peoples of the Austrian empire rose up in revolt. The emperor was forced to admit failure, above all in Hungary and the Austrian Netherlands.

It cannot be denied that "enlightened" absolutism realised many of the hopes which the philosophic thought of the Enlightenment places in the state and its rulers. In this way it succeeded in mitigating antagonisms which, especially in France, embittered relations between the estates and warped the attitude of the middle class and peasantry towards the state. But it was not capable of placing the state on a new footing; for this not only was equality of all before the law a prerequisite, but also the severance of the ties holding the estates together and keeping them in existence. Certainly Frederick the Great's conviction was that such a radical reform would have destroyed the internal stability of his state, and Joseph II was to learn by experience how many of his reforms met with the embittered resistance of the people. Notwithstanding, the Enlightenment exercised a decisive influence on German intellectual life and prepared the way for Germany's rebirth as a land of culture during the age of Goethe. This in its turn was the necessary preparation for Germany's rise and political unification during the 19th century.

Chapter Twelve

THE AGE OF GOETHE (1749—1832)

The Enlightenment and Classicism

The discovery of America had brought about the displacement of European trade to the western seaboard of the Continent. The middle classes of central Europe were thus abruptly halted in their economic expansion, before the intellectual movements known as Humanism and the Renaissance had been able to exert their transforming power fully. In addition, the intellectual and religious upheavals of the Reformation period had turned men's eyes inwards. The protracted religious conflicts together with the economic decline of the once flourishing cities strengthened the readiness of the middle classes to submit to the will of their territorial lord without too great resistance. In contrast, an economically strong middle class developed in western Europe. In Holland it gave rise in the religious and political struggle with Spain to a state and culture of its own; in England it took advantage of the political dispute with the crown to make an intellectual reappraisal of the relation man should have to religion, society, the state, and, finally, to himself. Here it was Newton's teachings especially which had thrown down a challenge to the traditional philosophy which until now had seen revelation as its guiding principle. The rejection of this principle, however, was a decisive prerequisite for the doctrine of man's autonomy, according to which man as a being endowed with reason was entitled to submit all fields of human existence to critical evaluation. Men called into question the traditional "religious" foundation of the state, and substituted therefore a purely utilitarian association with decidedly limited rights. "The Commonwealth[1] seems to me to be a society of men constituted only for the procuring, preserving and advancing of their own civil interests" (John Locke). Foremost among these interests was the protection of the natural rights to life, liberty and property. To guarantee these Locke developed the principles

---

[1] i. e. civil society, the state (TR)

of the representative system and of the separation of powers. This also meant that absolutism had been theoretically countered.

England's "Glorious Revolution" of 1688 as a practical example of revolutionary self-liberation by the middle classes and lesser nobility from the yoke of royalty and aristocracy, together with the theoretical justification of the new state on the basis of the philosophy of the Enlightenment acted as stimuli in France. The ready adoption of the new ideas by the French bourgeoisie is to be explained by its economic strength, which, as previously in England, made it more clearly conscious of its complete lack of political rights under the absolutist system. In 1718 Montesquieu, like John Locke, demanded the division of powers, and founded the necessity for this separation on the liberty of the individual. He interpreted liberty rather as "permission to do what the law requires and absence of obligation to do what it forbids"—a witness to the still unshaken faith in the harmony existing between positive and natural law.

However, the more men studied the true nature of man without bias, the more they were compelled to abandon the view that man's nature was determined by reason alone. Thus it was that the Enlightenment found in Rousseau the first considerable critic of its unadulterated belief in reason. In contrast to the one-sided domination of reason he emphasised—of course just as one-sidedly—the law of the "heart" and of the passions. But he remained true to the basic conceptions of the Enlightenment, at least to the extent that nature and an existence in keeping with nature constituted for him man's real happiness, by opposing nature and culture he gave the concept of nature a meaning that could no longer be equated with reason.

In Germany the ideas of the Enlightenment fell very early on fertile soil. But in the way the intellectual elite adopted them and made them the basis of a philosophic and artistic development peculiarly German revealed the divergent historical paths followed by Germany and her western neighbours. A state or society which could be both the cause of far-reaching problems and the goal of their solution did not exist in Germany. All attempts by an individual of strong personality to liberate himself from the dominion of one of the numerous small princes were doomed to remain without hope of rousing a response from a self-confident middle class, for the very simple reason that there was no such class. A crusade conducted with the pen against the political conditions created by absolutism could also only be directed against one particular prince, never against the system as a whole, because this varied from state to state in a way unknown, for example, to the France of Louis XVI. Whereas some of the small German states persisted in their absolutist narrowness and backwardness, others had through their rulers been opened to the new ideas and had tried to give their subjects a modest share in them. Since, for this reason, a desirable political or economic aim which would be the same for all Germans was not immediately available, men's eyes were easily concentrated on an imaginary "Reich" of the future, or on a great past. Even scholars from the middle classes were seldom successful in gaining a social status equal to that of the nobility and clergy. For this reason in Germany the philosophy of the Enlightenment was often transformed in the beginning into a rationalistic subjectivism, which is reflected in numerous autobiographies and "confessions". Parallel to this ran a strong pietistic subjectivism which, in contrast to the Enlightenment, strove to understand religion solely on the basis of the feelings of the individual. Their common relationship to the individual gave both these tendencies their special stamp. In art, too, it was this relationship which was first and foremost sought; it was found in the liberation from social and moral ties. The lyrical and epic poetry of Klopstock (1724—1803) provides an early example of this.

The work of Gotthold Ephraim Lessing (1729—1781), on the other hand, represents an attempt to give appropriate artistic expression to the philosophic ideas of the Enlightenment, with which he shared the ever-present thirst for truth and the optimistic faith in man's continuous progress. Over and above that, however, he wanted, through his artistic activity, to give its ideas universal validity, achieving in the process a universal appeal transcending all religious and national barriers ("Die Erziehung des Menschengeschlechts"; "Nathan der Weise"). Nevertheless, the power to reflect life in its entirety is absent from his works, a shortcoming which he became aware of especially through his study of Shakespeare. This explains why it was at first not granted to him to exercise a greater influence on his contemporaries, who anyway saw in commitment to the Enlightenment far too great a restriction of their artistic subjectivism and their vital power of artistic creation. Many of them believed with Rousseau that man's real roots are in nature, which would imply a life based on the incomprehensible and inconceivable as opposed to a human life formed by morality and law. Between the true and the violated nature of man lies a contradiction which is the cause of the problematic character of human existence. What we know as the *Sturm und Drang* (Storm and Stress) attempted to give expression to this in all its varied manifestations.

Like Rousseau, this movement also saw its ideal in natural man. However, it not only depicted him as a contrast to eighteenth-century civilised man but discovered him at a particular point in the historical existence of every people. Peoples, like individuals, pass through the periods of youth, maturity, and old age, and have an unmistakable individuality of their own. Through this tenet the *Sturm und Drang* had invested the people or nation with peculiar significance and a distinctive character of its own, a new departure in European thought which was to have a lasting effect on the intellectual and political life of Europe, expecially through a treatise by Herder (1744—1803): "Ideen zur Philosophie der Geschichte der Menschheit". A direct result of this new outlook was, on the one hand, the spiritual return of the *Sturm und Drang* generation of writers to Germany's early days and, on the other, the rediscovery of Shakespeare, Homer, folk-songs, and Gothic, as the expression of an art rooted in nature, by Herder and J. W. Goethe, and later by Friedrich Schiller (1759—1805), too. In contrast to the Enlightenment with its lack of history and belief in the future, the *Sturm und Drang* was permeated by a vigorous historical consciousness and looked back in retrospect on a past in union with nature. Its goal became the restoration of the past from the untapped powers of the ordinary people of the present.

The realisation of such a poetically conceived goal was of course outside the bounds of political possibility. Where a creative will felt the urge for "expression", it had to seek other fields for its exercise. The change which took place early in the age of Goethe was rooted in many respects in the Enlightenment and the *Sturm und Drang* (cp. here Herder: "Briefe zur Beförderung der Humanität"; Goethe's and Schiller's classical period). The influence of Greek antiquity as seen through the eyes of Johann Joachim Winckelmann (1717—1768) was to prove of paramount importance in this very respect.

German Classicism in proclaiming its ideal of humanity was the attempt, and as such the last, to lay down a norm binding for all men. That this undertaking was essentially a failure lay to a great extent in the entirely changed historical circumstances of the 19th century. The most noteworthy achievements of German Classicism were attained in the fields of literature (Goethe, Schiller), of music (Ludwig van Beethoven, 1770—1827), and of philosophy (Immanuel Kant, 1724—1804). Their genius was of such wide variety and comprehensiveness, however, that no details can be given within the limits of this book.

While Goethe and Schiller still stood at the height of their artistic productiveness, Classicism was faced by its most important critic, Romanticism. Like the Enlightenment, this movement extolled liberty. But whereas at the beginning of the 18th century this meant the completely concrete desire for liberation from the bonds of outdated political and social conditions, Romanticism proclaimed absolute freedom, according to which no objective restrictions are placed on man other than those he is himself prepared to set on his thought and actions. The only determining factor in man is an infinite striving by which he attains the infinite. Although man is limited by his finitude, he can transcend this through his striving, which is infinite.

The most fundamental idea in Romanticism was accordingly the intense longing for an ideal which aimed at the conquest of matter by spirit. That involved complete absorption in one's self since that longing for an ideal is alone worthy of expression. The romanticist made himself the constant object of his efforts to express this infinite longing. In the process he burst all the fetters of external form in both literature and music. At the same time, however, he widened the field of psychological perceptions to an extent till then unknown. In addition the extreme variety this longing took in each individual led to the conception that the individual represents something utterly unique and unrepeatable. In connection with the notion of freedom this view gave birth in its turn to an ultra-subjectivism, the rule of pure arbitrariness, which recognised no binding norm. Representatives of this viewpoint were Friedrich Schlegel (1772—1829) and Ludwig Tieck (1773—1853) during their early periods.

This marked the high point of Romanticism with its teaching, now exaggerated beyond all limits, on the autonomy of each individual. The development which the movement now underwent accepted the doctrine of the absolute superiority of the spirit over matter, of the uniqueness and "irrepeatability" of the individual, and of freedom, and recognised man's longing as the formative principle, but it also tried to keep in touch with concrete realities. This led to a new absorption in the secrets of the past or in the idealising view of a future world. This change took place most easily in the field of music. True, the work of Franz Schubert (1797—1828) still had strong links with Classicism, nevertheless he too interpreted the world from the viewpoint of man's longing, as also did Felix Mendelsohn-Bartholdy (1809—1847), the greatest of the Jewish romanticists, and Carl Maria von Weber

155

(1786—1826). In literature, the preoccupation with the past at first took the form of an absorption in Greek antiquity, though not in the same sense as for Winckelmann and Goethe, especially in the work of the young Friedrich Schlegel, Friedrich Hölderlin (1770—1843), and Heinrich von Kleist (1777—1811). Certainly the last two can only be spoken of as romantics with some qualification. The idealising presentation of the Greeks, their history and their political development was paralleled by an equally one-sided extolling of the German Middle Ages. At first this was concerned only with the artistic and religious aspects of medieval culture and had begun with Wackenroder's (1773—1798) "Herzensergiessungen eines kunstliebenden Klosterbruders" and Tieck's "Franz Sternbalds Wanderungen". These were shortly followed by Tieck's translations of Minnesongs and von der Hagen's German History of the Middle Ages which inaugurated the scientific study of that period. Novalis and the Schlegel brothers saw new hope for Europe in medieval civilisation and universalism (Novalis: "Die Christenheit oder Europa", 1799).

Finally the great historical past of the Germans, as seen in its supposedly ideal realisation in the Middle Ages, was contrasted with their own present time with its multiplicity of small states and domination by Napoleon. The romanticist became a political poet. However, since he had no concrete notion of the form the state would take which was one day to form the framework of political activity for the Germans, the "people" as a living organism was transformed into the mystical architect and pillar of an "empire" of indeterminate definition. This new preoccupation with the "people" and its tradition, its "spirit" and its "soil" undoubtedly proved of uncommon poetical fruitfulness and developed forms unknown till then (fairy tales, folk-songs and folk-art), but was not bereft of all political danger since one's own people could easily be elevated to an absolute value. Romanticism succumbed to this danger in only a few of its lesser exponents of second-rate importance. On the whole a nationalistic strain was foreign to it. On the contrary, its most magnificent and abiding results were its devoted study of the cultures of other peoples, its preoccupation with the spirit and nature of language, and the unprecedented impetus it gave to historical studies. The greatest works of world literature were integrated into the German intellectual heritage through outstanding translations (e.g. the Schlegel-Tieck translation of Shakespeare). W. von Humboldt and the Brothers Grimm were pioneers in the field of philology. And truly universal was Leopold von Ranke (1795—1886), "the patriarch of German historical studies".

From the viewpoint of the history of ideas the age of Goethe had, as a consequence of the particular sociological conditions under which it developed, given rise to completely characteristic results. During its Enlightenment period it had, as in western Europe, first laid the foundations of a purely rational consideration of the world. In the *Sturm und Drang* period it gave the Germans a historical and national consciousness for the first time. In this respect Romanticism was most closely related to the *Sturm und Drang*. During its classical period it rose above people and state in favour of an intellectual cosmopolitanism. In all phases of its development, however, it strongly emphasised the individual in the uniqueness and autonomy of his existence. The political happenings connected with the French Revolution and the Napoleonic wars compelled the intellectually leading classes to reexamine the political relevance of the liberty demanded by the Enlightenment, by Classicism, and Romanticism. The result was a dichotomy between cosmopolitan and nationalistic thought which was to persist in German history throughout the 19th century.

Chapter Thirteen

GERMANY AND THE FRENCH REVOLUTION

The Revolutionary Wars and the End of the Empire

The American War of Independence against England and the formation of the sovereign "United States of America" had not passed without repercussions in Germany. The interest aroused by the events on the other side of the Atlantic had been fed by the engagement, on the insistence of some German states, of German mercenaries on England's side against the insurrectionary colonists, and the not insignificant achievements of some Prussian officers in Washington's army. Moreover, shortly before his death, Frederick the Great had recognised the United States and entered into diplomatic relations with them which blossomed into an American-Prussian friendship. The effects of the French Revolution (1789) were to prove more enduring. This is to be accounted for not merely by the close relations existing between the two countries as neighbours but chiefly by the unbroken cultural influence that France had exercised on Germany for nearly 150 years, an influence scarcely diminished by the attention directed by German classical writers to French literature.

For this reason the revolutionary happenings which began spectacularly with the storming of the Bastille were greeted with an almost equal enthusiasm by broad sections of the educated German middle classes as in France. They saw heralded in these events a new epoch in the history of mankind. The suppression of aristocratic and clerical prerogatives, the abolition of the personal serfdom of the peasants, the proclamation of the liberty and equality of all men, the emancipation of the Jews from the ghetto, and the constitutional limitation of the monarch's absolute authority corresponded to demands made by German authors (e. g. Lessing and Schiller) in their writings. Nevertheless, even Schiller's positive approach to the revolutionary happenings in France was of short duration. A true estimation of the revolution was obscured here by ideals and political convictions. Germany's writers and thinkers showed themselves to be, in the last resort, thoroughly non-political precisely in their vacillating attitude to the French Revolution. That this, the first movement of the masses, so portentous in its effects and disruptive of all accepted forms, produced results not in keeping with the original inspiration was judged with too hasty criticism as a betrayal of that inspiration. In addition, revolutionary interference in the affairs of other countries provided the traditional powers of Europe with a welcome pretext to nip the revolution in the bud by a war to restore the historically accepted order. It was only too easy to unmask the faith of many Frenchmen in France's destiny to carry the new ideas over the whole of Europe as continuation of the French policy of conquest since the days of Louis XIV. The initial approval thus gave way to severe criticism which was far from objective. Germany became the new home of numerous noble and clerical emigrés who taxed the political relations between the two countries still further.

In 1792, as an answer to the threats of Austria and her princely allies in Germany that they would come to the help of the French king if his rights were limited still further, the Legislative Assembly in Paris forced a declaration of war on Austria and her comrades-in-arms. The enemy was at first successful in invading northern France. Prussian troops took Verdun. At Valmy, however, they were faced by a French army of revolutionary volunteers who held their ground in the face of the Prussian advance. The Prussians determined on retreat, the Austrians were defeated in Belgium and that country was overrun, so that soon the French armies were in Mainz and Frankfurt-on-Main.

The Austro-Prussian coalition did not last long. Prussia needed to secure its western flank in order to be able to proceed to the partition of the rump of Poland with Russia and to annex Warsaw, and therefore treated for a separate peace with France at Basle in 1795. A secret clause in the treaty ceded the left bank of the Rhine to France. As compensation Germany was declared neutral, so that it was spared the disturbances of war for the next ten years. In addition, Prussia was to receive right-bank gains in a future general peace treaty as indemnification for its losses west of the Rhine. Utterly oblivious of the dangers entailed in a victorious France, Prussia pursued a purely egoistic policy of domestic aggrandizement in the old style. In this way Prussian policy paved the way for the French subjugation of the whole of Europe and accelerated the dissolution of the empire.

As early as 1793 there was another partition of Poland between Russia and Prussia. Prussia took the towns of Danzig, Thorn and

CASPAR DAVID FRIEDRICH

Greifswalder Hafen nach Sonnenuntergang
Le Port de Greifswald après le coucher du soleil
Greifswald Harbour After Sunset
Puerto de Greifswald después del crepúsculo
O pôrto de Greifswald após o pôr do sol

1819. Stiftung Preußischer Kulturbesitz, Berlin-Dahlem

Posen with the surrounding territories. Whereas the countryside was populated by Poles, the percentage of Germans in the towns was appreciably high. To Russia's share fell an extensive area with a population of 3.5 million. Two years later, Russia, Prussia and Austria divided what was left of Poland almost equally among themselves. The Prussian frontier now ran east of Warsaw. Polish inhabitants of Prussia now outnumbered the German. Prussia could scarcely claim to be still a German state. This third partition of Poland, by which a sovereign state was erased from the map of Europe, has rightly been dubbed a crime.

After Prussia's withdrawal from the war against France, Austria, allied with some smaller German states, carried on the war against the French armies, now under the command of Napoleon and became much more effective. The French offensive was directed mainly against the Austrian possessions in north Italy, which fell into Napoleon's hands. In the Peace of Campo Formio, signed in 1797, Austria too ceded her possessions on the left-bank of the Rhine to France. The price for this was neutral Venetia. What the Bourbons had coveted in vain throughout centuries of war, the armies of the revolution had achieved after a war lasting five years: France's "natural frontier" was the Rhine.

Two years later Napoleon's abortive Egyptian adventure and the destruction of the French fleet in Aboukir Bay brought together again the former allies, with the exception of Prussia. But again Napoleon was able to carry the day on land. In a public declaration the emperor was compelled in the name of the empire, to recognise the Rhine as the frontier between Germany and France. Almost four million Germans or one seventh of the German population of the empire, became subjects of the French Republic. In 1802 England was also forced to sue for peace with France.

As heir of a revolution against the ancient thrones of Europe and of France's traditional anti-Habsburg policy, Napoleon, First Consul since the coup d'état of 1799, had to attempt not only to weaken the empire still further but to extirpate the imperial idea once for all. The terms of the peace treaties of Basle and Lunéville (1801) with Austria provided him with the opportunity. In Napoleon's view, in order to provide a counter-balance to Austrian imperial policy, Prussia had to be enlarged so that it could pursue a policy independent of Austria. A possible union of the two great German powers was to be obviated by strong buffer states which could at any time hinder a policy comprehending the whole empire. The Diet of Regensburg appointed a special commission or "Imperial Deputation" to determine the indemnification those powers should receive which had forfeited possessions on the left bank of the Rhine. Under pressure from France and also from Russia, which was likewise interested in weakening the empire because of the unsolved problems in the Balkans (the "Eastern Question"), the commission arrived at its final decision in 1803.

Following the French pattern, all ecclesiastical principalities were secularised, and 45 free imperial towns as well as the territories of 1500 knights of the empire lost their independence and were converted into mesne-towns and territories under a local ruler. This secularisation cost the Catholic Church the largest part of its worldly possessions, which fell for the most part to German Protestant princes. Only the three *Hanse* towns of Hamburg, Bremen and Lübeck, and the imperial cities of Nuremberg, Augsburg and Frankfurt-on-Main retained their independence. Baden, Württemberg and Bavaria received considerable territorial additions; Prussia received as a reward for its losses left of the Rhine and for its neutrality policy a territory now five times larger in extent.

Certainly the Regensburg decision meant first and foremost the collapse of the "Holy Roman Empire". Nonetheless our judgement of it cannot be purely negative. After all, it also provided the basis for the final victory over feudalism and led to a clear separation of the spheres of Church and state.

Under pressure from Napoleon sixteen medium-sized and small German states to the west and south united in the Confederation of the Rhine in 1806 and announced that they had ceased to be members of the empire. They placed their fortresses and troops at the disposal of France. The German empire had ceased to exist, and with it the heritage of Charlemagne and Otto the Great, the crown of the "Holy Roman Empire of the German Nation", had lost its symbolical value for all Germans. Accordingly, on August 6th, 1806, Emperor Francis II (Francis I of Austria) laid aside the imperial crown and took the title of "Emperor of Austria" for his hereditary lands. Napoleon, however, believed that he could continue the tradition of Charlemagne in another form as "Emperor of the French". His visit to the former imperial city of Aix-la-Chapelle shortly before his coronation in the cathedral of Nôtre Dame in Paris in 1804 and the revival of the kingdom of the Lombards bear eloquent witness to this.

The precarious peace Austria and England had concluded with Napoleon's France was only short-lived. The superiority of the English fleet and the uncompromisingly hostile attitude which England had shown again and again towards France as the leading power on the Continent moved Napoleon to make preparations for an invasion of England. But England found allies in Russia and Austria, who would have forced a two-front war on France in the event of an invasion of the island kingdom. To avoid this danger, Napoleon called a halt to his invasion preparations at Boulogne and faced the united armies of the Russians and Austrians at Austerlitz (1805). His brilliant victory there, however, was overshadowed by the defeat which Nelson had inflicted on the French fleet at Trafalgar barely six weeks earlier. Napoleon had to give up all thought of attacking and subduing England by direct means.

The Battle of Trafalgar, however, decided at the same time the fate of Europe for the next ten years. As long as Napoleon's policy was dictated by his fear that any strong military power in Europe was a potential ally of England, he held a preventive war against such a power as justifiable. Thus the grounds of the Napoleonic War against Prussia in 1806/7, which led to the collapse of Frederick the Great's state just 20 years after his death, are of no consequence. At its conclusion the French empire extended to the Elbe; Hamburg was administered by the French, and Napoleon's brother Jerome reigned in Cassel over the newly created Kingdom of Westphalia. Poland was resurrected as the duchy of Warsaw under the king of Saxony. Danzig became a free city garrisoned by the French. Russia, which had continued its support of Prussia after Napoleon had marched into Berlin, had likewise made peace with Napoleon and joined the continental blockade against England in 1806.

In order to ruin the British Isles economically, Napoleon had prohibited all the states of Europe from trading with England. English ships docking in continental harbours were seized together with their cargoes. As a counter-measure England captured the fleet of Napoleon's ally, Denmark, without a declaration of war, and set Copenhagen in flames by naval bombardment. The blockade was dangerous for the agricultural lands of Prussia and Russia, whose corn and timber became worthless. But other lands too had to suffer losses. On the other hand, European industry flourished, because the English factories could not deliver their goods. In Germany sugar beet was cultivated for the first time, and a flourishing textile industry sprang up in the Rhineland. The continental blockade led to a serious sales crisis in England, but it won the far-flung markets of the world as a compensation. Napoleonic rule had at first met with anything but downright rejection among the German population, for both economic and ideological reasons. The numerous reforms which France carried through in the spirit of the revolution of 1789 in the occupied territories as well were regarded as a welcome release from the oppressive rule of the feudal state. The introduction of the Code Napoléon in the Rhenish states provided the indispensable basis for the equality of all citizens before the law. The freeing of trade and economy from the ties which in part dated from the Middle Ages laid the foundations for free enterprise. Personal serfdom, the division of the population into estates, and the prerogatives of the nobility and clergy were all things of the past. In the occupied territories, too, there were to be only free citizens.

However, the further afield the campaigns of conquest extended the more oppressive became the burdens which Napoleon had to lay on the occupied territories in order to keep the wheels of his war machine turning. Equality before the law meant not only equality of rights but also of obligations, which for Napoleon meant that non-Frenchmen, too, could be called upon to serve in his armies or make economical sacrifices for his wars. Moreover, his intention to draw the occupied territories closer to France by introducing the French language and thereby robbing them of their German character became ever more obvious. In the struggle to ward off these measures of an alien conqueror, which they found unjust, the national consciousness of the Germans was born.

The relationship of the Germans to their country had hitherto consisted of an unthinking love of their homeland. There was no unified patriotic feeling for the empire. In the larger territories like Prussia, Bavaria or Austria, a certain pride had also developed among the people in the outstanding achievements of their rulers. The discovery of the "people" by the *Sturm und Drang* had been restricted to a small circle and was soon forgotten in the later profession of cosmopolitanism. The experience of foreign rule first effected a change in the attitude of Romanticism and partly of Classicism, especially in the dramatic writings of Schiller. Fichte (1762—1814) and Hegel (1770—1831) both laid great stress on the state and the community. With the axiom "There is no virtue other than forgetfulness of self; only one vice, mindfulness of self" the subjectivism which had also been the inspiration of early German Romanticism was finally mastered.

For the *Sturm und Drang* and the classical and the romantic movements, however, the notion of liberty was at the very centre of all philosophic and artistic endeavour. This conviction they shared with the leading minds of the French Revolution. The problem of the real nature of liberty split men into camps not only in Germany but in nearly all parts of French-occupied Europe. This cleavage was to be seen in the first place in the objectives which men set themselves in their struggle for freedom from the Napoleonic yoke, which had come to be regarded to an ever greater extent, even by many Frenchmen, as the expression of one man's megalomania.

In Germany several broad streams of thought formed. On the one side were those politicians who saw their ideal state in the community of free, responsible and self-dependent persons who find their fulfilment in the service of that same community; such thinkers felt themselves most strongly drawn to German Classicism's conceptions of man's mission. Among them were to be reckoned a number of the Prussian reformers. It was not rejection of France or of the ideas of the French Revolution which motivated their hostility towards Napoleon. On the contrary, they saw these as betrayed by Napoleon. This also explains why such reformers were almost indistinguishable from the champions of an early German liberalism, whose ideal was a German national state formed on the pattern of France and according to the ideas of the French Revolution. At the same time the German liberals were not aware that the most dangerous threat to the realisation of their notion of liberty was that very "messianic nationalism" which had developed in France as a result of the revolution and had been a contributory cause of the French wars of conquest. Another school of thought was represented by those under the spell of Romanticism, who aspired after the freedom of the "people" in a resurgent German empire and who championed the restoration of the "German" empire on the medieval model. Among these, too, were to be numbered some of the great reformers of Austria and Prussia, and above all the eloquent writer Joseph von Görres (1776—1848), whose newspaper the "Rheinischer Merkur", Napoleon described as "la cinquième puissance" (fifth great nation).

All efforts, however, were at first united and directed towards casting off the Napoleonic fetters. In this sense, Napoleon became the great unifier of the German as well as of the other European peoples. But this unity was from the start aimed at a very restricted objective and did not arise in Germany from a unified political outlook.

Prussia's recovery is associated with the names of Baron vom und zum Stein and Karl August von Hardenberg, who was raised to the rank of prince in 1814. Both were non-Prussians in the service of the Prussian state. As servants of the king they could only convert their reforms into reality if their plans also served to guarantee the prerogatives of the crown and to maintain the privileged position of the great landowning Junkers. Thus, in Prussia, reform involved a compromise between the old powers with their roots in history and the new which were obtruding from below and striving for freedom and responsibility. The question whether the middle classes and petty peasantry in Prussia would have been strong enough to force a reformation of the state must be answered in the negative for the early 19th century, because an economically strong middle class, which could have been the protagonist of such a conception, did not exist. For this reason reforms could only be set in motion from above, in the interest of the state. The state therefore stood at the centre of all considerations in the development towards greater freedom, which was initiated in Prussia at the beginning of the 19th century. It was the state which, by a governmental act, granted its citizens special rights, in return for which they were obliged to perform clearly defined services for the state.

Baron vom und zum Stein was born in Nassau in 1757. In 1780 he entered Frederick the Great's service and was at first employed in the Westphalian administration. After a few years he rose to the directorship of the Westphalian mines and later to be supreme president of the chambers of commerce and mining in Cleve, Minden and Brandenburg. In 1807 he was dismissed from the service of the Prussian state because of grave differences of opinion with King Frederick William III (1797—1840) but, after Prussia's defeat, was reinstated at Napoleon's request in the same year.

His work of reform was a combination of the experience which he had gathered in Westphalia and the convictions which he had acquired from his study of Enlightenment philosophy, especially of Montesquieu, and from his observation of the English and French political scenes. The result he attempted to merge with existent conditions in Prussia in such a way that the state's foundations, the monarchy and army, were not shaken, and the willing devotion and interest of every citizen in respect of the state were nevertheless assured. In the prosecution of his plans he was able to lean on a civil service relatively strongly imbued with the ideas of the Enlightenment, especially in the western parts of the Prussian kingdom. One obstacle to the realisation of his plans was the dissimilar social stratification of the population in East and West. This was exemplified in the eastern part of the kingdom, the former territory of the Teutonic Knights. Whereas the citizens of the town of Königsberg were extremely responsive to the ideas of Adam Smith, as were the professors of the university of the same town to the teaching of Kant, the landowning Junkers of the countryside objected to any innovation whatsoever. Thus Stein was faced with the problem of whether he should continue to entrust the army and the administration of the state exclusively to the class of landed nobility, or whether he should, and could, successfully apportion responsibility in the state to the middle classes and peasantry as well. In Prussia's westerly possessions he could rely on the support of a middle-class population that had gained a measure of self-confidence as a result of the incipient industrialisation there. The peasantry of these areas was also relatively free.

The centrepiece of his reform was the emancipation of the peasants throughout all Prussia's dominions. "On St. Martin's Day 1810 (11th November) all serfdom shall cease in all our states. As from St. Martin's Day 1810 all persons shall be free". In this way all personal restraints, domicile restrictions, the compulsory manorial service of tenants' children, corporal punishments, manorial approval of marriage and regulation of succession were abolished. All economic restrictions and burdens, such as field service and the obligation to supply agricultural draught-animals and implements and pay dues and rents, remained in force, since these were not binding on the person but on the holding. The purchase of aristocratic property by middle-class and peasant buyers and of peasant holdings by nobles was admitted, as also was the partitioning, merging and leasing of larger properties. The soil, however, was placed under the special protection of the state. Royal permission was required for the sale of knightly estates.

The same edict also lifted all restrictions on the free choice of profession. This meant that the caste system of Frederick the Great's state was in theory a thing of the past.

Up to that date the towns had been governed in the name of the king by "directors". For this system Stein substituted the self-government of the towns by a body of town delegates who were elected by all landowning townsmen according to the same law of franchise. The town delegates then elected from their number the town council, which required the king's confirmation. These measures granted the town the right of self-administration in all municipal affairs and the character of a democratic community.

Ministers answerable to the king and fully responsible in their departments took the place of the General Directory instituted by Frederick the Great. The provinces were administered by supreme presidents, who were placed over the district presidents in the administrative districts.

Stein also attempted a reform of the nobility. His plan was that the title should in each case pass with the property to the eldest son; all other members of the family were to lose the title. At the same time the nobility was to be constantly renewed by the elevation of commoners who were distinguished by special merit. But these efforts at reform came to nothing because of the united resistance of both king and nobility.

One of Stein's letters in which he mentioned his hope of liberation from the Napoleonic yoke fell into the hands of the emperor's agents. Napoleon obtained Stein's dismissal. Declared an enemy of France, Stein found refuge in Austria and later in Russia, while in Prussia he was succeeded by the Hanoverian Hardenberg. Hardenberg introduced complete freedom of trade. Workshops could now be opened by anyone, whereas until now this right had been reserved to gild-members. Jews were placed on a completely equal footing with Christians and became citizens enjoying full equality of rights.

The same tension between reactionary and progressive elements was apparent in the reorganisation of the army as in the civil reforms of Stein and Hardenberg. Both the crown and the nobility insisted on a regular army to ensure the stability of power in the state and to safeguard their own privileged position; Scharnhorst, too, was a champion of the standing army. Gneisenau, Clausewitz and Boyen, in contrast, were advocates of a citizens' army, a national militia.

Scharnhorst and Gneisenau, likewise non-Prussians, had not held positions of importance in the Prussian army until after the defeat of 1806/7. Only then were they able to improve their standing both in the eyes of the king and among the old military leaders, an improvement they owed to their promise to imbue the army with a new spirit by tapping the moral reserves of the people; this they hoped to achieve by developing a new concept of the Prussian state and fatherland. Scharnhorst and to an even greater extent Gneisenau and Clausewitz were heirs of the tradition of Herder and the romantics.

The army reforms, too, were the result of a compromise. In addition to the standing army, a national militia (*Landwehr*) and final levy (*Landsturm*) were created in conformity with the idea of the general

168

32. The Wartburg.

33. Tischbein: Goethe in Italy.

34. Runge: The Hülsenbeck Children.

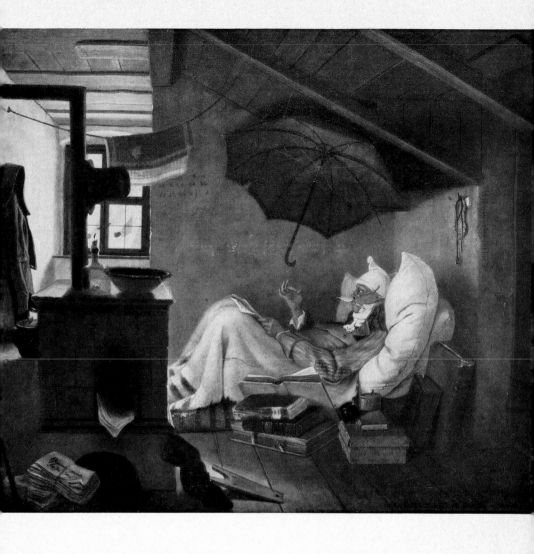

35. Spitzweg: The Poor Poet.

36. Corinth: Inn Valley Landscape.

mobilisation of the people. At the same time the establishment of a war ministry, a military academy and a general staff supplied the leaders of the Prussian army both a centralised command and training.

An essential complement to these organisational reforms was the new appreciation and esteem enjoyed by the army. The victories won by French arms were in a large measure the consequence of the morale prevailing among the Napoleonic soldiers, and it was the great aim of the reformers to inject this same spirit into the Prussian soldier, too. To this end all degrading punishments were abolished; the officer career was also opened to the more highly educated strata of the middle classes.

In this way Prussia fashioned, in readiness for a new trial of strength with Napoleon, an instrument of military strength that had a broad enough basis to make a reality of the idea of the "Nation under Arms". Only thus could it be a match for the French armies. Early German liberalism combined the ideal of the free autonomous individual with that of humanity. A cosmopolitan attitude of mind came more natural to it than nationalistic aspirations, and, like the Enlightenment, it believed in the infinite potential of education. In this respect Wilhelm von Humboldt (1767—1835), as one of the few members of the intellectual elite who took an active part in public life, also showed his affinity with early German liberalism when he founded the university of Berlin in 1810, during the course of the Prussian Reform. Here the intellect was to be cultivated in an atmosphere which would serve the great end of a free humanity by educating the youth of the nation to free moral responsibility. In these efforts Humboldt was in full agreement with the great educationalist and teacher Pestalozzi (1746—1827). Like Humboldt, Pestalozzi concentrated on the individual in order to arrive at a large community of free individuals with a sense of responsibility and self-reliance.

After the military fiasco of 1805 efforts had also been made to reform the Austrian state from the base up. These endeavours were directed by the Graf (Count) von Stadion, a descendant of an ancient family of imperial knights. He had studied law at Göttingen before entering the Austrian diplomatic service. In 1794 he retired from the service at his own wish, when he recognised that the absolutist system was powerless to solve the problems of the time. In 1805 the emperor appointed him one of his chief ministers. Von Stadion was opposed both to the French Revolution and to Napoleon. He accepted the difficult task of simplifying the unwieldy apparatus of government and of rousing the more highly developed German-Austrian middle class to take a responsible part in political life. The greatest obstacles to the work of reform proved to be the insolvency of and corruption in the state, the disordered administration and the political indifference of the population. Moreover the reforms could only be carried through in the German-speaking areas of the monarchy, since the concession of full administrative autonomy to the non-German peoples would have augured the dissolution of the Habsburg dominions. In addition von Stadion had to make concessions to the rich and powerful nobility; there could be no question of abolishing their class privileges in spite of the precedent of Joseph II's attempts at reform. For these reasons the main efforts of the reform were directed towards an early liberating war of revanche. The creator of the Austrian army was the popular Archduke Charles, who had covered himself with glory in the earlier campaigns. He inaugurated general conscription in Austria; exemption from military service was only possible when it was in the economic interests of the country. The barbarous punishments in the army were mitigated. The regular army was reinforced by a reserve *Landwehr* (territorial reserve).

The reform movement inspired by the freedom-loving von Stadion remained but a short interlude in the history of the Habsburg monarchy. After the Austrian defeat in 1809 von Stadion was removed from office, his place being taken by the Rhinelander, Count Metternich. The new minister skilfully steered the state back into absolutist waters and regarded every attempt to shake off the Napoleonic yoke with the help of citizens' armies as a threat to the existence of the Austrian monarchy.

Liberation from Napoleonic Domination and the New Order in Europe and Germany

The friendly Franco-Russian relations which Napoleon had viewed as the necessary presupposition for the pacification of the continent and for English recognition of France's supremacy in Europe did not survive the strain of the economic hardships occasioned by the continental blockade. Russia made approaches to England again in order to avoid economic ruin. Napoleon's answer to this change in Russian policy was a carefully prepared invasion of Russia in 1812. A huge French army, strengthened by German and Italian reinforcements, was intended to break Russian resistance by a rapid victorious advance calculated to reach Moscow before winter set in. Napoleon did march into Moscow, but the great distances, the Russian winter, and the bravery of the

Russian soldiers made it impossible for him to consolidate his gains. The greatest part of the French army perished.

In this extremely serious situation for Napoleon the Prussian General von Yorck concluded the Convention of Tauroggen with the Russian General von Diebitsch on 30th December 1812, neutralising the troops under his command, which were in French service. This was a violation of the obedience which bound him to his king. But Yorck believed that he had to place the interest of his country above his oath of loyalty and obedience; in his eyes Napoleon's defeat was a foregone conclusion if Prussia fought with Russia. The Prussian king, however, decided on a final break with Napoleon only after long hesitation. In the spring of 1813 he concluded a formal alliance with Russia, which was joined a few months later by Austria and the majority of the states of the Confederation of the Rhine, with the exception of Saxony. The "Battle of the Nations" at Leipzig in 1813 sealed Napoleon's fate. He returned to France with the remnants of his army, a broken man, and abdicated at Fontainebleu, renouncing both sovereignty and the imperial crown. The victors assigned him the island of Elba as a sovereign principality. France was granted the boundaries of 1792.

In the lack of harmony between the victorious powers about the reorganisation of Europe and in French dissatisfaction with the restored house of Bourbon Napoleon thought he saw his chance to seize power again in France. But his defeat at Waterloo and his exile to St. Helena brought an end to his "Rule of a Hundred Days".

The statesmen of the victorious nations assembled at Vienna to decide on the future of Europe. The original plan envisaged that only England, Austria, Prussia and Russia should take part in the deliberations, but both the Tsar and Prince Metternich, Austria's chancellor, saw no advantage in excluding France from the "Concert of European Powers". Thus Talleyrand, the astute plenipotentiary of humbled France, was able to work his country back into the circle of the five great European powers, although he himself had as a responsible minister served both the Republic and, at the beginning, Napoleon.

The most important matters to be decided by the Congress were the new disposition of Europe and the solution of the "German Question". Where territorial problems were concerned, all the European powers were in some way interested; the solution of the German question remained predominantly an internal domestic issue.

There could be no doubt but that the great victor in the struggle to break France's hegemony in Europe was England. This explains why her statesmen had, with Metternich, such a decisive say at the Congress. It was England's declared aim that no great power should come into possession of the coastline opposite hers. Since Austria was no longer willing to take on the defence of Germany's western frontier against France but rather strove to round off the Habsburg possessions in the south-east, the Congress created a Kingdom of the United Netherlands under the Dutch crown. In this way Austria renounced her sovereignty over Belgium. It was a consequence of Prussian renouncement of the districts of Sundgau in Upper Alsace and of Breisgau in Baden, and of its refusal to see Alsace as a duchy ruled over by a member of the house of Habsburg that, at the suggestion of Castlereagh, England's representative, Prussia succeeded Austria as the defender of Germany's western flank. The Congress granted Prussia the two important regions of the Rhineland and Westphalia, thus making Prussia France's immediate neighbour. The waiving of Prussian claims in Alsace, which baffled German patriots, was only in conformity with the wish of Metternich that the Bourbon monarchy should not be encumbered at the outset with territorial losses, a wish which also corresponded to his own political vision. Although the Alsatians were conscious of cultural links with Germany, politically they regarded France as their fatherland.

The adjustment of Austria's south-eastern frontier proved particularly difficult. Russia desired to expand still further to the west. In 1809, before the peace settlement, the Tsar had already wrested Finland from Sweden and incorporated it into Russia. The conference confirmed him in this possession and united Norway to Sweden as a consolation. The long-standing Danish rule of Norway was thus at an end. Heligoland, until now under the Danish crown, was transferred to England. Poland, which was the particular object of power-hungry Russia, was revived with diminished territory, and united to Russia in the person of the Tsar under an imperial lieutenant. Prussia received Posen, Thorn and Danzig. Austria received Salzburg and the Tyrol back from Bavaria; Venetia and Lombardy, too, came under direct Austrian rule.

The territorial changes inside Germany had almost completely reversed the state of affairs obtaining before the wars. Prussia, a definitely eastern power, had expanded into Germany so that its centre of gravity now shifted westwards, especially as a result of later industrialisation. The political tasks now imposed upon it also linked its lot more and more to that of western Europe. In contrast, Austria expanded eastwards, out of Germany. Though it still wanted to enjoy its sovereign position in Germany, it was unwilling to carry any responsibility. It no longer desired to be burthened with the "Watch on the Rhine", without the security of being able to engage the other powers in Germany for this end.

But neither Prussia nor the central states of Germany, whose self-importance had been inflated by the rise in status of their princes under Napoleon and the pseudo-sovereign policy which they had been able to pursue as France's allies against Prussia and Austria, were willing to relinquish even a fraction of their sovereign independence and subordinate themselves to Austria. This meant that the hoped-for restoration of a united empire on the medieval pattern, a dream cherished by German patriots, was impossible to realise. The problem of German dualism, buried under the union of interests in the struggle against Napoleon, reappeared. The final outcome of innumerable negotiations to decide the new order in Germany was the "German Confederation", a loose association of thirty-nine sovereign states, among which Austria enjoyed a sort of primacy of honour. Three foreign sovereigns were also represented in the Confederation: the King of England as King of Hanover, the Danish King as Duke of Holstein, and the King of the United Netherlands as Grand Duke of Luxembourg. East and West Prussia, Posen, Schleswig, bound in indissoluble union to Holstein, and most of the non-German possessions of Austria were not members of the Confederation.

The deliberative assembly of the Germanic Confederation was the federal diet established at Frankfurt-on-Main, a permanent congress of envoys. This body was, however, only rarely capable of effective action, since a two-thirds majority, at times even unanimity, was required for its resolutions to be binding.

Certainly the so-called Acts of the Confederation envisaged a written constitution for all member states. But this provision was not observed except in a few of the minor states.

The idealistic aims of those opponents of Napoleon who had gone to war for the cause of freedom and unity therefore remained unrealised. As a result, there followed a period of bitter disillusion and deep disappointment. More than ever before, any participation in public life which aimed at bringing about a change in existing conditions seemed doomed to frustration. The only sphere left for the exercise of the productive forces of the German people seemed to be that of the spirit and imagination.

This view of the situation was confirmed by the steps taken in their domestic and foreign policy by the leading European powers. In 1815 Austria, Russia and Prussia signed the "Holy Alliance", the brain-child of Tsar Alexander I of Russia, to act as a stalemate on revolutionary efforts to undermine the "legitimate order" and as a check on nationalism and aspirations for liberty, and to guarantee the status quo. The state of the absolute prince was everywhere restored; the divine right of kings reiterated still more emphatically, and the holy alliance of "throne and altar" backed by the solidarity of crown and nobility renewed. All revolutionary tendencies were nipped in the bud by the "Carlsbad Decrees" agreed by the German princes in 1819. Representatives of liberal ideas were henceforth regarded as demagogues. Thus, for the time being, the principle of legitimacy triumphed over the revolution, and the keynotes of the period after 1815 became restoration and reaction.

Still it cannot be denied that the Congress of Vienna, through the wise moderation of the participating nations, whether conquerors or conquered, accorded Europe a long period of peace. The historical credit for this must go to Metternich. His far-sighted supranationalism and clear grasp of the needs of the West determined the shape of Europe for several decades to come. Russia's sphere of influence did not extend west of the Vistula. With the assistance of the five great powers a new age of order and quiet on the international political scene dawned. Of course this newly created order did not bring the free development of political life within the framework of independent national states that the peoples of Europe had hoped for. Metternich's lack of sympathy for the motivating ideas of his age and the incapability of the leading politicians after 1815 to move with instead of resisting these same ideas was to bring about the collapse of Metternich's system a generation later. The dissolution of the old order began first in the west and split Europe for a time into a liberal western bloc (France and England) and a conservative und reactionary bloc (Prussia, Austria and Russia). In the end the forces of liberal progress prevailed in Germany, too. There were economic as well as national political reasons to explain why this process was more gradual in central than in western Europe.

Chapter Fourteen

CONSERVATISM AND LIBERALISM

The Romantic movement had a considerable share in providing the ideological foundation on which the backward-looking and partly reactionary internal orders of the individual states in the Germanic Confederation were based. Not only the people but the state, too, was regarded as a living organism whose healthy functioning depended on the collaboration of its members. Adam Müller (1779—1829), the political philosopher and economist, was a romantic thinker who argued from this tenet that the body politic is not an artificial formation, the result of a contract between individuals entered into on purely rational grounds, but the natural growth from small cells. The family had evolved in the course of time through the clan and tribe into the state. The more vigorous the life of this state the greater its claim to *Lebensraum* (living space), a line of argument which also provides the justification for war. In addition to the natural division of society, there is another: that of class based on calling, which in turn decides the function of the individual within the framework of the whole.

These thoughts were developed still further by the German conservative movement which arose after 1815. Friedrich Julius Stahl (1802—1861), a Jewish convert to Protestantism and professor and politician in Berlin, provided conservatism with the basic elements of its theory of state and society in his book "Die Philosophie des Rechts" (The Philosophy of Law). In his view both state and law are of divine origin, a fact guaranteed by divine revelation. The uniqueness and distinctiveness of the national character of each people is in conformity with the divine plan and order of creation. Inside the nation, class distinctions are the expression of this divine order and are to be accepted as so many given facts. Stahl's views became the official ideology of Prussian and German conservatism. Through the intermediary of the conservative parties, they exercised a considerable influence on political thought and life. Stahl himself became a member of the *Herrenhaus*, the Prussian upper house, and the leader of the conservative party. German liberalism became the most telling critic of this concept of the state. The liberals in Germany had developed, under the impetus of the post-1815 reaction and the nascent industrialisation of western Germany, political objectives which differed little from those of the west European liberal movement. Nationalistic aspirations were interwoven with the desire for freedom. The close association of "throne and altar" led also, as in France before 1789, to a campaign to throw off man's spiritual subjection to the churches of both confessions. In this the authors of the post-romantic *Biedermeier* period who became known as "Young Germany" took an active part. They fought for the emancipation of the citizen, equality of the sexes, full civil rights for the Jews, freedom in literature, press and theatre, constitutional limitation of the powers of the prince and, as their long-term objective, the transformation of the absolutist state into a free democratic republic. Their most gifted spokesmen were Heinrich Heine (1797—1856) and Ludwig Börne (1786—1837), both Jews, though Heine had embraced Protestantism in his early years. Heine was, with Goethe, the most important lyrical poet of the nineteenth century. As a consequence of Prussia's ruthless suppression of all activities in the cause of freedom, both emigrated to Paris, where, in the first political masterpieces written by Germans, they brought their critical, indeed often hypercritical, powers to bear on conditions in Germany. Their avowed political aim was a revolution which was to harbinger the institution of a free democratic state which would deliver the citizen from his present bonds. In this point, certainly, they far exceeded the demands made by German liberals.

It was German liberalism's tragedy during the first half of the nineteenth century that it could not count on the support of a numerically and economically strong middle class. It remained essentially the preserve of theoreticians. Its doughtiest protagonists were professors and men of letters, who for the most part fell victim to the myrmidons of the reaction and paid for their free speech and writings with imprisonment or exile. Since a free press was not tolerated, every attempt to found one was doomed to be thwarted by the strictly imposed censorship laws. But there could be no change in the political scene without a decisive change in the economic and, as a consequence, in the social conditions in Germany.

Central Europe after the Congress of Vienna (1815)

Chapter Fifteen

INDUSTRIALISATION AND THE SOCIAL QUESTION

The Industrial Revolution in Germany

The years 1815 to 1848, the latter a date momentous in its consequences for Germany, must be regarded as a period of transition. These are years almost entirely devoid of significant political events. The struggle against reaction and retrospective political immobility led by various liberal groups, especially the student associations in the universities, appeared more important after the event, in the light of the 1848 revolution, than it actually was at the time. The political set-up which the Congress of Vienna had created for Germany was not seriously threatened even by the 1830 French Revolution which sent out tremors all over Europe.

The economic changes taking place under the surface of this seemingly stable political order were of greater significance. They were the result of the gradual industrialisation in progress in western Germany, where, during the first half of the 19th century, the English industrial revolution first made itself felt. The lead was given by the Cockerill brothers, English industrialists, who became the founders of Belgium's industry when they set up at Liège mixed manufactories consisting of ironworks, collieries, and rolling mills; they built model factories in Prussia, too, and became the "teachers of the Continent". This explains why the slowly developing heavy industry also lay in the hands of foreigners, mainly of English and Irish entrepreneurs. A serious obstacle in the way of a German-owned heavy industry was the lack of capital, which could not be overcome for a long time because of the state prohibition against the formation of joint-stock companies. Even in a go-ahead city like Hamburg commerce was, until the end of the 18th century, almost entirely in the hands of the Dutch, to whom the city also owed the establishment of a clearing bank and, in consequence, its introduction to world trade.

The early German contributions to the industrial process are coupled with the names of prominent entrepreneurs. In Westphalia, the industrialist Friedrich Harkort set up iron- and copperworks, and did much to advance the construction of canals and railways and to promote steam navigation. Almost contemporaneously Friedrich Krupp founded the first German steel works in Essen, a town still insignificant at that time.

It was not just the want of capital which caused difficulties: the attitude of the German workers severely handicapped the development and spread of the factories. They were either completely disinterested, even when presented with the inducement of higher wages, or unsuitable because of their lack of specialised knowledge. For this reason Germany's young industry had to rely on specialised workers from England. Again, the multiplicity of small states in Germany rendered traffic and the extension of trade in manufactured articles more difficult. These obstacles to any improvement in the economic situation were at the back of the demands which were made by nearly all entrepreneurs during the early stages of the industrial revolution: the extension of primary education to all children, the construction of railways, and the conversion of the Germanic Confederation into one constitutional state embracing all Germans. Here Friedrich List, the Tübingen professor, was their most eloquent advocate.

In 1819 he had presented the petition of an association of south German industrialists to the Frankfurt Diet and argued without success for the abolition of all tariff barriers between the individual German states. In doing this, his long-term objective was the formation of a central European economic union which should include Austria, Luxembourg, the Netherlands, Belgium, Switzerland, and Hungary. Political difficulties forced him to emigrate to the United States of America. On his return he set down his thoughts on economic reform in his "Nationales System der politischen Ökonomie" (National System of Political Economy, 1840). In this work he examined the conditions necessary for the development of the German economy. He regarded an increase in prosperity as the decisive factor, but by this he understood an increase not in material possessions but in the "productive forces". Among these he numbered science, art, and educational establishments in so far as they formed men who placed their intellectual abilities at the service of the people. His political demands were concerned especially with the build-up of communications and the institution of a unified customs and economic area. He held tariff protection against foreign competition to be necessary during the initial stages in order to stimulate the development of the national economy. Free trade was his economic ideal. Relatively soon after the conclusion of the wars of

178

liberation, men had come to the fore in the Prussian Ministry of Commerce who approached the problems raised by the nascent German industry without bias. What they aimed at was the formation of a German customs union which should include all German states with the exception of Austria, an objective which was made a reality in all essentials on 1 January, 1834. From that date onwards, there was some sense in speaking of a national German economy. One year later a group of Bavarian capitalists built Germany's first railway line, from Nuremberg to Fürth. In the course of the next years the railway network was extended. In 1837 Borsig founded the first German engineering works in Berlin. The Krupp plants succeeded in producing a new cast steel which was as good as its English counterpart.

It is true that the greater part of the population of Germany still belonged to the peasant class, but there was a gradual movement of the population which ended with the industrial workers in the majority. Since social conditions made it difficult for a man to improve his social standing in the areas east of the Elbe, many peasants had moved west. And many craftsmen who found it impossible to compete with the cheap factory-produced goods were absorbed into the ranks of the mass of industrial workers. In this way, the "social question" became a problem for Germany. And once again it was Prussia that made the first attempts to mitigate by law those cases of too great hardship caused by the reshuffling of the population. As early as 1839 the maximum number of working hours per day was fixed at ten for persons under sixteen years of age. Five years later the rising of the Silesian weavers showed how greatly the accepted order had been shaken by the industrial revolution in Germany, too.

The Social Question

Doubtless the social question was not so acute at the beginning of the industrial revolution in Germany during the first fifty years of the last century as to necessitate decisive political steps being taken for its solution. Greater preoccupation with the realities of this world was a noticeable characteristic of intellectual life in Germany after the deaths of Hegel (1831) and Goethe (1832). Nevertheless, the great systems of thought which were so typical of the period of German idealism continued to exercise an enduring effect on the immediate heirs of this greatest period of German philosophy. To systematize the whole of the universe still remained their chief concern.

Theoretical preoccupation with the social question first began in France and spread to Germany, whereas practical attempts to find a solution were first made in England. Indeed, here the industrial revolution had been very much more far-reaching in its effects. Karl Heinrich Marx, the most important theoretician on the social question, was given first-hand experience of both these countries by his expulsion from Germany. It was from German philosophy, and in particular from Wilhelm Friedrich Hegel (1770—1831), that he received the inspiration for the scientific socialism which he founded.

Hegel's system owes much to a stream of western thought which had its origin far back in Greek antiquity. Heraclitus (c. 540—c. 480 B. C.) was the author of the aphorism: "War is the father of all things"; life therefore comes into existence and continues to exist as the result of polarities or tensions. Heraclitus had thus expressed for the first time a thought which for Hegel contained the key to the understanding of all the phenomena in nature, history, art and science: the thought of the dialectic. The same law is universally valid: the thesis gives way to the antithesis, which is in turn followed by the synthesis which contains both. The world was for Hegel the revelation of reason, so that he could make the well-known and notorious statement: "What is real is rational, and what is rational is real". Now, if emphasis was laid on the first part of the clause, the conservative state received its philosophic justification; if on the second, then the conclusion that the rational must of necessity become real, justified revolution. In fact, Hegel's own ideal was the Prussian state of the reform period because it was the "most progressive", since in it a perfect synthesis seemed to have been arrived at between the claims of the whole and the rights of the individual. In his efforts to harmonize reason with reality Hegel also sought to allocate a place in his system to the negative manifestations of the life of the peoples. Marx both developed and transformed this system.

In the former Roman cities on the Rhine and Mosel, German Jewry could look back on the longest tradition of German-Jewish coexistence and was accordingly there most thoroughly at home with German culture. Karl Marx was the son of a Prussian lawyer resident in Trier, a Jew who had embraced the Christian faith. Therefore, Karl too received Protestant baptism. Having passed his final examinations at a *Gymnasium* in Trier, he went on to study philosophy and history at Berlin University in preparation for an academic career. However, as a baptised Jew, he gave up this idea and started work as a journalist for the "Rheinische Zeitung" in Cologne. His concern with economic questions dates from this time. A year later he was expelled from the

Prussian state because of his radical democratic views. He emigrated to Paris, where he founded the "Deutsch-französische Jahrbücher". At the same time he edited "Vorwärts" in collaboration with Heinrich Heine and made his first critical examination of Hegel, his beloved master in philosophy, in the light of his own views. At the instigation of the Prussian ambassador in Paris he was forced to leave France. Via Brussels, where he spent some time, he travelled to London. Here he lived with his wife and family in straitened circumstances, supported by his friend Friedrich Engels (1820—1895), until his death.

Karl Marx was a scholar, not a politician. Nor was his background proletarian. Indeed his upbringing and his marriage to the wellborn Jenny von Westphalen tended rather to exclude him from all proletarian influence. Yet in spite of this he became the founder of a movement which has not only won the support of the proletariat of many nations but has continued to grow in significance. The reasons for this are to be sought both in his own make-up and in the system he evolved.

One of the decisive factors in the formation of his character was undoubtedly his Jewish origin. His forefathers both on the paternal and the maternal side had for generations been rabbis. Thus, his soul, too, had been fashioned by the agelong experience of his people, who, in spite of innumerable attempts to be accepted by their German neighbours, had always been repelled and ostracised. This explains Karl Marx's deep sympathy for all those similarly oppressed. But he was not content with sympathy; he was possessed by the will to change. It was this which inspired the radical demands he made as a young journalist and as author of the "Communist Manifesto", which appeared in 1847. This revolutionary pamphlet criticised with singular forcibleness the capitalist order, to which it opposed, in words reminiscent of the Old Testament, a prophetic vision of the future communist world order, mankind's true promised land. His exhortation "Workers of the world, unite!" became the battle-cry of all those attacking the existing social set-up.

It is impossible to understand Marx's intellectual development without Hegel or the study of the form capitalism took in England. Marx never wavered in his view that Hegel's thought represented "the quintessence of German philosophy", but he believed that the Hegelian system contradicted its own great contribution to philosophy, the dialectic. He began by criticising Hegel's interpretation of dialectical progression as the self-realisation of the objective spirit, rejecting this as an "idealistic fancy". Nevertheless he took over the dialectic method from Hegel, and by applying it was able "to see in the proletariat not only the negation of man, but in this very insight, in this extreme dehumanisation of man, the conditions for a negation of the negation".

Feuerbach's criticism of Hegel was of similar importance for Marx. Here the Hegelian reinterpretation of Christianity was replaced by open criticism, and for Marx "the criticism of religion is the prerequisite of all criticism", since the idea of God hinders a man from attaining his own self-perfection. Marx also admired Feuerbach for taxing Hegel with his inability to explain the infinite variety of concrete reality. But reality is alone true, since the concept is but an image of what is tangibly real. In this way Hegel's philosophy was "turned upside down". Marx went a stage further: he in his turn accused Feuerbach of having devoted far too much thought to man in the abstract in his search for what was genuinely human in man, instead of taking man in the concrete, in his definite social and temporal context. He arrived at the conviction that a man is a man in the full sense of the term only when he can freely dispose of himself and all he produces. The fragmentation of the work process through the division of labour has deprived man of this "self-expression" and is threatening to deprive him of it more and more. The worker finds himself up against an anonymous power which robs him of his human right to enjoy the fruits of his labour: capital. Only when this "alienation of man" ceases will reason truly become reality ("What is rational is real", Hegel).

This alienation, however, has come about as the result of economic conditions, which we must investigate if we want to understand their significance for man. This examination very soon led Marx to the conviction that man's thought changes with his working conditions, i. e. is dependent on the "material conditions of production". "It is not men's consciousness that determines their existence, but their social existence which determines their consciousness". Marx made this concept the corner-stone of his view of history. In this he was greatly supported by his friend Friedrich Engels, who had made an exhaustive study of class tensions, particularly between the proletariat and capitalist classes in England. History thus becomes for Marx a record of class warfare, of the struggle of slaves against their owners, of serfs against spiritual and temporal lords, of apprentices against their masters, of workers against entrepreneurs. Every crack in the social superstructure was a sign that the relationship between production methods and forms of exchange was not as it should be.

Marx did not stop at a purely historical consideration of the past. "The philosophers have only given various interpretations of the world; the real task, however, is to change it!" This is the task of the proletariat, which the inevitable development of capitalist society will one day in the foreseeable future transform into the ruling class. Only when that day comes will true democracy become a reality, because then class warfare will be replaced by the classless society. This will provide the basis for the free development of the individual in accordance with his mental, spiritual and physical abilities. In Marx's view the state, which is nothing else than the organ and expression of the rule of one class, will just wither away as soon as the classless society becomes a reality.

In their criticism of capitalism there were two theories especially which Marx and Engels evolved to show the need to abolish private ownership. These were the theories of surplus value and increasing misery. The worker sells his labour power to the capitalist in return for a wage that is just sufficient to supply the means of subsistence. However, the worker produces during his working hours goods which are worth more than the wage which he has been paid. The value of these additional goods is called the surplus value. This means that the employer grows rich at the worker's expense; in other words, we have the exploitation of labour. This point led Marx to contest the entrepreneur's right to possess the means of production, since this ownership only assists him to appropriate goods obtained by the labour of the workers. The accumulation of capital in the hands of a few at the same time makes it possible for an entrepreneur to step up the production capacity of his plant, because it enables him to develop the means of production still further (investment). When this stage is reached, the factory will dismiss workers who have become redundant as a result of labour-saving machines. The result: marketing crises, unemployment, universal misery. Thus, all capitalism is doing is raising its own grave-diggers. "Centralisation of the means of production and socialisation of labour at last reach a point where they become incompatible with their capitalist integument. This integument is burst asunder. The knell of capitalist private property sounds", because capitalism will no longer be able to master the crises which arise as a result of the overproduction of goods without a corresponding demand. The inevitable outcome of this process will, according to Marx, be the collapse of the entire capitalist system of private ownership, and the transfer of the means of production from the hands of the last capitalist magnates to society. "The expropriators are expropriated!" The working class will take over the government in all states as soon as the proletariat becomes aware of its power and unites as a political force.

"The cessation of class warfare within the nation will also mean the end of hostility between nations". Only the "dictatorship of the proletariat" can place an obstacle in the way of wars, which serve no one but the owners. The "Communist Manifesto", therefore, closed with the words: "Let the ruling classes tremble before the communist revolution. The workers have nothing to lose except their chains; they have the whole world to win. Workers of the world, unite!"

In 1867 the first volume of Karl Marx's major work, *Das Kapital*, appeared in Hamburg.

No matter how minimal the direct influence exercised by Marx's work in his own day may have been, it still cannot be denied that as early as 1848 fear of proletarian radicalism had thoroughly damped the revolutionary enthusiasm of the bourgeoisie to change the existing social order. The 1848 June revolution in Paris, the first communist rising, hamstrung the efforts of the German middle classes, too, in their resistance to the authoritarian state and strengthened the property-owning bourgeoisie in their inclination to conclude a pact with it. Since the appearance of the "Communist Manifesto", Karl Marx and his theories have helped to shape the course of German, as well as of world history.

The Christian churches' first attempts to relieve the misery resulting from the industrial revolution were on the purely practical level. On the Roman Catholic side, the Society of St. Vincent de Paul was founded in 1833 for the service of the poor and sick. In 1848 Father Adolf Kolping founded his "Gesellenverein" to encourage independent handicraft. From the middle of the century onwards Wilhelm von Ketteler, Bishop of Mainz, took up, in the spirit of Christianity, the theoretical study of the social question, which he recognised as the most pressing problem of the day. In contrast to the views popular among broad circles of the bourgeoisie he conceded the right of the worker to fight for a human wage and for the recognition of his human dignity, if these were not freely granted him by the social order of the day. In this respect von Ketteler prepared the way for Christian trade unionism.

In the year which saw the foundation of the Society of St. Vincent, Johann Heinrich Wichern, a Protestant, founded the "Rauhe Haus" in Hamburg to take care of children from poverty-striken homes. In 1848 the foundation of the central committee for the "Innere Mission" of the German Evangelical Church provided the organisational basis for large-scale charitable work. In 1854 the first "Herberge zur Heimat", a home for itinerant craftsmen and workers, was founded. In 1867 Bodelschwingh laid the foundation stone of his life work, Bethel, near Bielefeld in Westphalia, a home for the care of the mentally defective. These were undoubtedly admirable achievements on the part of the churches of both confessions. But it must be admitted that they intervened in the social issue only hesitatingly; they were long content to leave the solution either to radical thinkers or to political bodies. The result was the alienation of the working class from the churches.

Chapter 16

1848: THE YEAR OF REVOLUTION

Prologue •

In 1840 Frederick William IV came to the Prussian throne. The news of his accession was everywhere received with enthusiasm because it was remembered that as crown prince he had shown sympathy for several of the progressive ideas of his day. Liberals and nationalists throughout Germany, not just in Prussia, regarded him as the nation's great hope for a united and free fatherland.

The first acts of the reign did not disappoint expectations. A general amnesty released the "demagogues" from prison, and by the intervention of the King of Prussia the persecution of political suspects was discontinued in the other states of the Confederation, too. In his foreign policy Frederick William IV was guided by an overriding desire for peace. Thus, although the military and political situation favoured Prussia, the king avoided war in 1841 in spite of France's menacing attitude towards the Rhine and obtained a peaceful solution, in agreement with the other great powers of Europe.

Still, it must not be thought that Frederick William IV was a liberal; indeed he dissociated himself from the ideas of 1789 in no uncertain terms. He was a royal romanticist cast in the mould of Adam Müller. His ideal state was a sort of medieval states-general gathered around the divinely appointed king. He was so obsessed by this doctrine of the divine right of kings that he was the declared opponent of any constitution which might limit the royal power.

In 1847 he summoned the representatives of the Prussian estates to attend the "United Diet of the Monarchy" in order to win their approval for a loan to build the eastern railway from Berlin to Königsberg. But the liberals in the assembly demanded that work should begin on the formulation of a constitution. The king would hear nothing of this and addressed an emotional appeal to the members of the diet adjuring them to approve the loan in "obedience for God's and their consience' sake", and to abandon all thought of effecting a change in the existing order. The liberals refused to bow to the royal will, however, so that the outcome was conflict between the representatives of the estates and the crown.

The most notable feature of the situation in Austria, where Metternich still held the reins and dictated policy, was a huge financial deficit which crippled the monarchy. Austria had lost its German market as a result of its exclusion from the German *Zollverein* (customs union), and, to make matters worse, industrialisation was almost at a standstill. Intellectual life had been stifled by Metternich's strictly imposed censorship. Even a great dramatic poet like Grillparzer, whose works were read throughout the German-speaking world, had to conform to these censorship rules. A national consciousness, quickened by the writings of Herder and the romantics, had awakened in the Czechs, Hungarians, and Italians, and threatened to force the disintegration of the monarchy. These separatist aspirations among the subject peoples represented a far greater menace to the Austrian empire than any movement for German unification.

The Revolution

In February 1848 France was again torn by revolution and the Republic once more proclaimed. This news triggered off an outburst of enthusiasm all over Germany. Popular assemblies met. Freedom of the press, arming of the people, the utilisation of lay burghers in the administration of justice (trial by jury), popular assemblies and, above all, a German parliament, were demanded in practically all states. The governments dared offer little or no resistance. In most of the smaller states the ministers were dismissed and new liberally-minded men appointed. And in Munich King Ludwig I was forced to abdicate in favour of Maximilian II.

Events within the two great German powers were to prove decisive. In Vienna burghers, students, and workers rose in common cause against the hated Metternich, who was forced to seek refuge in England. The emperor reacted by promising a constitution, but at the same time transferred the seat of government to Innsbruck. The revolution in Vienna was the signal for revolutionary uprisings in other parts of the monarchy. In contrast to Austria proper, the cause of the unrest here was twofold: a desire for political freedom and a yearning for national independence of Vienna. The Austrian liberals presented a common front with the revolutionaries in Prague, Budapest, Bratislava (Pressburg), Milan and Venice in the struggle to obtain their first aim; their second aspiration came up against the united resistance of the Germans in the empire. Thus Austria was faced, at the beginning of the revolution, with exactly the same situation as in 1815. On Austria's decision depended not only the integrity of its possessions but also the freedom of its subjects, for a new order conceding freedom seemed inevitably to entail the disintegration of the multi-national state.

Vienna therefore decided to employ force against the insurgents in Bohemia, Hungary, and Italy. The revolutionary movements in Prague and Italy were put down in that same year of 1848; in Hungary the emperor had to call in Russian troops, which the tsar, a relentless opponent of the revolution, was only too willing to place at the emperor's disposal. By August of the following year the Hungarian struggle for independence had also been decided in Austria's favour.

In Prussia it looked as though the king wanted to meet the liberal demands of his own free will, when in a royal patent of 18 March 1848 he conceded freedom of the press and a constitution. On that same day a great part of the population of Berlin assembled on the square in front of the palace to thank the king. Two shots were accidentally fired from the ranks of the military who had been sent to clear the square. The Berliners taking part in the demonstration felt that they had been betrayed. They raised barricades and rose against the army. The fighting continued unabated until the next day with the loss of many lives. At this stage the king felt it his duty to call a halt to the fighting. In an appeal addressed to "my dear Berliners", Frederick William IV informed them of his decision to withdraw the troops. On 21 March he paraded the streets of the capital, unwillingly wearing the black, red, and gold of the revolution, and made his memorable statement that "Prussia is merged into Germany". There can be no doubt that he hoped to get the upper hand of the revolutionary movement in the long run.

At this juncture Schleswig-Holstein broke out in insurrection against Denmark, because the Germans of those territories feared that Denmark was planning the forcible incorporation of Schleswig into the Danish dominions. Danish troops marched into the duchies. A provisional government was set up at Kiel. The Prussian king took the part of the Schleswig-Holstein population; his troops crossed the Eider and advanced into Jutland.

The revolution sought not just a constitution for the individual states of Germany, but their unification in a single national state. Fifty men had assembled in Frankfurt as representatives of the movement for national unity; they were charged with preparations for a freely elected constituent national assembly. When their resolution was approved by the Federal Diet and the individual governments, the legal basis for the "Frankfurt Parliament" which assembled in the Paulskirche on 18 March 1848 was provided. The assembly included members of the intellectual elite of Germany; university professors sat side by side with men of letters, law and commerce.

The common goal of the members was national unification and a constitution. Their first action was to elect an imperial vicar who was to continue in office until such time as the final form of the central executive power had been decided. Their choice fell on Archduke John of Austria, a prince with liberal convictions. He proceeded to form an imperial ministry, but it very soon became obvious that the revolutionary tide was on the turn in the individual states. The crucial question which would decide the fate of the Frankfurt Parliament was whether the greater and lesser princes of Germany were prepared to forfeit their sovereignty, partially or entirely, in favour of a united Germany. As long as the princes resisted any attempt to restrict their independence, both the central executive and parliament lacked the army and police force needed to enforce their will.

Without having clarified this essential question, the men at Frankfurt formulated a constitution. Their resolutions on the "basic rights" of men were passed unanimously. The territorial extent of the new kingdom, its relationship to the individual states, and the division of powers caused differences of opinion. Austria represented the chief obstacle in the way of the solution to these questions. Prince Schwarzenberg, Metternich's successor, was determined not to jeopardise the Danube monarchy in any way. This led him to insist that the entire Austrian empire should be incorporated as a single entity in a united Germany, with Austria recognised as the leading power. The members of the Frankfurt Parliament realised fully that the acceptance of this suggestion would seriously imperil the cause of German unity. It was therefore resolved by 267 votes to 263 to drop what was known as the "Great German" settlement and to unite Germany under Prussian leadership with the King of Prussia as hereditary emperor. This "Little German" empire should then form an alliance with Austria. The powers of the future emperor were to be limited by the constitution they had already passed and by a freely elected parliament (the Imperial Diet).

The Victory of Reaction

While the National Assembly was meeting in the Paulskirche at Frankfurt and theoretically achieving freedom and unity almost without any thought for the political feasibility of its resolutions, important political changes were taking place in the German states. In March 1848, even before the imperial government in Vienna had crushed the revolutionary outbreaks in the non-German parts of the empire, Schwarzenberg had imposed a constitution designed to transform the Austrian multi-national state into a unitary one. It contained no concessions to nationality and thus rendered any collaboration between the representatives of the various racial groups impossible from the very outset. Schwarzenberg prorogued his own constitution in 1851 when the various insurrections had finally been put down. Austria thus entered the second half of the 19th century as an absolutist state. Nevertheless the revolution of 1848 had brought some changes for the better: serfdom had been abolished once and for all; the monarchy had been converted into a single economic unit.

In March 1848 a national assembly met in Prussia as the result of general elections. The liberals won more seats than the conservatives. Their demands were radical and calculated to realise all those ideas that had been the inspiration of liberalism since the days of the French Revolution. Their most resolute opponents were the Prussian nobility and the Prussian Conservative Party it had founded. The voice of the latter was the "Neue Preussische Zeitung" (later called the "Kreuzzeitung") which was to remain the organ of Prussian conservative opinion down to the Third *Reich*. Among the conservative extremists of 1848 Otto von Bismarck was also to be numbered.

After the happenings of March 1848, Frederick William IV nominated the conservative general, Frederick William Count of Brandenburg, as his minister-president. Prussian troops reentered the capital, and the national assembly was moved to the quiet little town of Brandenburg, which had already proved its disinclination to rebel. In December the assembly was dissolved. On the fifth of that same month the king issued a constitution by royal proclamation which was to remain in force in Prussia with little alteration until 1918. It incorporated some of the liberal demands, such as the equality of all before the law, and the freedom of the press and conscience, but the upper house it created, the *Herrenhaus* (house of lords), with its members nominated by the king, placed an obstacle in the way of progress, since in order to become law a motion required the unanimous approval of both *Herrenhaus* and *Landtag* (provincial diet). In spite of the limited franchise which favoured property, the liberal-minded were generally in the majority. An observer could not but conclude, however, that taxable income gave more political rights than education. The executive was still in the hands of the king, who also named the ministers and decided on matters of war and peace.

The Counter Revolution had thus won the day in both great German countries. The army and civil service had proved their loyalty to the king. This victory of the Counter Revolution inevitably had repercussions in the other German states.

On March 28, 1849, the National Assembly in Frankfurt elected the King of Prussia emperor. A delegation was dispatched to Frederick William IV to offer him the imperial crown in the name of the German people. However, the Prussian monarch made his acceptance dependent on the consent of the other German princes—a condition which was tantamount to a refusal. Frederick William was unwilling to become emperor by the grace of the people. He referred to the crown as the "dog-collar by which they want to chain me fast to the revolution of 1848". Immediately after the imperial election the Austrian delegates were recalled. The Frankfurt Parliament disintegrated, though the rump moved to Stuttgart, where it was forcibly ejected from the city. In Dresden, the Palatinate, and Baden there were popular risings which had in the end to be put down with the help of Prussian troops. In Dresden Richard Wagner and in Baden Carl Schurz fought in the ranks of the insurgents; Wagner afterwards emigrated to Switzerland, Schurz to America.

Frederick William IV had explained his rejection of the imperial crown with the statement: "I am not Frederick the Great". With these words he probably meant to imply that he did not feel himself equal to the difficulties which his acceptance would have involved both in Germany and abroad. Russia had already dropped a hint that it was not in favour of German unification, and in those days a hint from Russia carried great weight in Prussia. How France and Austria would act in the event was also uncertain. Prussia might have found itself a second time in Frederick the Great's situation during the Seven Years War.

That this fear was not entirely groundless could be seen by the reaction Frederick William IV aroused when he tried, on the advice of his friend von Radowitz, to carry out plans for German unification which envisaged the Prussian king as hereditary head. This step was opposed by Austria, Bavaria, Württemberg, Saxony, Hanover and the Prussian conservatives, with Bismarck among them. Russia took Austria's side. Marx and Engels regarded this Russian decision as the crucial reason for the collapse of the revolution of 1848. Prussia was forced to abandon its ambitions in the Olmütz Convention. The Federal Diet was reconvened at Frankfurt with Austria presiding. Bismarck, whose loyal bearing the king had not forgotten, was sent to Frankfurt as Prussia's deputy.

The victory of the Counter Revolution also marked the end of nationalist aspirations in Schleswig-Holstein. In the "London Protocol", 1852, the great powers agreed on the status of these duchies. Their decision excluded the incorporation of Schleswig in Denmark.

Chapter Seventeen

THE NEW GERMAN REALISM

Both the Revolution of 1848 and the efforts of the Frankfurt Parliament to place a united Germany on a new footing had come to nothing. A deep sense of disillusionment took the place of the idealistic enthusiasm of revolutionary days. Many now looked to America and emigration as alone offering the opportunity for a meaningful life, with the result that the number of Germans settling in the United States grew from year to year.

At home, Germans were more than ever inclined to leave their country's fortunes in the hands of professional politicians. The view that the state is primarily and of its very nature synonymous with power was finding more and more supporters. Now although this theory had the attraction of offering a ready-made explanation for the 1848 fiasco—the politicians of the revolution had failed because of their incapacity to gain control of the organs of power in the individual states—it also led many to turn their backs on politics in disgust. Another conviction becoming widespread, especially among the liberals, was that German unity could not be won by economic forces alone. The middle classes were thus encouraged to believe that it was their duty to throw in their lot with the military might of the state. A political course which made calculated and unemotional use of the power of the state for its own ends was regarded by many as the only feasible course, since after all it did take account of things as they really were.

Since the deaths of Goethe and Hegel, a more realistic approach to the world and to natural phenomena had also won through in science and the arts. At the beginning of the century, Schopenhauer (1788—1860) had questioned idealism's blind faith in the formative power of the intellect. In his work "Die Welt als Wille und Vorstellung" (The World as Will and Idea), published in 1819, he had presented his view of life as a chain of sorrows. A man can only win release from the vicious circle of desire and its satisfaction by a denial of his will to live. After Hegel's death, the philosophical criticism of the "left-wing" Hegelians displaced traditional views. In his "Life of

Jesus", David Friedrich Strauss (1808—1874) conducted a critical examination of the gospels to determine their value as sources. His conclusion was that they contained a myth, a product of the unintentionally creative legend deriving from the Christians of the first two centuries. Ludwig Feuerbach converted theology into anthropology and maintained that religion is nothing more than the embodiment of the wish projections of human egoism. Man creates his God or gods after his own image and likeness. Immortality is only to be understood as a man's survival in his children or in what he has made.

All this prepared the way for a purely materialistic view of the world. And this *Weltanschauung* (philosophy of life) found confirmation, in its turn, in the conclusions of the natural sciences with their basis in experience and highly-refined experimental methods. In the field of physics, Robert Mayer, a German doctor from Heilbronn, discovered the law of the conservation of energy; Theodor Schwann proved that cells form the basis of both animal and vegetable tissues (1839); Mendel, an Augustinian monk, explored the laws of heredity in plants; and Justus Liebig turned the laws of metabolism to account to increase agricultural production by the application of artificial manures (1843). At the same time, his research gave a decisive impetus to the development of German chemistry. Ampère's work on electromagnetism (1826) made possible both the needle telegraphy of the Göttingen professors Gauss and Weber (1833), and the recording telegraphy of the American Morse (1835).

In literature, too, writers were meeting the challenge of the real world and making this the main theme of their works. This was not the result of any supra-personal conviction; it was much more a reflection of the personal vision of the individual writer. Whereas art during Goethe's time wanted to be at the centre of life, it now became just another facet of life's many-sidedness—thus sharing the fate which had already overtaken religion to some extent. A deep-seated pessimism was the basic feature of the entire German literary production of this period. Lenau, Grabbe, Büchner, and Hebbel never tired of showing how even the exceptionally gifted individual is broken by the petty trivialities of life. Even where the simple man acts in accordance with his deepest instincts, as in Büchner's *Woyzeck*, no solution is offered. It was in ordinary people and their simple way of life and in a conscious surrender to the sober realities of existence that Immermann and Jeremias Gotthelf saw a means of escape from the agonizing unrest which has assailed man as a result of his vacillation between the desires of his own ego and the higher demands made on him from outside. Man's salvation is to be sought in obedience to the laws which have been imposed on him by nature.

This outlook on life was shared by the two most considerable poets and novelists of the middle of the last century, the German-Swiss Gottfried Keller (1819—1890) and the Schleswig-born Theodor Storm (1817—1888). The main characters in their writings are heroes of everyday life who are deeply rooted in clan and country and absorbed by the work which is their lot, and who prove time and again that true human greatness is to be found in the quiet of a simple and in itself insignificant life.

In Eduard Mörike (1804—1875) and Annette von Droste-Hülshoff (1797—1848) alone did something of the Goethe period seem to survive; both of these writers found the inspiration for their works in an undoubtedly highly personal faith. For them poetry was still the expression of human desires mirrored in nature and myth, and looking to a release by some supra-human power. But their poetry was out of tune with their time; for long they went their way, unknown and unrecognised.

There were few representatives of note in the field of fine arts in Germany. Painters sought their subjects in history. The Prussian Adolf Menzel was the only painter to rise somewhat above the general mediocrity.

At a time when German philosophy was languishing, when classicism and romanticism had lost their attraction, when technological progress and science were laying the foundations of their future significance, and the incipient industrialisation was just beginning to reveal its power to work changes on man and countryside, Otto von Bismarck was preparing himself for his political career as a Prussian minister and the creator of the German empire.

Chapter Eighteen

BISMARCK

Origins and First Political Endeavours

Otto von Bismarck, born into an ancient *Junker* family at Schönhausen in Brandenburg on 1 April 1815, made his first acquaintance with the period of Prussian reaction while still a schoolboy at the "Graues Kloster" (grey monastery) in Berlin. He rejected it and was a convinced republican by the time he left school. As a law student at the university of Göttingen he was, like the other undergraduates, interested in the revolutionary ideas of the day. The brief interlude in Prussian service as a judicial administrator in Potsdam (1837—1838) only served to show that it did not suit him. His decision to throw up his career in the Prussian civil service brought him back into the main stream of his family's centuries-old tradition. Bismarck now became a member of the landed gentry not merely by birth but also by profession. He gained firsthand experience of the duties, rights and obligations of a landed gentleman. The task of mastering them gave him the mental image of the life of such a gentleman which was to remain with him until his death. His life as administrator of the family property harmonised completely with his desire for self-development through achievement, but also developed his conviction that any more-than-personal achievement must be rooted in the distinction between master and servant, between those who command and those who obey. Although it was his opinion that the special significance of the landowning *Junker* class was to be seen in its obstinate attachment to its privileged position within the state, he still felt that it was the obvious duty of the nobility to place their property at the service of the state. Such a social order could only be guaranteed by a strong monarchical head. The service of the king, the representative of the power within the state, thus took on twofold significance: dedication to the supra-personal idea of the state and the protection of an order which by implication also safeguarded one's own position. Bismarck therefore resolved to take up politics primarily to play his part in the strictly conservative defence of the existing order against any assault, convinced as he was that any participation of the bourgeoisie in the government of the state represented a peril to the traditional structure of the Prussian state with its privileges for the property-owning nobility.

His Protestant religious convictions, however subjective these may have been, strengthened his Prussian conservative viewpoint in politics. In his youth, Bismarck, like the rest of his contemporaries, had not been proof against the scepticism of the Enlightenment. But his love for Johanna von Puttkamer, who was later to become his wife, brought him once again under the influence of practical Lutheran Protestantism. From this arose his—in many respects—exemplary loyalty to the service of his king and to his convictions of the stateman's duty to spend himself in safeguarding the interests and powers of the state. Apart from the Prussian King Frederick William I, no other man has so outstandingly embodied the type of a convinced Christian statesman who regards the state, in accordance with Luther's ideas, as forming a completely autonomous world of its own, which cannot be ordered and ruled according to the standards of Christianity. Nevertheless it was his firm conviction that the ethos of Christianity and that of the Prussian state could not stand in contradiction to each other.

An ardent determination to put his ideas across was the motive, and *Junker* Prussianism was the basis of his dealings. In 1847 he made his debut on the political stage as representative of his class in the Prussian Diet. In 1848 he was the most determined opponent of the revolution and the most vigorous champion of anti-revolutionary ideas. The full glare of public interest was not yet focused on him. Nevertheless he attempted, through the conservative press and through other members of the nobility, to induce the Prussian king to change the attitude he had adopted towards the Prussian Diet and the Frankfurt Parliament. The victory of the Counter Revolution in Prussia and throughout Germany gave him great satisfaction.

The revolution of 1848 in opening the way for Napoleon III's rise to the position of "Emperor of the French" (1852) marked a decisive turning-point in European politics. The "Holy Alliance", that expression of the need of the European princes for political peace and stability after the close of the Napoleonic Wars, had lost its effectiveness; it became a completely dead letter during the Crimean War. When the Treaty of Paris was signed in 1856 to mark the conclusion of the war, France was lined up on the side of Russia's vanquishers, England, Turkey and Sardinia. France saw this as finally squaring accounts for her defeat in 1814/15, which she regarded as essentially Russia's work.

During the Crimean War Bismarck was Prussian respresentative at the Frankfurt Diet. Although he did not start by being anti-Austrian, his contact with the Austrian diplomats at Frankfurt soon led him to conclude that Austro-Prussian dualism would one day have to be replaced by Prussian hegemony. Austria's ambiguous attitude during the Crimean War, when, contrary to Russian expectations, she remained neutral, isolated the Danube monarchy. Russia broke off her close relations with Austria and made overtures to Prussia. The Western powers, especially France, had anticipated Austria's active participation in the war. The admission of Sardinia, Austria's great rival in Italy, added fuel to anti-Habsburg feelings in Italy, which looked to Napoleon III as her strongest ally.

In 1859 a second Italian war broke out between Austria and Sardinia to decide the possession of Lombardy. Within a few months the Austrian armies were forced to admit defeat. The centenary celebrations of Schiller's birthday unleashed a great wave of national enthusiasm throughout the whole of Germany. Prussia felt it could no longer afford to hold aloof, and was prepared under certain conditions to enter the war on Austria's side in order to defend the "Po on the Rhine" against France, Sardinia's chief ally. At this juncture Napoleon offered an armistice. Austria lost Lombardy; Savoy and Nice fell to France. Bismarck, now ambassador in St.Petersburg, was never tired of admonishing Prussia to remain neutral. The surprisingly rapid conclusion of the war was completely in accord with his own political desires. In St. Petersburg he saw it as his main objective to do everything to cement Russo-Prussian friendship.

In 1862 he was sent to Paris for a few months as ambassador. This short stay in the French capital gave him a deep and valuable insight into the political ambitions of Napoleon III.

Minister President in Prussia

The ailing King Frederick William IV had handed over the regency to his brother William, who succeeded to the throne in 1861 when Frederick William died. After the Austro-Italian war of 1859 the Prussian Diet called upon the king to strengthen the army. William complied and requested Albrecht von Roon, his Minister of War, to make the necessary preparations. Von Roon's proposals envisaged strengthening the combatant regiments by the addition of an aristocratic officer corps, whereas the *Landwehr* or national reserve with its many middle-class officers was to be reduced. He also wanted to raise the period of military service from two to three years. The liberal majority in the Prussian Diet, which had combined to form the "German Progressive Party", resisted these governmental reforms. They wanted to see the royal army transformed into a people's army. Every increase in the regular army represented an increase in the number of commissions available and, by the same token, of the royal influence. The diet declared its readiness to authorise the necessary grant for the reorganisation of the army but demanded that the king should realize his plan only in accordance with the changes proposed by the members of the diet. In 1862 the diet refused to authorise the army budget because the king obstinately stuck to his demands. A general election only resulted in an even stronger liberal representation being returned. The conflict between king and people was now common knowledge. William felt inclined to abdicate in his son's favour. At this juncture a man came to his aid who promised to carry the royal plans into operation even without the diet: Otto von Bismarck. William nominated him minister president.

Since the diet still resolutely refused to give way, Bismarck governed without a budget by appealing to his extremely questionable theory of the "gap in the constitution". This meant, according to him, that the government was permitted to collect and spend taxes without a budget if no agreement could be reached between the Prussian chamber of deputies and the upper house. Such an eventuality had not been envisaged by the constitution. The army reforms were put into operation. The army and civil servants remained loyal to the government.

Bismarck now sought successes in foreign policy in order to become master of the precarious situation at home. He had influential opponents even inside the royal family: Queen Augusta and the Crown Prince and his wife (a daughter of Queen Victoria) disapproved of his policies. But he did not allow this to deter him from keeping his objectives in view. He strengthened Prussia's close ties with Russia by coming out unambiguously against Poland on the occasion of a Polish revolt against Russian overlordship, a step which cost him the last liberal sympathies in Prussia and Germany.

At this point a foreign political event came to his aid. In 1863 a new constitution was adopted in Denmark in which Schleswig was to be severed from Holstein and incorporated into the Danish dominions. This was a clear breach of the 1852 Treaty of London. Bismarck was able to gain Austria's support for united intervention. The two great powers declared war when Denmark refused to make any concession.

The Danish armies were defeated and Denmark was compelled to cede Schleswig, Holstein, and Lauenburg to Prussia and Austria. Both Austria and Prussia agreed to a later popular referendum. In the meantime they intended to administer the territories jointly.

The joint administration could not but be temporary. Public opinion in Germany favoured the reorganisation of the territories as an independent state. Austria supported this proposal as a means of preventing the duchies from falling into the hands of Prussia. Bismarck, however, opposed the scheme by demanding that the duchies should enter into a closer relationship with the Prussian state, subordinate all military and naval matters to Prussian supreme command, and cede the important harbour of Kiel to Prussia for development as a naval base. Austria was prepared to turn a blind eye in return for the restitution of part of Silesia and a guarantee of its Italian possessions. Bismarck, however, was trying at this time to enter into an alliance with Italy and therefore refused. In the end they arrived at a provisional agreement known as the Gastein Convention, according to which Austria was charged with the administration of Holstein, and Prussia of Schleswig.

Bismarck, far from considering this treaty final, rather regarded it as a means of realising *his* solution of the German question. His main objective was to isolate Austria from possible allies in the event of war between the two countries. For this reason he started negotiations with Italy (1866) to gain its support and with France to obtain a guarantee of neutrality. In a secret agreement Napoleon III committed himself to non-interference in a war against Austria, in the event of Prussia fighting in alliance with Italy. Bismarck thereupon proposed to the Frankfurt Diet that the Federation should be reformed and a German parliament be elected by universal and secret suffrage. This was intended as bait to win the support of the liberals. However, like most of the German princes, they rejected his proposal. Austria countered by demanding from the Federal Diet a decision about the future of the lands between the North Sea and the Baltic. Bismarck regarded this as a violation of the Austro-Prussian agreements, gave the command for Prussian troops to overrun Holstein, and urged the Diet to expel Austria from the Federation. Austria's next move was to propose the mobilisation of the Federation's troops against Prussia. War between the two leading German states now looked inevitable. Prussia was allied with Italy. With the exception of Mecklenburg and a few of the smaller north German states, the whole of Germany was lined up with Austria. Bismarck invited the rulers of Hanover, Saxony, Hesse and Hesse-Nassau to accept the Prussian plan for a reform of the Federation. But they still refused. Whereupon Prussian troops occupied their territories.

The Prussian army was now poised to smash Austria. The two armies joined battle on 3 July 1866 in the Battle of Königgrätz (or Sadowa as it is known in France and England). The Austrian army had to leave Prussia in possession of the field. The war had been decided within three weeks.

The Prussian king had been very reluctant to give his consent to a war with Austria. The feeling of solidarity had become so strong among all Germans since the Wars of Liberation and under the influence of nationalist ideas, that even dynastic considerations gave way before it. Bismarck had to make it clear to his sovereign that Austria aimed at undermining Prussia's position in Germany and at destroying her supremacy in north Germany. However, having given the royal consent to a recourse to arms, he also wanted to savour the fruits of victory after Austria's decisive defeat. He insisted on territorial concessions by Austria and Saxony and the entry of Prussian troops into Vienna. In contrast, Bismarck's main preoccupation was to prevent any feeling of bitterness from arising in Austria. He wanted her to remain unimpaired as "a piece on the chess-board of Europe", but William proved immovable. Bismarck thought of resignation, of suicide. He found an ally in his opponent, the crown prince. He finally succeeded in wringing the preliminary Peace of Nikolsburg from the king, shortly before Napoleon III laid claim to the Palatinate and parts of Hesse. In the Peace of Prague Austria gave up all claims to Schleswig-Holstein and Venetia, which was ceded to Italy, undertook to withdraw from Germany, and gave her consent to the formation of a North German Federation under Prussian leadership. She also declared her readiness to pay an indemnity. Prussia concluded a peace treaty with the south German states without annexations. Hanover, Electoral Hesse, Frankfurt, and Schleswig-Holstein were annexed by Prussia, although William had some qualms of conscience about the legitimacy of this act. Bismarck's *Realpolitik*, aiming at transforming Prussia into a territorially unified state in north Germany, overcame the unwillingness of the crown; the gap between Prussia's east and west German possessions was closed.

In secret military agreements the south German states placed their troops under Prussian supreme command. Bismarck was able to persuade them to take this step by informing them that Napoleon III had demanded the Saar, the Bavarian Palatinate, and Rhinehesse with Mainz in recompense for his neutrality.

The Peace of Prague had broken the bonds which had for centuries linked the Germans of Austria to those of the rest of Germany. Seen from the viewpoint of the history of the Habsburg empire, this seemed to be the logical outcome of its development. Since the 17th century the continual tendency had been for Austria to expand "out of" the empire. Her interests in the Balkans and in Italy had prevented her from effectively defending Germany's western border. Her claim to be integrated as a whole in a united Germany had seemed impracticable even to the parliamentarians of 1848. In any case such a solution would probably have aroused the decided opposition of Russia and France: Russia's Balkan aspirations would inevitably have seemed illusory, and France would have been compelled to consider her position in Europe threatened.

Austria herself did not regard her definite exclusion from the empire as involving any change in her position as a great power in Europe, since, in spite of her losses in Italy, she was convinced that nationalistic aspirations did not, as yet, endanger the monarchy as a whole. This was why, just one year after her defeat, she undertook the constitutional reorganisation of the Habsburg dominions. In 1867 the dual monarchy of Austria-Hungary came into being. From this time on Austria and Hungary formed two autonomous states, under the crown of Habsburg, each with its own government and administration and nationality laws. The emperor of Austria was at the same time king of Hungary, where he was represented by a viceroy. Each state had its own parliament, in which the national tongue was the official language of parliamentary business. Foreign affairs, the army, and finance were under joint administration. Croatia's special position within Hungary was recognised by the concession of a Croatian diet. Slavonia and Transsylvania were subordinated to Hungary; the other regions of the monarchy, divided into 17 provinces, were placed under Austria. The Slav problem remained unsolved. The Czechs, Slovaks, and Serbs saw themselves treated as second-class citizens and were more and more attracted to Pan-Slavism. Here lay Austria-Hungary's Achilles' heel.

The outcome of the Austro-Prussian War meant that Prussia alone had the decisive say about the future of the German people. No other German state could now venture to oppose Prussia with hope of success. Accordingly Bismarck's proposal that the states north of the Main should unite in the North German Federation under Prussian leadership was rapidly converted into reality. On 1 July 1867 a constitution approved by both the North German *Reichstag* and the various governments of the Federation was published. It had been drafted by Bismarck and was a not unskilful attempt to synthesise monarchic and democratic conceptions. The *Reichstag* was elected by universal, equal and direct suffrage. For legislation to become law, the approval was also required of the *Bundesrat* (Federal Council), composed of delegates sent from the individual states of the Federation. The Prussian king headed the Federation as hereditary president. He nominated as Federal Chancellor a man who had won his confidence. Otto von Bismarck became first chancellor of the Federation.

Without a doubt all Germans realised that the first step towards German reunification had been taken. A change began to take place in their attitude to Bismarck, the man who at a dark moment during his life-and-death struggle with the Prussian parliament had said that the great questions of history can only be solved "by means of iron and blood". Further members of the liberal middle class were now inclined to make their peace with the creator of the North German Federation because of the remarkable progress in German industry and commerce which characterised the sixties and was still further augmented by the creation of larger markets. Bismarck met these desires half way by asking in the Prussian Diet in 1867 for a "bill of indemnity" (exemption from incurred penalties) for the unconstitutional expenditure of state revenue over the past years. In so doing he recognised the budgetary right of Parliament. The diet granted him his wish by 230 to 75 votes. The liberals split into a "Progressive Party" and the "National Liberals". From now on the National Liberals were to lay greater emphasis on considerations of prestige and economy and less on the freedom ideals for which they had fought for years. They became the most doughty champions of Bismarck's policies.

Founder of the German Empire

Napoleon III, Emperor of the French and bearer of such a fateful name, needed, the longer he reigned, political successes abroad in order to secure his rule at home. The failure of his Mexican adventure in which he had involved his country during the American Civil War in an attempt to consolidate its position in Latin America had not only cost Archduke Maximilian of Austria both crown and life but had damaged Napoleon's international standing as well. At home he was faced by impending conflicts with the Catholic Church because the latter regarded him as a friend of Italian nationalism which was threatening the states of the Church as an obstacle to unification. And now Austria had been defeated without the slightest intervention of France.

Napoleon thus continued his efforts to secure a favourable adjustment of France's north-eastern frontier. In 1867 he tried to purchase Luxemburg from Holland for cash. The grand duchy had been a member of the Germanic Federation and Prussia had garrison rights in the fortress at Luxembourg. Bismarck would have countenanced the transaction, but the North German Federation raised protests. In London the great powers agreed to guarantee the grand duchy's neutrality. Prussia withdrew her troops; Luxembourg remained within the German Customs Union.

In 1870 Spanish politicians thought of offering their country's vacant throne to a prince of the Catholic branch of the Hohenzollern family. Bismarck seconded the Hohenzollern candidature. The French immediately began to recall the encirclement of their country under Charles V. Tough words uttered by the French Foreign Minister, Gramont, created an atmosphere of crisis. However, without prior consultation with Bismarck, the Hohenzollern prince refused the honour. It seemed that the crisis had blown over. Bismarck had suffered a personal defeat.

At this point the French foreign minister overreached himself. He requested his ambassador to speak with the Prussian King William I, asking him to guarantee that the candidature of the Hohenzollern prince would in no event be renewed. The interview took place in a street of Bad Ems where William was staying at the time. William refused and afterwards let the ambassador know that he had nothing more to say to him on the subject. He also sent a telegram to Bismarck informing him of the incident. Bismarck published the text of this communication in a condensed and ruder form (the "Ems Telegram"). As he worded it, it looked as though the French ambassador had insulted the Prussian king. The Prussian population was incensed; the French believed that their country had suffered a resounding defeat in foreign policy. War was talked of in both countries and on 18 July 1870 France declared war on Prussia.

Napoleon III hoped that the south German states, Bavaria, Baden and Württemberg, would join him after the first battles had been won. In the event they declared en bloc for Prussia. Within a short time the united German armies advanced across the Rhine. The fighting raged heaviest around Metz; here the French were confined within the town's defences. Hardly seven weeks after the outbreak of war the German armies emerged victorious from the Battle of Sedan and Napoleon was taken prisoner.

In France this led to a change in the constitution. The Third Republic succeeded the empire. The new government sued for peace but the negotiations broke down because of Prussian insistence on the cession of Alsace-Lorraine with the fortresses of Strassburg and Metz. The war therefore continued. The German armies laid siege to Paris and on January 28, 1871, the city was forced to capitulate because food supplies had run out. On the same day the armistice was signed. The final peace treaty was concluded at Frankfurt-on-Main on 10 May, 1871. France was obliged to pay an indemnity of five million frs and to cede Alsace-Lorraine. Nine French provinces were occupied until such time as the indemnity was paid.

The decisive considerations which led Bismarck to demand the cession of Alsace-Lorraine to Germany were of a military and not of a nationalistic nature. He always felt that the overemphasis on the fact of "the Alsatians having once been Germans and speaking German" was a "professor's brain-child". On the other hand, since he regarded "Strassburg and Metz as France's sally-port", and feared French influence in south Germany, the military reasons for annexing the fortified regions and the provinces seemed obvious to him.

Alsace had formed part of the empire for centuries and its inhabitants spoke a dialect of German. But the close links with France, both political and cultural, had always been indisputable, and had become closer since the French Revolution. Quite apart from the numerous members of the population of Alsace and Lorraine who chose voluntary exile, the majority of those who stayed behind did not feel at home within the empire. The measures taken by the new German Empire, too, were such as could only encourage this dissatisfaction. Alsace-Lorraine was declared a "Reichsland" by a law of 9 June, 1871, a status which did not carry the rights enjoyed by the other states of the empire. It was not granted the franchise until 1874 and from then on consistently sent delegates to the *Reichstag* that to a man opposed the German regime. Later the inhabitants aspired to the status of autonomy within the empire, but this was refused. From 1879 onwards the land was administered by an imperial *Statthalter* (governor) assisted by one secretary and four undersecretaries of state. Not infrequently Prussian Protestant officials were appointed to this predominantly Catholic land. In 1911 it was granted a constitution and three seats in the Federal Council.

The annexation was to embitter Franco-German relations considerably, especially as the attitude of the Alsace-Lorraine population was almost continuously one of repudiation. It merely served as fuel for the French policy of revanche which had as its main objective the reversal of the 1871 decision.

The final collapse of France and the signing of the armistice were preceded by an event of crucial significance for Germany and the world: the foundation of the German empire in the palace of Versailles on 18 January 1871. This was the fruit of Bismarck's painstaking negotiations with the south German princes. Württemberg and Baden proved amenable enough, but Ludwig II of Bavaria, the friend of Richard Wagner, could only be persuaded with the greatest difficulty to relinquish some of his sovereign rights. After protracted negotiations Ludwig agreed to offer the imperial crown to the King of Prussia. Now it was the latter's turn to have misgivings: as a Prussian he had more respect for the royal dignity that had been his till now and did not relish exchanging this for an empty title.

After agreement had been reached in November 1870 on the "reserved rights" of the south German princes, Ludwig of Bavaria copied out a letter drafted by Bismarck and sent it to the King of Prussia, offering him the imperial crown in the name of the German princes. This was followed shortly afterwards by a delegation of the north German *Reichstag* headed by the same man who had offered the imperial crown to William's predecessor in Berlin in 1849, Eduard Simon, the national-liberal descendant of a Königsberg Jewish family. He embodied the longing of the German people for a unified German *Reich*. William accepted the crown. In his first speech composed by Bismarck for the opening of the *Reichstag* of the new empire he declared: "May God grant us and our successors on the imperial throne that we may at all times augment the German empire not by force of arms but by imparting the advantages and gifts of peace in the field of national prosperity, freedom and civilisation."

Now that Germany had achieved unity it wanted to enjoy peace. How little the imperial throne meant to the Prussian king in the last analysis he showed eloquently enough by not even giving his chancellor Bismarck a grateful handshake on the day of his imperial coronation, 18 January, 1871.

The constitution of the German empire differed little from that of the North German Federation. The main stress of the constitution continued to be placed on the Federal Council, that is on the princes. The army and navy, legislation covering civil and penal law, customs matters, and trade and commerce, the regulation of weights, measures and coinage, and the postal services, were under the jurisdiction of the empire. Other matters were regulated by the individual states. The Imperial Chancellor (*Reichskanzler*) stood alone at the head of the imperial administration and under him were all the government departments (*Reichsämter*). The imperial chancellor was at the same time Prussian minister president.

The German empire was a national state in so far as it united most of the German-speaking inhabitants of Europe within its frontiers and sheltered only a few minorities (Poles, Danes, and French). Bismarck himself had always regarded with equanimity the way Germans were scattered over certain parts of Europe and never dreamt of making political capital out of this fact. It was reserved to a later period to demand that these cultural links should be made the basis of state membership.

The German empire took its place as a new great power among European powers that had enjoyed constitutional stability for centuries. It had therefore at first to expect that it would be greeted with a measure of reserve and mistrust. More than ever before everything would depend on the character of the new power's foreign policy.

Securing the Empire

The relations of the new German *Reich* to its neighbours was governed by Bismarck's conviction that Germany would have at all times and in all circumstances to count on France's antagonism on account of the Frankfurt peace treaty. Since in Bismarck's opinion Germany itself was "satiated", so that a policy of expansion in any direction was entirely out of the question, he had to direct his efforts towards preventing France from becoming the centre of a coalition. German foreign policy after 1871 could, therefore, only aim at isolating France. The contemporary international scene seemed to favour such a policy. Russia had maintained an attitude of benevolent neutrality towards Prussia during the wars for German unification. Prussia had shown its gratitude while the Franco-Prussian War was still in progress and had used its influence to see that Russia was granted the right of free navigation on the Black Sea at the conference which led to the signing of the Treaty of London in 1871. Count Julius Andrássy, the Hungarian Foreign Minister of Austria-Hungary, advocated a policy of friendship with Germany and was backed in this by both his own sovereign and Bismarck. A meeting of the emperors of Russia, Austria, and Germany in Berlin in September 1872 was a preliminary to negotiations leading to a consultative pact known as the "Alliance of Three Emperors".

This was signed in 1873 and provided for mutual consultations in the event of attack by a third state. When three years later, alarmed by French armaments, Bismarck thought it necessary to warn France in a newspaper article entitled "War in Sight?", French diplomatic efforts were successful in prevailing upon Britain and Russia to make representations in Berlin to save the peace. Both Britain and Russia were under the misapprehension that Germany was planning a preventive war against France. Bismarck saw in this incident unmistakable confirmation that these two powers at the extremes of Europe were no longer, in contrast to 1870, prepared to stand by and see Germany augment her power at the expense of France. This only served to strengthen him in his conviction that any threat to European peace must automatically be disadvantageous to affect Germany's position in Europe.

Russia claimed to have saved the peace in 1875. Now she brought pressure to bear on Germany to give unreserved support to her Balkan claims over Turkey. Bismarck was not prepared to cooperate, so that Russo-German relations were bound to cool. The pan-Slav movement in Russia was also unfavourable to a Russo-German rapprochement because it saw in Austria, with its close links with the *Reich*, one of the biggest obstacles in the way of Russian expansion in the Balkans. When Russia attacked Turkey in 1877 and pressed forward as far as the gates of Constantinople, Bismarck was faced with the prospect of allowing Austria to draw him into a war with Russia. Austria, like England, could not countenance an extension of Russian power at the expense of Turkey without seriously jeopardising her own existence. The international respect enjoyed by the chancellor and the trust placed in him as an "honest broker" was demonstrated by his ability to assemble all the powers concerned in the eastern question at the Congress of Berlin (1878), under his own presidency, to seek a compromise agreeable to the conflicting interests. This could only take place at Russia's expense because England, on account of her own position in the Mediterranean, was interested in the continued existence of a weak Turkish empire, and because Austria rejected any decisive increase in Russian influence in the Balkans. Russia felt that Prince Bismarck had played her false, and that the outcome of the Berlin Congress had cheated her of the fruits of victory; after all, Bismarck did confirm England in the possession of Cyprus, left Macedonia in Turkish possession and thus robbed Russia of her coveted access to the Aegean Sea via Bulgaria. Montenegro, Serbia, and Rumania were declared independent; Bosnia and Herzegovina were placed under the administration of Austria-Hungary. Russia received Bessarabia as far as the Danube delta and Kars, Ardahan, and the free port of Batum in Asia. A much reduced Bulgaria was declared an autonomous but tributary state under Turkey. Against Russian wishes the Bulgarian national assembly elected Prince Alexander of Battenberg of the House of Hesse-Darmstadt to the Bulgarian throne. All that the Congress of Berlin brought Germany was a considerable deterioration in Russo-German relations. The political situation of the *Reich* abroad had worsened, particularly as international respect for France had increased.

From this time on Bismarck's foreign policy was dictated by the thought that a Franco-Russian entente was not out of the question. For this reason he was anxious, in spite of Russian reserve, to "prevent connections being entirely severed with Petersburg". On the other hand, he also sought an alliance with one of the other great powers in Europe. Of the five European powers Austria-Hungary was the only state which came into question as a partner, since England was unwilling to renounce its policy of "splendid isolation". A change had taken place in Austro-German relations. The vanquished nation of 1866 was now in a position to dictate the terms of an alliance with the *Reich:* Austria was only prepared to enter into a defensive alliance against Russia and her allies. Bismarck had to agree to these conditions in order to prevent Germany being isolated (1879). Another consequence was the empire's entanglement in Austria's Balkan policies. In the event of French aggression against Germany Austria merely engaged to observe benevolent neutrality.

This two-power alliance was converted into the Triple Alliance by the admission of Italy. But even this coalition was hampered from the outset by Italian mistrust of Austria, since regions of Italy were still under the dominion of the dual monarchy. For this reason Italy had first sought to draw closer to France. But when France established a protectorate over Tunis in 1881, an area which Italy had hoped to acquire, it threw in its lot with the central European camp (1882). He had to admit failure here, not only because of the English policy of united aggression by France and Russia. Italy insisted on the inclusion of the one reservation that it could not be called upon to go to war with England. Rumania also adhered to the Triple Alliance by a secret treaty in 1883.

Bismarck's desire was to woo England into an alliance. Although he had to admit failure here, not only because of the English policy of "splendid isolation" but also because of England's misgivings about the internal stability of the Austro-Hungarian state, Bismarck avoided

212

any step that could prove detrimental to Germany's relations with England. Only late in the day did he yield to the pressure of German business and trading circles and acquire colonies for the empire. In 1884 he declared the south-west African concession of A. Lüderitz, a merchant of Bremen, a protectorate of the German empire. This measure was the basis of German South-West Africa, the only colony at all suited to German settlement. At roughly the same time Togoland and the Cameroons were proclaimed German protectorates. Later the *Reich* acquired German East Africa and some islands in the Pacific.

Bismarck's relations with Russia were determined by the same sort of considerations as were decisive in the case of England. His main concern was to avoid even the slightest suspicion of anti-Russian tendencies. Even the Three Emperors' League was revived in 1881, although it had to be treated with the greatest secrecy in Russia on account of the pan-Slavists. However, the Balkan rivalries between Austria-Hungary and Russia made the chances of harmonious relations between the three powers look extremely remote. Bismarck therefore concluded a secret neutrality pact with Russia, whereby both powers engaged to observe benevolent neutrality if either of the two signatories were attacked by a third state (the so-called Reinsurance Treaty). This gave security to Germany against possible French aggression and to Russia in the event of attack by England. Anglo-Russian relations were strained at the time because of their conflicting colonial interests. However, the supplementary protocol allowing occupation of the Dardanelles by Russia was in contradiction to the Mediterranean agreements made under Bismarck's auspices with the intention of preserving Turkey's existence.

Bismarck was convinced that his policy of alliances prevented a war which could threaten his life's work. In his opinion direct danger of war could only arise from France, which had been isolated in Europe since 1887. This led him to regard peace as assured on the one hand and the treaty with Russia as an absolute necessity on the other. He regarded the imposing military might of the German empire, to which he had given every financial support while it was being built up, as a means of raising Germany's value as an ally and as a deterrent to would-be aggressors. He had always insisted that the military should acknowledge the primacy of the political considerations. The best guarantee of this he saw precisely in the perfect understanding existing between him and von Moltke, the Chief of General Staff. The position which he allotted the empire among the five great European powers was determined by purely continental considerations and was in no sense dictated by hope of advantage on the world political scene. Bismarck had also dissociated himself completely from the widespread view abroad that Germany "had to follow the Napoleonic lead, if she wanted to be, if not the arbitrator, at least the schoolmaster in Europe". Till the end his model as a statesman remained Metternich. Like him Bismarck, too, was opposed to any policy which tried to break with the old established order or which violated the legitimate rights of other nations in the crudest way. Even in success he never lost his sense of proportion. This was one of the most important reasons not only for the international respect he himself enjoyed but also for the European position of Germany, which was tolerated and respected as an influence for peace in Central Europe.

Problematic Domestic Policy

Bismarck had given the German empire a constitution which incorporated many democratic features. For all this, it was nothing more than a skilful attempt to merge the new democratic ideas with the claims of the emperor, as advanced by his trusted chancellor, to independent leadership of the state, without actually founding a new democracy. There were, it is true, political parties and a national assembly, the *Reichstag*, elected according to democratic principles and composed of members of these parties. But the *Reichstag* had no influence whatsoever on the formation of the government. Never could one of the parties alone expect to carry the full responsibility of government. Certainly the elections and their results reflected the will of the people but neither the emperor nor his chancellor was compelled to respect the will of the majority so long as the chancellor was able to find varying majorities to carry his legislative measures. On the other hand, the chancellor was in no way dependent on the division of power in the *Reichstag*.

At first, Bismarck found his main support in the National Liberals, the representatives for the most part of the middle class. They did not see eye to eye in every respect with the Bismarckian conception of the *Reich*—it was too federalist and authoritarian for their liking—but still in many points of practical day-to-day politics National Liberalism had much in common with many of Bismarck's ideas. This agreement extended to both economic and politico-cultural matters. As early as 1869 complete freedom of enterprise, guaranteed by the commercial code of the North German Federation, had been granted, thus satisfying

214

Liberalism's main economic demand. Free trade, too, which was practised throughout a large market since the foundation of the new empire, was at first in the interest of the German entrepreneurs. Thus with the help of his party the chancellor succeeded in getting through the *Reichstag* a whole mass of important legislation which helped to unify the *Reich*. The party's readiness for compromise made it possible for the annual grants of military credits urged by the English-orientated liberals to be converted into a "Septennate" (1874), which meant that the military grant only came up for consideration by the *Reichstag* once in every seven years. He was divided from the Conservatives, the representatives of his own class, by their narrow-minded, traditional Prussian way of thinking. The Guelph, Polish, Danish, and Alsatian delegates, too, were his sworn opponents. They worked hand in hand with two parties which often met Bismarck's measures with the most determined opposition, the Centre and the Social Democrats.

Catholic delegates had joined forces for the first time in the Frankfurt Diet. They called themselves the Centre after the position they occupied in the diet. The most important objective of their first political programme was the creation of Greater Germany; in the domestic field they showed a strong inclination towards federalism. The party was markedly confessional in character. The 56 Catholic *Reichstag* delegates of the year 1871 came for the most part from the west of the empire. The party's main concern in the diet was the protection of ecclesiastical institutions against the power pretensions of the state.

Bismarck did not think the sovereign rights of the state were guaranteed in the ecclesiastical sphere as fully as they should be. His opinion here was the result of purely political and not religious considerations, even if it is true that as a Lutheran he did not understand the Catholic concept of the nature of the state and its position within the terrestrial order established by God. For him the dogma of papal infallibility in matters of faith and morals, defined in 1870, represented a curtailment of the authority of the state and a threat to his work.

The conflict between Bismarck and the Church arose when the latter placed a ban on all Old Catholic teachers, who refused to accept the dogma of papal infallibility, forbidding them to impart religious instruction. The teachers affected countered by declaring they were the servants of the state and therefore not subject to ecclesiastical jurisdiction.

Many Liberals would have welcomed the foundation in Germany of a national Church independent of Rome and thought they perceived the beginnings of such a movement in the ranks of the Old Catholics. The Old Catholics therefore enjoyed the special patronage of the state.

In his struggle with the Catholic Church, Bismarck joined forces with liberalism, as represented in the National Liberal party. Liberalism, as the heir of the Enlightenment, regarded the influence of the Church as an obstacle in the way of cultural progress and hoped to see it finally broken. One of its adherents therefore dubbed Bismarck's struggle the *Kulturkampf*, the conflict of cultures. Bismarck himself did not share these views. And most active Protestants considered the *Kulturkampf* a mistake. The laws passed in the *Reichstag* and the individual states presented German Catholics with many problems of conscience. Diplomatic relations between the Vatican and Prussia were broken off. The number of seats held by the Centre Party rose to 93, a sure sign that Bismarck's ecclesiastical policy was encountering strong opposition. In spite of the state use of force against the clergy, the Catholic population of the *Reich* remained true to the Church. A spiritual power could not be broken by a state authority which recognised the limitations imposed on a constitutional state.

The *Kulturkampf* also explains why a large proportion of the Catholic population regarded the Prussian-dominated *Reich*, long after the dust of battle had settled, in a light that was perfectly intelligible from the viewpoint of this struggle with the state, but which was characterised by a certain one-sidedness. This attitude made it difficult for many Catholics to feel more than a cool loyalty towards the *Reich*.

The realisation that he had embarked upon a mistaken political course, together with other considerations dictated by his *Realpolitik*, led Bismarck to annul the laws of 1873/74 one by one. Civil marriage, civil registration of births and deaths, the law providing for state inspection of schools, the expulsion of the Jesuits, and the "Pulpit Paragraph", which forbade clerics to make declarations of a political nature from the pulpit, were retained.

Bismarck's economic legislation had followed the lines of the free trade doctrine championed by the Liberals since the foundation of the North German Federation. The Conservatives also lent their support to these measures in order to gain an outlet for Germany's excess grain. However, the changes which had taken place in world trade and communications, the rapid industrialisation of Germany, and the growth in her population, had a detrimental effect on agriculture and the iron and steel industry. From 1878 onwards German agriculture was no longer able to meet market needs. Cheap grain poured into Germany from Argentina, America, and Russia. English iron products were cheaper than their German counterparts and flooded the German market after the last tariffs on iron had been annulled in 1877. The doctrine of free trade now began to come up against strong criticism. The large landowners of the east and some branches of industry pressed for the introduction of protective tariffs, whereas the Liberals clung to their free trade teaching. Bismarck successfully found a majority in the *Reichstag* for a new customs tariff. His supporters here were the Conservatives and his erstwhile enemy, the Centre. This protectionist legislation came into force in 1879. Grain and cattle, iron and wood were to be subject to import duties in the future. These measures certainly caused a rise in prices at the time, but wages did not follow suit.

The reasons for Bismarck's break with the Liberals, with whom he had cooperated so long, lay in the financial insecurity of the empire and in his efforts to win for his state the support of the Conservatives, the former governing classes. According to the constitution the *Reich* had no sources of income of its own; it was a mere "boarder of the federal states". The customs dues now gave it financial independence. Bismarck believed that for the good of the *Reich* he was justified in using the parties in this way to obtain his political ends. In 1862 Ferdinand Lassalle, the son of a Breslau merchant, had come into political prominence with a programme of social reform. In his view the state not only had the duty of protecting the freedom and property of the individual but was bound to see that all shared in its benefits, i.e. to find a solution for the social problem. Lassalle differed from Marx in holding that the state could win its working classes by granting them universal and equal suffrage, if at the same time it took care that the workers were given a share in the profits of capitalism. This latter provision could only be realised by the formation of productive associations or collective worker-undertakings; the necessary credits were to be placed at their disposal by the state. Lassalle did not lay such emphasis on the constitutional form of the state as did Marx, who was a republican on principle.

In 1863 Lassalle founded the "Universal German Worker's Union", which only had some 5000 members at first and two seats in the North German parliament. The moment for a "social monarchy" seemed to have arrived when Bismarck and Lassalle met for personal talks about the possibility of dethroning the middle-class liberal majority in the Prussian diet by granting universal suffrage. But Lassalle's death in a duel put an end to any hope of collaboration.

In 1864 the "First International" was formed in London. Its aim was the implementation of the demands of the proletariat in all countries and by any means. Karl Marx played an important part in drafting its statutes. Its effectiveness was, however, diminished by conflicts

217

within the "General Council" about the line to be followed. Not until the congress at Basle in 1876 did Marx's conceptions of communism gain the upper hand. The "First International" was dissolved just two years later at a congress in Philadelphia, U.S.A.

William Liebknecht, who had taken part in the 1848 rising in Baden and then fled to England, propagated Marx's ideas in Germany. His chief collaborator here was August Bebel, a turner. Together they founded the Social Democratic Party. The first congress was held at Eisenach (1869). It was to prove of decisive importance that in the Gotha Programme (1875), on the basis of which the Universal German Workers' Union and the Social Democrats merged, "orthodox" Marxist teaching won the day over Lassalle's state socialism. Nevertheless, the Gotha Programme also incorporated a number of proposals for state reform which were tantamount to a democratic remodelling of the constitution.

In 1871 the Social Democrats held two seats in the *Reichstag*, in 1877 twelve. Bismarck saw a threat to the *Reich* in this party because of its internationalism and its opposition to the monarchy, and wanted to prohibit its press. But middle-class liberalism at first remained true to its principles and voted against the measure.

Two attempts on the life of Emperor William I caused the tide to turn in Bismarck's favour. Exceptional legislation recalling the Carlsbad Decrees of 1819 was accordingly passed by a Conservative-Liberal majority, although there was absolutely no evidence to show that the Social Democrats had been behind the assassination attempts. All associations which aimed "at the subversion of the existing state or social order on account of social-democratic, socialist or communist tendencies" were dissolved, their members threatened with banishment, and its press banned, though it still remained possible for social democrats to stand for election.

In 1887 the Social Democratic Party received three quarters of a million, and in 1890 as many as one million votes. The Gotha Programme had manifested a real, if qualified, will to cooperate with the existing state order; the Erfurt Programme of 1891 no longer mentioned the state. The German working-class movement had turned its back on the national state. Even the Bismarckian social legislation which was intended to win the working class was powerless to change this. In contrast to politicians in England, Bismarck failed to recognise that the social problem was no mere financial one. It was far more a question of how to integrate the proletariat sensibly in the intellectual, economic and political life of the existing state, while at the same time protecting the freedom of the individual.

Even as early as the time when he was Minister President of Prussia, Bismarck had thought about improving the often insecure lot of the worker. As imperial chancellor he considered it in the interest of the state to do something for the physical well-being of the worker. An imperial directive of 17 November, 1881, announced a string of laws "to provide the needy with greater security and a more extensive share of the assistance which is their due". The social legislation of the following years—insurance against sickness (1883), accidents (1884), and old age and disability (1889)—gave Germany the lead in this field but did not reconcile the working class to the Bismarckian state.

The Fall of Bismarck

On 9 March 1888 William I, the emperor whom Bismarck had served for practically the whole of his reign, died. Undoubtedly there had been many an occasion when he had not shared his chancellor's opinions, but he had in the end always followed the advice of the more experienced Bismarck. He was succeeded by his son Frederick, a man already dying of a fatal disease of the throat. His sympathies were on the side of the liberal middle class so that he had on a number of occasions opposed Bismarck. Still, he had had a considerable share in getting Bismarck's political ideas realised both in 1866 and at the foundation of the empire. His death, 100 days after ascending the throne, precluded all possibility of putting his liberal political views into action. His successor was William II, a man of 29 years of age. In the course of one year the throne passed from grandfather to grandson. An entire generation which was acquainted at first hand with the numerous unsolved problems of the 1871 period was thus excluded at a stroke from taking a responsible part in the direction of the country.

Bismarck greeted the young emperor with unconcealed scepticism. He was himself perfectly well aware that all was not as it should be in the *Reich*. In spite of the recently signed Reinsurance Treaty, he had not got rid of his "coalition nightmare". His social legislation, generous as it was in the context of the day, had not succeeded in winning the working class for the *Reich*. The young emperor, who liked to think of himself as the "roi des gueux" (king of beggars), wanted to see the protection of the worker extended by a ban on Sunday work. Bismarck called this "sentimental humanitarian claptrap" and was determined to crush the Social Democrats by force, to dissolve the *Reichstag* and, if need be, to govern without any parliamentary support whatsoever. William II, in contrast, demanded the lifting of the ban on the Social Democrats at home and, as an act of friendship to Austria, the non-renewal of the Reinsurance Treaty abroad. This amounted to more than a mere withdrawal of the imperial confidence; it called into question the aged chancellor's entire domestic and foreign policy. On the afternoon of the same day on which the Russian ambassador Shuvalov had talked with Bismarck about extending the Reinsurance Treaty, the chancellor informed the council of ministers that he had submitted his resignation. The emperor had urged this step upon him. He was empowered to do this by the constitution, which stipulated that the chancellor must enjoy the confidence of his sovereign. Bismarck became in this way the victim of his own constitution. He worded his resignation in such a way as to lay the blame squarely on the emperor's shoulders if his lifework should be brought to nothing. On 20 March, 1890, his political career in a responsible position came to end. He sullenly retired to Friedrichsruh in the Saxon Forest near Hamburg. There he died on 10 July 1898. His tomb bears the epitaph he had himself devised: "A Loyal German Servant of Emperor William I".

Bismarck's dismissal by the new emperor marked the end of an epoch in the evolution of the German *Reich*. For close on thirty years Prince Bismarck had been the sole arbiter of Germany's entire domestic and foreign policy. He had been the architect of German unity realised in a league of princes under Prussian leadership and with the exclusion of Austria. An ingenious system of alliances had gained external security for the new great power. The unification achieved did not measure up to the expectations entertained in 1848, but the nation resigned itself to this because the vigorous upward surge in the political and economic spheres did conceal the numerous defects in the empire's structure. These only became obvious from time to time on the home political front, and did not represent a direct threat to Bismarck's work. Certainly he was always able to find a majority for his political measures, which accorded with his idea of the responsibility he bore towards both *Reich* and *Kaiser*. He was, in any case, more than a match for parliament and the parties, and often used them in a way which only served to lower them in the eyes of the people. His *Junker* conservatism and Prussian monarchism prevented him from seeing that the German people were willing to share responsibility in the state, a willingness which had already led to a progressive democratisation of political life in all west European countries. He was only prepared to grant parliament the function of seeing that power was not usurped by one man; it was not to develop initiative.

That explained why the men who were at first resolved to accept their share of responsibility withdrew from politics because they were denied any voice in the government of the state. In foreign politics Bismarck had much in common with his much admired ideal, Metternich. Both successfully safeguarded their political creations from war and its ensuing dangers by steering a well-balanced political course. They therefore bestowed a long period of peace on Europe, indisputably one important outcome of their cool and skilled diplomacy. But both lacked the insight to perceive the broad pioneering trends at work on the slopes below the rarified heights of diplomacy. Metternich understimated the liberal and national movement; Bismarck did not grasp that the economic forces and social concepts active at the close of the century would also be able to determine the direction to be taken by the entire policy of the state. He kept to the beaten track of traditional absolutist politics, which had not yet taken into consideration the dynamic element represented by the economy. His conviction that Germany was "satiated" and therefore a factor for European stability won for his foreign policy world-wide trust, but at the same time showed its limitations when this conviction no longer proved defensible. Although Germany's economic development had already begun to take on world-wide dimensions and seek new possibilities for development, his policy could easily come into conflict with powers which, while willing to aquiesce in Germany's position as the strongest power on the Continent, would resist German imperialism.

Like many great statesmen before him, Bismarck loved power. During the struggle for Prussian supremacy in Germany he had often misused it and employed it to bend the law to his own will. But he was also well aware of the limitations of power and did not believe that it alone could achieve everything. The sensible moderation of the peace treaty of 1866, his policy of safeguarding the peace after 1871, and many a volte-face in domestic politics show that he did not want unrestrained power for its own sake but merely regarded it as a tool.

Chapter Nineteen

SOCIETY, THE ECONOMY, SCHOLARSHIP AND SCIENCE, AND THE ARTS IN GERMANY DURING THE SECOND HALF OF THE NINETEENTH CENTURY

Social Changes

It was not without reason that Bismarck's peers in Prussia and the other states of the *Reich* had offered the most concerted and prolonged resistance to the policy of German unification under Prussian leadership. After all, ever since the days of the Prussian reforms which had prepared and made possible the wars of liberation from the Napoleonic yoke, the middle classes had tried, in the course of their struggle for national unity and a constitution, to curtail the social and political privileges of the nobility. The 1848 revolution was thwarted in Germany mainly because officialdom and the officer corps, both drawn from the aristocracy, resisted it to a man. But the rise in the economic prosperity of the middle classes after 1850 had already served to reduce the political influence of the nobility as a consequence of the strength of the Liberal party in the parliaments of the various states. It was inevitable that the influence of the economically up-and-coming middle classes would increase as a result of the enlarged marketing possibilities offered by the political union. Unlike their English counterparts, the members of the German nobility had hardly participated in the industrialisation that was sweeping the country. In keeping with long-standing tradition they still looked upon their large landed properties as the economic foundation of their position in society. Here was another ground of discontent: the yield of their estates fluctuated considerably and was dependent, especially in east Prussia, on the conditions obtaining in the world market, as a direct consequence of the economic policy of the Liberals. This could deprive them of the basis of their existence.

All this caused them to be extremely reserved in their attitude to Bismarck's policies. Only after Bismarck's break with the Liberals, his protectionist legislation, and his campaign against the Social Democrats, and finally after the inauguration of William II's political system, did the nobility become reconciled to the new empire. This was rendered all the easier for them since in Germany there was no attempt to assail their privileged position. On the contrary, this was further accentuated by the favoured treatment accorded them in the army, navy, diplomatic service and higher offices of state administration. The nobility could take comfort from the certainty that a definite percentage of the leading positions in these fields were reserved for them as their special privilege. In Prussia the "Three-Class" electoral system buttressed the privileged position of the nobility still further.

The middle class now became the real promoter of Germany's economic development, and the economy in its turn opened the door to decisive positions in many spheres of state, society and culture. The middle class very soon split into a purely property-owning and a decidedly intellectual, cultural group, a division which at first entailed no distinction in social respect and standing. Indeed each of them was fully conscious of its dependence on the other. Throughout the whole of the nineteenth century the conception was kept alive that progress in technology and economics was synonymous with progress in science and culture.

After the emancipation of the Jews at the beginning of the 19th century, German Jews gained access more readily to the society of the propertied middle class than to the "academic" cultural middle class with its consciousness of tradition. For this reason, and because of the legislation of the "Christian state", civil service positions were at first not open to Jews. But the situation was different after 1869. In the newly founded empire Jewish lawyers, physicians and scientists were often prominent in university life as well.

The craftsmen and small farmers felt themselves most menaced by industrialisation. A number of them had to give up their former calling and seek a new livelihood in industry. By uniting in cooperatives and associations numerous branches of the handicrafts and of the peasant community with medium-sized farms were able to adapt to the changing circumstances and maintain a "middle-class" standard of living.

The dispossessed craftsmen and peasants moved into industry and formed the industry proletariat in Germany as in all other industrial states. Since the wage was nothing but the expression of the marketable value of their capacity for work, it stood in no relationship to the worker's needs as a human being or as the family bread-winner. The size of the wage was dependent on fluctuations in the market, and its regularity on the worker's willingness and capacity for work. The employment of female and child labour was for this reason perfectly

MAX LIEBERMANN

Die Netzflickerinnen
Les ravaudeuses de filets
Women Mending Fishing Nets
Las remendadoras de redes
Remendeiras de rêdes

1887—1889. Kunsthalle, Hamburg

normal. The greater the number of children the larger the family income. The position of the proletariat in Germany remained grim in spite of the Bismarckian social legislation.

With the advance of industrialisation the number of women employed in industry also increased. This destroyed the original unity of family, home and work much more than the factory work of the husband. By 1899 the number of married women permanently engaged in factory work had risen to some 250,000 and the number continued to grow year by year until the beginning of the Great War. This meant that entirely new problems arose for women and their position in society. Conservative circles tried to stem this development by allowing women to enter only those employments "suitable" for them. However, as early as 1865 the "Universal German Women's League" had demanded the admission of women to the academic professions. But women were not allowed to study at the universities until 1891. In 1896 the first doctorate examinations for women were held. In 1908 Prussia was the first German state to approve grammar school education for girls with a state leaving examination (Abitur) at the end. In keeping with the situation peculiar to Germany, the efforts of the German feminist movement were directed less towards political than towards social equality with men. Political equality was only granted them by the "Weimar Constitution" in 1919.

Towards the end of the 19th century a development entirely peculiar to Germany was the rise of the youth movement. In 1898 pupils of the Berlin-Steglitz Gymnasium founded the "Wandervogel". This association of young people was in the first place a protest against the middle-class civilisation which had grown up in the course of the second half of the 19th century under the influence of the economic prosperity and the widespread materialistic, non-religious *Weltanschauung*. It was also a fight for those elements of the cultural legacy not reducible to rational terms. German youth wanted to develop a new and more genuine way of life based on the experience of comradeship, unexplored nature, carefree rambling, and the beauty of old traditions in folk drama, song, and dance.

This movement soon spread to the rest of Europe. International youth rallies became more common. There was an attempt to give new impetus to international understanding inspired by the spirit of youthful comradeship and far removed from the political questions of the day. Under the influence of the *Jugendbewegung* a new appreciation of the intrinsic value of youth was also awakened in the older generation, which bore fruit especially in the general movement for school reform.

225

One year before the outbreak of the First World War the various German youth organisations combined to form the "Free German Youth", whose aim it was "to mould their lives on self-determination, personal responsibility, and inner sincerity".

The Economy

Since the 1850's Germany had been passing through a process of conversion from an agricultural country into an industrial state. The industrial revolution had rapidly swept through the whole of Germany and begun to refashion people's lives. The basis of this speedy industrial development was coal, the energy source in which Germany was the wealthiest country in Europe. First the heavy industries grew up around the coal fields. By the end of the century Germany had outstripped England in steel production although she had only small iron ore deposits of her own. Still more impressive was the foundation and extension of the chemical industry: by the outbreak of the First World War Germany was the biggest producer in the world. In spite of the reduction in land under cultivation, agricultural production increased to an extent never before known as a result of the use of artificial manures. The following table gives an idea of the rise in production in important basic branches of industry and agriculture:

Anthracite and lignite
| 1870 | 34 | mill. metric tons | 1913 | 277 | mill. metric tons |

Pig iron
| 1870 | 1.391 | mill. metric tons | 1913 | 16.7 | mill. metric tons |

Rye
| 1870 | 5.8 | mill. metric tons | 1913 | 10 | mill. metric tons |

Wheat
| 1870 | 2.4 | mill. metric tons | 1913 | 4.03 | mill. metric tons |

Barley
| 1870 | 2.2 | mill. metric tons | 1913 | 3.03 | mill. metric tons |

Oats
| 1870 | 4.3 | mill. metric tons | 1913 | 8.6 | mill. metric tons |

Germany's foreign trade (exports and imports) amounted to 5,726 million marks in 1880. It had risen to 7,473 million in 1890, to 10,377 million in 1900, and had reached 20,867 million marks in 1913.

The German population, which totalled 40 million in 1870, numbered 66 million in 1913.

Clearly these figures reflect an economic expansion unparalleled in German history. They are the mathematical expression not only of a strong will to work and of undiminished creativeness but also of astonishing advances in scientific research and a no less remarkable capacity to convert the results of this research into ever more refined industrial techniques. The significance of this close collaboration between research and technology was to be most clearly seen in medicine. If chemical knowledge and the chemical industries had not gone from strength to strength, medical science could not have registered such successes in the field of healing. The brilliant discovery of X-rays by the physicist Wilhelm Conrad von Röntgen (1845—1923) was soon to prove one of medicine's greatest aids.

The dynamo invented by Werner von Siemens opened up a source of energy of enormous potentiality, while the light internal combustion engine built by the two mechanical engineers Daimler and Benz in 1885 gave the impetus to automobile production. In the years 1898—1900 Graf Zeppelin, continuing where his French predecessors had left off, began experimenting in an attempt to conquer the air for man, too. Shortly before the outbreak of the First World War he had achieved a certain measure of success with his rigid airships.

The national economy seemed to be determining the fate of man more and more. In 1870 there were eight towns in Germany with more than 100,000 inhabitants; in 1913 there were forty-eight, while Berlin's population had passed the million mark. The Ruhr—formerly an agricultural region—became the industrial centre of the *Reich*. The small and medium-sized factory, where the owner could easily supervise production personally, became an anonymous giant concern. German industry organised, as in other countries, in cartels, syndicates and combines. Whereas in 1882 there were only 127 concerns employing more than a 1000 hands, there were 255 by 1895.

In spite of the mark "Made in Germany" which England had insisted on, German goods continued to conquer the world market. Contrary to the English intentions these words became a guarantee of quality.

Scholarship and Science

In German philosophy the reaction against idealism continued for the time being. The widespread outlook was one rejecting all metaphysical speculation. Monism became the *Weltanschauung* favoured by the cultured and learned. Ernst Haeckel (1834—1919), its main advocate, was not far from atheistic materialism. In his view all reality is essentially one. The earth and man are but tiny specks of dust within a mighty cosmos. "Die Welträtsel" (1890, "The Riddle of the Universe"), his most widely read work, puts forward the view that mind cannot exist without matter, or matter without mind.

Haeckel believed that his thesis that God and the world are identical, made the great concept of a personal God, human freedom and the immortality of the soul superfluous, and substituted for them a religious view bounded by this world. However, very often philosophers were no longer philosophising but merely pursuing the history of philosophy or ideas (Wilhelm Dilthey, 1833—1911), or epistemology. This latter was raised to a universal methodology of all scientific thought in the Marburg School of Neo-Kantianism (H. Cohen, 1842—1918) and in the Heidelberg or South-West German School with its sharp distinction between the physical sciences and historical and social studies (H. Richert, 1863—1930). A later offshoot of the Heidelberg School was the "phenomenological" axiology of M. Scheler (1874—1928); but its most noteworthy thinker and scholar was the sociologist Max Weber (1864—1924). Weber's herald was Karl Jaspers (b. 1883) who has since achieved fame as an existentialist. Weber carefully distinguished between the amoral and objectively scientific establishment of facts and causes, on the one hand, and the rationally unjustifiable subjective value judgments, on the other. He differentiated distinctly between the *Verantwortungsethik* (responsibility ethics) of the politician who must be prepared to put up with "lesser evils" for the sake of avoiding larger-scale ones, and the *Gesinnungsethik* (conviction ethics) of the uncompromising "mystic".

Historical and social studies developed in the shadow of the natural sciences. Procedures were borrowed and adapted from the natural sciences where this was feasible (word statistics, sociological and psychological literary analysis). In particular, historical science compared the facts established by a critical examination of the sources in order to discover parallels ("laws") in the historical process. It was very much under the influence of Auguste Comte (1798—1857), who coined the name "Positivism" for his new way of philosophising. This sought explanations in immanent causes and represented, according to him, the third and final stage (succeeding to the theological and metaphysical) in man's understanding of himself and the world. For Comte history was sociology, i.e. the science which deals with certain typical phenomena which can be observed to recur constantly in the social life of human beings.

History also conformed to the general tendency towards specialisation, so that now only certain periods of history and limited fields of study were treated by scholars thoroughly versed in them. But such historians were not able to free themselves completely from contemporary views when they got down to passing judgments on the events and figures of the past, even if this only manifested itself in the choice of the facts deemed worthy of note. Theodor Mommsen's "Roman History" (1854/55) was the work of a man full of democratic sentiments and with nothing but contempt for the senatorial patrician families of ancient Rome. Julius Ficker (1826—1902) presented the "Greater German" viewpoint in his book "Das deutsche Kaiserreich in seinen universalen und nationalen Beziehungen" (1861, "The German Empire in its Universal and National Relations"), whereas Heinrich von Sybel (1817—1896) assessed the German imperial policy of the Middle Ages from the "Little German" standpoint. Heinrich von Treitschke was, in Germany, the first of those historians who tried to turn the history of their own people to educational advantage. Although a Saxon by birth, he moved to Berlin because of his enthusiasm for Prussia and Bismarck. He wanted to awaken respect for the state and a pride in its achievements, power and greatness through the history of the German people, in order to strengthen the people's readiness to serve the *Vaterland* in disinterested loyalty. He achieved this end not only through his book "Deutsche Geschichte " (1879, "German History"), but even more by his inspiring lectures as a professor in Berlin. The generation of teachers he formed educated young people who saw the Bismarckian *Reich* as the most significant expression not only of the German spirit, but also of the objective (in the Hegelian sense). Social history advanced alongside political history. The Swiss historian Jakob Burckhardt from Basle brought "The Civilisation of the Renaissance in Italy" to life (1860). Heinrich Schliemann laid the foundations of Germany's later archaeological fame. In 1871 he began his excavations at the site of Hissarlik and soon uncovered the remains of ancient Troy. He also rediscovered Mycenae and Tyre. Between the years 1878 and 1881 Wilhelm Dörpfeld laid bare the ruins of Olympia.

An anti-materialistic reaction in philosophy accompanied by greater emphasis on the subconscious gave rise in an extremely problematic way to ideas which, in spite of their rejection by serious scientific scholarship, found increasing support in the political field. Although the real originators were not German, the pseudo-scientific character of the new theories won them a good reception in Germany. The origins of racialism are to be sought in France, especially in Comte de Gobineau's (1814—1882) book "Essai sur l'Inégalité des Races" (Essay on the Inequality of Human Races). The British-born political thinker Houston Stewart Chamberlain (1855—1927), Richard Wagner's son-in-law, popularised these views in his book "Die Grundlagen des 19. Jahrhunderts" (The Foundations of the 19th Century). In it he maintained that all the major cultural achievements are to be attributed to the higher races, and in particular to the Nordic, whose present-day representatives are the Germanic peoples. The human mind is determined by race (biological materialism). The highly gifted Nordic race is opposed to the Jews, who are quite simply inferior. Anti-Semitism, the natural offspring of this teaching in pseudo-scientific guise, was thus given a new lease of life. It had survived beneath the surface in Germany and had even played a role in the struggle against Bismarck because of his links with the Jewish banking-house of Bleichröder. Treitschke had supplied it then with his insane slogan: "The Jews are our misfortune". Both the Protestant Adolf Stöcker, cofounder of the *Evangelisch-Sozialer Kongress* (Evangelical Social Congress, 1890) and court and cathedral preacher in Berlin, and the Catholic Karl Lueger in Vienna, politician of the Austrian Christian Socialist Party, encouraged anti-Semitism for political and religious reasons in their opposition to liberalism; Schönerer, the great advocate of Pan-Germanism in Austria, used the pseudoscientific racialist foundation of anti-Semitism in his political fight. He also rejected Christianity as a Judeo-Semitic creation. Nevertheless, anti-Semitism did not gain decisive significance either in Germany or Austria.

The Arts

No great art was produced in Germany during the second half of the 19th century. The foundation of the *Reich* had left no noticeable effect anywhere in the entire realm of artistic production. Only C. F. Meyer (1825—1898), a Swiss, was influenced by it to write in German and not in French. However, apart from his novel "Huttens letzte Tage" (The Last Days of Ulrich von Hutten), there were no further points of contact in either his own works or those of his contemporaries. Independent of all political happenings, literary creation at first continued to follow the course which had been set when the second half of the century had opened. Many an individual achievement was noteworthy but the arts were no longer the arbiters of man's life. They satisfied rather the middle-class need for an idealisation of life which appealed to the senses (thus Spielhagen and Heyse in literature; Piloty, Mackart, and Achenbach in painting).

Painters could not remain completely indifferent to the more realistic, less "idealising" contemporary view of the world. They broke new ground never entered on before when they began to paint subjects from the world of industry and labour (Adolph Menzel, 1815—1905), and did not hesitate to present proletarian reality in all honesty and candour (Käthe Kollwitz, 1867—1945).

Yet this was a mere side current in the painting of the age. Impressionism played a far more decisive part in the content and form of artistic expression. Max Liebermann (1847—1935) with Max Slevogt (1868—1932) and Lovis Corinth (1858—1925) headed the German impressionistic school of painting. Liebermann's pictures are characterised not just by the influence of French impressionism but by their social message as well.

Naturalism in literature—its founders were Heinrich and Julius Hart, during the eighties; its leading representatives: Sudermann, Halbe, Liliencron, Gerhart Hauptmann (1862—1946)—sought new fields of expression far more in keeping with the spirit of the age. It must be admitted, though, that naturalism often represented nothing more than a feeble imitation of reality and held aloof from the spirit everywhere at work. Still it was not without significance because, like the youth movement, it brought home to the middle classes the shallowness and sham morality of their world. However, naturalism exhausted itself in criticism; it lacked the vitality to present an alternative compelling philosophy of life.

Music continued in the tradition of Beethoven. Thus Brahms (1833—1897) and Bruckner (1824—1896) were hardly touched by the spirit of the age. The restraint of Brahms, the north German, was in marked contrast to the vigorous, elemental character of Bruckner, the Austrian. Although Bruckner's debt to Wagner is unmistakable, he had much more in common with Bach in the religious inspiration of his music than with his model.

The age found its most powerful artistic expression in the "unified work of art" of Richard Wagner (1813—1883). No doubt opinions are still extremely divided on the subject of his dramatic and musical production, but it can hardly be denied that Wagnerian music and writing struck such an answering chord in his contemporaries because it offered his godless and materialistic age new gods and new myths. Although the question of man's salvation formed the background of all his endeavours, the answer he gave remained, in the last analysis, vague. In clothing the great problems of life in the language of mythology he failed to shake and transform men.

231

No one was more conscious of the artist's responsibility to his own age than Friedrich Nietzsche (1844—1900), the poet and philosopher. He was the declared enemy of all that could be called the spirit of his age: he rejected traditional religion, the national state, liberalism, philosophy, and artistic production up to and including Wagner. In this sense he overthrew all traditional values. Sincerity and honesty led him to declare quite openly as the final presupposition for the natural and historical sciences: "God is dead". The world is purposeless. He saw it as his duty to oppose his "master morality" to Christianity's "slave morality", his courageous, affirmative attitude to life and the earth to the belief in another world.

Chapter Twenty

GERMANY UNDER WILLIAM II

The Character of the New Emperor

The period between Bismarck's fall and World War I receives its name in German history books from Germany's third emperor, William II. This is unwarrantable in so far as William was by no stretch of the imagination the type of man to dominate and form his time. It was not he that moulded the age but the age which moulded him. In its vacillation between a tendency to yield and an overemphasis of power, between readiness for peace and sabre-rattling, between sentimental social impulses and a domineering impersonation of kingship by divine right, between idealism and realism, between romantic gush and an unfeeling cynicism, his reign was nothing if not the reflection of his time. William was extremely sensitive to the changing winds of opinion in Germany and registered them infallibly. Since in his self-overestimation he laid claim to being the leader of his people in everything, he often made the mistake of confusing the changing views of the day with his own political insight. Because he was himself inconsistent and his aims vague and irresolute, the political course he steered was often inconsistent and puzzling. Confident that he possessed a special instinctive feeling for politics he rarely hesitated to base national policy on his own conceptions. In the process he liked to lay the main stress on military power, since he was convinced that Germany was invincible on the field of battle. Whenever he thought it opportune and useful to his purpose, he would threaten the world with Germany's military might without ever seriously desiring war.

He prided himself in being the "people's emperor", and curried the favour of the masses. His speeches, therefore, aimed more at the popular touch than at politically responsible formulations. Wherever he went, wherever he made a public appearance, his main concern was to convey the impression of a ruler especially favoured by God. This meant that he had a ready ear for flattery. Whoever shared his views

233

enjoyed his confidence; if anyone dared to criticise he could count on the emperor's displeasure.

It was his conviction that both France and Russia were hostile to Germany. His relations with England were poisoned by his deep distrust. In spite of his outward display of self-assurance the feeling was never far from him that both he and his empire were threatened and imperilled from all sides. His reaction was to make provoking references to Germany's military might and continually to step up the armaments programme. The result was that Germany's neighbours began to look upon him and his country as a threat to peace. What Bismarck had prevented by his moderate policies and William II had always feared but as good as provoked by his clumsy political dealings, became a reality: alliances were formed against the heavily armed *Reich* which surpassed even Germany in military might.

Dangerous Tendencies

The remarkable economic advances which Germany had made since 1871, the world-wide respect which German science and scholarship enjoyed in many fields, and the empire's undisputed position as a great power in Europe caused those German voices to grow more audible and urgent with the passing of time which asked whether history had not reserved some special destiny for such a gifted people. This question appeared perfectly justified, especially against the background of England's historical development. Whereas the British nation could look back with satisfaction on centuries of steady growth in her power, her industry could count on more than ample commodity and outlet markets, and the British navy was the unchallenged lord of the seas, Germany's power was still confined to the European Continent even after national unification. Bismarck had aimed at reconciling Germany's neighbours to the existence of the *Reich* by giving them the feeling that Germany represented a threat to no one. This seemed far too unambitious a programme to a generation personally unacquainted with the laborious process which had been crowned by unification. The heady wine of victories won against militarily weaker opponents so intoxicated men's minds that they were blind to the difficulties which Germany would have to face if the European great powers were united against her. Men thought, in complete misunderstanding of the bases of Bismarck's policy as also of his words, that the policy of "iron and blood" could be pursued with a certain hope of success even if the

234

vital interests of other peoples were threatened. The dream of a "place in the sun" was no longer confined to the colonial possessions already acquired but aimed at genuine rivalry with England and France in the partition of the world. The frenzy aroused by imperialistic aspirations after world power befuddled not only the clear vision of level-headed leaders of the economy but blighted the pages of the scholarly works of numerous professors. The schools, too, all too easily became forcing-beds of a fervent and blind nationalism to which nothing appeared too hazardous or out of reach.

Three associations, relying for their support mainly on the middle classes, were hotbeds of these imperialistic and nationalistic tendencies: the "Pan-German League", founded in 1891 as a protest against the Heligoland-Zanzibar treaty with England, the "German Colonial Union", and the "German Navy League" (1898). It is true that their membership was never particularly high, but this did not prevent the "Pan-German League" in particular from sucessfully propagating its ideas by means of pamphlets and lectures by its supporters. The League's political objectives were the incorporation of all European Germans in the *Reich*, a dynamic and aggressive colonial and emigration policy, and the special protection by the empire of German traditions and way of life throughout the world. Over and above this they further aimed at fanning the flame of German territorial aggression and acquisitiveness in an effort to win the support of broad sections of the population for the *Weltpolitik* (world politics) of William and his responsible ministers.

Until well into the 1850s the attitude of the ordinary German to the army was negative, if not actually antipathetic. Military service was looked upon rather as a degradation of the free man than as a distinction. Public opinion began to change here as a result of the numerous victories in the field and the privileged social position accorded the officer. It became an honour to wear a uniform, and in time the "lieutenant of the reserve" held the key to middle-class respect and professional advancement. The soldier class was given the first place in the scale of values, the military mentality began to predominate.

This change was exploited to Germany's undoing by two men who succeeded in subordinating the *Reich's* essential political interests to military calculations: von Schlieffen and von Tirpitz. General Alfred Count von Schlieffen was appointed chief of the general staff in 1891 and entrusted with the task of elaborating a plan of campaign to be put into operation in the event of a war on two fronts with Russia and France. He was convinced that German military supremacy could make short work of France, on condition that the right flank of the German army were deployed in a large-scale enveloping movement which would encircle the enemy. Logically he was willing to infringe Belgian neutrality since his plan was otherwise unworkable. If the responsible statesmen in the *Reich* wanted to adopt this plan they would have to accept the political consequences and be prepared for England, one of the signatories to the 1831 Treaty of London which guaranteed Belgium's permanent neutrality, to take up arms against Germany. And yet not a single high-placed political voice was raised to oppose the general staff. When von Moltke succeeded Count von Schlieffen in his office in 1905, he took over the Schlieffen strategic plan. It did, in fact, form the basis of the German assault on France in 1914 and not only involved the breach of Belgian neutrality but exercised a decisive influence on political developments in the period immediately preceding the First World War.

Grand Admiral Alfred von Tirpitz (1849—1930) was the architect of the German navy, which was pivotal to William II's wishful thinking. William believed that the mere existence of a powerful navy would make it possible for him to realise his world political aspirations. Germans looked upon it as the symbol of their nation's importance in the world and as the proof of the *Reich's* equality with Great Britain. Tirpitz's own view was that the navy should make it clear to England that it would be a "risk" to attack Germany. Naval construction was stepped up yearly from 1898 onwards, so that in 1914 the German navy was the second largest after that of Great Britain. England's pride was wounded and she felt forced to increase armaments. In spite of repeated efforts on the part of the English to call a halt to the naval arms race, Germany's political leaders could not bring themselves to come to an agreement with England because of the pressure exerted on them by Tirpitz and the emperor. Here again it was the armed services that had the last word in deciding Germany's political course.

During World War I the German navy could do nothing to protect the colonies and took no active part in the struggle with England. While its military significance was almost negligible, it played an extremely important part in bringing about a deterioration in Anglo-German relations.

William II rightly sensed that one of the most important issues of the day was the solution of the social problem. The first thing he tackled, therefore, with his imperial chancellor Caprivi was the extension of the *Reich's* social legislation. Industrial courts were created to deal with disputes between employers and employees. They were intended to guarantee workers greater security in the event of industrial disputes. The coverage provided by state insurance against sickness and accident was widened in the workers' favour. The legislation concerning Sunday work, and female and child labour, and the measures to protect the worker's health met the main demands of the unions and the Social Democrats.

At the same time a new economic policy aimed at improving the state of German industry and raising the standard of living of the worker masses. Long-term commercial treaties, especially with other European states were intended to guarantee steady production to German industry and to give greater security to the worker in his job. As a reciprocal gesture Germany had to open her frontiers and lower some of her customs tariffs, especially those intended to protect German agriculture. This move, in its turn, promoted a policy of "cheaper bread" for the industrial masses.

The German farming community, especially in the east, resisted this policy. The "Farmer's Union" created an effective political mouthpiece in the Conservative Party. The farmers' threat to scuttle the emperor's naval plans was sufficient to get the customs reductions revoked. The half-hearted attempt to lead Germany back into the ranks of free-trading states thus came to nothing.

There can be no doubt that military considerations also contributed towards this development. Germany's access to the seven seas was extremely limited. In the event of war Germany would be thrown back almost entirely on her own agricultural resources. Intensive farming alone could lead to the increased production made necessary by the constant diminution in the area under cultivation caused by progressive industrialisation. German agriculture was able to meet this challenge with the help of that same industry and the application of scientific knowledge. But this also presupposed that agricultural prices were artificially maintained.

William II failed to win the support of the workers and the Social Democrats for his *Reich* and its foreign policy by his "cheap bread policy". This can be partially explained by the German Social Democratic Party's being more completely dominated by the Marxist dogma of world revolution and the collapse of the capitalist system. But it was also to be accounted for by William's own attitude to the Social Democratic Party. He was already disillusioned as early as 1894 because his policy of social concessions did not produce an immediate change in the political climate among the workers. He immediately began to advocate a campaign in defence of "religion, morality and sound order" against the parties of subversion, by which he meant the Social Democrats. He referred to their supporters in public speeches as *vaterlandslose Gesellen* (rootless good-for-nothings). When the emperor attempted to limit the constitutional rights of the Social Democratic Party in order thus to put a brake on the socialist campaign for a more equitable social order, the *Reichstag* refused to cooperate—which shows what progress the concept of a democratic, constitutional state had already made in the other parties, too. Still this does not alter the fact that the middle-class attitude to the Social Democratic Party, now the strongest party in the *Reichstag*, was extremely reserved. Since the government and middle classes were not prepared to recognise the importance of constitutional reform as a preliminary to thorough-going social reforms, all attempts to gain the support of the broad masses of the population for a policy of nationalist imperialism were doomed to failure.

Foreign Policy Under William II

A decisive factor in German foreign policy was her relations with Russia. The "era during which the alliance with Russia formed the gospel of Prussian politics" came to an end. Now German foreign policy was based on the conviction that an alliance with France would be of no value to Russia as long as the latter was unable to gain England's participation; but the United Kingdom would only be prepared for rapprochement with Russia if the tsar were to abandon his ambitions in Asia. The author of this diplomatic assessment was Friedrich von Holstein, the determined critic of Bismarck's foreign policy, director of the political department in the German foreign office and Germany's *Graue Eminenz* (grey Eminence). As he saw it, Germany should preserve freedom of action within the Triple Alliance and choose the opportune moment to come down on the side most favourable to German interests. This gave German foreign policy a very unstable character, which earned it the name "zigzag policy".

The Heligoland-Zanzibar treaty of 1890 had eliminated certain colonial differences with England. Germany approved the proclamation of the island of Zanzibar as a British protectorate in exchange for Heligoland. The mainland possessions of the Zanzibar sultanate were ceded to the *Reich* as German East Africa. In 1892 Russia concluded a military convention and in 1894 a formal treaty with France. Although both agreements were plainly directed against the *Reich*, the arbiters of German foreign policy were not disturbed by them and continued to believe that Germany could draw near to Russia again whenever necessary. An opportunity for a rapprochement seemed to be offered by the Sino-Japanese conflict. However, the unfriendly attitude Germany here adopted towards Japan, Russia's potential enemy in the Far East, produced exactly the opposite effect to that intended: instead of bringing about a Russo-German entente, it drove Japan into the arms of England. Germany entered the world political stage by protesting against the 1895 Peace of Shimonoseki, which concluded the Sino-Japanese war. The other world powers were inevitably puzzled by this intervention, especially as Germany had no interest of her own to protect in the Far East. Germany allowed herself to be drawn into the rivalries between Russia, China and Japan because she thought there was a need to assert her political importance as a great power before the whole world. The acquisition of Kiaochow Bay with its port, two years later, seemed to justify the Far Eastern adventure after the event, but it made an enemy of China and only aroused bewilderment in Japan.

Germany had hoped to make the Heligoland-Zanzibar treaty with England the point of departure for negotiations leading to an alliance, especially as Great Britain had been given the assurance that the *Reich* would "resist any Russian attempt to gain free passage through the Dardanelles". England still believed she could adhere to her policy of "splendid isolation". When, as a consequence of the Boer War, she was later brought to see that this policy was impracticable in the long run, she decided to make overtures to the *Reich*, notwithstanding William II's moral support of the Boers. However, these efforts were not from the beginning hamstrung by Germany's championship of the Boers, for which England showed understanding, since it was, she thought, the "natural sympathy for the weak against the strong". England's attitude to Turkey had changed since 1895. Lord Salisbury, the English Prime Minister, backed by his Colonial Secretary, Joseph Chamberlain, was toying with the idea of connecting the African colonies with India in a world empire. In this scheme the Near and Middle East were to form the connecting land-bridge. This would have meant the incorporation of Asiatic Turkey, Arabia, Mesopotamia, and Persia in the British empire. Austria-Hungary was to be compensated in the Balkans, Russia by the grant of free passage to the Mediterranean. Germany, however, was interested in the continued existence of Turkey for economic reasons. On a voyage to the East in 1898 William II assured 300 million Muslims that they could always count on him as their protector. One year later work began on the Baghdad Railway, financed by private German interests. The route from Berlin to Istanbul and Baghdad passed through the Balkans and affected areas within the British sphere of interest in the Near East.

In 1898, too, Germany had started on the great build-up of her navy. Thirty-four battleships were to be launched over a period of sixteen years.

In spite of this naval programme with its undoubtedly harmful effect on British prestige, the British Colonial Secretary, Joseph Chamberlain, reopened negotiations with Germany in 1898. His intention was to reach a general understanding as a step towards a closer working relation, which "would amount to England's joining the Triple Alliance". The negotiations dragged on for three years. England was from the outset unwilling to enter into formal treaty obligations; Germany could not shake off the suspicion that she was merely cast for the role of "England's sword on the Continent because of Anglo-Russian differences in eastern Asia, and expected to "fight England's battles in the Far East", a task for which her geographical position made her unfitted. Germany also feared that she would not be able to rely on effective help from Great Britain in a European war with Russia and France. On Holstein's advice the talks were discontinued, in the face of England's undisguised threat to seek a settlement with France and Russia if her overtures met with a rebuff. England did in fact enter into closer relations with France and Russia. Germany's isolation at the side of two weak allies, Austria-Hungary and Italy, had begun.

These developments led to a decided deterioration in Germany's diplomatic position. The first consequences of this were to be seen during the various European crises which preceded World War I. One year after the Anglo-French entente, Bülow, Chancellor since 1900, persuaded the emperor to put in an unexpected appearance at Tangier, and recognise the sultan as an independent ruler. This was certainly in keeping with the 1850 and 1880 treaties by which all the great powers

Central Europe before World War I

Central Europe after World War I

were accorded an equal voice in Morocco, but it was also clearly intended as a timely reminder to France, which was then seriously thinking of converting Morocco into a French protectorate.

In accordance with the treaties, the great powers assembled at Algeciras in 1906 to confer on a settlement of the Moroccan question. English fears that France and England would be isolated proved entirely unfounded: the other great powers, with the one exception of Austria, all came out against Germany. The principle of the "open door" was proclaimed, but never observed. Germany had suffered a decisive reverse in foreign policy.

A year later England and Russia were also able to come to an agreement about their colonial differences.

Relations between the *Reich* and the Turkish sultanate had grown ever closer as a result of the economic support accorded by Germany. In 1908 the precarious situation in Turkish domestic politics gave rise to the young Turk revolution, which was backed by the army. Austria-Hungary took advantage of Turkish weakness to annex Bosnia and Hercegovina in violation of the stipulations of the Berlin Congress. In so doing, the dual monarchy deprived Serbia of its access to the sea, interfered with Russia's Balkan plans, and placed a severe strain on Germany's relations with Turkey. Bülow nevertheless declared: "Our attitude to all questions concerning the Balkans is determined in the first place by the needs, interests, and wishes of Austria-Hungary". A mistaken conception of Austro-German solidarity thus involved Germany in the Balkan conflict of interests.

Since the armament costs were placing a severe strain on the resources of all the great powers, a peace conference was called at the instance of the tsar. It met at The Hague in 1899, and had as its main objective the limitation of armaments. Germany was reluctant to agree to such a reduction because of her "encircled" position in central Europe. The second Hague conference of 1907 also broke up without agreement on essential questions.

Britain made another move in the same direction in 1911. The Haldane mission to Berlin also hoped to obtain some reduction in armaments. Germany, however, demanded a declaration of neutrality from England in the event of war with France. England, for her part, desired some moderation in the German shipbuilding programme. Since Germany was only willing to make concessions if England first gave the coveted promise, the negotiations ended in a deadlock. When another trip of Haldane's to Berlin in 1912 also proved abortive, Great Britain transferred her Mediterranean fleet to the home waters of the North Sea. Nevertheless, England still continued to evade a formal treaty with France even at this stage.

In 1909 Bethmann-Hollweg replaced Bülow as imperial chancellor. He did not change his predecessor's course in foreign policy. In 1911 the French occupied Fez, the capital of Morocco. The chancellor induced the German emperor to dispatch the gunboat "Panther" to Agadir, where it accordingly appeared in the harbour. But a fighting speech by Lloyd George, England's Chancellor of the Exchequer, caused Germany to have second thoughts. After long drawn-out negotiations Germany gave France carte-blanche in Morocco and received in exchange a strip of territory ceded from the French Congo. Thus, the second Moroccan crisis also resulted in a defeat for German foreign policy. In that same year Italy occupied Tripoli, although Germany entertained friendly relations with Turkey. But the *Reich* was forced to condone this step, too, in order to avoid losing an ally.

Encouraged by Turkish weakness the Balkan states united in an attack which nearly succeeded in driving Turkey out of Europe. Russia and Austria-Hungary did not intervene, and Germany even managed with England's help to localise the conflict. The result of the Balkan Wars of 1912/13 was that the Balkans fell more and more into Slav hands. Austria-Hungary was the only power which numbered Slav regions among its dominions. Young Serb nationalism regarded the Austro-Hungarian monarchy as its greatest enemy. And behind Serbia loomed the threatening presence of Russia.

Chapter Twenty-One

THE FIRST WORLD WAR

The Causes

On 28 June 1914, a Sunday, Serbia first observed the annual commemoration of the Battle of Kossovo, at which a Serbian nobleman had killed the Turkish Sultan Murad I, as Greater Serbia's day of liberation. On that same day Archduke Francis Ferdinand, the heir to the Habsburg throne, was visiting Bosnia and Hercegovina, the provinces annexed by Austria-Hungary in violation of international law. The population of these regions contained a high percentage of Serbs, whose political goal was union with the kingdom of Serbia. The archduke's fame had preceded him. It was said that he desired, after his accession, a reorganisation of the dual monarchy which would grant autonomous status to the individual ethnic groups within Austria's dominions. If this plan, rejected by the ruling classes in Germany and Austria, had ever become effective, it would automatically have drawn the claws of pan-Slav agitation and probably have frustrated Belgrade's hoped-for formation of a Greater Serbian kingdom. Such considerations as these led Serb extremists to assassinate Archduke Francis Ferdinand and his wife on that same day. This outrage aroused feelings of the greatest abhorrence throughout the entire world.

Vienna decided to make the most of this opportunity to come to a final reckoning with the hated Serbs. On 5 July the Austrian ambassador to Berlin delivered a hand-written letter from Emperor Francis Joseph to the German emperor, in which German support was requested for Austria's projected action against Serbia. Believing that it would be possible to localise the conflict, both the German emperor and the imperial chancellor expressed their unreserved agreement with the Austrian plans. Austria declared that her intention was "to eliminate Serbia as a political power in the Balkans". The government of the *Reich* gave its approval. It also added the urgent advice that Austria should take action against Serbia without delay and with inflexible determination. In Berlin they certainly anticipated Russian intervention but hoped that

243

Russia was still not strong enough militarily to win a war. Italy and Rumania were not informed of the contents of the Austro-German exchange of views, although they were the allies of the two great powers. As Poincaré, the President of the French Republic, happened to be paying a state visit to Petersburg at the time, the policy-makers in Vienna judged it advisable to delay the despatch of an ultimatum to Serbia until after Poincaré's departure. Russia and France agreed to make joint representations in Vienna on behalf of Serbia. England was to be asked to do the same. But the British government first planned to persuade Serbia to give satisfaction to Austria and was not in favour of any alteration of the *status quo* in the Balkans. On 22 July the German ambassador to London could still inform Berlin that the British government would use its influence to gain Serbia's agreement to the Austrian demands "as long as they are moderate and compatible with the sovereignty of the Serbian state". On 23 July, however, Austria delivered a strongly-worded ultimatum in Belgrade which demanded a full legal enquiry into the assassination, with the collaboration of Austrian officials. The full text of the ultimatum was only communicated to the German government in Berlin after its presentation in Serbia, an omission which was all the more serious as the Austrian demands clearly infringed the sovereign rights of the Serbian state. Nevertheless the Serbian government sent a conciliatory reply two days later which satisfied Austrian requirements in all essential points. It rejected any violation of its sovereignty but was willing, even here, to abide by the decision of the Hague tribunal. On the same day it ordered the mobilisation of its troops.

William II regarded the Serbian reply as "a great moral success for Vienna" and was convinced that "this caused all grounds for war to disappear". However, on 28 July Austria declared war on Serbia. The German government expressed itself in full agreement with this step, although just two days earlier, on 26 July, the British foreign secretary had put forward the suggestion that the dispute should be settled at a conference of ambassadors in London. A further English move in favour of mediation was rejected by Austria with the backing of the *Reich*. On 29 July the Russian government ordered general mobilisation, only to cancel it, in response to a telegram to the tsar from William II, and substitute partial mobilisation against Austria-Hungary. On the evening of 30 July the tsar issued the definitive decree for total mobilisation. Before news of this Russian step had been received, Austria also gave orders for general mobilisation. Berlin proclaimed a "state of war emergency" (*Zustand drohender Kriegsgefahr*), a preliminary to mobilisation, and sent an ultimatum to Petersburg demanding to call a halt to her mobilisation preparations against Austria within 12 hours. At the same time Berlin also asked in Paris whether France "would remain neutral in a Russo-German war". Russia ignored the ultimatum, and France answered evasively that "she would do what her interests dictated". Whereupon, on 1 August 1914, Germany's representative in St. Petersburg delivered Germany's declaration of war to the Russian foreign minister. Germany and France ordered mobilisation on the same day. Two days later Germany also declared war on France.

The Course of the War

In the event of a war on two fronts the Schlieffen plan envisaged that German arms should first knock out France and then crush Russia. The execution of this plan involved a preliminary approach march through Luxembourg and Belgium, both neutrals, in order to circumvent the French frontier fortifications. By 2 August Germany had already occupied Luxembourg and demanded the free passage of imperial troops through Belgian territory. On that same day the British navy assumed responsibility for the defence of France's northern coastline. Belgium refused to grant the German request and was invaded on August 4. This step evoked a Belgian declaration of war. England dispatched an ultimatum to Germany demanding the restitution of Belgian neutrality. The *Reich* did not comply. Accordingly, as from midnight of that day, England was lined up on the side of Germany's opponents. The First World War had begun.

The following day Austria-Hungary also declared war on Russia. Italy and Rumania did not regard this as fulfilling the *casus foederis* and remained neutral for the time being. In August 1914 Japan also entered the war as England's ally. Bulgaria and Turkey joined the central powers.

Immediately after the violation of Belgian neutrality by German troops, the imperial chancellor made the following promise in the *Reichstag:* "The injustice which we thereby do we shall make good as soon as our military objectives have been obtained". These words provide a revealing, if partial, insight into the tragic development of German policy under William II. This was characterised by the subordination of political to military considerations by the astonishing false assessment of the *Reich's* situation in Europe and the world by responsible politicians in Germany, especially the emperor, and by the uncritical following of the political course adopted by the Austrian monarchy. Nevertheless, it cannot be maintained that German policy aimed at a war in 1914; but no more can German policy be absolved from its share of the responsibility for the outbreak of World War I and its world-shattering consequences, though these could not be foreseen, of course, in all their appalling significance for our planet, by any of the belligerents. Again it should not be forgotten that nearly all statesmen alive at the time looked upon war as a justifiable, if last, resort to obtain political ends.

In Germany, as in all nations in time of war, both the troops at the front and the civilian population at home were confident that they were fighting a just war. Even the Social Democrats, until now the determined opponents of imperial policy, voted with only a few exceptions for a grant of war credits. The oft-vaunted solidarity of the Socialist International did not survive its first test.

For the first time in the long history of Europe there was a question in 1914 not of gladiatorial combat between armies but of total warfare between peoples. Accordingly the individual nations mobilised to the full all the resources at their disposal. The economic and political preparation and conduct of the war were to prove just as decisive, if not more so, for the success of the war effort as the military achievements of the warring powers. The economic superiority of the enemy, even if accompanied by initial inferiority in the field, was bound to bring victory in the long run. This meant that the final triumph must inevitably be denied Germany and its allies in the case of a protracted struggle.

The Schlieffen plan as modified by von Moltke, the chief of the general staff, seemed to justify the faith of its supporters. Belgium and northern France were overrun as the victorious German advance pushed forward rapidly. Paris was soon in sight. But the German high command did not succeed in completing the encirclement manoeuvre and thus had no enclosed French army to annihilate. French resistance made a determined stand at the Marne. The German advance was brought to a standstill in a three-day battle (6—9 September). The German troops were thus compelled to dig themselves in along a line stretching from Flanders to the Swiss frontier. This marked the beginning of the stalemate of trench warfare. The German plan of campaign had failed; the outcome of the war was open, at least for the time being. From this time onwards economic factors were going to assume increasing importance.

In the east the "Russian steam-roller" rumbled over the borders of East Prussia sooner than anticipated. But the resounding victories of Hindenburg and Ludendorff at Tannenberg and the Masurian Lakes soon put a stop to this advance. When Russian troops later threatened to overrun Hungary from conquered Galicia, the German Dunajec-San offensive (May 1915) relieved the hard-pressed Austrian troops and forced a breakthrough as far as Warsaw. The conquest of Serbia and Bulgaria's entry into the war at the end of 1915 meant that a direct connection had been established between Berlin and Istanbul. Shortly before, Turkish contingents had just managed with German backing to contain the Allies' attempt to break through in the Dardanelles.

On the western front the German army had to rest content with beating off repeated attempts by superior forces to dislodge them from their positions. The foolhardy attempt, conceived by von Falkenhayn, the German Chief of Staff, and approved by the emperor, to "pulverise" the French reserves "in the Meuse mill" in a western offensive directed against Verdun (1916) cost the attackers extremely heavy casualities, too, despite the bravery manifested in the execution of the plan. It was almost a miracle that the Allies' Somme offensive with enormous troop concentrations was held (at the end of 1916) and that the Russian General Brusilov's full-scale offensive launched at the same time in the Bukovina could be beaten back by the Germans after it had scored initial successes against the Austrians. The German armies also succeeded in a brillantly executed campaign in crushing Rumania, which had entered the war at a very critical moment for the central powers.

Thus, the military balance to be drawn at the close of the first phase of the struggle was that the mobile war had petrified into a trench war of attrition on all fronts, even against Italy, which had declared war on the central powers in 1915. The enemy's attempts to force a breakthrough had proved unsuccessful.

From now on the war progressively developed for the central powers into a race against time. Although, on account of military successes, a German-dominated *Mitteleuropa* (Middle Europe), rich in agricultural products and industrial raw materials, now appeared to have become a reality, the strain of the British blockade was beginning to make itself increasingly felt. Since the government of the *Reich* had not reckoned with a prolonged contest, it began relatively late in the day with economic planning; the industrialist Walter Rathenau organised the supply and management of all raw materials and agricultural products vital to the war effort. But even this measure could only mitigate, not eliminate, the supply crisis at the front and at home.

The military leaders thus felt called upon to try and force a quick decision. The military situation at the time rendered this impossible in the theatres of war on land. The high command therefore came to the conclusion that unrestricted submarine warfare was the only possible reply they could make to the English blockade. On 9 January 1917 a crown council decreed the commencement of unrestricted submarine warfare as from 1 February. England's overseas supply-lines were to be cut with complete disregard for neutral shipping. The country primarily affected by this resolve was the United States of America. The responsible politicians within the *Reich* thus realised clearly that this step made America's entry into the war almost inevitable. They were, however, unable to drive home their doubts about the advisability of this course of action, as William II was in full agreement with the military's calculations that such unrestricted submarine warfare would force England to her knees within six months.

The military developments at the turn of the year 1916/17 took place against the background of various moves for peace. The initiative here was taken by the central powers, who judged that the prospects for peace would be good in view of Rumania's recent defeat. The Entente powers, however, doubted the sincerity of these attempts since the peace note addressed to France, Great Britain, Japan, Serbia and Rumania on 12 December 1916 did not contain a single concrete proposal which could serve as a basis for negotiation. The allies were clearly hoping that time was on their side and that they would later be able to force the central powers to sue for peace.

In that same month Wilson, the President of the United States, had offered his services to the powers at war as "an honest broker". Whereas the Entente powers accepted the president's offer of mediation with some reserve, the central powers rejected all "American interference" outright, especially as Germany was not prepared to surrender Alsace-Lorraine. When Wilson renewed his offer in January 1917 in spite of this rebuff, Bethmann-Hollweg informed Washington on 29 January that Germany was only prepared to negotiate a peace under the following conditions: Alsace-Lorraine must remain in the *Reich*, an eastern frontier would have to be drawn which gave Poland and Germany security against Russia, the German colonies must be restored, and France would have to agree to some corrections in the Franco-German frontier. Belgium's independence was to be restored, though Germany felt obliged to demand certain guarantees in the interests of her own security.

248

Since the German ambassador delivered with this declaration a note informing the Americans of Germany's decision to step up submarine warfare, diplomatic relations between the United States and the *Reich* were severed. On 6 April 1917 America intervened actively in the war for the first time.

The note which Germany sent in reply to the American president's efforts on behalf of a peace without conqueror and conquered, represented the first official statement of what the political leaders hoped for from the conclusion of the world-wide conflict. Bethmann-Hollweg was nevertheless severely criticised for the moderation of his war aims by those circles led by the Quartermaster-General Ludendorff. As far back as 1915 leading industrialists, German intellectuals, and members of the Pan-German League had consigned Germany's war aims to paper in a memorandum. Their demands included the annexation of Belgium and northern France roughly as far as the mouth of the Somme, the incorporation of the metallurgical districts around Longwy and Briey, the shifting of the *Reich's* eastern frontier in the direction of Russia by the inclusion of at least parts of the Baltic Provinces, and, finally, an extended colonial empire. In September 1917 these circles amalgamated into the "Fatherland Party" in order to give their views greater political efficacy.

In contrast, broad sections of the German people who looked to the Social Democrats, the Liberal Progressives and the Centre as their political representatives supported the standpoint that the general state of the war made a peace by agreement imperative. Unrestricted submarine warfare had disappointed the hopes of even the naval chiefs. These political parties therefore considered that the time had come to use the *Reichstag* to influence the country's political leaders in favour of a peace agreement. A peace resolution which envisaged the conclusion of hostilities without annexations and indemnities was passed in the *Reichstag* on 19 July 1917 by 212 to 126 votes with 17 abstentions. The Imperial Chancellor Bethmann-Hollweg had resigned five days previously and been replaced by Michaelis. The latter gave his agreement to the resolution but only after appending the reservation "in the sense that I understand it". The resolution achieved nothing. A similar fate awaited the peace efforts Pope Benedict XV made in the same year. The central powers were not ready to make genuine concessions; the Entente allies, however, were even less prepared to do so.

It was at this point that the Bolshevist revolution of 7 November 1917 seemed to herald a decisive alleviation in the situation for the central powers. Russia had already been shaken by the revolutionary unrest caused by the enforced abdication of the tsar and the assumption of power by the moderate leftist parties during the early days of March of that year. This had not at first produced any noticeable change on the eastern front. The new government abode by the alliance with the western powers. It was even able to launch a new offensive against the central powers, which was to prove ineffective. Since Bolshevist propaganda was entirely directed towards restoring peace and partitioning the land, the central powers looked upon the Bolshevists as their natural allies. This explains why the high command, with the agreement of the German civil government, allowed Russian emigrés in Switzerland free passage through the *Reich* on their way back to Russia. It was hoped to strengthen in this way the "radical wing among the revolutionaries in Russia". Among the Russians who benefited was W.I. Lenin, who had already enjoyed German financial assistance at an earlier date.

The aftermath of the Bolshevist revolution appeared to justify the central powers' hopes. On 15 December 1917 an armistice was signed between them and Russia, which was followed in March 1918 by the peace of Brest-Litovsk. Although the military situation on all fronts and the economic situation at home looked decidedly unfavourable to Germany, the military leaders, strongly influenced by Ludendorff, forced a dictated peace on the Bolshevists which separated the Baltic states, Finland, Poland and the Ukraine from Russia. This meant that the Russian empire lost 26 % of its population, 26 % of its railways and 75 % of its iron and steel industry. The peoples thus liberated from Russian domination at first welcomed their new freedom and independence. When it became clear, however, that Germany planned to place them under German sovereignty, though with differential rights, the sympathy which they at first felt for the *Reich* disappeared. The allies took advantage of the peace of Brest-Litovsk to intensify their propaganda against Germany and to increase their own war efforts in the conviction that this peace made plain what fate awaited them if they lost the war.

Military Defeat and End of the "Reich"

The relief which the armistice and peace had brought in the east led the high command to entertain hopes of successfully forcing a breakthrough by a large-scale western offensive. They hoped in this to force a peace on the allies on the basis of manifest military superiority. In March 1918 German troops were able to make appreciable territorial gains in an extended "Spring Offensive", but the breakthrough intended to sever the British and the French lines near Amiens failed. On 4 April the attack was brought to a standstill. Ludendorff tried to continue the offensive elsewhere, but French counter-attacks directed by General Foch with English and American reinforcements forced him to discontinue his attempts on 17 July, 1918. On 18 July the Entente powers launched their counter-offensive with still stronger American backing. As Ludendorff put it: "The initiative now lies with the Entente."

The troops of the quadruple alliance had now passed the point where they could still offer serious resistance. In 1916 Francis Joseph, the Austrian Emperor, had died. Under the Emperor Charles, his successor, the disintegration of the dual monarchy continued apace. In September 1918 Bulgaria, Turkey, and Austria-Hungary, Germany's allies, sued for peace.

The fighting on the western front confirmed Ludendorff's assessment of the situation. Certainly German troops were always able to fall back on prepared positions, but there was no longer any question of taking the offensive. The war was already lost militarily. The high command was now faced with the question whether they should turn Germany itself into a battlefield. On 28 September 1918 Hindenburg and Ludendorff had both recognised the hopelessness of further re-sistance; they demanded that the German government initiate peace negotiations and introduce a constitutional monarchy. This was to avoid having to bear the responsibility for the inevitable military ca-pitulation themselves.

On 3 October Max, Prince of Baden, who enjoyed the reputation of being a liberal-minded politician, was entrusted with the task of form-ing a government. A day later he sent a note to the president of the United States requesting an armistice on the basis of Wilson's Fourteen Points. Wilson replied by demanding the abdication of the emperor—undoubtedly a wrong allocation of the real responsibility for political developments in Germany under William II—and the capitulation of Germany's armed forces. When Ludendorff wanted to carry on the struggle, he was dismissed by the emperor. Hindenburg remained Commander-in-Chief. The German naval authorities made a final attempt to force a conclusion in Germany's favour by ordering the fleet to seek a trial of strength with the Royal navy. The members of the German navy, however, felt that this order contradicted the peace efforts of their political leaders and refused to obey, because they regarded further resistance as hopeless so late in the day. On 4 November this refusal to obey orders developed into open rebellion which soon spread to the larger German towns and was fanned by radical leftist elements. On 5 November Wilson informed Germany's statesmen that the allies were agreed to a peace on the basis of the Fourteen Points on condition that the emperor abdicated.

William II need not have abdicated on account of the revolutionary radicalism, which could anyway claim the support only of an insignificant minority of the population. The parties of the left centre did not aspire after a republic but a constitutional monarchy in which the ministers were responsible to the *Reichstag* and not to the emperor. But William's advisers considered the monarchic cause lost and counselled him to flee the country. On 9 November William II crossed the frontier into Holland and began his life in exile. Philipp Scheidemann proclaimed the republic in Berlin. The monarchy had ceased to exist because its last representative, William II, was too weak to fight for it.

Two days later the armistice was signed in the Forest of Compiègne. The head of the German delegation was not a soldier but a politician of the Centre, Erzberger. The bloodshed which had lasted more than four years had come to an end. The German *Reich* was now at the mercy of its former foes.

At first the armistice was restricted to a period of 36 days. Afterwards it was continually renewed, amidst constant complaints about infringement by the Germans and repeated protests by the German government, until the signing of the peace treaty. The Entente's blockade of Germany remained in force. German prisoners-of-war were not repatriated, whereas those from allied countries were allowed to return home immediately. During the famine winter of 1918/19 the American Relief Administration under Herbert Hoover began its work. Five million tons of food supplies to a value of one $ 1,000,000,000 were sent to a devastated and starving Europe in the course of eight months. This organisation continued its work until 1922. Smaller states like Sweden, Holland, and Switzerland also helped to feed hungry German children.

The world, whether conqueror, conquered or neutral, believed that a new era was about to dawn. The foundation stone of this new order was to be laid in Paris.

Chapter Twenty-Two

THE WEIMAR REPUBLIC

A Difficult Start

The Germans acquired their new, republican form of government more or less by chance. The new system was not a goal they had struggled to obtain. Many took it to be a consequence of the defeat suffered by the German army. Many thought it was a malicious plot hatched by the victorious powers. Even the political parties who had criticised the *Kaiserreich* for the most varied of reasons were not in principle champions of the republican form of government. But they lost no time in accepting the situation. It was their historical achievement that they very quickly sized up the possibilities of preserving the unity of the *Reich* within the framework of a libertarian and democratic constitution, and of defending it against extremists either on the Bolshevist left of the radical camp or in the ranks of the diehards eager to see imperial power restored. Here, the chief responsibility fell to the Social Democrats, whose leader at the time, Friedrich Ebert, enjoyed the confidence of the working classes. He succeeded in firmly establishing the idea of democracy among the workers, thus erecting a stout bulwark against communist infiltration. Many of the Social Democratic Party's aims were supported by the Catholic Centre and the Liberal Democrats. The latter, most of whose members sprang from the middle classes, had succeeded to the Progressives, who had opposed both Bismarck and William II.

It was possible to hold free elections for the national assembly as early as January 1919. The majority of the candidates elected belonged to the parties left of centre who favoured a democratic and republican form of government. Their principal task was to work out a constitution. They met at Weimar, a choice motivated by two considerations: they wished to repudiate all connection with the "military spirit of Potsdam" and to affirm their loyalty to the great tradition of the German spirit which had been known and honoured throughout the globe when Goethe and Schiller had lived at Weimar.

The constitution drafted by Professor Hugo Preuss came into force in August 1919. It was formulated on the lines of the *Paulskirche* constitution of 1849 and consisted of two sections. The first of these regulated "The Structure and Tasks of the *Reich*", while the second laid down "The Basic Rights and Duties of Germans". Although the Weimar constitution also stressed the federal character of the *Reich* and retained the *Länder* as developed by history, the unity of the *Reich* was strengthened, and important rights were transferred to it which had hitherto been prerogatives of the *Länder*. Even in the cultural sector the *Reich* could lay down certain principles which legislators in the *Länder* were bound to respect. It was to be expected that the increased strength of the central government would soon provoke criticism, particularly in Bavaria. All this was grist to the mill of those who regarded the *Reich* with disfavour or hostility.

The "Basic Rights and Duties of Germans" were founded on concepts fixing the relationship of the individual to community and state which were part of the heritage of the Enlightenment and liberalism. The rights and freedoms of the individual which had already been demanded in 1848 were now given constitutional validity. In addition, the constitution guaranteed the so-called "fourth estate" rights for which political parties, trade unions and the churches had been clamouring ever since the emergence of the social question.

Friedrich Ebert became the first president of the *Reich*.

Thanks to its spirit of freedom and social justice, the Weimar constitution was worthy of a place beside the constitutions of the great western democracies. But it takes more than a constitution to shape the life of a people and of a nation. Even in the very hour of its birth, German democrats were forced to acknowledge that democratic thought, feeling and action were still very alien to the way of thinking of the broad masses of the people. The German people were no longer capable of distinguishing between the valuable and the worthless in the world of politics. When the Weimar constitution suddenly presented Germans with a fullness of freedom scarcely conceded in the old democracies, they did not know how to use it. It was generally welcomed by those engaged in politics or in forming public opinion as giving them a free hand to ridicule or fight against the democratic system of government. The republic was burdened with the odium of defeat. Proportional representation, introduced in order to secure the fairest possible distribution of seats, facilitated the formation of an increasing number of parties and made it possible in certain circumstances for a party to be represented in the *Reichstag* by only one member. Germany became a multi-party state in which party interests frequently came before the good of the state as a whole. Chancellor and ministers being dependent on possessing the confidence of a majority in the *Reichstag*, no government could function without a coalition of several parties, since no single party ever secured an absolute majority during the whole of the Weimar era: the more numerous the parties required to form a majority, the weaker the government. The active hostility towards the Weimar system of government shown by the opposition on both right and left wings, and tolerated by the republic almost without protest, inevitably paralysed the authority of the state the moment these parties secured a majority in the *Reichstag* without themselves being in a position to form a government.

Another aggravating factor was the equivocal attitude of the Germans to the authority of the state as such. Whereas this had scarcely played a part in the efforts of the politicians to achieve unity in 1848/49, Bismarck's policy had made the Germans aware of the power of the state to such an extent that, contrary to Bismarck's intentions, it had already become an important plank in the political platform in the time of William II. Militarism dominated all sectors of public life. The disastrous overemphasis put on military power in Germany produced a militarist mentality which was regarded abroad as something typically German. When this mentality distintegrated in consequence of the defeat of 1918, there seemed to be some justification for the widespread view that the curse of militarism was the sole cause of the German catastrophe. Those who entertained this idea, blind to the fact that the state always represents power, were too easily inclined to deny the state all right to substantiate its legitimate claims by employing a constitutional instrument of power.

This explains why the young republic, threatened by communist risings, had to avail itself of services whose attitude to the new state was, to say the least, ambiguous. The "Free Corps", a volunteer association of privates and officers who had fought in the war, did indeed manage to quell the risings, but they regarded themselves not as instruments of the republic but as the saviours of the fatherland with the right to a special status. This they secured in the *Reichswehr* (armed force), which was established later, partly with the tacit tolerance of officials in responsible positions. As a "state within the state", the armed forces, small as they were by decree of the victorious powers, did not form an instrument to be wielded by the republic. The claim voiced by their leaders, particularly by General von Seeckt, their organiser, that they were non-political was stronger proof of their aloofness from the

Weimar Republic than of their neutrality in the party political arena. Actually, their sympathies were with those who thought that the liquidation of "Weimar" by a "national revolution" would provide the foundation for German recovery. The tardy recognition of this threat to the republic, latent in the *Reichswehr,* is a failure to be laid at the door of responsible politicians from 1919 to 1933.

How dangerous to the republic the *Reichswehr* might become was evident as early as 1920. In March of that year General Freiherr von Lüttwitz, commander of Berlin, installed Wolfgang Kapp, an East Prussian official, as chancellor. Kapp had been one of the founders of the "Fatherland Party" during the war, and the advocate of extravagant German annexations in the event of a German victory. The government of the *Reich* had to leave Berlin. It is true that the *Reichswehr* was not seriously involved in the Kapp *Putsch,* but neither was von Seeckt prepared to call out loyal *Reichswehr* units against the rebels, because he did not want to have "*Reichswehr* shooting against *Reichswehr*". The *Putsch* eventually foundered on the united resistance of the civil servants and the workers, whom the Social Democratic Party and trade unions induced to stage a general strike. This, however, was not the end of domestic unrest. Groups of communists made the Kapp *Putsch* an excuse to mobilise workmen in the Ruhr district against legitimate authority. Since in this case the *Reichswehr* was called out against the rebels, military know-how soon got the better of what was merely a revolutionary flare-up.

Considerably more lasting and more injurious in their long-term effects on the stability of democracy in Germany were the differences of opinion in Germany and abroad about the structure of the peace treaty concluded by the western allies in Paris.

The Treaty of Versailles

The Treaty of Versailles, the peace treaty dictated to the Germans by the allies, came into force on 10 January 1920, after it had been accepted under vehement protest by the national assembly on 22 June 1919 and signed in the hall of mirrors at Versailles on 28 June. It decreed that Germany should cede the following territories (in some cases after a plebiscite): Alsace-Lorraine to France, Eupen and Malmédy to Belgium, Posen (Poznan) in West Prussia, small areas of East Prussia and part of eastern upper Silesia to Poland, part of north Schleswig to Denmark and the area known as the "Hultschiner Land" (part of

FRANZ MARC

Turm der blauen Pferde

Tour des Chevaux Bleus

The Tower of Blue Horses

Torre de los caballos azules

Tôrre dos Cavalos Azuis

1913/14

Ehemals Nationalgalerie, Berlin. Im Kriege verschollen.

Autrefois Galerie Nationale, Berlin. Perdu au cours de la guerre.

Formerly in the National Gallery, Berlin. Missing since World War II.

Anteriormente en la Galería Nacional de Berlín. Desaparecido en la guerra.

Antiga Galeria Nacional, Berlin. Extraviado durante a guerra.

the district of Ratibor, with Hlucin) to Czechoslovakia. The Saar basin was subjected to a government appointed by the League of Nations, France being allowed to exploit its economy. After fifteen years the population was to decide by vote whether it wished to become French, or German, or remain under the international regime appointed by the League. The Hanseatic town of Danzig became a "Free City" under a high commissioner appointed by the League of Nations. The town was incorporated into the Polish customs area and its foreign affairs were to be directed by Poland. The city and hinterland of Memel were ceded to the allies; the area was later awarded to Lithuania. The former German colonies were handed over to the league and administered by the allies as mandatory powers.

In order to prevent the outbreak of another war, Germany had to promise to reduce her army to 100,000 men and to limit her armaments to a minimum. The general staff was disbanded, conscription abolished, and military training outside the army, that is in schools, associations and the like, forbidden. The German navy was reduced to six smaller battleships, six light cruisers, 12 destroyers, and 12 torpedo boats. The fighting strength of the navy was fixed at 15,000. The naval harbour on Heligoland was dismantled.

Germany acknowledged that, being the originator of the war, she was responsible "for all the loss and damage to which the allied and associated governments and their nationals have been subjected", i.e. for all the costs of the war, for the devastation of northern France and Belgium, and for all ships which had been sunk. Germany was thus to bear all extra expenditure incurred as a result of the war. A reparations commission was appointed to assess the damage inflicted and the obligations of Germany. The *Reich's* entire property and all its sources of income were impounded for the payment of reparations. The reparations commisson was endowed with unlimited authority in carrying out its duties. Germany herself had at the outset little or no say in its decisions. Similarly, committees of the allies supervised the disarmament of Germany. The German rivers, the Rhine, the Elbe, the Oder, the Vistula, the Memel, and the Danube, were placed under international control.

The Treaty of Versailles did not represent either the spirit or the letter of Wilson's Fourteen Points, on which Germany's willingness to cease hostilities had been based. It reflected the victor's hatred and desire for revenge which, pent up for the long war years and nourished by the immeasurable sufferings and losses inflicted, particularly on the French people, and by the knowledge of Germany's jingoistic war aims, here found drastic expression. This in itself suffices to explain the

257

harsh terms of the treaty. Its severity was criticised even by members of the allied nations. Indeed, the criticism aroused in the United States was so strong that Congress refused to ratify the Treaty of Versailles and the United States concluded a separate treaty of peace in 1921. Nor was the Treaty of Versailles a burden only for Germany. It was in many respects responsible for the chaotic conditions prevalent in Europe after World War I. The allies had promised to end the war as champions of right. Wilson's Fourteen Points had expressed the principles of this justice, but they were not embodied in the treaty of Versailles. The treaty, therefore, was not calculated to increase the German people's respect for the priority of right in international relations. By refusing the Austrians the right of self-determination, by demanding exorbitant reparations, by redistributing German colonies for no cogent reason, by demanding that the emperor and the leaders of the German army should as a result of Germany's alleged sole responsibility for the war be handed over as war criminals, the treaty supplied ammunition to those Germans who declared that might is the only criterion respected by statesmen. The Treaty of Versailles would of necessity boomerang, unless it were revised in good time so as to secure the victors just compensation for their losses without imperilling the vanquished nation's bare existence. It was the tragedy of the allied statesmen at Versailles that they did not realise that a verdict based on might can only be carried out at the cost of great sacrifices on the part of its pronouncers; it was the tragedy of allied statesmen between 1920 and 1933 that their mitigations of the treaty always came too late to win the gratitude of the Germans; it was the tragedy of the German people not to have learnt that it always takes time to reach political decisions and that it is often better to wait than to act in haste.

The Weimar Republic's Foreign Policy

At the start, German foreign policy had to operate within the restrictions imposed by the Treaty of Versailles. No other course was open. The necessity to regain the confidence which the world had completely lost in the sincerity of Germany's actions and intentions handicapped operations severely. For it was only when that hurdle had been crossed that Germany could hope to be admitted to international negotiations on an equal footing with the other partners.

Formidable difficulties attended the negotiations to settle the question of reparations. In 1921 an inter-allied conference had decreed that German payments were to be made for a term of 42 years. When the German government found itself unable to assume such a burden, a series of conferences, most of them barren, were held. One of these was attended by delegates from the new Bolshevist state of Russia, the invitation having been prompted by the allies' desire to allow the Bolshevists to share in the reparation pickings. The German delegation was given no details of the deliberations between the western and the eastern partners. When the Russian foreign minister invited Rathenau, his German colleague, to a meeting at Rapallo, the German foreign minister felt obliged to accept. It was Germany's first opportunity to break through her isolation, and, in the event, the negotiations quickly led to results satisfactory for both sides. Germany was the first western state to recognise the new Bolshevist government. A ten-year treaty of friendship was concluded between the two countries, in return for which Russia abandoned all claim to compensation for war damage. All trade and business was to be transacted on the basis of the "most-favoured-nation" principle.

The Rapallo Treaty had an extremely unfavourable effect on Germany's relations with the western powers. The French were convinced that the treaty contained secret military clauses, by means of which Germany wished to circumvent the severe disarmament terms of the Treaty of Versailles.

Though this was not the case, secret discussions between the chiefs of the German army and the Russian general staff resulted in Russia allowing members of the *Reichswehr* to experiment and gain experience in Russia with certain arms which had been forbidden to Germany. In addition, General von Seeckt advocated a course of German foreign policy with an eastern bias in order to burst the fetters of Versailles with the help of Russia and perhaps recover the territory lost in the east. These plans, however, did not have the support of responsible statesmen in the Weimar Republic.

But quite apart from the future aims of German foreign policy, France imagined that her claim to reparations was imperilled by the Rapallo Treaty. As her distrust of the *Reich's* policy increased, France sought to restrict Germany's freedom of action by demanding what were called "productive pledges" and at the same time to solve the reparations problem once and for all.

Meanwhile Germany's economic situation was deteriorating in consequence of the increasing inflation of the currency. This was not primarily due to the unsolved problem of reparations, but to the *Reich's* financial and taxation policy during the war; it was, however, aggravated by the reparations payments. Germany could pay acceptable compensation for the war only if her balance of trade or payments was favourable. The war had robbed her of all assets abroad and her economy was weakened to such an extent that it would take years to achieve a favourable balance of trade. So the German Mark depreciated ruinously. The most disastrous effects of the inflation were felt by the middle classes, those with modest savings, and old-age pensioners; they considered that the Treaty of Versailles and the Weimar democracy were responsible for their misfortunes.

Here the seeds of radicalism fell early on fruitful soil. The assassination of politicians, openly propagated by rightist radicals, throve in such circles. In 1921 Erzberger, the leader of the Centre, was the first to be murdered. The ground for this crime was that he had signed the armistice. A year later, Rathenau, Foreign Minister of the *Reich*, was assassinated in Berlin. He was the first victim of the wave of anti-Semitism that was engulfing the extreme rightist youth of Germany in particular. Although his policy and his patriotism were above reproach, he had to die because he was a Jew. It was the first manifestation of a spirit which was to become a political principle under the Nazis and to find expression in the unspeakable cruelties of the ghettoes and extermination camps.

At the end of 1922 the inter-allied reparations commission discovered that Germany was in default in her deliveries of coal and timber. France, under Poincaré, immediately seized this as an excuse to send French and Belgian troops into the Ruhr, an action which won England's disapproval. In January 1923, 100,000 French and Belgian troops occupied the Ruhr. The *Reich* government protested, the Ruhr workers reacted with passive resistance, all work came to a standstill. Protected by French bayonets, German separatists attempted to separate west Germany from the *Reich* and to establish close political connections with France. An ancient French dream appeared to be coming true. But the patriotic loyalty of the Germans in the Ruhr and on the Rhine proved stronger than France had expected. It is true that passive resistance only added to the hardship, inflation increased prices to astronomical heights, the entire economy of Germany was paralysed. Nevertheless, the occupation of the Ruhr brought France no nearer to either her long-term political or her economic aims. Both sides were forced to realise that a permanent solution of the problems arising from the Treaty of Versailles could only be reached by way of sane negotiation. The hour had struck for Gustav Stresemann, the German statesman.

Later on, his efforts towards a settlement of the differences between France and Germany were to be wholeheartedly supported by Aristide Briand, the French socialist.

The Franco-German Settlement

Dr. Gustav Stresemann came from the world of business. Since 1907 as a member of the National Liberal Party, he had advocated a definitely national and monarchist policy in the *Reichstag*. During the war he pursued the expansionist, nationalistic aims of the Fatherland Party. After the war he founded the German People's Party which at first was passively opposed to the Weimar Republic. It was the flood of extreme rightist propaganda, which did not even shrink from advocating the assassination of politicians, that induced Stresemann and his party to support the republic and eventually to accept the Weimar constitution.

When passive resistance in the Ruhr was abandoned, a change of government became necessary. In August 1923, *Reich* President Ebert called upon Gustav Stresemann to form a new government. Stresemann based his government programme on what he viewed as the undeniable right of the victors to reparations; payments, however, depended on the economic strength of the *Reich,* which was bound to remain weak as long as nothing was done to boost the currency and as long as domestic unrest imperilled all economic progress. The government secured its first successes in the struggle against the regime in Saxony and Thuringia, which was under communist influence, and against the first *Putsch* staged in Bavaria by the then unknown leader of the National Socialist Party, Adolf Hitler. It was the stabilisation of the Mark in November 1923, however, that marked the real beginning of Germany's recovery and of the consolidation of domestic interests.

Stresemann thus felt that he now had a sound basis for successful negotiations with the victors, particularly with France. He recognised clearly the difficulty of France's situation. The cataclysm of the war had left the people of France and their statesmen convinced that Germany was their eternal enemy and that France would be victimised by Germany as long as no brake was put on that country's energy. French hopes of a close union with the two great Anglo-Saxon powers in order to safeguard French hegemony in Europe had been disappointed. Her efforts to cripple her dangerous opponent in war by means of the Treaty of Versailles and a system of alliances to isolate

Germany in Europe overstrained the political and economic resources of the country; they even provoked severe criticism from her Anglo-Saxon allies, who condemned the Ruhr action, being interested in a limited recovery of the *Reich's* economy. Stresemann's starting-point was therefore that his first task in the sector of foreign policy was to satisfy France's need for security without sacrificing justifiable German interests. His views received energetic support, above all in England. After Aristide Briand became French foreign minister, France appeared to be willing, if not enthusiastic, to cooperate with her former enemy. Stresemann sought to ease the reparations problem by reducing its political implications and emphasising its economic aspects. Since the allies had to use the reparations paid them for the discharge of their war debts to America, the United States were interested in a Germany with a healthy economy. Stresemann's policy won its first victory, therefore, when Charles Dawes, the American financier, succeeded in persuading France to accept his plan for reparations based on Germany's real economic capacity. At a conference in London in 1924, the first to be attended by a German delegation (under Stresemann) as a partner, the Dawes Plan was accepted by all the powers concerned. This marked an important step towards the establishment of international confidence.

The settlement of the reparations problem was followed by the first stage in Franco-German reconciliation. In the Treaty of Locarno (1925) Germany voluntarily guaranteed the inviolability of her frontiers with France and Belgium and undertook to demilitarise the Rhineland. Although Germany was not willing to regard her frontier with Poland as final, she agreed that it should not be altered by force.

The Locarno Pact, which seemed to usher in a period of understanding between the nations of Europe, had significant consequences for Germany. The victorious powers affirmed their readiness to evacuate the area they had occupied round Cologne, and, by withdrawing occupation troops stationed elsewhere, to restore to the *Reich* full supremacy over its territory before the date fixed in the Treaty of Versailles (1935). In addition, Germany was to be admitted to the League of Nations in 1926.

The League of Nations resulted from the peace conference in Paris; its statutes were incorporated in the Treaty of Versailles. In accordance with the plans of its orginator—America's President Wilson—its purpose was to promote peaceful understanding between all the nations of the world in respect of all questions which hitherto had been apt to lead to war. It did not, however, include all states: the defeated countries were not members nor were the United States and Russia.

In spite of President Wilson's urgent appeals, America had refused to join because of the fear that membership of the League might involve America in European wrangles. Soviet Russia had not been invited to become a member.

The absence of those two great powers, the exclusion of the defeated nations and the fact that the League was anchored in the Treaty of Versailles were weaknesses which paralysed activity and provoked criticism, particularly from the defeated nations. Nevertheless, it could not be denied that the new international organisation with its headquarters at Geneva provided an important forum for the promotion of international understanding in many provinces. Moreover, the membership of the defeated nations was tantamount to their inclusion on a basis of equality in the community of nations. When, therefore, Germany was admitted to the League of Nations in 1926 and accorded a permanent seat on its council with the unanimous approval of the member countries, she once more joined the ranks of the great powers. In the same year the *Reich* concluded in Berlin a treaty of friendship with the Soviet Union. The treaties of Locarno and Berlin thus seemed to guarantee the *Reich's* security in both east and west. The Kellogg Pact, the multilateral pact renouncing recourse to war, was signed in 1928 by the *Reich* and most of the nations of the world; war as an instrument of policy seemed to have been excluded for all time from international relations. With the withdrawal from the Rhineland of the last of the occupation forces on 30 June 1930, five years before the date stipulated in the Treaty of Versailles, the most difficult chapter of post-war German foreign policy could be regarded as closed. Stresemann did not live to see the most striking results of his foreign policy: he died in 1929.

The premature evacuation of the Rhineland seemed, however, to the German nationalists of all shades of opinion to have been purchased too dearly. The Dawes Plan, it is true, had fixed the amount of the annual payments, but at too high a figure. So, in 1929, a committee of experts under the chairmanship of another American, Owen Young, and including eight German bankers and eminent industralists, fixed German payments until 1988. In spite of considerable doubts in respect of the amount and duration of the German payments, Stresemann had agreed to the plan and recommended the *Reichstag* to accept it on condition that the allies evacuated the Rhineland. He thought that Germany's recovery of complete sovereignty was worth the price. The *Reichstag* accordingly accepted the Young Plan, which came into force in 1930. But the economic crisis which had befallen the whole world soon cast its shadow over Germany, too. The plan, violently rejected from the very outset by German nationalists, thus became unworkable. In view of Germany's inability to pay, *Reich* Chancellor Brüning had to request President Hoover to allow payments to cease. In 1931 the notion, born of the world-wide economic crisis, that the reparation payments threatened to bring ruin on the entire economy of the world led first to the Hoover Moratorium and eventually to the conference at Lausanne, at which it was decided to put an end to reparations. This happened in 1932, just a few months before Hitler came to power.

Domestic Policy in the Weimar Republic

It was not till inflation ceased and the problem of reparations was settled—if only temporarily—by the Dawes Plan that it became possible to stabilise the German economy and to quell unrest throughout the country. The propaganda of rightist radicals lost its potency, particularly after Hitler's unsuccessful *Putsch* in 1923. Moreover, there was a slow but steady decline in the Communist vote at the elections. The troublesome controversy over the form of government was also settled for the time being; many who had hitherto unwillingly adapted themselves to the changed system of government in Germany now became convinced advocates of the Republic. This brought no mitigation, however, to the heated contest between the parties. Rightist parties detected in the programmes of the Social Democrats and the Communists merely a difference of degree in their adherence to Marxist principles, principles which the majority of the middle classes were still determined to eschew.

At this point, when the future of German policy at home and abroad still hung in the balance, Friedrich Ebert, first President of the *Reich* and responsible with others for the foundation and continuance of the Weimar constitution, died. The choice of his successor lay, according to the constitution, in the hands of the people. The Republican candidate was Wilhelm Marx, former Chancellor of the *Reich*, while the opponents of the Weimar constitution put up Field Marshall von Hindenburg, now an old man. His supporters hoped that his election would deal the republic a fatal blow. Hindenburg did in fact win the election, but he swore to uphold the constitution, though it was alien to all his political principles. As a Protestant, however, he felt himself bound by his oath and he remained loyal to it until, at an advanced age, he yielded to those around him by appointing Adolf Hitler, the strongest

37. Barlach: The Avenger.

38. Marcks: Prometheus Bound II.

39. The Hansa Quarter, Berlin.

40. Pylon of the Severins Bridge, Cologne.

opponent of the Weimar Republic, Chancellor of the *Reich*. This was the first step in the course that was to plunge Germany into the abyss.

Though the German economy began to recover when inflation ended, supplies of foreign capital were necessary to repair the damage of the war and post-war years. By 1930 foreign loans amounting approximately to 26,000 million marks flowed into Germany. About 10 % of the total was appropriated by the *Reich*, the remainder being allocated to private industry and the municipalities. Thanks to this aid German industry quickly recovered to such an extent that it soon reached the technical level of industry in the United States. The consequences of this complete reorganisation were astounding.

The daily per capita output of the German miner rose

from   950 kg in 1913

to   1350 kg in 1930.

The figures for the production of coal, steel and potash amounted to:

	Coal	Steel	Potash
1913	277 mill. metric tons	17 mill. metric tons	11.5 mill. m. tons
1924	240 mill. metric tons	9.7 mill. metric tons	8.1 mill. m. tons
1927	280 mill. metric tons	16.1 mill. metric tons	11.1 mill. m. tons

The merchant navy, which in 1913 had a total tonnage of 5.7 million tons, had already reached 3.2 million tons by 1927.

From 1925 on, the export of electrical apparatus was the highest in the world; the German chemical industry ranked first among the world's producers.

These results are all the more amazing when we remember that the Treaty of Versailles had deprived Germany of 26 % of her coal, 79 % of her iron ore, and 90 % of her merchant shipping. The high level reached by German industry in such a remarkably short space of time signified a victory for big capital. Its distinguishing characteristic was the concentration of industry in a few hands. The union of capital and technical science was complete. Huge combines—the *Rheinisch-Westfälische Kohlensyndikat*, the *Vereinigte Stahlwerke AG*, the enterprises of Krupp and Stinnes, *IG Farben*, the *AEG*—were developed still further. Since the big concerns fixed the prices, they controlled all medium-sized and small enterprises as well. The research promoted by these great industrial concerns could point to successes in many fields.

Furthermore, this economic progress was accompanied by comparative prosperity in all classes of German society. Credit for the improvement is due to the trade unions and to those political parties whose main concern had always been the welfare of the masses, and also to a number of employers with a sense of social responsibility. Social legislation developed as state and municipalities extended the scope of their social services. The underprivileged were thus given a share in the country's economic prosperity. This led to a rise in the general standard of living, evident particularly in the increased consumption of quality foodstuffs and in the annual rise in private savings. Changes in the occupational distribution of the population which had set in before the world war continued. More and more people were employed in industry and trade, while at the same time the number of white-collar workers increased considerably, too. Factories having been largely mechanised, there was less demand for manual labour and more for brain workers in technical and administrative offices.

The following table illustrates the changes in the occupational distribution of the population:

	Agriculture	Industry and Crafts	Trade and Commerce
1882	42 %	33 %	8,6 %
1907	34 %	39.1 %	13.9 %
1925	30.5 %	41.4 %	16.5 %

The progress of Germany's economy in the years 1924—1928 was due both to the industry of the population and to the huge loans from abroad. In 1929, when the world-wide depression set in, the German boom collapsed. On 24 October 1929 Wall Street crashed. The immediate consequence was the withdrawal from Germany of American credits, most of which had been granted subject to recall at short notice. The effect on German industry was catastrophic, since its capital reserves were extremely small. Many factories had to shut down. Already in December of that same year there were 2.8 million unemployed in Germany. As the critical economic situation continued to deteriorate in the other industrial countries, there was no hope of improvement. This well-nigh desperate situation was seized by Adolf Hitler and his party —the *Nationalsozialistische Deutsche Arbeiterpartei* (NSDAP) or National Socialist German Workingmen's Party—as an opportunity to replace the detested democratic system by a state modelled on that erected by the Italian Fascists.

The order of freedom established for almost fifteen years in Germany as the result of the Weimar constitution proved to be extremely fruitful, particularly in the province of culture. The designation "golden twenties" is justified in that for one short decade Berlin became in the field of drama, music and the cinema a centre which for a short time replaced Paris as the cultural capital of Europe. It is impossible to list all the names of the many German producers, theatre managers, conductors and actors who achieved world-wide fame. The most eminent of them was Max Reinhardt, the founder of a new style of dramatic presentation. In addition to brilliant performances accepted as setting new standards, many experiments revealed the potentialities of stage, screen and, later, radio as vehicles of literary expression. Bert Brecht's early plays were given an interpretation worthy of them in Berlin, whence their influence spread throughout Germany and Europe. The art of music was richly stimulated by Richard Strauss (1864—1949), and still more by Hindemith and Schönberg, the pioneers of atonal music.

Under the influence of Walter Gropius and his *Bauhaus* at Weimar (later transferred to Dessau), a new style of architecture was founded. Characterised by functional design and the use of modern materials, it found expression above all in blocks of flats, business offices, concert and congress halls, sports centres and schools, all built to harmonise with the austere setting of a modern industrial city. Vigorous sculpture exemplified, say, by the work of Barlach, Marcks and, above all Lehmbruck enriched such functional structures by enlivening the architectural design both outside and in.

Literature and painting in Germany after World War I received fresh impetus from expressionism, a style developed in Germany just before 1914 in reaction to impressionism. The expressionist artist deliberately rejected "natural" colours and forms; he intensified his modes of communicating the essence of his themes—religious, social or abstract—so that his statement should stand out as clearly as possible. Line, surface, and colour were regarded as the main vehicles of expression. Eminent representatives of this tendency were Nolde, Heckel, Kokoschka, Schmidt-Rotluff, Kirchner, Marc, and Beckmann. Rudolf Belling is still active in the province of "absolute sculpture".

It was much harder in literature than in visual art to put the theory of expressionism into practice. Though the war took its early toll of young writers of note, our period produced lyric poetry and drama of permanent value (Ernst Stadler, Georg Heym, Gottfried Benn, Else Lasker-Schüler, J. R. Becker, Fritz von Unruh, Georg Kaiser, Ernst Barlach, Alfred Döblin, Franz Werfel).

On the whole, the intellectual creative spirits in the Germany of 1918 had welcomed the revolution and birth of the republic as providing congenial conditions for their activity. This also applied to those writers who had made a name for themselves before the war, men like Thomas Mann, Gerhart Hauptmann, Franz Werfel and Jakob Wassermann. Others such as R. M. Rilke and Stefan George and his circle, had refused political commitment by withdrawing into an exclusively "poetical existence", though this did not debar George's disciples, for instance, from criticising the course of Germany's development. Already in the twenties, however, we find writers beginning to repudiate the results of the change-over in 1918. For such writers, possessed as they were by the idea of a "conservative revolution", the Weimar Republic promised, not the rejuvenation of the German people and national life, but the dissolution of all order. Though scarcely any of them supported Adolf Hitler, they made a decisive contribution towards undermining resistance to National Socialism, particularly in conservative and national-istic circles. Their works provided the Nazi spokesmen with valuable propaganda material (Ernst Jünger: "Der Arbeiter", "In Stahlgewit-tern"; Moeller van den Bruck: "Das Recht der jungen Völker", "Das Dritte Reich"; O. Spengler: "Der Untergang des Abendlandes"; H. Johst, H. Grimm, and others).

Max Scheler (1875—1927) was an innovator in the sphere of philos-ophy. He broke away from the view that philosophy is nothing more than epistemology and reestablished objectivism. For him ethical values are constant and permanent. They are genuine facts and do not depend on the mental attitude of the individual. Scheler thus rescued ethical values from the relativism which they had fallen prey to chiefly in consequence of Freud's psychoanalysis and Max Adler's individual psychology. Scheler also gave religion its own special significance again. If for him metaphysics could achieve nothing more than probability, he did nevertheless try to restore it to its proper place in philosophy.

Of more lasting effect, however, was the discussion on existence, or rather on man's relationship to the truth of existence, which was ini-tiated by Martin Heidegger's early work "Sein und Zeit". This book made Heidegger the most important exponent of German existentialism. The literary productions of Camus and J. P. Sartre, to mention only French authors, witness to Heidegger's impact on international thought.

Early in the twentieth century the implications of philosophic thought constrained scientists to widen the horizon of the physical sciences. An overall view of human knowledge was adopted, which, however, did not mean the abandonment of exact scientific research. Science acquired a greater prominence than ever, particularly in Germany, where the work of Albert Einstein and Max Planck revolutionised the physical image of the universe.

Chapter Twenty-Three

FROM WEIMAR TO POTSDAM

The Presidential Government of Heinrich Brüning

No majority could be found in the German *Reichstag* of 1930 to meet a financial crisis that had arisen. The government, headed by Chancellor Hermann Müller, a Social Democrat, was composed of members of those parties which Stresemann's efforts had held together for years now in the "Grand Coalition" (Social Democrats, Democrats, and politicians of the Centre and of the German People's Party). Government expenditure for the unemployment insurance fund had been rising, since the world economic crisis was already beginning to have repercussions in Germany, too. The People's Party and the Social Democrats could not reach agreement on who should be made to bear the increased burdens, the employers or the workers. On this issue the coalition split. The government resigned.

For the first time in the short history of the Weimar Republic, it proved impossible to find a majority to form a new government. In this critical situation President von Hindenburg called upon Dr. Heinrich Brüning, *Reichstag* member for the Centre Party, to form a government not based "on coalitional ties". On 30 March 1930 Brüning accepted the responsibility with some misgivings; Hindenburg had finally overcome his reluctance by appealing to his "sense of duty as a soldier". Thus, the first presidential government came into being.

Brüning was unquestionably a man of sterling integrity. As an officer in the reserve during the First World War, he had proved his "national reliability" well enough even for the ultra-national circles in the country. By his financial policy he had made a name for himself both within and without his own party. He scorned empty phrases and loud-mouthed demagogy, by now the stock-in-trade of the extremist parties. Stern with himself, he believed that he could gain the good will of the German people by the example of his own devotion to duty and thus bring them to cooperate in combating the crisis facing the nation and the economy by their spirit of sacrifice and readiness to economise. This belief in a reasonable, far-sighted majority among the people was to prove his undoing.

To master the financial crisis, Brüning adopted a method then considered classical: he pursued a policy of deflation. He intended to balance the economy by applying drastic cuts. He was well aware that the economic situation would deteriorate as a result of these measures, but believed that considerations of domestic and foreign policy left him no alternative. His deflationary policy was aimed at proving to the world that Germany was in no position to bear the burden of the reparations imposed by the Young Plan without ruining her own economy and disturbing the economic balance of the country. At the same time he hoped that, by patient negotiation with the victor powers, he would be able to obtain some relaxation of the armament restrictions imposed by the Treaty of Versailles, and thus force equality for the *Reich* in this respect, too. He viewed the economic crisis as a natural healing process by which the economic organism would cure itself of the unhealthy outbreak of inflation caused by the excessive demand which had followed upon the First World War. His view was that government intervention in this process would be useless, until some signs of recovery were already apparent.

In order to carry through his financial reforms, he presented a series of laws to the *Reichstag* which were promptly rejected. Whereupon he had them enforced by the president of the *Reich* as emergency decrees for the "protection of the economy and finances". He now had to obtain the *Reichstag's* subsequent ratification for his measures. He therefore submitted them a second time, but they were again thrown out. For this reason Hindenburg decided to dissolve the *Reichstag* and fix new elections for 14 September 1930. In the meantime, the unemployment figures had risen to four million.

The elections only served to underline the crisis facing German democracy. The two radical parties, the Communists and the National Socialists, recorded a notable increase in their vote. The National Socialists had changed overnight from an insignificant splinter party to one of the strongest parties in the *Reichstag*. Both the conduct of the party's leader, Adolf Hitler, and its programme gave clear warning that a ruthless war against parliamentary democracy and a determined struggle for the sole power in Germany could now be expected.

The outcome of the elections only increased Brüning's difficulty in finding a majority for his programme of German restoration from within and for his foreign policy aimed at reversing Versailles. The economic crisis grew more acute as a result of the distrust aroused in foreign

OSKAR KOKOSCHKA

Amsterdam, Kloveniersburgwal

1925. Kunsthalle, Mannheim

investors by domestic developments in Germany. Brüning thus felt that he must make even greater use of the president's emergency powers. Hindenburg thus became a decisive factor in German politics. From now on, the chancellor could only govern in practice as long as he enjoyed the confidence of the president, who hat to sign and promulgate his laws in virtue of the emergency powers granted him by the constitution. At this juncture, the democratic parties, alarmed by the success of the radical parties, decided to tolerate Brüning's cabinet and give their subsequent approval to the emergency measures in order to prevent a government coming into power in which the National Socialists would have a decisive say.

On the domestic front Brüning's efforts to reverse Versailles and its consequences were designed to create the conditions for a well-balanced budget in the *Reich*, the *Länder,* and the local administration. His drastic measures to deflate prices and wages were all directed to this one end. The cost of living index did fall as a result, but the actual crisis only became more acute. Even his outstanding success in foreign policy in 1931, the Hoover moratorium for all debts, did not bring any alleviation. The progress of the opposition continued un-checked, since the unemployment figures had now risen to the five million mark. Communists and Nazis were still more successful in all pro-vincial and local elections. But as long as the parties, rejecting any kind of dictatorship, continued to tolerate Brüning's programme and the president signed his chancellor's emergency decrees, the government had nothing to fear in parliament, in spite of the fact that it did not enjoy more than a small measure of the people's confidence.

The dissolution of the dual monarchy, a consequence of Austria's defeat in the First World War, meant that German-speaking Austria had lost the economic hinterland which she had built up over the centuries. Czechoslovakia had inherited most of its industrial centres. As an agricultural country with negligible supplies of natural resources and raw materials, Austria was even more dependent on the world market than Germany. The Austrian processing industry was concentrated around the capital, Vienna, which now had a population out of all proportion to the size of the country. The high tariff barriers erected by the "Successor States" hindered the exchange of goods which had been normal before the war in the large marketing area represented by Austria-Hungary. Economic crises had thus been the order of the day since 1919, though until the world depression international monetary aid had staved off disaster. But this aid was discontinued in 1929, so that the small country was hit much harder by the breakdown in international trade than the other states of Europe. Just one year later, one of Austria's leading banks crashed, because foreign credits amounting to 80 million Marks had been withdrawn within a short time. The percentage of Austrian unemployed far exceeded the world average and was even higher than the figures in Germany.

Austria therefore concentrated her efforts on forming a customs union with Germany, attracted by the enlarged trading area that this would create. Since the peace treaties disallowed the right of self-determination in this point, so that political merger with the *Reich* was forbidden, Austria's negotiations with Germany aimed at a customs union between the two states. In March 1931 a treaty was signed which envisaged such a union. France, Italy and Czechoslovakia remained most strongly opposed to the scheme, even though both America and England had given their approval. A questionable decision of the international court at The Hague, to which France had appealed on the basis of the terms of the peace treaties concerning Austria, was against the proposed economic union. The two German states had suffered a major defeat in foreign policy, for which the nationalists in Germany and Austria justifiably blamed the 1919 treaties. Embitterment grew as the unemployment figures in both countries rose (in Germany now almost six million).

In 1932 Hindenburg's seven-year term of office expired. The Democratic-Republican parties decided, greatly influenced by Brüning, to renominate Hindenburg as their candidate. The first poll brought no constitutional decision, since none of the candidates received the required absolute majority of the actual votes cast. In the second election between Hindenburg, Hitler and Thälmann, the Communist candidate, the German people clearly decided for Hindenburg (19.4 million) and against the candidates of the right wing (Hitler 13.4 million) and of the left (Thälmann 3.7 million).

Shortly after the presidential election, Brüning introduced an emergency decree "for the protection of the authority of the state"; it banned the Nazi Storm Troopers organisation (*Sturmabteilungen*). At the same time the percentage of votes cast for the radical parties in various state elections continued to rise. This occasioned General von Schleicher to start intriguing to influence the president against Brüning. Schleicher felt the hour had come to put his scheme into execution for a renewal of the *Reich* by the right-wing parties with the support of the Centre. But the various associations of army veterans had an essential part in his plan. As he saw it, they alone provided the necessary basis for a future expansion of the army by general conscription.

Hindenburg sympathised with Schleicher's line of thought, especially as he had always regarded his reelection with the support of the left-wing parties as an election with "reversed fronts". The great landowners of East Prussia, Hindenburg's peers, also supported this line of reasoning; they regarded Brüning as an "agrarian Bolshevist", since he had made it known that he was unwilling to subsidise the bankrupt estates of the *Junker* aristocracy east of the Elbe with further *Osthilfe,* the state agrarian relief scheme providing agricultural quotas for the east. Indeed, Brüning had already started settling such estates with peasant lads from the overpopulated west. Hindenburg demanded that his chancellor also forbid the *Reichsbanner,* the Social Democrat organisation of old soldiers dedicated to the defence of the republic. Brüning refused. He was therefore dismissed by the president on 30 March 1932, without being able to summon up the resolve to appeal to the *Reichstag* to find out whether a majority from the right or the left could be mustered against him. The new man who enjoyed the president's confidence was Franz von Papen.

Papen, Hitler's Precursor

Brüning's resignation met with the approval of the Right, but was sharply criticised by the Centre and Left. Abroad it was greeted with amazement. Papen was numbered among Hindenburg's closest friends. Politically he had adopted a position on the extreme right-wing of the Centre Party and had definite inclinations towards the German National Party. His cabinet was composed mainly of members of the aristocracy, so that it became known as the "cabinet of barons". Schleicher was appointed Minister of Defence.

Shortly after von Papen took office, the reparations conference for which Brüning had prepared the way met in Lausanne from 16 to 19 June. The payment of reparations was abolished. Although this could be considered a foreign political success for Papen, it did not strengthen his hand at home.

In order to achieve his goal in home politics of a "concentration of 'national' forces", i.e. a majority of the Right, Papen deposed, in a breach of the constitution, the lawfully elected Prussian cabinet of Social Democrats, Democrats and politicians of the Centre, and appointed himself *Reich* commissioner for Prussia. Hindenburg dissolved the *Reichstag.* But the elections did not result in a majority for Papen's government, since the National Socialists were able to increase their share of the poll to 37.2 %, whereas the German National Party was reduced to the status of an insignificant splinter party. In order to forestall an inevitable vote of no confidence, Papen influenced the president to dissolve the *Reichstag* yet again in September 1932. But these elections did not bring a workable parliamentary majority for Papen's government, either. Papen therefore offered Hindenburg his resignation.

Hindenburg appointed Schleicher successor to Papen. Schleicher now tried to achieve his "renewal of the *Reich*" by splitting the Nazi party and enlisting the support of the unions. Among the National Socialists he was able to win over Gregor Strasser and his supporters. A serious crisis arose in the leadership of the party, which was accompanied by a crippling lack of funds. But Hitler and Goebbels were able to isolate Strasser who lacked the decisiveness to carry his view. Organised Labour also disappointed Schleicher's plans. Hindenburg would not give his support to Schleicher's last resort of a *coup d'état* with the aid of the military.

Papen, who still enjoyed Hindenburg's confidence, exerted himself behind the scenes to bring about a reconciliation with the National Socialists. On 4 January he met Hitler for talks in the house of the Cologne banker von Schroeder. Here the broad outlines for the formation of a future government were agreed upon. On 28 January, Schleicher resigned from the chancellorship. Two days later, Hindenburg appointed the "Bohemian Corporal", as he liked to call Hitler, Chancellor of the *Reich*. As agreed beforehand, Papen became Vice-Chancellor and *Reich* Commissioner for Prussia. With the exception of Frick (Minister of the Interior) and Göring (Minister without Portfolio), both National Socialists, all the other ministers were either German National politicians or independents. It looked as though the National Socialist flood had been successfully "canalised", or, as Papen put it referring to Hitler, "We have enlisted his services for our cause". On 1 February the *Reichstag* was dissolved and new elections announced for 5 March.

Chapter Twenty-Four

GERMANY UNDER HITLER

Adolf Hitler

The wave of enthusiasm for the national cause which swept many sections of the German population in August 1914 also affected a 25-year-old Austrian who had been eking out a living in Munich for a year as an "independent artist" without regular employment. He despised Austria because of her multi-national character and this led him to evade military service in the Austrian army. However, he volunteered for a Bavarian regiment, saw action on the western front as a dispatch runner, and, as a common soldier, was awarded the Iron Cross, first and second class, for bravery in action. He was recuperating from the effects of gassing in a military hospital in Pomerania, when the news came through of the German defeat. Germany's capitulation brought his world crashing down in ruins. He had believed to the end in a German victory. Convinced that the defeat and the revolution were not the result of Germany's military and economic inferiority but rather of the political inadequacy of the emperor and the government, "he resolved to enter politics". The Austrian in question was called Adolf Hitler.

There had been nothing remarkable about Hitler's life before his participation in the war, unless perhaps the fact that a healthy young man should have loafed away his time in the men's hostels and doss-houses of Vienna out of work and with no profession should be considered out of the ordinary and worthy of mention. He was later to maintain, after he had already attained a certain measure of success in political life, that he had wanted to become an architect, after a short and unsuccessful beginning at a secondary school. But he had not been admitted to the Vienna Academy of Fine Arts, since he did not satisfy the preliminary scholastic requirements. This meant that he was forced to work as an "independent artist". During this period he devoted a great deal of his attention to political questions and extended his general education by a self-imposed course of study and wide reading.

After the war he returned to Munich where he came under the influence of the numerous "national" groups which all had one thing in common: antagonism to the Weimar Republic. He joined the "German Worker's Party", receiving membership card no. 7. He soon became well-known as a political speaker in the beer cellars and taverns of the suburbs. The party changed its name to *Nationalsozialistische Deutsche Arbeiterpartei* (National Socialist German Workingmen's Party) or NSDAP as it was generally known. Its programme was a hodge-podge of nationalist and socialist ideas. It laid particular stress on anti-Semitism. Its proclaimed goal in foreign politics was the liberation from "Versailles" and the foundation of a Greater German *Reich*. The party programme was silent about the form the state should take.

Inflation, communist risings, the occupation of the Ruhr by the French and general political apathy all seemed to confirm Hitler in his belief that he could follow Mussolini's lead and install a Nazi-dominated government in Berlin. But his first attempt to seize power in Munich on 9 November 1923 foundered, because of inadequate preparation and the resistance of the Munich police. The republic put Hitler and his accomplices on trial for high treason. The sentences imposed were extremely mild. An amnesty brought Hitler's confinement in the fortress at Landsberg to an end after only two years.

Now he showed a talent for organisation in building up his scattered party again and, at the same time, a strong will in pushing through without compromise the measures which he considered right. This meant that he was able to inject into National Socialism, in itself just another insignificant party among the many nationalist groups, a certain energy and drive which bore fruit in the elections. Nevertheless, between the years 1925 and 1930, his party polled hardly more than 3 % of the votes cast.

This period of political unimportance he employed to good purpose by making a careful study of modern political propaganda methods in practice. Certain of his power as an orator, he became convinced that he could capture and win the masses for his cause by the power of the spoken word; their votes would help him to attain the supreme power in the land. This meant, of course, that the demagogue must adopt the simplest style in his speeches and constantly repeat the same primitive line of argument. While appealing to the lowest instincts in men, he would also have to awaken their longing for the realisation of some great ideal. The spoken word was to be underlined by striking symbols. In Hitler's eyes the essential means to achieve his ends became the mass meetings, to which he imparted a style of their own. He preferred to arrange his political demonstrations for late in the evening. He had the waiting crowd, numbering tens of thousands, entertained with military music. He arranged for his proximate appearance to be announced several times. By the time he eventually showed up, the crowd was already in such a state of excited hysterical expectation that it was impossible for them to receive him and what he had to say with any measure of critical judgment. He thus became a master of propaganda technique at a time when the world of commerce was only just beginning to realise the importance of advertisement.

At the outset, his audience was essentially composed of all those whose lives had been thrown off balance by defeat, inflation, and the economic crisis: impoverished members of the lower middle classes, farmers, discontented petty officials, former members and officers of the free corps, all varieties of artists of average ability, out-of-work university graduates and students. They all tried to cover their own personal inadequacy with the mantle of some superhuman fate, identified by Hitler with "Versailles" or with "international Jewry". That certain influential and financially powerful circles in German industry also gave Hitler their support from time to time is to be accounted for less by their sympathy for him personally than by their antipathy for many of the dominant circles at the head of the Weimar Republic.

Nevertheless, Hitler's party would have remained insignificant if the economic crisis had not caused broad sections of the German population to join his party and vote for him. The number of enrolled members was still only 180,000 in 1928. From 1930 onwards, the year in which the unemployment figures topped the 4 million mark, membership rose by leaps and bounds, until it reached one million in 1932. The Nazi share of the poll rose just as astronomically, although it never amounted to anything like an absolute majority of all the votes cast.

Hitler's speeches revolved around a few central themes: international Jewry, which was represented as the source of both capitalism and Marxist Bolshevism indifferently, the "Weimar Set-Up", which was nothing more than an invention of the Jews to enslave Germany, and the Treaty of Versailles. The Jew was thus depicted as the cultural vandal par excellence; his one consuming aim was to displace the "Aryan" master race, which was the embodiment of human greatness, the positive creator of world history. The extravagance of his hatred for everything Jewish, the onesidedness of his propaganda against the Jews, whom he regarded as the one and only cause of all the misfortunes that had befallen the German people, gave the impression to those familiar with his teaching on the "one and only opponent" on whom all hatred should be focused that anti-Semitism was a propaganda gimmick rather than an essential objective. Many German Jews even took false comfort in this line of thought, for they simply could not credit that a far more terrible storm was gathering in the land of Lessing and Goethe than had overtaken the Jews during the expulsion from Spain during the course of the 15th and 16th centuries.

Hitler and his henchmen created out of their anti-Semitism a counterpart which they opposed to the object of their hatred. This was the myth of pure blood and of the Aryan race. They felt that they could base this myth on pseudo-historical and biological grounds.

Since Hitler wanted nothing other than "power, the whole power" (as he once informed Brüning), his words and actions were directed with singleness of purpose to this one end. An astonishingly unerring instinct for what served his purpose here and now helped him to the realisation of that end. This instinct determined his attitude in his personal intercourse, whether with a man of the people or with the representative of a friendly or hostile power. Although he himself recognised no ties and was scornful of every moral norm, he could, when he felt that the occasion demanded it of him, talk of the highest moral, religious or national values, as if he were their untiring champion. The next moment, however, the spirit of hate or his thirst for power could cause him to trample over the bodies of millions in the pursuit of his true aims.

The "Führer" State

After his appointment as chancellor on 30 January 1933, Hitler overrode the wishes of the German Nationals in his cabinet and proclaimed new elections for the *Reichstag*. There can be no doubt that he hoped that his party would obtain an absolute majority. The NSDAP and its leader conducted an election campaign such as Germany had never seen before. Radio and press were placed almost exclusively at their disposal. Yet, in spite of this, the majority of the German people did not cast their vote for Hitler and his party. Of the total poll the Nazis received 43.9 % of the votes, the German Nationals 8 %. However, this did mean that the coalition now had a majority in the *Reichstag*. The SPD (Social Democratic Party), the Centre and the Bavarian People's Party managed to maintain their previous share of the poll. The communists registered considerable losses.

Nevertheless, the elections had once again shown that the majority of the German people had voted against the democratic order established at Weimar, for the communists were also not prepared to rise to the defence of the republic. They thought that, after a short, barren Hitler regime, Germany would be ripe for a Bolshevist dictatorship. Their dogmatism had prevented them for years from pursuing a realistic policy.

Hardly one week before the elections, a Dutchman, M. van der Lubbe, set the *Reichstag* building afire in Berlin. No conclusive evidence has ever been produced to show that political forces were behind this arson. But Hitler and his cronies, at any rate, saw it was a heaven-sent opportunity to make the communists publicly responsible for this outrage and to whip up German fears of Bolshevism still more. At the same time the fire gave them a pretext to suspend with the approval of the president certain decisive basic rights enshrined in the German constitution. All German citizens, their homes and possessions, all political parties, associations and groups were placed at the mercy of police tyranny. Thus, even before the elections, Hitler had already taken the first crucial step towards eliminating his opponents by force.

The majority which the two coalitional parties, the National Socialists and the German Nationals, had obtained in the *Reichstag* was not sufficient to enable Hitler to rule without the *Reichstag*, as long, that is, as he still set store on an appearance of legality for his actions. This explains why his mind was so set on getting a two-thirds majority in the *Reichstag* for a "Law for Removing the Distress of People and Reich" (the so-called "Enabling Act"), which would empower him to enact laws for four years without parliamentary control. When the *Reichstag* assembled on 21 March 1933, Hitler's speech was a model of restraint. He spoke of the great importance of the Christian Churches and of keeping the law in Germany completely independent of politics. He vowed that he would never use his powers to abuse the law. He guaranteed the separate cultural and economic existence of the German *Länder*. The *Reichstag*, too, was to exercise its constitutional rights again after a period of four years. Trusting his word, all parties with the exception of the Social Democrats and the Communists, who had been excluded beforehand, cast their votes for the law. Wels, the leader of the SPD, gave the reasons for his party's attitude in a last courageous free speech before the assembled parliament. The *Reichstag*, however, surrendered its rights by a two-third's majority. Hitler could now commence the construction of the *Führer* state with complete constitutional legality.

But a few days later, Hitler made clear to Germany and the world what his word was really worth. In violation of the German constitution, all the *Land* diets were reconstituted on the basis of the *Reichstag* elections, without fresh regional elections being held; the governments of the German states were placed under "*Reich* Governors".

When it became clear that the Trade Unions were not willing to relinquish their position as the independent representatives of the workers, they were dissolved on 2 May 1933. Their funds were confiscated and placed at the disposal of the German "Labour Front". This measure formed the prelude to the proscription or self-dissolution of all parties with the exception of the National Socialists. A law was promulgated forbidding the formation of new parties and pronouncing the NSDAP the "State Party". From now on the *Reichstag* had but one function: to rubber-stamp all Hitler's decrees. It "prolonged" the "Enabling Act" twice, the third prolongation was effected by Hitler in 1945 by means of a "decree".

Within some six months of Hitler's assumption of power, the bases of the Weimar Republic had been thoroughly undermined. Hitler's own name for the violent destruction of the free framework of the constitutional state was "National Revolution". But whereas all previous revolutions—even the Bolshevist—had tried to replace the old order with a new, Hitler aspired to something quite different. The democratic and constitutional free state was replaced by the dictatorship of one man. The instrument of his power was terror, at first over his own people, and later over all those peoples who fell under his sway. That there were many willing helpers among the German people to assist Hitler in his criminal objectives was a disgrace to the German name and reduced Germany, in the historical sense, to an accessory to Hitler's acts.

The Reign of Terror

Already before Hitler's assumption of power, the Nazi Storm Troopers (the SA or *Sturmabteilung,* the "Storm Section" of the party) had tried to intimidate Hitler's political opponents by threats of death and economic pressure. From 30 January 1933 the regular police force was reinforced by members of the SA acting as "auxiliary policemen". They regarded the arbitrary arrest of political opponents and Jews as their primary duty. As the number of those arrested continued to rise, the prisons could no longer accommodate them all, so, by Göring's order, the first concentration camps were erected, in which at first only

Germans were placed. Party violence was given pseudo-legality in the state when the "Secret State Police" *(Geheime Staatspolizei,* abbreviated to the more familiar *Gestapo)* was made an executive organ of the state. What Nazi propaganda was not able to achieve, fear of arrest and confinement in a concentration camp was to make possible.

Ernst Röhm, a former captain in the army and now head of the Storm Troopers, had already planned before Hitler came to power to make his organisation, with its approximately 400,000 members, the core of a Nazi people's army. The officer corps in the army was inflexibly opposed to this plan. As long as Hindenburg was still alive, Hitler believed that he must ensure the good will and conduct of the army. Among the party leaders, Heinrich Himmler, the chief of the *Gestapo* and originally one of Hitler's personal bodyguard of Storm Troopers, was bitterly opposed to Röhm and his supporters. While he had the SA heads rounded up and shot in Munich, Göring and Goebbels, the *Reich* Minister of Public Enlightenment and Propaganda, took the opportunity to murder numerous personages of public life who were viewed as possible opponents of the new regime. Several hundred people fell victim to this "Blood Purge" directed by the party leaders— among others Schleicher, Gregor Strasser, collaborators of von Papen, and "Catholic Action" leaders. The *Reichstag* gave its blessing to these murders by pronouncing them "lawful" and necessary for the "defence of the state". Röhm's murder also left the way clear for the rise of the SS (*Schutzstaffel*) and Himmler. Two years later the police were also placed under Himmler. Hitler possessed in his "*Reichsführer* SS and Chief of the German Police" until the fall of the "Third *Reich*", as Germany was known under the Nazis, a willing tool for the execution of his insane scheme of extermination, which men had until now looked upon as inconceivable and impossible of realisation.

The death of the President of the *Reich*, Hindenburg, on 2 August 1934 released Hitler from the irksome necessity of having to show consideration for the office and authority of the president, although Hindenburg on account of his great age, his dwindling mental powers, and his isolation at Neudeck, his East Prussian estate, was hardly still able to exercise a decisive influence on the political scene. It cannot be denied that Hindenburg had played a fateful role in Germany's destiny since the dismissal of Brüning. Immediately after Hindenburg's death, Hitler nominated himself "*Führer* and *Reichskanzler*", thus combining the offices of president and chancellor, and caused the army to take an oath of allegiance to his person. In 1938, he added to the unrestricted power that was now his in Germany by abolishing the Ministry of War. Its place was taken by the Supreme Command of the Army. That same year he nominated himself Commander-in-Chief of the army as well.

The Campaign Against the Jews and the Christian Churches

German Jewry had won a position of respect for itself in Germany since its liberation from the ghetto by the Stein-Hardenberg reforms at the beginning of the 19th century and its full emancipation in 1869. The tendency to merge entirely with the German people had become more pronounced in proportion to the ever-increasing social, economic and professional equality. Conversions to either of the two great Christian confessions were not infrequent and marriages with non-Jews were no longer looked upon as something out of the ordinary. During the Great War, the percentage of Jews who laid down their lives for their country was completely in accord with their numbers in the population. Many of them left the army with high decorations. Since the war the Jews had provided a remarkable number of internationally recognised scientists like Einstein, artists like Max Reinhardt, musicians like Bruno Walter and Schönberg, writers like Kafka, and philosophers like Martin Buber. In spite of anti-Semitic speeches and writing before and after the First World War and in spite of the Zionist movement which only gradually took root among the broad masses of the Jews, the tendency towards assimilation had continued among the majority of German Jews.

This fruitful development was brought to an abrupt end, when Hitler assumed power. Completely misunderstanding Hitler's real intentions, only very few German Jews, mainly those active in politics, got out of harm's way. But as early as 1 April 1933 a public boycott hit Jewish shops, lawyers and doctors hard. The SA provided sentries to supervise its observance. By the law for the "Restoration of the Civil Service" all Jews and officials descended "from at least three grandparents of pure Jewish race", as well as political opponents, lost their posts. The Jews in the liberal professions were also deprived of their livelihood, for since the *Gleichschaltung* (the coordination of the *Reich*), all self-employed persons were obliged to enroll in a Nazi organisation.

The "Nuremberg Laws" of 15 September 1935 distinguished between "Aryan citizens of the *Reich*" enjoying full rights and mere "subjects", prohibited marriages between Aryans and Jews, and brutally punished

284

the so-called "racial stain". Thus, in one fell stroke, the Jews were cast back to their state of pre-emancipation days.

The assassination of a counsellor at the German embassy in Paris by the 17-year-old son of a Jewish family deported to Poland in the most shameful fashion was the opportunity for an organised outbreak of "spontaneous" terror by plain-clothes members of the *Sturmabteilung* against all Jews in the night of 9/10 November 1938 (called the *Kristallnacht* or "Night of the Broken Glass" on account of the shattered windows of Jewish shops). In this one night practically all the synagogues in Germany were set on fire, Jewish cemeteries desecrated, and brutalities practised on Jewish men, women and children. In addition a fine of 1,250 million Marks was imposed on the Jews. From now on, Jews were forbidden to take part in cultural events or attend German schools. Naturally they were regarded as "unfit for military service", too. In order to make any relations with a German impossible, in accordance with Hitler's will, they were bound as from 15 September 1941 to wear a "Star of David", several inches across, attached to their clothing on the left hand side of the breast, and to add "Israel" or "Sarah" to "Aryan" sounding names. Many Jews proudly conformed to this decree to bear the names of great biblical personages. A kind of "Jewish Renaissance" flowered out of the isolation into which the Jews were now forced. Hitler's final aim was the physical extermination of the whole of European Jewry, a goal for which he felt the time was not yet ripe merely for reasons of foreign policy. A war would, in his opinion, provide him with the opportunity he was looking for.

The two great Christian confessions, but especially the Catholic Church, had met Hitler's seizure of power with reserve or open disapproval. The assertion in the Nazi programme that the party "rests on the foundation of positive Christianity" was generally regarded as pure rhetoric. The Catholic Church had even attached penalties to membership of the National Socialist Party. After he came to power, Hitler's political conduct towards the Churches at first seemed to give the lie to this attitude. In July 1933 he concluded a concordat with the Catholic Church, in which he recognised the Church's right to its own Catholic youth organisation and to denominational schools. But immediately after signing it, he had Catholic youth leaders arrested in Berlin. A little later he tried to shake the Catholic population's confidence in its pastors by bringing "scandal cases" against Catholic priests.

Hitler thought the Protestant Church would be easy meat. Ludwig Müller, a former army chaplain, was placed at the head of a Hitler-inspired splinter group which called itself the "German Christians' Faith Movement". He had Müller appointed *Reichsbischof*. After Müller had been confirmed in this position by synodal elections which resulted in a German Christian majority in all the regional churches, with the exception of Westphalia, Hitler regarded him as the official representative of the Protestant Church. But now representatives of the Protestant Church in all the German *Länder* took up the struggle against the distortion of the Christian message by the German Christians. They formed the "Confessing Church", which took its stand on the bible and the creeds. The best brain among them was Karl Barth, their best known member Martin Niemöller, former submarine commander during the First World War and now pastor in Berlin-Dahlem. Niemöller was placed in a concentration camp in 1937 because of his resistance to the National Socialists, and remained there until the end of the Second World War. In 1934 at Barmen, and a year later in Berlin, the "Confessing Church" rejected the Nazi *Weltanschauung*. In 1937 the papal encyclical "Mit brennender Sorge" (With Burning Anxiety) condemned Nazi racialism and the glorification of the "Aryan Master Race" as heretical.

Nazi Economic Policy

Hitler came to power when the economic situation in Germany, as in all the other industrial states of the world, had already passed its crisis. Measures calculated to encourage the natural process of recovery were also passed in the democratically ruled countries of the world. The Papen government had already inaugurated, on the basis of plans prepared by Brüning, an economic policy which envisaged an economically feasible, accelerated solution of unemployment problems. Hitler, however, contended that he was the architect of the so-called "Battle against Unemployment", a scheme designed to eliminate unemployment by expanding public works. The German *Autobahnen*, for instance, were constructed within the framework of these plans, though at the time few people were aware of their strategic importance. The government also awarded a great many armament contracts in an effort to pave the way for rearmament. And, in fact, the regime succeeded—faster than in the other industrial states— in reducing unemployment considerably, a success which enabled the Nazis to consolidate their position at home and which also won them recognition among those circles which were most inflexible in their oposition to the Nazi *Weltanschauung.*

However, as early as 1936, the drawbacks of Nazi economic policy began to make themselves felt. The state programme of work provision compelled the German economy to import a greater proportion of raw materials and agricultural products. Such imports were not balanced by corresponding exports. The national reserves shrank. In order to bolster the value of the Mark at home, the regime developed a planned economy by which Germany was to be made as independent of other countries as possible. This economic coercion harmonised completely with Hitler's conceptions, for he believed that he would be able to brave an English blockade in a future war because of Germany's autarky. The entire industrial and agricultural production was re-organised from the military standpoint on the basis of a four-year plan elaborated by Göring. Steel production rose considerably. In spite of the high cost of production, new synthetic materials of military importance were developed to replace their natural counterparts. The import of agricultural products was cut so drastically that important basic foodstuffs became scarce ("Cannon instead of butter"). The policy of unrestrained public expenditure disorganised finances; the German economic dependence on other countries, which could not be entirely excluded, drifted ever closer to a dangerous situation in which production would have to be throttled, because the country's foreign exchange was exhausted. Hitler was able to escape this danger by unleashing the Second World War.

Successes in Foreign Policy

From the moment Hitler "resolved to enter politics", his goal in foreign politics was to cast off the shackles of the Treaty of Versailles, to efface the German defeat of 1918, and to acquire *Lebensraum* (living space) in eastern Europe for the "German master race". In this way Germany was to become the foremost power in Europe. All Hitler's measures, in the field of domestic policy also, served this prime purpose. Conscious that the European powers, including Fascist Italy, regarded him and his regime with marked reserve, he proceeded with the greatest caution in the realisation of his plans. During the early years, in order to avoid a premature war, which he had no hope of winning on account of Germany's military weakness, he protested again and again his desire for peace and his intention to achieve a peaceful settlement of all outstanding questions, especially in regard to France. However, in 1933, when England, France and Italy refused to extend the equality already conceded the *Reich* to military matters as well, Germany walked out of the League of Nations. A few weeks later Hitler unexpectedly signed a ten-year pact of non-aggression with Poland. The Weimar Republic had always refused to recognise the Versailles settlement of the border questions to Germany's east and had thus forced Poland to maintain a close alliance with France. However, when Poland found in 1933 that the western powers were not prepared to wage a preventive war, she drew away from France out of fear of Soviet Russia, and closer to Germany. Poland hoped to defend her possessions against her eastern neighbours, if need be, with the aid of the *Reich*. The signing of the treaty gave Hitler another welcome opportunity to demonstrate his peaceful intentions. With this treaty he also weakened the "Little Entente" (Yugoslavia, Czechoslovakia, Rumania) emphasizing the value of bilateral agreements as opposed to collective security.

In January 1935 Hitler achieved his first convincing success in foreign politics when nearly 90 % of the inhabitants of the Saar voted for the return of the region to the *Reich,* in a plebiscite provided for in the Treaty of Versailles. Hitler regarded the vote as a confirmation of his policy, which was true only with qualifications. However, the plebiscite did show with absolute clarity that the right of self-determination, the safeguarding of which Wilson had already proclaimed in 1918 as one of the essential war aims of the allies, could no longer be denied to the German people. This viewpoint found support especially in England, where it weakened the spirit of resistance to National Socialist policy. Moreover, Hitler's efforts to present Germany as the uncompromising opponent of Bolshevism and as the "defender of western culture and civilisation" succeeded in winning ever more sympathy and understanding for Germany. The anti-Semitic excesses, the concentration camps, and the travesties of justice were dismissed only too lightly outside Germany as passing, subsidiary excesses in a great people's revolutionary awakening.

Still Germany remained politically isolated until 1935. This was to be seen especially when universal military service was reintroduced in March of that year. Italy, France, and England countered this move with the Conference of Stresa (16 April). It looked as though a period of close collaboration between these three powers was being heralded. Shortly afterwards France concluded a treaty of mutual assistance with the Soviet Union. Czechoslovakia also joined the treaty.

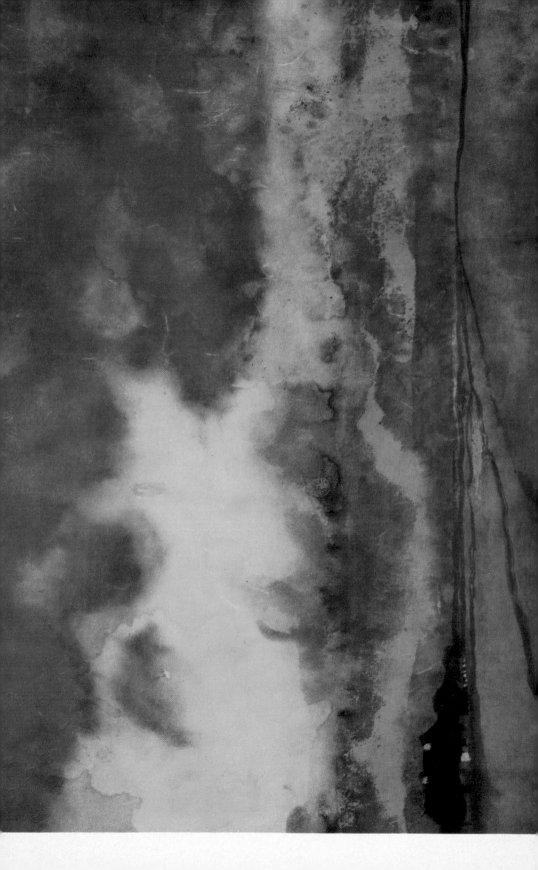

EMIL NOLDE

Abend im Gotteskoog

Le soir à Gotteskoog

Evening in Gotteskoog

Atardecer en Gotteskoog

Anoitecer no Gotteskoog

1945. Sammlung Dr. Harald Busch, Frankfurt a. M.

But by June 1935 Germany's situation had changed considerably. Great Britain announced her readiness to sign a naval treaty with the *Reich*. Hitler's demands seemed moderate: the German navy should not exceed 35 % of British naval forces; submarine tonnage was to be limited to 45 %, under certain conditions to 100 %, of British submarine strength. In this way Britain was the first power to give legal recognition to German rearmament and to express its approval by treaty.

When the League of Nations imposed sanctions in answer to Italy's attack on Abyssinia, Mussolini drew closer to Hitler for economic reasons. Hitler's recognition of Italy's African conquests and the grant of German economic aid to Italy led to a hesitant re-orientation of Italian foreign policy.

Hitler judged the new political situation in Europe appropriate for a daring political and military undertaking: the remilitarisation of the Rhineland (7 March 1936). This was not only a clear breach of the Versailles Treaty, but also of the Locarno Pact, which Germany had freely signed. But the western powers responded with nothing more than a weak protest.

Germany had successfully reasserted her full sovereignty over her territory; now rearmament transformed her into one of the strongest military powers in Europe. This meant that she came into consideration as a possible ally and as an important figure in European power politics. At the same time she pursued a vigorous anti-Bolshevist policy, which she shared with Italy, and Japan, and also with influential circles in western and eastern Europe. At this time, too, ideological considerations were often placed above national interests. Hitler exploited this attitude for his own ends. This explains why Hitler, in union with Mussolini, supported Franco, an extreme anti-Bolshevik, in his struggle against republicans, communists, and anarchists.

To overcome Mussolini's mistrust of Nazi foreign policy, Hitler dropped the Austrian policy he had followed till now. Very soon after coming to power, Hitler had exerted economic pressure on his smaller German neighbour to force her into his camp. The attempt had ended in failure, because Italy gave her support to Austria. Even the assassination of the Austrian dictator Dollfuss by Austrian Nazis in 1934 did not force a change in Austrian foreign policy, which was intent on safeguarding Austria's independence for as long as Hitler was in power. Austria could rest assured of Mussolini's support, precisely in this respect, because Italy feared a common frontier with a Greater German *Reich*. For this reason Hitler aspired after a provisional normalisation of his relations with Austria. He therefore recognised Austria's independence in an Austro-German treaty of 11 July, 1936. In this way another obstacle to closer Italo-German cooperation had been removed.

This cooperation found expression not only in the combined support of Franco mentioned above, and the closer economic relations between the two countries, but also in an ideological pact. In November 1936, Japan and Germany had concluded the Anti-Comintern Pact, which bound both lands to an ideological war against the Communist International. It expressly emphasised that the struggle was not directed against the Soviet Union. For this reason the treaties of both parties with the Soviet Union remained intact.

The following year Mussolini also signed the pact. In the meantime, the relations between the two dictators had grown so close that there was talk of a Berlin-Rome Axis. The Soviet Union was weakened by internal political and economic crises. Stalin's "purges" had also hit the officer corps of the "Red Army" hard. In France, the popular front government was incapable of pursuing a clear line in foreign policy. In England influential political and business circles regarded National Socialism in Germany with a certain measure of benevolence, no matter how emphatically they rejected any form of totalitarianism for their own country.

All this formed the foreign political background to Hitler's next steps in domestic and foreign policy, which he prepared with the greatest care. The key positions in the diplomatic corps and the army he filled with men who enjoyed his confidence. J. von Ribbentrop, a man whose ambition was matched by his blind devotion to Hitler, was appointed foreign minister.

Since the dissolution of the dual monarchy after the First World War, the *Anschluß* or union of German-speaking Austria with the *Reich* had formed part of the programme of nearly all political parties, even of the Left, in both Austria and Germany. The drafts of the democratic constitutions of both these countries even envisaged such a union. However, the victors vetoed this plan for reasons of military policy, which were strongly advocated especially by France, Italy and Czechoslovakia. The populations of both countries reconciled themselves to this arrangement only with marked reluctance. Austria's economic weakness strengthened the hand of those agitating for the *Anschluß*, which the Austrian Nazis had made the fulcrum of their political programme. Hitler could therefore be sure of the approval of nearly all the inhabitants of both countries if he succeeded in achieving a peaceful union. Instead, in keeping with his entire mental outlook, he achieved it by subjecting the smaller state to the will of the government of a great power.

To strengthen the influence of the Austrian National Socialists in the government of their country, Hitler requested the Austrian Chancellor to pay him a visit in 1938. The Austrian Chancellor declared under pressure his willingness to reorganise his cabinet, but he was not prepared to renounce Austria's independence. When he then tried to thwart the German dictator's demands by suddenly announcing a plebiscite, Hitler ordered German troops to march into Austria on 13 March 1938. They met no resistance; on the contrary, they were given an enthusiastic reception by the population. The Austrian government had to yield to this pressure. A plebiscite taken later showed that Hitler's action was approved by the peoples of both lands. The Austrians still had no inkling of the sacrifices they would be called upon to make for the realisation of the century-old dream of all-German unity.

The west European powers answered this new surprise development again with feeble protest notes. Italy gave its approval to Austria's incorporation in the *Reich*. Hitler declared in the *Reichstag*: "The period of surprises is now closed. Peace is our supreme good." But at the same time he was elucidating to the bigwigs in the party and army his plans to smash Czechoslovakia and for the construction of the "West Wall".

The *"Sudeten* German Party" led by Konrad Henlein now adopted a threatening attitude towards the Czechoslovakian state. Prague ordered the mobilisation of its armed forces on 20 May 1938 out of fear of German aggression. A new crisis began to build up which was to bring Europe to the brink of war in the autumn of that year.

Czechoslovakia was one of the successor states to the Austro-Hungarian Monarchy; like the latter it was also a multi-national state, though on a much smaller scale. The two constituent peoples, the Czechs and the Slovaks, who were not even united among themselves, were offset by Hungarian, Ruthenian, Polish and German minorities. The Germans alone numbered 3.5 million. The intention of the founder of the state, Masaryk, to make Czechoslovakia another Switzerland could not be realised. The composition of the German parties represented in the Czech parliament in Prague was more or less the same as in Germany until 1930. But here the German left-wing parties also aspired after greater independence from Prague for the German regions within the Czechoslovakian state. The Nazi Sudeten German "Home Front" headed by Henlein made capital out of Czechoslovakia's close alliance with the Soviet Union in 1935 and became the second strongest party. In the elections of May/June 1938 it polled 91 % of the German votes. On 12 September 1938 Hitler demanded self-determination for all Germans. Prague declared martial law, France called up the reservists, and the English fleet was concentrated. In this tense situation the English Prime Minister Neville Chamberlain sought to save the peace by personal negotiations with Hitler. When these threatened to break down because of Hitler's extravagant demands, President Roosevelt of America intervened and called upon Mussolini to use his influence with Hitler to avert a war. Hitler, who was set on military action against Czechoslovakia, was unable to resist this great pressure, so that the Munich Agreement was signed on 29/30 September 1938.

The result of the Munich Conference between Neville Chamberlain, Premier Daladier of France, Mussolini and Hitler was the cession of the German-speaking border regions of Czechoslovakia to the *Reich*. Czechoslovakia thus lost its most prosperous and, from the military and the industrial standpoint, most important regions. In the eyes of the Germans and the world, Munich represented Hitler's greatest triumph, especially as he had succeeded in completely ignoring the Soviet Union, Prague's most important ally. Hitler himself did not lay great store by this triumph. He nursed a grudge against the western statesmen whose spirit of compromise had made the military occupation of the whole of Czechoslavakia impossible. He looked upon their efforts on behalf of peace as cowardice, not as an expression of the western powers' recognition that the order created by Versailles could no longer be considered tenable. The denial to the Germans of the loudly proclaimed right of self-determination for peoples had proved the greatest cause of unrest since 1919. If the policy of the West was to inspire belief and trust in the peoples of the world and of their own countries, it could not afford to abandon moral principles. It was Chamberlain's tragedy that he was called upon to negotiate with a man for whom moral principles were mere empty phrases.

Chapter Twenty-Five

THE SECOND WORLD WAR

The Prague Prelude

Chamberlain had assured the English nation on his return to London from the Bavarian capital that the Munich Agreement represented "peace in our time". His words were enthusiastically received by the broad masses of the people. In his heart of hearts, however, Chamberlain was convinced that the demon in Hitler would not allow the world any rest. The optimistic face he put on things he considered justified because of an agreement by which Germany and England committed themselves to mutual consultation. A similar agreement was signed some weeks later between the *Reich* and France. The scepticism with which Chamberlain received Hitler's assurances of his peaceful intentions, however, led to English rearmament on a moderate scale. France also strengthened her armed might. For the first time since 1933, the western democracies realised that force was the only answer to a totalitarianism based on force. But even now both powers were again content with half measures, so that Hitler could afford to greet their menacing words with taunts and sneers.

Immediately after signing the "Munich Agreement" Hitler had ordered the army to make the necessary preparations for the occupation of the remainder of Czechoslovakia. When we consider that, after the cession of the *Sudeten* regions, Czechoslovakia was no longer in a position under any circumstances whatsoever to pursue an independent foreign policy, let alone one directed against Germany, it is astonishing that Hitler should still have insisted on military occupation of the country. The only possible explanation must lie in the deep-rooted hatred and the boundless contempt of Hitler, the Austrian, for all Slavs.

Now the incorporation of Bohemia and Moravia was accomplished according to well-tried methods. Although the Czechs offered no grounds for interference in their internal affairs, Nazi propaganda maintained that the Slovaks could no longer be expected to remain party to the Czechoslovakian state. Tiso, the Slovak premier, was invited to declare Slovakia an independent state under German protection. During the night of 14/15 March, Hacha, the Czech President, was summoned to appear before Hitler and place "the fate of the Czech people and country confidently in the hands of the *Führer* of the German *Reich*", under threat of the aerial bombardement of Prague. Bohemia and Moravia thus became a *Reich* protectorate. On 15 March Hitler made his entry into Prague with an ostentatious display of military strength. The country was now ruled from Hradschin Castle by a *Reich* Protector.

Under pressure of events in central Europe, the little country of Lithuania also declared its readiness to cede the Memel district to Germany.

By occupying Prague, Hitler had himself destroyed the bases upon which his Munich Agreement had been built. Again and again he had solemnly declared that nothing was more alien to his purpose than the incorporation in the *Reich* of non-Germanic lands. His annexation of Bohemia and Moravia not only discredited his words before the whole world but deprived his previous political actions of all moral foundation. If it was his conviction—and we have no reason to doubt this—that politics are, in the final analysis, merely a matter of naked force, then he had also to reckon with the possibility that one day, when the might of his enemies was greater than his own, his policy would be cruelly visited on his own people, in whose name he pretended to speak. And in fact the occupation of Prague marked a turning-point in the policy of the western powers. From now on they were resolved to take countermeasures.

The New Partition of Poland

Hitler could still maintain that there was no power in the world that was a match for his. No country came to Czechoslovakia's assistance. The Soviet Union did not make a move because of her crippling distrust of the western powers. The guarantee which England gave Poland on 31 March 1939, with which France also associated herself, might very well be dismissed by Hitler, on the basis of his experience so far, as of no importance. The German Chancellor also answered Roosevelt's appeal of 31 April 1939, calling upon him not to attack other European states, with the ironical sentence: "You will permit me to state that I can think of no end for which I should wage war." At the same time he denounced the German-Polish treaty of non-aggression and terminated the naval agreement with Great Britain. The open trial of strength to solve the Polish question had begun.

In autumn 1938 Hitler had already called upon Poland to return Danzig to the *Reich* and to approve the construction of an extra-territorial motorway through the "Polish Corridor". Poland had not troubled to answer this demand. The English guarantee seemed to assure Poland of a strong ally. Moreover, the two western powers were making efforts to form an alliance with Russia. These failed because no solution could be found to the problem of how Russia was to fulfil its obligations in case of an alliance if Poland refused to allow Russian troops right of transit through her territory. In any case Russia was not really convinced of the sincerity of the western powers' desire for a military pact. The Soviet leaders' mistrust of the western powers, which had existed since the October Revolution of 1917 and had only been aggravated by the Munich Agreement, gave Hitler the opportunity to take up a secret offer made by Stalin. After short negotiations a Russo-German pact of non-aggression — which surprised the world just as much as the German people—was signed on 23 August 1939. For the sake of his new-found friendship with the enemy, whom he had until now so vigorously attacked, Hitler signed a secret protocol in which he sacrificed the Baltic states, half of Poland, as well as Bessarabia. "The northern frontiers of Lithuania (form) at the same time the dividing line between the spheres of interest of Germany and the USSR."

Hitler thought that this new coup would cause England to allow him a free hand in regulating matters in eastern Europe, without herself going to war. But a mere two days later, on 25 August, England signed a formal treaty with Poland. As a consequence Hitler postponed the German invasion of Poland from 26 August to 1 September.

This brief respite was used in international diplomatic circles to make a renewed attempt to prevent the outbreak of another war. The pope, the Queen of the Netherlands, the King of the Belgians, and the President of the United States offered their good offices. On 28 August, the British ambassador to Berlin expressed the United Kingdom's readiness to hold talks about the German-Polish dispute. On 29 August, Hitler demanded that a Polish emissary with full powers should be dispatched to Berlin. When such a representative did not appear, the *Reich* Foreign Minister read to the British ambassador a proposal which sounded relatively conciliatory, but he refused to hand over the actual text. Hitler was willing to appear moderate, because, in his own words, he needed "an alibi, especially to satisfy the German people, that I had done everything to save the peace". Although Mussolini suggested, on

31 August, that a conference of the Great Powers should be summoned for 5 September, Hitler gave the command for his troops to invade Poland on 1 September. The invasion took place under the mantle of "Polish provocations".

On 3 September, Great Britain declared war on Germany in accordance with the terms of the treaty of mutual assistance. Her example was followed—though with reluctance—by France. Nevertheless both powers were content to remain entirely on the defensive on the western frontier of the *Reich*, much to the surprise of the German military und political leaders, who, on account of the numerical superiority enjoyed by England and France, had expected an allied offensive. This meant that Germany's full power in armoured divisions, air force and motorised infantry could be hurled against Poland. The campaign was over in 16 days. On 17 September, Russian troops attacked Polish territory. On 28 September, Russia's boundary with Poland was settled in a Russo-German Friendship Treaty. This frontier settlement is still in force today. Some 77,000 square miles were added to Russia. Great areas of Poland were incorporated in the *Reich*, the rump formed a "Government General" under a German as governor-general.

With the start of the Polish campaign, the history of the sufferings of the Polish people also began—sufferings which were greater than those of any other people with the one exception of the Jews. Hitler worked off his contempt for the Slavs in systematic campaigns to liquidate the Polish intelligentsia. It was the *Führer's* declared aim to reduce the entire Polish population to the level of semi-illiterates in order to smother the subject people's spirit of resistance and to exploit Polish workers ruthlessly in the service of the *Reich*. In the winter of 1939/40 the great resettlement and deportment programme was put into operation. The Polish regions incorporated in the *Reich* were settled with *Volksdeutsche*, i.e. with Germans drawn from German-language enclaves in other countries; the Polish inhabitants were deported. In those cases where these latter were resettled, they were assigned to the "Government General". Generally the political leaders had to call upon party functionaries and the *Gestapo* to execute these measures, since the army refused to go into action against the Polish civilian population and even tried, in individual cases, to circumvent Hitler's orders.

The western powers' declarations of war on Germany did not have the slightest influence on Poland's fate, because the relatively strong Anglo-French forces were not brought into action. Hitler thus felt that he was justified in concluding that England still placed her hopes on a peaceful settlement which would allow her to save face. This was why he again made peace overtures in October, without, however, giving up one inch of conquered territory. Indeed, he even demanded the return of the former German colonies. His offers were ignored. Still it is astonishing that the western powers were unable to find the resolve necessary to take some military action against him. This gave Hitler the opportunity to step up his armament production still further and to secure better bases for the struggle with England. The occupation of the neutral states of Denmark and Norway on 9 April 1940 brought him in possession of the North Sea coastline so important for action against England. Now he could conduct a still more concentrated U-boat and air assault on the British Isles. In this way he also ensured the import of Swedish iron ore via the Norwegian harbour of Narvik. In occupying Norway, he anticipated England by a mere matter of hours. England was about to carry out her plan to conduct the battle against the *Reich* from Scandinavian bases. Still, the occupation of Norway made greater demands on the German troops than had originally been expected. The Norwegian people's determination to resist was considerable. The small Norwegian fleet was given British backing, so that a large part of the German fleet had to be sacrificed. Still, the conclusion was inevitable because of the numerical inferiority of the Norwegians.

This prelude in the north was followed, on 10 May 1940, by the offensive in the west, which the Germans initiated by violating the neutrality of Holland, Belgium and Luxembourg, and by exploiting German superiority in men and materials. Without the slightest military necessity the heart of Rotterdam was shattered by a hail of bombs, ostensibly "to force Holland to capitulate", although the country had surrendered an hour earlier. Six weeks later France, too, was forced to lay down her arms (21 June). This success was followed by delay in ordering the advance of the German armoured divisions on Dunkirk. This delay, incomprehensible though it is, was by Hitler's express order. It enabled the English to evacuate troops to the number of 340,000 men, although they were forced to abandon all their weapons on the beaches.

In spite of the severe armistice conditions, which were dictated to the French delegation in the Forest of Compiègne, and which—in open violation of the internationally recognised right of asylum—included the extradition of German emigrés, Hitler did not insist on occupying the whole of France, contrary to all the fears of French politicians. Only northern and western France, including Paris, was placed under German rule. The French army and air force were disarmed. The navy was placed under the command of Germany and Italy. Italy had entered the war during the final phase of the offensive in the west. Vichy became the capital of unoccupied France.

Already in these days of France's greatest humiliation, forces opposed to the military and political collapse of France, which appeared just as inevitable as the Nazi dictatorship in Germany, began to assemble around General de Gaulle. He gradually managed to persuade more and more "free" Frenchmen, especially those living in the African colonies, to take an active part in the struggle at England's side.

In England, Winston Churchill had succeeded Neville Chamberlain as Prime Minister on 10 May 1940. In spite of the hopelessness of her situation after the French capitulation, England was still not prepared to take part in peace talks. On the contrary, she continued the fight for the defence of human freedom, Europe's bequest to mankind, with new resolve. Certainly she was borne up by the hope that Hitler's insatiable thirst for power would bring allies to her side sooner or later. The invasion of the British Isles, which the English awaited as a certainty for the late summer of 1940, did not take place. We still do not know beyond all doubt whether it was the Battle of Britain, which ended in July/August 1940 in a heavy defeat for the German *Luftwaffe*, or whether it was the preparations for the invasion of Russia that led Hitler to abandon his plans for the invasion of England. The numerous raids which the *Luftwaffe* flew against British towns were of practically no military significance; they only served to strengthen the English will to resist.

The rest of the year 1940 would have passed uneventfully from the military standpoint had not Mussolini extended the war to the Mediterranean basin. His plan to challenge England in Egypt came to nothing because of the resistance with which the British forces, in spite of their inferiority both in numbers and equipment, answered the Italian pressure on Egypt from the south and the north-west. Contrary to all expectations, the British even managed to throw the Italians out of Somaliland and to liberate Ethiopia. By December 1940, Cyrenaica was also in British hands. Mussolini's military operation against Greece, which he launched from occupied Albania, proved just as disastrous.

If Mussolini was to remain in the saddle in Italy, Germany would have to come to his aid, no matter how little the Balkans and the Mediterranean attracted Hitler's territorial ambitions. Anyway, since 27 September 1940, Japan, Italy, and Germany were bound by a formal treaty of mutual assistance. Only an attack by Russia on one of the signatory powers was exempted from the treaty.

The War With the Soviet Union

Until the close of the year 1940, the Russo-German "friendship" had survived even severe tests. Russia had fulfilled the obligations arising from the Russo-German trade agreement punctually, but, in the summer of 1940, had begun to interfere actively in the politics of the Balkans. Germany had observed with distrust the Soviet "Winter Offensive" against Finland (1939/40), the annexation of the Baltic states, and of Bessarabia, but there were no external signs of tension between the Russians and the Germans. From 12 to 14 November 1940, Molotov, the Russian Foreign Minister, paid an official state visit to Berlin. Hitler evaded Soviet demands for military bases in Bulgaria and the Straits. Even the invasion by German troops of Jugoslavia in the spring of 1941 and the occupation of Greece at the side of Germany's ally, Italy, did not cause Stalin to lend a more ready ear to British warnings about an imminent invasion of Soviet Russia. Above all, the occupation of Crete with such heavy losses seemed to justify the conviction of those who saw the Balkan campaigns as just another means of forcing England to her knees.

But as with all the other pacts which Hitler had concluded in the past, the Russo-German "Friendship Treaty" had been signed only to gain time, to lull the enemy into a false sense of security and to isolate him, so that, when the time was ripe, he could be taken off his guard and subdued so quickly that it would be impossible to engage all the reserves of strength at home and any help from abroad would arrive too late. The world had been given more than sufficient opportunity to study these tactics on numerous earlier occasions, and the point could hardly have escaped Stalin. That the lesson was not learnt becomes all the more incredible, when we consider that Hitler had expounded his views on the extension of Germany's "living space" in the east at great length in his book *Mein Kampf*. Although he had never made a public declaration to the effect that he now dissociated himself from the views expressed in that work, they were not taken seriously either at home or abroad. That he looked for this "living space" only in the east is to be accounted for by his views on the "racial inferiority" of the Slavs, to whom he denied any culturally creative potential in contrast to the Germanic peoples of Europe. On the other hand, he was convinced that only a country which ruled a large compact territory could hope to be a world power in the 20th century. Logically he considered colonial possessions superfluous, because the days of colonialism were already numbered, so that from this standpoint alone a renewal of William II's imperial policy was doomed to failure. How far the German "living space" should extend to the east he had not yet decided even in the wildest flights of his imagination. The few Slavs who still remained after the conquest were to be demoted to the level of a Helot class of slave workers in the service of the German "Master Race".

Hitler overrode the numerous warnings of the German generals against an invasion of Russia. German troops with Finnish, Rumanian, Hungarian and Italian reinforcements, invaded Russian territory. The campaign was to be over in five months at the outside. The offensive at first ran according to plan, because Russia was caught unawares. The Soviet losses in men and materials were beyond all expectation, the territorial gains considerable. Soon the German armies were at the gates of Leningrad and Moscow. At this point the Russian winter suddenly set in. For this, at Hitler's express order, the German army command had made no preparations. The advance came to an unforeseen standstill. Russia was given a respite to organise her armaments industry and to raise new troops in its great hinterland. Still more decisive, however, was the entry of the USA into the war. The European struggle had now taken on the dimensions of a Second World War.

America's Entry Into the War

As long ago as 1933, Franklin D. Roosevelt, the Democrat President of America, had broken with the former American policy of non-recognition of the Soviet Union and established diplomatic relations with Russia. As a determined opponent of right-wing totalitarianism either of the Italian or the German variety, Roosevelt had supported the policy of the western powers against the axis powers. To do this, after the outbreak of the war in 1939, he got round the American Neutrality Act of 1937 with great skill. By this act the USA had declared itself neutral in any international disputes. But this did not prevent the president from helping the belligerent western powers, especially England, with deliveries of goods of all kinds, aid which was extended to Russia in 1941. In contrast, the USA was extremely reserved in her trade relations with Japan, which was not only bound by treaty to the axis powers, but had also been on the offensive in East Asia since 1931. The United States were not prepared to conclude a new trade agreement with Japan in 1941, if the Japanese did not undertake to withdraw from China. The military party in Japan rejected this condition. The Japanese military leaders countered the intensification of the Anglo-Saxon economic war on their country with the successful attack on Pearl Harbour (Hawaii) on 8 December 1941. America's reaction was to declare war on Japan. Germany and Italy reiterated their solidarity with Japan a day later and declared war on the USA, too. Japan remained neutral towards the Soviet Union.

Although in this world-wide struggle the USA and England gave the greatest possible help to the Soviet Union in the form of supplies of materials of all kinds, the German troops were still able, in the summer of 1942, to gain considerable successes on all fronts. The advance in south Russia brought the German army as far as the Volga and the Caucasus. Under Rommel's generalship the *Afrika Korps* arrived with their Italian allies at the gates of Alexandria. But at the same time the allies were poised for a counter-offensive. On 24 October 1942, the north African offensive launched by the British under Montgomery as Commander-in-Chief and backed by superiority in materials and in the air achieved the breakthrough at El Alamein in Egypt. In early November American and British troops landed in Morocco, whence they advanced on Tunis, which the German troops had occupied as a counter-move. Russian troops, with strong backing in the air, were able in a determined counter-offensive launched against the units of Hitler's weaker allies to completely encircle an entire German army in Stalingrad (today Volgograd), which had to surrender on 2 February 1943. Hitler's stubbornness prevented the army from being saved; he forbade it to break through the Russian lines while there was still time. This marked the turning-point in the war on the Russian front. The German and Italian forces had to withdraw from north Africa. And in May 1943 the remainder of the *Afrika Korps*, till now accustomed only to victory, was compelled to surrender in Tunis.

The defeats at El Alamein, Stalingrad and Tunis together form the decisive turning-point in World War II. But they had a still more far-reaching significance as well. Hitler had embarked on the war in order to win for Germany that position as a world power of which, in his opinion, the whole course of history during the last 400 years had cheated her. The defeats proved that this second attempt during the first half of this century was also bound to end in failure, in spite of the heroic fight put up by the German soldiers and of the first-class military intelligence of the German generals. At the same time Hitler's ideology that the new ruling class of Europe would come from the ranks of the German people also collapsed. In the age of moribund European nationalism and colonial imperialism such a view was in fact an anachronism. The German people would have to pay dearly for this error, which was to prove as fateful as it was unnecessary.

At the same time, the "Home Front" also began to feel the material superiority of the enemy. Innumerable Anglo-American terror raids on the residential areas of German cities took extremely heavy toll of the German civilian population, but contributed nothing to a more speedy ending of hostilities. Moreover, these systematic raids on cities of no decisive military or economic importance for the war could only serve to confirm the Nazi propaganda among the German people that the allies were set on the destruction of the great monuments of German civilisation and culture (Würzburg, the heart of Nuremberg, Munich, Cologne, Hildesheim, Münster, and Potsdam, etc.). The raid on Dresden especially, which not only destroyed the magnificent monuments of Baroque architecture, but also claimed some quarter of a million dead (three times as many as at Hiroshima), because it was carried out at a time when long columns of refugees from the German east had assembled in the city, convinced the German people more and more that the war was not directed against Hitler but against all Germans without distinction.

The military objective of the western allies for the year 1943 was to sever Italy from Germany. Allied landings in Sicily led to Mussolini's arrest on 25 July 1943 at the instigation of the Fascist Grand Council. By August, secret armistice negotiations between the new government and the allies were already being conducted. But, for all that, the Anglo-American advance northwards dragged on until late in 1944 because of the German resistance. In June 1944, the allies were able to occupy Rome; the German troops withdrew without a fight. Northern Italy fell into allied hands only after the capitulation.

In Russia, too, the German army fought on during the year 1943 with varying military success. In the second half of that year, however, the initiative passed once for all to the Russians. They drove the Germans out of Leningrad and Stalingrad. When in 1944 the western powers launched the invasion in France, the Russians were once again in possession of the whole of their fatherland. Now began the battle for Germany itself.

The Soviet Union, which in spite of the material aid given by the USA still distrusted the English and the Americans, pressed for more active allied support in their struggle by the establishment of a second front in the west. The allies made extremely painstaking preparations for this and were only ready on 6 June 1944. In the successes which they achieved they were helped, as was also more often the case in the east, by Hitler's false assessment of the situation. In contrast to the generals and the soldiers at the front, he held that the allied landing in Normandy was merely a diversionary move; the main assault would come somewhere along the Pas-de-Calais coastline. For this reason he still held back the available reserves even after the allies had established a secure beachhead. The breakthrough came only after the allies had suffered heavy losses. On 25 August, the allies marched into Paris, their way prepared by the French Resistance. At the head of the regular French troops stood the champion of French freedom, General de Gaulle. The German commandant surrendered Paris into his hands, the French capital being almost unscarred. By mid September the troops of the western powers had reached the "West Wall". At the same time the Russians arrived at the Vistula and took Bukarest. Sofia was occupied by the "red army" without a shot being fired, after Bulgaria had formally withdrawn from the war. In Jugoslavia, the partisans, headed by the Communist Marshall Tito, who had been fighting against the Germans since 1941, were achieving even greater successes by their own unaided efforts. On 20 October, they took Belgrade. Budapest fell to the Russians in February 1945. When Bratislava, the capital of Slovakia, was taken by the "red army" in 1945, all the eastern states subjugated by Hitler had been eliminated from the contest.

The Climax of Nazi Terror

Hitler had from the beginning designated the war against the Soviet Union as a clash of ideologies, although undoubtedly the Bolshevist *Weltanschauung* was just as immaterial to him as that of National Socialism. But he had thought, not without good reason as events were to prove, that this ideological masquerade would enable him to persuade the other peoples of Europe to take part in the war. And in fact small, though undoubtedly insignificant, contingents were formed in all countries for the fight against the Soviet Union. But a far more decisive reason in Hitler's eyes was that he would thus be able to hide the brutality of his commands concerning the Russian civilian population, Soviet commissars, P.O.W's and the Slav slave labour under an ideological camouflage, and in this way steel his army to adopt measures of extreme severity against the Bolshevist enemy. However, by and large, the army tried to observe the code of war in the conduct of their engagements, although this was not always made easy for them by their Bolshevist opponents, for Stalin too had given the war an ideological veneer. Extravagant propaganda incited the Russian soldier to brutal conduct of the war against the "Fascist invaders". But, since the administration of the conquered east European regions was primarily the concern of the party and the SS, it was especially the population behind the lines who was made to bear the entire brunt of an inhuman regime. Himmler as *Reichsführer* SS was the main organ for the execution of Hitler's policy. On 4 October 1943 he cynically declared in public: "Whether 10,000 Russian women collapse from exhaustion while digging an anti-tank ditch is of interest to me only in so far as it affects the completion of the ditch for Germany." The fruits of such treatment were hatred of Germany and ruthless partisan warfare. Whereas at the beginning of the Russian campaign the inhabitants of the Baltic states, the Ukrainians and even numerous Russians had greeted the Germans as their liberators, Bolshevism soon appeared to them the lesser of two evils and its victory was hailed as the fulfilment of a great hope for the "Fatherland", a hope which was even shared by many Germans at times.

Hitler's insane view of the Jew as the author of all evil and of all that was inferior in history had led him to equate Jewry with Bolshevism. It was his declared aim to exterminate the Jews under cover of war. On 31 July 1941, Heydrich, who was assassinated one year later in Prague, was commissioned to take charge of the annihilation of the Jews. The gassings of Jews began in September 1941, at first in Auschwitz. On 20 January 1942, Hitler issued his instruction for the "Final Solution of the Jewish Question". In all German-occupied areas, Jews were herded together by the *Gestapo* at Hitler's command and deported to east Europe, where they were to meet their deaths by gassing in extermination camps specially erected for the purpose. By 1944, some 5.5 million Jews had fallen victim to this reign of terror. The fate of the Jews walled up in the Warsaw ghetto was appalling: after years of inconceivable physical and mental sufferings, they made a last

Central Europe before World War II

Central Europe after World War II

desperate stand against their SS guards from 18 April to 16 May 1943, until not one of them was left alive.

The representatives of both Christian confessions in Germany addressed strongly worded protests to the government against this barbaric extermination of the Jewish race which, like other inhuman measures carried out by the Nazis—such as the liquidation of mentally sick children—was kept secret as far as possible from the German people and soldiers. The protests were ignored. The more the situation at the front deteriorated the freer the rein given to the criminal instincts of a small, but ruthless, minority of the German people. It was precisely during the last years of the war that the concentration and extermination camps, in which numerous Germans were also interned, became centres of refined horror.

Allied Policy Towards Germany During the War

Even before the USA entered the war, Roosevelt had defined American policy towards a conquered Germany at his first conference with Churchill, which was held on board a warship in the Atlantic on 14 August 1941. Whereas the so-called "Atlantic Charter" promised the peoples of the world liberty both at home and abroad, and equality of access to raw materials and economic collaboration, Germany as the aggressor was to be completely disarmed and was explicitly excluded from enjoying the fruits of the realisation of these promises.

At Casablanca, at a conference lasting from 14—24 January 1943, the invasion of Sicily was resolved upon. At a press conference Roosevelt declared that it was the intention of the allies to demand the unconditional surrender of Germany. The German people was thus equated with National Socialism and its *Führer*; the war waged by the western powers was thereby raised to a crusade. Like Hitler, his opponents now also demanded total extermination.

Like the terror raids on German cities, this formula of "unconditional surrender" undoubtedly protracted the war. Both inspired hatred for their devisers and this hatred in turn strengthened the will to resist to the bitter end. Even those Germans who utterly abominated Hitler's policy were hardly prepared to approve the destruction of their own nation. On the other hand, it must also be admitted that the very composition of the alliance against Germany made it impossible to withdraw the Roosevelt formula. East and west were filled with deep mutual distrust. Neither Munich nor the Stalin-Hitler pact were forgotten. Each doubted the resolution of the other to wage the war until the German enemy was annihilated. To overcome this distrust, both sides vied with each other in giving vent to their hatred of Germany.

The first time the two western statesmen came into personal contact with the absolute ruler in the East, Joseph Stalin, was at the Conference of Teheran (28 November to 1 December 1943). Roosevelt supported Stalin's claims in the Balkans and promised the invasion of France for the summer of 1944. Russia's dream of undisputed hegemony over the peoples of the Balkans seemed close to realisation. The adoption of the Morgenthau Plan by Roosevelt and Churchill at the Quebec Conference in September 1941 was entirely in keeping with the demand for "unconditional surrender". According to this plan the entire industry of the *Reich* was to be dismantled and Germany converted back into a pastoral country.

At the all-important Conference of Yalta in February 1945, on the eve of the allied victory over Germany, Roosevelt, Churchill and Stalin laid down the new order of the world. All the attempts of the western statesmen to ensure the democratic right of self-determination for the states of eastern Europe by laying down definite conditions for the political set-up in those countries were frustrated. For fixing Poland's eastern and western frontiers Stalin's wishes were largely taken into consideration. The post-war occupation of Germany by the allies was agreed upon and the programme for the dismantling of Germany's industry approved in broad outlines. The remaining resolutions concerned Japan.

The German Resistance Movement and 20 July 1944

The military reverses suffered by the German forces and their allies made it only too apparent how senseless it was to continue the fight. But Hitler refused to admit defeat. On the contrary, he attempted to silence with brutality any contradiction of his insane commands.

Since Hitler's accession to power on 30 January 1933, there had been innumerable small resistance groups in Germany. At first the Communists were the strongest, but after the conclusion of the Russo-German pact in 1939 they gave up their opposition at Stalin's express wish. They only took up the struggle again after the invasion of Russia. Social Democrats, army officers, civil servants and trade unionists constituted the main element in the non-Communist opposition to Hitler. General Beck, Chief of the Army General Staff since 1935, resigned because he was not prepared to countenance Hitler's preparations for war. In 1938 he planned with other officers the assassination of Hitler if a war should break out as a result of the *Sudeten* crisis. The "Munich Agreement" caused them to abandon this plan, although the western powers had been kept fully informed about the intentions of the conspirators. But as long as Hitler could point to success after success in foreign policy, any opposition to him could not help but look like betrayal of the fatherland. A conspiracy against the *Führer* could only count on popular support if the situation at the front and at home became so menacing that a peace won by submission would be preferable, as a last resort, to any senseless continuation of hostilities. The Opposition led by the generals judged that these conditions were fulfilled after Stalingrad, as several unsuccessful attempts on Hitler's life during the year 1943 show. On 20 July 1944, Count von Stauffenberg, a colonel who had been seriously injured in action, tried to kill Hitler by planting a bomb in his headquarters in East Prussia. By removing the *Führer*, the conspirators hoped to obtain a more favourable peace. General Beck was again the key figure in the resistance group gathered around Stauffenberg. He was to become head of state after the assassination. Goerdeler, the former Lord Mayor of Leipzig, was to take over the office of chancellor. Among the high military personnel who belonged to the group were Field-Marshall von Witzleben, Generals von Stülpnagel, Halder and Oster, and Field-Marshall Rommel; Julius Leber and Adolf Reichwein represented the Social Democrats in the conspiracy. Members of the diplomatic corps and representatives of the Christian churches either joined the group or sympathized with its intentions. Chance saved Hitler's life, so that he escaped with only superficial injuries. Some of the officers standing near him were killed. Stauffenberg, however, presuming that the attempt had been successful, gave the go-ahead for the attempt to gain control in Berlin. This was nipped in the bud by order of Goebbels, the Minister of Propaganda. Beck and Rommel died at their own hand; Stauffenberg was shot in the general staff building in Berlin. All the other conspirators suffered a dishonourable death or died in concentration camps or prisons. The victims of Hitler's revenge numbered thousands.

During the course of the war, the resistance in Germany had tried on many occasions to obtain the recognition and help of the western powers. But Roosevelt and Churchill always refused to offer any hope of support. In addition to the local resistance groups formed by many members of the Christian churches, former trade unionists or members of the proscribed democratic parties, the "Kreisau Circle" gathered around Count von Moltke in Silesia, and the student revolt centred on Hans and Sophie Scholl in Munich are worthy of mention. They tried to combat the moral decline instigated by Hitler in the German people and in the younger members of the population grouped in the "Hitler Youth". They, too, paid for their opposition to Hitler with their lives.

The End

The unsuccessful *coup d'état* of 20 July 1944 unleashed a new wave of terror, this time directed especially against the army. Himmler was appointed Commander-in-Chief of the Replacement Army (*Ersatzheer*). A final levy of boys and old men was to call a halt to the allied advance. The hope of a destructive wonder weapon was to brace all at home and at the front for one last supreme effort before the predicted final victory of the *Reich*.

In fact, German scientists working at Peenemünde under General Dornberger and Wernher von Braun had succeeded in constructing guided missiles. These were put into action against England from June 1944 onwards and had a considerable psychological effect. Their military significance, however, was small. Jet aircraft also boosted the German war effort, but too late. Atomic weapons, however, were not planned. Indeed, no German nuclear physicist had ever prostituted his knowledge by indicating to Hitler that the construction of such weapons was possible.

In the spring of 1945 the western allies broke through the German lines of defence. The Russians took Vienna on 13 April. The day before, Roosevelt had died; he was succeeded by H. S. Truman.

After the fall of Vienna, the final struggle for Berlin began. By 25 April Berlin had been completely encircled. On 28 April Mussolini was put to death by Italian partisans. Two days later, at half past three in the afternoon, Hitler shot himself in his bunker in the Chancellery. His wife, married to him some days before, took poison.

In his "Last Will", Hitler had handed over the supreme authority in the state to Grand Admiral Dönitz. On 7 May, General Jodl, acting on behalf of the German Supreme Command, signed Germany's unconditional surrender in the allied H. Q. at Reims. This act was confirmed in the Russian H. Q. at Karlshorst near Berlin on 8 May. The ceasefire was set for 9 May.

Germany paid for Hitler's war with the loss of more than three million soldiers, the disablement of two million servicemen, more than half a million air-raid victims, and more than four million dead and missing among the 16 million refugees who were expelled from their homes in east Germany, the *Sudetenland*, and other regions.

It is precisely this expulsion of Germans from their homelands which shows the appalling moral decline into which Europe had allowed herself to drift. In the course of her long history Europe has seen many changes of national boundaries, but never before, at the conclusion of a war, had inhabitants been denied their right to the homelands they had lived in for centuries. The fate which Hitler had decreed for the Jews and the Slavs now rebounded on the heads of the Germans.

Hitler had promised Europe that he would destroy Bolshevism; his war opened Europe as far as the Elbe to Communism. Hitler had promised to transform Germany into a world power; his war even gambled away Germany's position as a great power in Europe. The clock had been turned back a thousand years: the free part of Germany extended only as far as the eastern frontier of the Carolingian and early Saxon emperors.

Chapter Twenty-Six

GERMANY AFTER WORLD WAR II

The Rule of the Victors

Once again Germany had arrived at a turning-point in her history, but this time one more radical than any she had ever seen in the past. One could maintain now that Germany was a "monster, hardly a geographical entity still" with even more truth than at the conclusion of the Thirty Years War. Even the frontiers assigned at Versailles were no longer certain. No one could say when the stream of refugees from the east would cease, or what regions the victorious powers would determine for further expulsions, or whether the West, too, was not interested in seeing German living-space limited still further. As if to symbolise that any claim Germany might have to continued existence in international law had been extinguished, the "Dönitz Government" was arrested in north Germany just a few weeks after the capitulation. All economic activity which did not serve the interests of the allies ceased; the dismantling of Germany's industrial machinery began. Most German men were either in internment camps or imprisoned; women and children eked out a scanty existence from the savings the war had not devoured, or from money earned by the work of their own hands. Certainly the high-sounding phrases which had been hammered into the Germans for the last twelve years were dead, but with them all hope had perished, too.

The lack of clarity about the future of conquered Germany made a conference of the victors necessary. To this end the "Big Three"— President Truman of America, Prime Minister Attlee of England, and Stalin, the Russian dictator—met at Potsdam, a town which was a symbol both of Prussian greatness and of Hitler's extravagant ambitions. In an agreement signed on 2 August 1945 they undertook to disarm Germany, to root out National Socialism and militarism from the German people, and to build up a decentralised Germany on a democratic basis. However, Germany was still to be treated as a single economic unit. The East Prussian city of Königsberg together with its hinterland was placed under the administration of the Soviet Russians. All the remaining German regions east of the Oder-Neisse line were to be administered by Poland. The resettlement of the German population which this involved was to be carried out in "a humane fashion". The final delimitation of Germany's frontiers was left to a future peace treaty. The Potsdam Agreement, therefore, maintained the fiction in international law of a Germany within the frontiers of 1937.

In contradiction of the agreement, no government for the whole of Germany was created. The four occupying powers, the Soviet Union, Great Britain, the United States and France, set up state administrations in their zones, from which in the course of time new *Länder* developed. Berlin was divided into four zones and granted its own statute of occupation.

Austria suffered the same fate as Germany, but the federal government which the victorious powers allowed the Austrians to form preserved the country's unity.

While the war was still raging, the allies had agreed to cite the major war criminals before a military tribunal at the conclusion of hostilities and put them on trial for their crimes. The military tribunal set up at Nuremberg was composed of judges drawn from the four occupying powers. The indictment was threefold: crimes against peace, war crimes, and crimes against humanity. German lawyers undertook the defence of the accused. These lawyers did not dispute the right to judge war crimes—such crimes, for instance, as the total destruction by the *Gestapo* of the villages of Lidice in Czechoslovakia and of Oradour in France together with their inhabitants—but they disputed the legality of the other two points of the indictment, since they were based on retroactive law created specially for the purpose. The international court did not sustain this objection, however. Judgment was passed on 30 September 1946. Twelve of the accused were sentenced to death by hanging and seven to periods of imprisonment, while three were acquitted. A number of Nazi organisations were declared criminal in nature. Their members were obliged to produce evidence to show that they had not been guilty of any crimes; inability to do so rendered them liable to punishment.

The holders of various military or political positions had to account for their actions before military tribunals, too. Even distinguished National Socialist doctors and judges were put on trial.

The Nuremberg trials have often been criticised because the victors acted there as "judges in their own cause", without attempting to condemn their own war criminals. The trials also infringed the legal principle recognised by all peoples "nulla poena sine lege". Above all, the participation of the Soviet Union seemed highly questionable, since the Russians had been guilty of the same crimes in 1939 when they annexed parts of Poland, and in the Finnish War. This criticism, though it may be justified in individual points, does not give sufficient consideration to the dimensions of the crime the condemned had been guilty of both in regard to other peoples and also to their own. Moreover, no one can deny that the judges at Nuremberg did their utmost to ensure a fair trial.

After the disbandment of the Nazi Party and its various affiliated organisations, all Germans above a certain age had to submit themselves to a process known as "denazification". A questionnaire containing 131 questions was to establish the individual's share of responsibility for National Socialism and its policies. This "purge" was intended to ensure that all former Nazis should be excluded from responsible positions in the state and in the industrial and business life of the country. It was hoped to facilitate in this way the task of reestablishing democracy in Germany. The western allies especially overlooked the fact that after 1933 membership or non-membership of the National Socialist Party or its affiliated organisations was hardly a matter left to the free discretion of the individual. Moreover it was impossible to establish by a questionnaire an individual's moral complicity in National Socialism and its crimes, which anyway was often shared by those who were members neither of the party nor of its affiliated organisations. The "denazification" process came as a welcome opportunity to the Russian victor, who used it as a cover for changes in a communist direction wrought in the social structure of the Soviet zone.

The Foundation of the German Federal Republic

Between the years 1945 and 1947 the unnatural alliance between the Soviet Union and the western powers split. It became ever clearer that the Soviet Union did not intend to rest content with the gains brought by the successful outcome of the war, but would continue to work for a world revolution. She was aided in her plans by the disarmament carried out by the western allies and the unstable economic conditions obtaining in all the lands of Europe as a direct consequence of the six years of war. It was precisely these economic difficulties which made the Communist ideology appear so attractive to a large proportion of the European population. In spite of numerous conferences, no agreement could be reached on the German question, either. For this reason America decided to alter the course where Germany was concerned. This course had been determined by the spirit of the Morgenthau Plan. In 1948 the United States developed a programme of economic aid known as the Marshall Plan designed to bring about an amelioration in the economic conditions of the countries hit by the war and to cut the ground from under the Communist agitation against the capitalist system. This led to the European Recovery Programme, which made still further aid available to Europe; Germany was included among the countries to benefit from the new aid. In order to put the German economy on its feet again, a monetary reform had to be carried through, for only in this way could the currency in circulation be reduced to reasonable limits. This currency reform was carried through in the three western zones, with the assistance of American financial experts, in June 1948.

Before this date, the western powers had already come to an agreement by which their three zones of occupation were to be amalgamated to form a German state which should be ruled by a government of Germans and slowly but surely raised to the status of an equal partner. Only the Saar was not to come under the new state. This region had been economically attached to France as a semi-autonomous region at a conference held in Moscow in 1947. The plan of the western powers had the approval of all the political parties which had reformed in Germany after 1945. They saw it as an opportunity to mitigate the severity of the occupation regime and to make the extravagant demands of the victors, especially in respect of the dismantling of German industry, more tolerable. Thus, representatives of the various state parliaments under the chairmanship of Konrad Adenauer formed the "Parliamentary Council", which drafted a constitution for the western half of Germany. The constitution was, in accordance with the desires of the victors, pronouncedly federalist in character. Kurt Schumacher, the chairman of the Social Democratic Party, successfully opposed the tendency to exaggerate the federalist structure of the new state; he thus ensured to the central government the necessary freedom of movement. This constitution came into force as the "Basic Law of the German Federal Republic" on 25 May 1949. It laid claim to speak on behalf of all Germans, although for the time being it regulated the political life of west Germany only.

Bundestag (Federal Diet) elections, as provided for in the Basic Law, took place on 14 August 1949. The short, hotly disputed election was contested mainly between the Christian Democratic Union and the Social Democratic Party. The Christian Democrats were sent to the *Bundestag* with the strongest representation, the Social Democrats as the second strongest party. On 15 September 1949, the German *Bundestag* elected Dr. Konrad Adenauer Federal Chancellor of the new Republic; Professor Theodor Heuss became its first president.

In this way, western Germany regained a certain measure of autonomous statehood. But the new state was faced, like the German people itself, with the distrust of Europe, indeed of the whole world. In the sober realities of state, this distrust was reflected in the powers which the allies had reserved to themselves and in the controls placed on foreign policy. It would therefore be the task of the new government to pursue a consistent policy designed to prove, at least to the western world, that the change wrought in the German people as a result of the experience of Nazi dictatorship and the ensuing defeat was so profound that western Germany might even be accepted as a partner by the western powers. This policy fitted exactly the American viewpoint that America's power would itself be strengthened if the economic and population potential of the Federal Republic of Germany was carefully incorporated in the western defence system. This incorporation was to be carried out in such a way, however, that the economic and political interests of the European victor powers were safeguarded. Adenauer's political aim was to counterbalance the justified rights of the victorious powers with the equally justified vital interests of the German people by a union of all European peoples. Only a united Europe seemed capable of dealing the deathblow to nationalism and petty political thinking. Robert Schuman, the French politician and enthusiastic advocate of the European idea, had perhaps more supporters in Germany than in his own land. The first result of his endeavours, which were actively supported by Chancellor Adenauer and Premier de Gasperi of Italy, was the Council of Europe, which came into existence in 1950 and to which all the non-Communist European countries belonged, with the exception of Finland, Spain and Portugal. Of course, the Council of Europe enjoyed no state rights. More effective politically and economically was the integration of the heavy industries of France, the German Federal Republic, Italy, Belgium, Holland and Luxembourg in the European Coal and Steel Community (ECSC), a sort of common market for coal and steel, which was followed by further economic integrations of the six countries during the following years. The final objective of all these efforts was the European Economic Community. The Rome treaties governing the

Common Market were signed on 25 March 1957 and came into force on 1 January 1958. The attempt to place the military potential of the German Federal Republic at the service of a "European Defence Community" ended in failure because of French opposition to the plan (August 1954). The Paris Agreements of October of the same year, however, placed the German armed forces under NATO command and envisaged that Germany should be granted the rights of a sovereign state. At the same time the Western powers bound themselves to a policy calling for the reunification of Germany and protecting the freedom of west Berlin. After the Paris Agreements had been ratified by all participating states, the Federal Republic of Germany was granted sovereignty by the western victor states on 5 May 1955. The Soviet Union approved this step in practice also, for the Kremlin agreed to establish diplomatic relations with Germany on the occasion of a state visit to Moscow of the Federal Chancellor, Konrad Adenauer, in September 1955.

One of the primary objectives of Adenauer's foreign policy was a Franco-German rapprochement. In his opinion the realisation of this aim provided the key to the future of Europe. Here, too, he could be certain of having the west Germans behind him. But imposing obstacles stood in the way of his efforts here. In France, the distrust of the eastern neighbour was still far from dead; in Germany, resentment roused by the separation of the Saar impeded any amelioration in relations with France. After protracted negotiations both powers signed a special agreement known as the "Saar Statute". According to this statute the Saar was to be "Europeanised" and placed under a Saar commissioner, who was to be appointed by the council of the "Western European Union". The Saarlanders were to be given the opportunity of accepting or rejecting the agreement in a referendum. On 23 October 1955, 68 % of the votes cast were against the statute and thus *ipso facto* for the return of the Saar to Germany. France bowed to the voice of the people. On 1 January 1957 the Saar formally returned to Germany. A state visit of President de Gaulle to the German Federal Republic in 1962 made the profound change in the relations between the two peoples only too obvious for all the world to see. The treaties signed in Paris in 1963 not only set the political seal on this new relationship but also marked the beginning of a close Franco-German friendship within the framework of a united Europe.

The Marshall Plan, the currency reform and the creation of the German Federal Republic also laid the foundations for the gradual surmounting of the economic chaos which was the aftermath of National

Socialism and the war. All levels of the German population played an equal part in the astonishing economic recovery in western Germany, which is today the third strongest industrial power in the world. The spirit of enterprise and business acumen of the employers was balanced by the employees' readiness for hard work and spirit of sacrifice, which was especially manifest in the moderate wage policy pursued by the trade unions. The national product rose from year to year and attained a level of more than 300,000 million Marks in 1961. The consistently pursued policy of a "socially orientated freemarket economy", which was initiated by the former Minister of Economics and later (until 1966) Federal Chancellor, Professor Erhard, had proved its superiority to any Communist planned economy and had made it possible for West Germany to become one of the richest countries in the world within a relatively short time. It is still too soon to say whether Germany will also be able to win back her former position of importance in the intellectual and cultural life of the world.

The Division of Germany

The Soviet Union countered the currency reform carried out in the allied zones with the introduction of the east German Mark (*Deutsche Mark-Ost*) in their zone of occupation. When the three western sectors of Berlin refused to recognise this east German Mark as the only valid legal tender within their limits, the Soviet Union enforced a total economic blockade of west Berlin to force the western powers to abandon Berlin and to gain control of the whole of the former capital. The West answered this move by organising an Anglo-American air lift, which kept Berlin supplied with the necessities of life. The Berliners stood firm against this economic and moral pressure from the east for 11 months. At the end of this period, the Russians yielded and once again allowed the provision of Berlin within the limits laid down in the "Potsdam Agreement".

During the days of the blockade, preparations were being made for the creation of the "German Democratic Republic". The Soviets officially handed over power to the new government on 7 October 1949. The new "state" drew up a constitution which leaned heavily in formal details on that of Weimar but which followed in practical political issues the example of the totalitarianism characteristic of the Bolshevist east. The only party with any say in the government of the "German Democratic Republic" is the *Sozialistische Einheitspartei Deutsch-*

lands or SED (Socialist Unity Party of Germany), which arose, under pressure of the occupying power, out of a fusion of the Communist and Social Democrat Parties, a merger which Kurt Schumacher was able to prevent in West Berlin and West Germany. In this way he saved West Germany from Communist infiltration.

How little the policy of the SED represents the will of the people in the Soviet zone was shown on 17 June 1953, when the industrial workers rose spontaneously against government by compulsion and demanded its discontinuance in the future. The "Government of Workers and Peasants", as the government of the "German Democratic Republic" proudly entitles itself, was only able to put down the rising with the aid of Soviet tanks.

In keeping with the wishes of the Soviet occupying power, the Soviet zone follows the Russian example in its economic policy. All large undertakings were transferred to public ownership by nationalisation. The economy and its development is governed by a plan drawn up by the state, generally for a period of five years. The administrative apparatus directed by the Communists determines and controls every aspect of life. As in the days of Nazi terror, it is impossible for the individual to escape state regimentation. For this reason the inhabitants of central Germany left their homes and fled to the West in hundreds of thousands. By the late summer of 1962 two million had turned their backs on the "German Democratic Republic". In order to stem the flow of refugees to the West, the rulers in the Soviet zone have sealed off their state with barbed wire, minefields and watch towers. Any attempt to leave the eastern zone was branded as "desertion of the Republic" and made punishable by imprisonment with hard labour. And yet the number of refugees still continued to rise, for there was still one loophole in the "Iron Curtain": West Berlin. What Stalin had not attained by his blockade, Khrushchev hoped to achieve by his Berlin ultimatum of November 1958. In it he threatened a separate peace with the Soviet zone and unilateral denunciation of the four-power status of Berlin. He demanded that West Berlin should be converted into a "free city" by the withdrawal of western occupation forces. The Soviet Union gave way before the determined attitude of the western powers and of the population of Berlin, but threats regarding Berlin as well as the denial of the right of self-determination to Germans living in the Soviet zone of Germany continue to impede relations between East and West, especially between the German Federal Republic and the Soviet Union. When, in addition, Moscow and its Communist allies gave the Ulbricht regime of east Germany permission to build a wall right through Berlin on 13 August 1961, they brought the western world and especially Europe face to face with the question whether or not they want to come to terms with a divided Germany and a Europe in two camps. On the answer they give depends not only the future of all Germans on both sides of the Berlin Wall and the barbed wire barriers but also that of Europe, for the simple reason that Europe does not end at the Elbe. More strikingly than ever before, however, the Wall has once again provided evidence that only the iron hand of constraint prevents the Germans in the "DDR" (*Deutsche Demokratische Republik*, German Democratic Republic) from leaving the "First German Socialist State of Workers and Peasants".

Certainly the Germans in East and West Germany have become extremely sober in their expectations. Big words and ideologies they greet with scepticism. However, it would be a mistake to forget that all Germans are vitally interested in two objectives: the reunification of their fatherland and the creation of a United Europe.

LIST OF ILLUSTRATIONS

1. Porta Nigra, Trier. Built in 3rd century A.D. as the northern gate of the Roman city of Augusta Treverorum.

2. The Imperial Throne of Charlemagne in the Imperial Chapel, Aachen. Throughout the whole of the Middle Ages German kings ascended this throne after their coronation.

3. The Imperial Chapel of Charlemagne was erected between 790 and 805 and was later enlarged, during the Gothic period, into Aachen Cathedral.

4. The Lothair Cross. The Cross was made in 10th century. An ancient cameo bearing the likeness of the Emperor Augustus was inserted at its centre. The Cross received its name from the seal with the portrait of King Lothair (840—855) which is set in the base. Aachen, Münster.

5. Ivory Book Cover, c. 870. Christ on the Cross, the Women at the Sepulchre, and the Resurrection of the Dead. Bavarian National Library, Munich.

6. The Bernward Portal of Hildesheim Cathedral. The bronze door was donated by Bishop Bernward in 1015 A.D. (detail)

7. St George's, Oberzell, on the Island of Reichenau, Lake Constance. Building commenced in the first half of 9th century. The decoration of this colonnaded basilica dates from 10th century.

8. Maria Laach. Benedictine abbey on the Laacher See in the Eifel region. Date of construction: 1093—1156.

9. Speyer Cathedral. Building was started in 1030 under Emperor Conrad II and completed under Emperor Henry IV in the year 1100.

10. Worms Cathedral, c. 1180.

11. Bronze grave slab of Bishop Friedrich von Wittin's tomb, 1152, Magdeburg Cathedral.

12. The Margravine Uta. One of the statues of the founders in the choir of Naumburg Cathedral, c. 1250.

13. Trumpeting angel from a "Last Judgement" group on a column in Strassburg Cathedral, c. 1220.

14. The Bamberg Rider. Royal equestrian statue on a pillar in Bamberg Cathedral, c. 1230.

15. Freiburg Minster. This Gothic cathedral was erected between 1280 and 1320.

16. Festal Refectory of the Marienburg on the Nogat, 1340. The Marienburg, a fortress of the Teutonic Order, was built between 1274 and 1398.

17. The Town Hall, Thorn. This edifice, constructed in the Brick Gothic style about the year 1250, was the largest town hall of its day.

18. Tilman Riemenschneider: Adam and Eve. From the portal of the Marienkapelle in Würzburg, 1493. Main-Franconian Museum.

19. Michael Pacher: Coronation of Mary. Centrepiece of the Late Gothic altar in St Wolfgang's, Salzkammergut, Upper Austria, 1478—1481.

20. Peter Vischer: a portrait figure of the artist himself, on the Sebaldusgrab (Shrine of St Sebaldus) in the Church of St Sebaldus, Nuremberg. Bronze, 1508.

21. Albrecht Dürer: The Artist's Mother. Charcoal drawing, 1514. Berlin.

22. Hans Holbein, the Younger: Portrait of Thomas Howard, Duke of Norfolk, 1539. Windsor Castle.

23. Heidelberg Castle. On the right the Otto Heinrich wing erected in the Renaissance style in 1556—1559. A ruin since the end of the 17th century.

24. Nördlingen. An example of a medieval city layout which grew up around a central core and was protected by an enclosing defensive wall.

25. Karlsruhe. Example of a city built according to a systematic plan during the Baroque period. Founded in 1713 by Karl Wilhelm, Margrave of Baden.

26. St Michael's, Munich, 1583—1588.

27. Residence Theatre, Munich. The Rococo court theatre built by François Cuvilliés in 1750—1753. Faithfully restored after destruction during World War II.

28. The Zwinger, Dresden. Augustus II the Strong, King of Saxony, had this palace built by M. D. Pöppelmann in 1711—1722. Restored after destruction during World War II.

29. Belvedere Palace, Vienna. The summer residence of Prince Eugène was built by Lucas von Hildebrandt in 1721—1722.

30. The Frauenkirche, Dresden. Built by Georg Bähr, in 1726—1738. Totally destroyed in World War II.

31. Andreas Schlüter: equestrian statue of the Great Elector, Frederick William of Brandenburg. 1696—1709. Charlottenburg Palace, Berlin.

32. The Wartburg near Eisenach, Thuringia. The castle was built in 1067 and extended during the following centuries. In 1207 the Minnesingers competed here in the traditional minstrels contest, the "Sängerkrieg". In 1521/22 Luther, who had taken refuge in the castle, translated the New Testament into German, thereby providing the German people with a uniform language. In 1817 the German student association, the "Deutsche Burschenschaft", demonstrated for a national and autonomous Germany at a commemorative celebration held at the Wartburg.

33. Johann Heinrich Tischbein: Goethe in the Campagna. 1786/87. Städelsches Kunstinstitut, Frankfurt.

34. Philip Otto Runge: The Hülsenbeck Children. 1805/6. Kunsthalle, Hamburg.

35. Carl Spitzweg: The Poor Poet. 1839. Nationalgalerie, Berlin.

36. Lovis Corinth: Inn Valley Landscape. 1910. Staatliches Museum, Berlin-Dahlem.

37. Ernst Barlach: The Avenger. Bronze. 1914—1922. Wallraf-Richartz-Museum, Cologne.

38. Gerhard Marcks: Prometheus Bound II. Bronze. 1948. Wallraf-Richartz-Museum, Cologne.

39. The Hansa Viertel, Berlin. Built on the occasion of the "International Building Exhibition 1957". Famous architects from all over the world collaborated on the Hansa Viertel project (Gropius—U.S.A., Vago—France, Niemeyer—Argentinia, Aalto—Finland, and many others).

40. Pylon of the Severinsbrücke, Cologne (1956—1959). In the background Cologne Cathedral.

LIST OF COLOURED PLATES

ACKNOWLEDGEMENTS

Thanks are due to the following for kind permission to make reproductions:

Ars Liturgica, Fine-Art Publishers, Maria-Laach; Bartcky-Titzau, Frankfurt-on-Main; Max Baur, Aschau/Chiemgau; Bavarian Public Library, Munich; Bruckmann Publishers, Munich; Dr. Harald Busch, Frankfurt-on-Main; Niko Haas, Trier; Hamburg Art Gallery, Hamburg; Franz Hanfstaengl, Munich; R. N. Ketterer, Campione/Switzerland; Ralph Kleinhampel, Hamburg; Louvre, Paris; Foto Marburg; Werner Neumeister, Munich; Photographic Archives of the Rhineland, Cologne; Helga Schmidt-Glassner, Stuttgart; Art Institute Städel, Frankfurt-on-Main; Foundation Preussischer Kulturbesitz, Public Museums, National Gallery, Berlin-Dahlem; Foundation Ada and Emil Nolde, Seebüll; USIS, Bad Godesberg; Tourist Office of the city of Cologne; Wallraf-Richartz Museum, Cologne.

INDEX OF NAMES

D

N

Naples 67, 78, 93, 100, 122, 123
Napoleon I, 161 f., 173, 214
Napoleon III, 200, 201, 203, 204, 206, 207
Narvik 297
Nassau 166
Naumburg 88, 101
Neckar 13
Nelson 163
Netherlands 80, 93, 107 f., 110, 114, 115, 116, 120, 122, 123, 145, 178
Neumann, Balthasar 136
New Mark 74
Nibelungenlied 69
Nice 201
Niemöller, Martin 286
Nietzsche, Friedrich 232
Nikolsburg 204
Nördlingen 114
Nogat 76
Nolde, Emil 267
Normandy 303
Normans 26, 42, 53, 54, 59
North America 143, 144
North Mark 55
North Sea 18, 23
Norway 84, 85, 172, 297
Novalis, Friedrich 156
Nowgorod 84
Nuremberg 104, 105, 162, 284, 392, 302, 312

O

Oder 14, 31, 35, 56, 257, 312
Odo of Champagne 42
Old Mark 74
Oliva 60
Olmütz 122, 193
Olympia 229
Opitz, Martin 136
Oradour 312
Orange 108
Orkneys 47
Osnabrück 101, 115
Oster, colonel 307
Otto the Great, German emperor 32 f., 39, 40, 59, 65, 71, 162
Otto II, German emperor 38
Otto III, German emperor 37, 38, 39
Otto of Brunswick, German king 65
Otto of Wittelsbach 61

Ottokar, king of Bohemia 76, 77
Ottomans 100, 121, 123

P

Pacher, Michael 88
Paderborn 61
Palatinate-Neuburg 110
Palermo 64, 67
Palestine 13
Papal States 20, 21, 33, 38, 59, 65, 100
Papen, Franz von 275, 283, 286
Paracelsus 108
Paris 27, 28, 122, 135, 176, 181, 184, 200, 201, 208, 245, 246, 252, 298, 303, 315
Pas de Calais 303
Passarowitz 126
Passau 30
Pavia 20, 36, 41
Pearl Harbour 301
Peenemünde 308
Pepin 18, 19, 20, 21, 23
Persia 239
Pestalozzi 169
Peter the Great, tsar of Russia 121
Peter of Holstein-Gottorp, tsar of Russia 144
Peterlingen 42
Petersburg 201, 212, 245
Petrarch 79
Peter, Simon 19, 20, 39, 52
Philadelphia 218
Philipp II, king of France 62
Philipp of Swabia, German emperor 65
Philipp II, king of Spain 82, 102, 107, 110
Philipp, landgrave of Hesse 100
Piasts 39
Piloty, Karl von 230
Pilsen 114
Pirkheimer, Willibald 104
Planck, Max 269
Podolia 123
Pöppelmann, Daniel 136
Pioncaré 244, 260
Poitiers 18
Poland 37, 39, 40, 55, 57, 74, 80, 122, 123, 128, 129, 144, 145, 160, 161, 172, 202, 210, 215, 248, 250, 256, 257, 262, 288, 294, 295, 296, 306, 312, 313
Pomerania 55, 56, 60, 74, 75, 77
Poppo of Stablo 44
Portugal 315
Posen 161, 172
Potsdam 135, 142, 147, 199, 253, 302, 311

Western Pomerania 116, 129, 139
West Franks 25, 26, 28
Westphalen, Jenny von 181
Westphalia 31, 61, 110, 166, 172
Westphalian Peace 115, 129
West Prussia 80, 145, 256
Wettins 74
Wichern, Johann Heinrich 184
William, king of Sicily 62
William of Holland, German king 68
William, Count of Nassau-Orange 107
William of Orange, king of the Netherlands 125
William I, king of Prussia, German emperor 201, 204, 207, 218, 219, 220
William II, German emperor 219, 220, 223, 244, 245, 248, 251, 252, 253, 255, 300
Wilson 248, 251, 252, 257, 258, 263, 288
Winckelmann, Johann Joachim 154
Wismar 84
Wittelsbach 61, 74, 111, 145
Wittenberg 91, 92, 96, 105

Witzleben, Erwin von 307
Wolfram von Eschenbach 70
Worms 44, 50, 51, 54, 65, 81, 87, 93, 95, 99
Württemberg 31, 72, 73, 162, 207, 209
Würzburg 44, 61, 88, 135, 302

Y

York, general 171
Young, Owen 263, 272
Yugoslavia 288
Yalta 306

Z

Zähringe 73
Zanzibar 235, 239
Zeitz 38
Zeppelin, Count of 227
Zürichgau 73
Zwingli, Ulrich 100